Literature
in
Canada

Volume 1

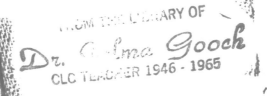

Literature in Canada

Volume 1

Edited by

DOUGLAS DAYMOND   LESLIE MONKMAN
Department of English   *Department of English*
University of Guelph   *University of Guelph*

Gage Educational Publishing Limited

TORONTO

ISBN 0-7715-1156-6

Design by Robert Burgess Garbutt

Printed and bound in Canada
by John Deyell Company

1 2 3 4 5 6 7 8 9 0   JD   86 85 84 83 82 81 80 79 78

Contents

Preface

The predilection of Canadians for what Northrop Frye has called "relentless cultural stock-takings and self-inventories" is nowhere more evident than in the many anthologies that serve as points of reference throughout the literary history of Canada. In the latter half of the nineteenth century, William Hartley Dewart's *Selections from Canadian Poets* (1864) and William Douw Lighthall's *Songs of the Great Dominion* (1889) reveal a concern with establishing the existence of a national literature. In the early decades of the twentieth century, *Canadian Poetry in English* (1922), edited by Bliss Carman and Lorne Pierce, and *A Book of Canadian Prose and Verse* (1923), selected by E.K. and E.H. Broadus, illustrate a developing literary tradition extending over more than one hundred years. At mid-century, the anthologies of Ralph Gustafson, A.J.M. Smith, C.F. Klinck and R.E. Watters combine modern critical standards with an enlarged historical perspective. Just as each of these anthologies illustrates a review of Canadian literature in the light of the ideas and concerns of a particular era, *Literature In Canada* reflects an examination of our literature in terms of contemporary attitudes, interests and evaluations.

Literature In Canada traces the evolution of Canadian literature from the narratives of exploration of the sixteenth century to the poetry, fiction and drama of the nineteen-seventies. It is intended for the English-speaking reader and emphasizes the development of Canadian literature in English. However, translated texts from more than two dozen authors writing in French have been included and, within the limits of translation, these selections introduce some of the major writers of French Canada. Authors whose creative imaginations have been predominant forces in shaping a Canadian literary tradition are extensively represented, but we have also included secondary figures of importance to a more complete understanding of the evolution of our literature. In addition to poetry, fiction and drama,

Literature In Canada represents such genres as the travel book, the captivity narrative, the newspaper sketch, the missionary report and personal journal. Works originating in oral traditions have not been included since their special qualities and significance can be better examined within the larger context of folklore, a context provided by Edith Fowke's *Folklore of Canada* (1976). Critical essays have also been excluded on the grounds that the reader now has a wide choice of accessible material as indicated in the bibliography of secondary sources appended to each volume.

The two volumes are arranged in chronological order according to the birth date of each author. Volume 1 extends from Jacques Cartier in the sixteenth century to Stephen Leacock and his contemporaries in the early decades of the twentieth century. Volume 2 begins with Frederick Philip Grove, E.J. Pratt and other writers involved in the rise of modernism following World War I; it concludes with writers such as Tom Wayman and Susan Musgrave who have come into prominence in the nineteen-seventies.

The date appearing at the left margin after a selection indicates the time of first publication of that work in a volume by the author. The date at the right margin identifies the publication date of the text used by the editors. Where more than one selection by an author appears, the texts have been arranged in chronological order according to the date of first publication in a volume by the author. Archaic spelling, punctuation and abbreviations have been normalized in several cases but the language of each selection has not been altered except for the correction of obvious errors in the original text. Titles are those of the original except where printed within square brackets.

We wish to thank Conrad Wieczorek, our editor, and Laura Damania, our copy editor. We are also grateful to Grace Martin for her assistance in the compilation of the bibliography and to the secretaries of the Department of English and the library staff at the University of Guelph. Finally, we are indebted to Elizabeth Waterston for her encouragement and to our wives for their assistance and support.

DOUGLAS DAYMOND
LESLIE MONKMAN

Jacques Cartier
1491-1557

———◆———

BORN IN ST. MALO, Brittany, Jacques Cartier was first commissioned by King Francis I of France in 1534 to explore the gulf of the St. Lawrence River. On a second voyage in the following year, he sailed up the St. Lawrence as far as the island of Montreal. After spending the winter near present-day Quebec, Cartier returned to France in 1536. His last expedition to Canada was made in 1541. The narratives of Cartier's voyages were widely circulated and translated during the sixteenth century and became best known in English when they appeared in Richard Hakluyt's *Divers Voyages* (1582). *The Voyages of Jacques Cartier* (1924), edited by H. P. Biggar, provides modern translations of the accounts of Cartier's voyages.

From
The Voyages of Jacques Cartier

[The First Voyage, 1534]

Of the harbour called St. Anthony's Harbour,
of Port St. Servan, Port Jacques Cartier,
of the river called St. James's River; of the costumes
and clothing of the inhabitants on the island
of Blanc Sablon

THE NEXT DAY, Friday, June the twelfth, we continued our way through these islands, and at the end of the thickest portion of them we found a good harbour, which was named St. Anthony's Harbour. And further on, about a league or two, we came to a small, very deep passage with the land running south-west and with very high shores. It is a good harbour; and a cross was set up there, and it was named St. Servan's Harbour. About a league to the south-west of this harbour and passage,

1

there is an islet, round like an oven, with several other small islets about it, which give indication of the said harbours. Ten leagues farther on there is another good opening somewhat larger where there are many salmon. We named it St. James's River. While here, we saw a large ship from La Rochelle that in the night had run past the harbour of Brest where she intended to go and fish; and they did not know where they were. We went on board with our long boats and brought her into another harbour, one league farther west than the said river St. James. This harbour is in my opinion one of the best in the world. It was named Port Jacques Cartier. If the soil were as good as the harbours, it would be a blessing; but the land should not be called the New Land, being composed of stones and horrible rugged rocks; for along the whole of the north shore, I did not see one cart-load of earth and yet I landed in many places. Except at Blanc Sablon there is nothing but moss and short, stunted shrub. In fine, I am rather inclined to believe that this is the land God gave to Cain. There are people on this coast whose bodies are fairly well formed but they are wild and savage folk. They wear their hair tied up on the top of their heads like a handful of twisted hay, with a nail or something of the sort passed through the middle, and into it they weave a few bird's feathers. They clothe themselves with the furs of animals, both men as well as women; but the women are wrapped up more closely and snugly in their furs, and have a belt about their waists. They paint themselves with certain tan colours. They have canoes made of birch-bark in which they go about, and from which they catch many seals. Since seeing them, I have been informed that their home is not at this place, but that they come from warmer countries to catch these seals and to get other food for their sustenance.

How, when our people had sent two men on
shore with goods, about three hundred Indians
met them in great glee; of the nature
of the country and of its products; and of a bay
named Chaleur Bay

ON THURSDAY, THE eighth of the said month [July], as the wind was favourable for getting under way with our ships, we fitted up our long-boats to go and explore this Chaleur bay; and we ran up it that day some twenty-five leagues. The next day at daybreak, we had fine weather and sailed on until about ten o'clock in the morning, at which hour we caught sight of the head of the bay, whereat we were grieved and displeased. At the head of this bay, beyond the low shore, were several very high mountains. And seeing there was no passage, we proceeded to turn back. While making our way along the shore, we caught sight of the Indians on the side of a lagoon and low beach, who were making many fires that smoked. We rowed over to the spot, and finding there was an entrance from the sea into the lagoon, we placed our long-boats on one side of the entrance. The savages came over in one of their canoes and brought us some strips of cooked seal, which they placed on bits of wood and then withdrew, making signs to us that they were making us a present of them. We sent two men on shore with hatchets, knives, beads and other wares, at which the Indians showed great pleasure. And at once they came over in a crowd in their canoes to the side where we were, bringing furs and whatever else they possessed, in order to obtain some of our wares. They numbered, both men, women and children, more than 300 persons. Some of their women, who did not come over, danced and sang, standing in the water up to their knees. The other women, who had come over to the side where we were, advanced freely towards us and rubbed our arms with their hands. Then they joined their hands together and raised them to heaven, exhibiting many signs of joy. And so much at ease did the savages feel in our presence, that at length we bartered with them, hand to hand, for everything they possessed, so that nothing was left to them but their naked bodies; for they offered us everything they owned, which was, all told, of little value. We perceived that they are people who would be easy to convert, who go from place to place maintaining themselves and catching fish in the fishing-season for food. Their country is more temperate than Spain and the finest it is possible to see, and as level as the surface of a pond. There is not the smallest plot of ground bare of wood, and even on sandy soil, but is full of wild wheat, that has an ear like barley and the grain like oats, as well as of peas, as thick as if they had been sown and hoed; of white and red currant-bushes, of strawberries, of raspberries, of white and red roses and of other plants of a strong, pleasant odour. Likewise there are many fine meadows with useful herbs, and a pond where there are many salmon. I am more than ever of opinion that these people would be easy to convert to our holy faith. They call a hatchet in their language, *cochy,* and a knife, *bacan.* We named this bay, Chaleur Bay.

Stephen Parmenius
c. 1555-1583

———————◆———————

BORN IN HUNGARY, Stephen Parmenius set out in 1579 on a tour of
European universities in order to complete his education. In 1581 he
arrived in England where he met Richard Hakluyt while studying at
Oxford. Introduced by Hakluyt to Sir Humphrey Gilbert, Parmenius
accompanied Gilbert's expedition to Newfoundland in 1583. Within a
few weeks of his arrival he was drowned during the shipwreck of an
expedition from St. John's, Newfoundland, to Sable Island. His letter
to Hakluyt, written in Latin after his arrival in Newfoundland, appeared in an English translation in Hakluyt's *Principall Navigations*
(1589). Translations of Parmenius' work, together with an account of
his life, appear in *The New Found Land of Stephen Parmenius* (1972),
edited and translated by David B. Quinn and Neil M. Cheshire.

[LETTER TO RICHARD HAKLUYT]

To the worshipful, Master Richard Hakluyt
at Oxford in Christchurch,
Master of Art, and Philosophy,
his friend and brother

I HAD NOT purposed to write to you, when the promise of your letters
came to my mind; you thought in June last to have followed us yourself,
and therefore I had left order that you should be advertised of my state
by Master Doctor Humfrey,* but so you would not be satisfied. I will
write therefore to you, almost in the same words, because I have no
leisure at this time to meditate new matters and to vary or multiply
words.

The 11th of June we set sail at length from England in good earnest,
and departed, leaving the haven and land behind us at Plymouth. Our
fleet consisted of five ships; the greatest, which the Admiral's brother
had lent us, withdrew herself from us the third day, we know not upon
what occasion; with the rest we sailed together till the three and twenty

*Lawrence Humfrey, a friend of Parmenius and Hakluyt at Oxford.

of July, at which time, our view of one another being intercepted by the great mists, some of us sailed one way, and some another. To us alone the first land appeared, the first of August, about the latitude of fifty degrees, when as before we had descended beyond forty-one degrees in hope of some southerly winds, which notwithstanding, never blew to us at any fit time.

It is an island which your men call Penguin, because of the multitude of birds of the same name. Yet we neither saw any birds, nor drew near to the land; the winds serving for our course directed to another place, but we met all together at that place a little before the haven, whereunto by common counsel we had determined to come, and that within the space of two hours by the great goodness of God, and to our great joy. The place is situated in Newfoundland, between forty-seven and forty-eight degrees, called by the name of Saint John's. The Admiral himself by reason of the multitude of the men, and the smallness of his ship, had his company somewhat sickly, and had already lost two of the same company which died of the flux;* of the rest we conceive good hope. Of our company (for I joined myself with Maurice Brown, a very proper Gentleman), two persons by a mischance were drowned; the rest are in safety and strong, and for mine own part I was never more healthy. We arrived at this place the third of August, and the fifth, the Admiral took possession of the country for himself and the kingdom of England, having made and published certain laws concerning religion and obedience to the Queen of England. At this time our fare is somewhat better, and daintier, than it was before; for in good sooth, the experience of so long time hath taught us what contrary winds we have found and what great travail we may endure hereafter. And therefore we will take such order that we will want nothing, for we found in this place about twenty Portingale and Spanish ships besides the ships of the English, which being not able to match us, suffer us not to be hunger starved. The English, although they were of themselves strong enough and safe from our force, yet seeing our authority by the Queen's letters patent, they showed us all manner of duty and humanity.

The manner of this country, and people, remain now to be spoken of. But what shall I say, my good Hakluyt, when I see nothing but a very wilderness? Of fish here is incredible abundance, whereby great gain grows to them that travel to these parts; the hook is no sooner thrown out, but it is eftsoons drawn up with some goodly fish. The whole land is full of hills and woods. The trees for the most part are pines and of them, some are very old and some young. A great part of them being

*dysentery

fallen by reason of their age doth so hinder the sight of the land, and stop the way of those that seek to travel, that they can go no whither. All the grass here is long and tall and little differeth from ours. It seemeth also that the nature of this soil is fit for corn for I found certain blades and ears in a manner bearded, so that it appeareth that by manuring and sowing, they may easily be framed for the use of man. Here, are in the woods bush berries, or rather strawberries, growing up like trees, of great sweetness. Bears also appear about the fisher's stages of the country, and are sometimes killed, but they seem to be white, as I conjectured by their skins, and somewhat less* than ours. Whether there be any people in this country I know not, neither have I seen any to witness it and to say truth who can, when it is not possible to pass any whither. In like sort it is unknown whether any metals lie under the hills; the cause is all one, although the very colour and hue of the hills seem to have some mines in them. We moved the Admiral to set the woods afire, that so we might have space, and entrance to take view of the country which motion did nothing displease him, were it not for fear of great inconvenience that might thereof ensue. For it was reported and confirmed by very credible persons, that when the like happened by chance in another port, the fish never came to the place about it, for the space of seven whole years after, by reason of the waters made bitter by the turpentine and rosin of the trees, which ran into the rivers upon the firing of them. The weather is so hot this time of the year that except the very fish which is laid out to be dried by the sun, be every day turned, it cannot possibly be preserved from burning. But how cold it is in the winter the great heaps and mountains of ice in the midst of the sea have taught us. Some of our company report that in May they were sometimes kept in with such huge ice for sixteen whole days together, as that the islands thereof were threescore fathoms thick, the sides whereof which were toward the sun when they were melted, the whole mass or heap was so inverted and turned in manner of balancing, that that part which was before downward rose upward to the great peril of those that were near them, as by reason we may gather. The air upon land is indifferent clear but at sea towards the east there is nothing else but perpetual mists. And in the sea itself, about the Banks (for so they call the place where they find ground at forty leagues distant from the shore, and where they began to fish), there is no day without rain. When we have served and supplied our necessity in this place, we purpose by the help of God to pass towards the south, with so much the more hope every day, by how much greater

*smaller

the things are that are reported of those countries which we go to discover. Thus much touching our estate.

Now I desire to know something concerning you, but I fear in vain, but specially I desire out of measure to know how my patron, Master Henry Umpton, doth take my absence. My obedience and duty shall always be ready towards him as long as I live. But indeed, I hope that this journey of ours shall be profitable to his intentions. It remaineth that you think me to be still yours and so yours as no man's more. The son of God bless all our labours, so far as that you yourself may be partaker of our blessing. Adieu, my most friendly, most sweet, most virtuous Hakluyt. In Newfoundland, at Saint John's Port, the sixth of August, 1583.

Stephen Parmenius of Buda,
yours.

(1972)   (1589)

Marc Lescarbot
c. 1570-1642

———————◆———————

BORN NEAR LAON, France, Marc Lescarbot studied the classics and then law. In 1606 he accepted an invitation to accompany Jean de Poutrincourt to Port Royal, Acadia, where in November of that year he composed *Le Théâtre de Neptune,* the first theatrical production in North America. This entertainment was staged to welcome de Poutrincourt back to Port Royal after a voyage into the Bay of Fundy. A nautical masque, the work consists of poetry, songs and dances honoring France, her king and her colonizing agents.

From
The Theatre of Neptune in New France

Presented upon the waves of Port Royal the fourteenth day of November, sixteen hundred and six, upon the return of Sieur de Poutrincourt from the Armouchiquois country.
Neptune speaks first robed in a veil of blue, with buskins, gray hair and a beard worn long. He holds his trident in his hand and is seated upon his chariot adorned with varied colors. The chariot is drawn over the waves by six Tritons and so they come in state to the side of the shallop in which Sieur de Poutrincourt is sitting with his company ready to leave the boat and go ashore. As the shallop grapples, Neptune speaks as follows.

NEPTUNE: Hail to you, Sagamos,* rest and remain awhile!
Come, listen to a God who welcomes with a smile!
And if you know me not, great Saturn was my sire,
Brother am I to Jove, and Pluto, God of fire.

* * *

Fine courage you have had, that has led you to explore
With a bold constancy this strange and fog-bound shore,

_____
* Leader.

8

That you may here establish a wide realm for France
And carefully may guard my laws from all mischance.
    By my sacred trident, by my sceptre, I now swear
That to favor this high project shall be my happy care!   10
Even though you override me I shall never take my rest,
Until you bring the burden and the toil to my breast,
Of ten thousand busy ships that with noisy hue and cry
Shall carry out your orders in the twinkling of an eye.
    Go, then, with happiness, and follow on your way
Where ever fortune leads you, since I foresee the day,
When a prosperous domain you will prepare for France
In this fair, new world and the future will enhance
The glory of de Monts,† so too, your name shall ring
Immortal in the reign of Henry – your great king.   20

Neptune having finished speaking, a trumpet sounds loudly,
to encourage the Tritons to do the same.

* * *

THIRD TRITON: France, with fairest reason
Your praises are in season
For sons whose love and loyal courage
Appear more grandly in our age
Than in the centuries of old.
Through eager care and action bold
They seek to honor you and place
In Farthest lands, to a strange race,   30
The codes of your immortal law
That mortal world shall hold in awe.
    Then give your help and prospering favor
Unto so wonderful a labor!
Neptune, himself, gives godlike power
To you and yours in this great hour.
No human force can bring you harm
Whatever threat may bring alarm
'For man should never lose or spend
Good fortune that a god shall send.'   40

* * *

SIXTH TRITON: Hail King of France, Henry the Great!
Under your law New France holds her state.

---

† Pierre Du Gua De Monts (1558?-1628), explorer, trader and sponsor of de Poutrincourt's expedition to Port Royal.

New nations are yours, rich in your name,
And we, the bold Tritons, hope that the fame
Of Neptune, in reverence, here you may hold
High, as when in the days of old
The God was praised and worshipped by all
The dwellers upon the coasts of Gaul.
In regions where courage and hardiest daring
Called heroes abroad to fearless sea-faring   50
These, their descendants, for unselfish labor
Our God will cherish in his special favor
And prosper the end of their splendid emprise
Upon the great waves where his empire lies.

> *After this, Neptune withdraws a little to give place to a canoe, in which are four Indians who approach, each bearing a present to Sieur de Poutrincourt.*

FIRST INDIAN:
> *The first Indian offers a quarter of a moose or deer, speaking as follows:*

In the name of the peoples uncouth
Whose homeland is bound by their seas,
We come to give our vows in truth,
Unto the sacred Fleur-de-lis
Unfurling from your faithful land.
You act in princely majesty,   60
Watchful to tend in this rude land
The habit of sweet piety
And gentler ways, to foster all
That should secure establishment
Of common good, or what may fall
To build a Royal Government.
So, Sagamos, in every act
You find us friends, in verity,
And true devotion, in our pact
With you and your posterity.   70
Our little talent in the chase
We beg you use, from hearts entire.
To live forever in your grace
Is all our wish, our whole desire.

* * *

> *After Neptune had been thanked by Sieur de Poutrincourt for his offers toward the good of France, the Indians were also thanked for*

their good wishes and devotion, and they were invited to come to Fort Royal and to take bread. At this moment the troupe of Neptune sings in music of four parts the verse that follows.

FOUR PART SONG

Give us your pledge, great God Neptune,
Against wild ocean arrogance.
And grant us all, as your high boon
That we may meet again in France.

The music having finished, the trumpets sounded again and each man took his several way. The cannons broke forth on all sides and it seemed as though Proserpine were in birth pangs for her child. This effect was caused by the innumerable echoes sent back against one another from these hills and which continued for a quarter of an hour. The Sieur de Poutrincourt having arrived before Fort Royal habitation, a companion in a merry mood who was waiting for him patiently, spoke as follows:

Sagamos, the days of loneliness are past.
An angry heaven ordains your safe return at last,   80
And with relenting pity has shown to us your face,
Dispersing all our care with kind, surprising grace.
Come, then, chefs, cooks, and boys – all you who make good
    cheer.
Scullions and pastry cooks, let soup and roast appear,
Ransack the kitchen shelves, fill every pot and pan
And draw his own good portion for every eager man!
I see the men are thirsty, SICUT TERRA, SINE AQUA
Come, hurry boy, and pour for each his beaded measure.
Bestir yourselves, be brisk. Are the ducks on the spit?   90
What fowl have lost their heads? The goose, who cares for it?
Hither have sailed to us a band of comrades rare;
Let portions and their hunger be matched with equal care.
Enter within, messires, your welcome gaily seize,
Let each man drain his cup! Let each man strongly sneeze!
That never a frosty humor his person may contain
And only sweetest vapors may crowd his merry brain.

(1609)   (1927)

Robert Hayman
1575-1629

ROBERT HAYMAN WAS born in Devonshire, England, and educated at Oxford University. In 1621 he was appointed governor of a colony at Harbour Grace on Conception Bay, Newfoundland, where he wrote *Quodlibets* (1628), one of the earliest volumes of verse in English about life in North America.

From
Quodlibets

79.   The four elements in Newfoundland.

To the worshipful Captain John Mason, who did wisely and worthily govern there divers years.

> The Air in Newfoundland is wholesome, good;
> The Fire as sweet as any made of wood;
> The Waters, very rich, both salt and fresh;
> The Earth more rich, you know it no less.
> Where all are good, Fire, Water, Earth, and Air,
> What man made of these four would not live there?

80. To all those worthy women, who have any desire to live in Newfoundland, especially to the modest and discreet gentlewoman, Mistress Mason, wife to Captain Mason, who lived there divers years.

> Sweet creatures, did you truly understand
> The pleasant life you'd live in Newfoundland,
> You would with tears desire to be brought thither:
> I wish you, when you go, fair wind, fair weather:
> For if you with the passage can dispense,
> When you are there, I know you'll ne'er come thence.

81. To a worthy friend, who often objects the coldness of the winter in Newfoundland, and may serve for all those that have the like conceit.

> You say that you would live in Newfoundland,
> Did not this one thing your conceit withstand;
> You fear the winter's cold, sharp, piercing air.
> They love it best, that have once winter'd there.
> Winter is there, short, wholesome, constant, clear,
> Not thick, unwholesome, shuffling, as 'tis here.

101. To the first planters of Newfoundland.

> What aim you at in your plantation?
> Sought you the honour of our nation?
> Or did you hope to raise your own renown?
> Or else to add a kingdom to a crown?
> Or Christ's true doctrine for to propagate?
> Or draw savages to a blessed state?
> Or our o'er-peopled kingdom to relieve?
> Or show poor men where they may richly live?
> Or poor men's children goodly to maintain?
> Or aim'd you at your own sweet private gain?   10
> All these you had achiev'd before this day,
> And all these you have balk'd by your delay.

117. A Skeltonical continued rhyme in praise of my Newfoundland.

> Although in clothes, company, buildings fair,
> With England, Newfoundland cannot compare,
> Did some know what contentment I found there,
> Always enough, most times somewhat to spare,
> With little pains, less toil and lesser care,
> Exempt from taxings, ill news, lawing, fear,
> If clean, and warm, no matter what you wear,
> Healthy, and wealthy, if men careful are,
> With much much more, then I will now declare,
> I say if some wise men knew what this were   10
> I do believe they'd live no other where.

(1628)   (1628)

Paul Le Jeune
1591-1664

———◆———

BORN AT VITRY-LE-FRANÇOIS in the diocese of Châlons sur Marne, France, Paul Le Jeune entered the Jesuit order at Rouen in 1613. The second Jesuit superior of Quebec (1632-1639) and chief founder of the Jesuit missions in Canada, Le Jeune came to Canada in 1632 and remained until 1649 when he returned to France. During the first year of his residence in Quebec, Le Jeune initiated what eventually became the *Relations des Jesuites de la Nouvelle-France* (1632-1673), a series of annual reports sent by the missionaries of the Company of Jesus in Canada to their superiors in France. These reports were translated in *The Jesuit Relations and Allied Documents* (1896-1901), edited by Reuben Gold Thwaites.

From
A Brief Relation of the Journey to New France

ON PENTECOST DAY, just as I was ready to preach, as I usually did on Sundays and great Fête days, one of our sailors began to cry out, "codfish! codfish!" He had thrown in his line and had brought out a large one. We had already been on the banks several days, but had caught very little. On that day we drew in as many as we liked. It was a pleasure to see so great a slaughter, and so much of this blood shed upon the deck of our ship. These fresh supplies were very welcome to us after such continuous storms.

On the following Tuesday, the first day of June, we saw land. It was still covered with snow, for the winter, always severe in this country, was extremely so this year. Some days before, to wit, the 15th and 18th of May, being still distant from land about two hundred leagues, we had encountered two icebergs of enormous size, floating upon the sea. They were longer than our ship and higher than our masts, and as the sunlight fell upon them you would have said they were churches, or rather, mountains of crystal. I would hardly have believed it if I had not seen it. When a great number of them are encountered, and the ship finds itself caught among them, it is very soon broken into pieces.

On Thursday, June 3rd, we passed into the country through one of the most beautiful rivers in the world. The great island of Newfoundland intercepts it at its mouth, leaving two openings whereby it can empty into the sea, one to the north and the other to the south. We sailed in through the latter, which is about 13 or 14 leagues wide. Upon entering, you discover a gulf 150 leagues wide; going farther up, where this grand river begins to narrow, it is even there 37 leagues wide. Where we are, in Quebec, distant over 200 leagues from its mouth, it is still half a league wide.

At the entrance of this gulf we saw two rocks, one appearing to be round, the other square. You would say that God had thrown them into the midst of the waters, like two dovecotes, as a retreat for the birds that withdraw there in such multitudes that you would almost tread upon them; and if you do not obtain a good foothold, they rise up in such numbers that they may knock you over. Boats, or little skiffs, full of them are brought back to the ships, when the weather permits approach to these islands, which the French have named the Isles of Birds. Ships come into this gulf on whaling expeditions. We have seen a great many fishing also for cod. I saw here a number of seals, and our people killed some of them. In this great river, which is called the St. Lawrence, white porpoises are found, and nowhere else. The English call them white whales, because they are very large compared with the other porpoises; they go up as far as Quebec.

On the day of Holy Trinity, we were compelled to stop at Gaspé, a large body of water extending into this country. It was here that we trod land for the first time since our departure. Never did man, after a long voyage, return to his country with more joy than we entered ours; it is thus we call these wretched lands. We found here two ships, one from Honfleur and the other from Biscay, which had come to fish for cod. We begged the people from Honfleur to raise an altar for us, that we might celebrate the Holy Mass in their cabin; and there was a strife among them as to who should work upon it, so greatly were they pleased. So I said to them, laughingly, that in building their cabin they did not think they were building a chapel. When I came to the Gospel appointed for that day in the Mass, and which was the first that I had read in these lands, I was very much astonished in hearing these words of the Son of God to his Disciples, *Data est mihi omnis potestas in cœlo & in terra, euntes ergo docete omnes gentes baptisantes eos in nomine Patris,* etc. *Ecce ego vobiscum,* etc. I took these words as a good omen, although I clearly saw that they were not addressed to so poor a person as I. But it is my opinion that I come here like the pioneers, who go ahead to dig the trenches; after them come brave soldiers, who besiege and take the place.

Christophe Regnaut
1613-1697

———————◆———————

TRAINED AS A shoemaker, Christophe Regnaut arrived in Canada about 1640 and became one of the *donnés*, or lay brothers, of the Jesuit mission to the Huron Indians living east of Georgian Bay. In the spring of 1649, Regnaut was sent with a party to recover the bodies of Jean de Brébeuf and Gabriel Lalemant after their torture and death at the hands of the Iroquois. He returned to France in the following year and presented an account of the martyrdom of the Jesuit missionaries to the Order at Caen in 1678. This account appears in *The Jesuit Relations and Allied Documents* (1896-1901), edited by Reuben Gold Thwaites.

A Veritable Account of the Martyrdom and Blessed Death of Father Jean de Brébeuf and of Father Gabriel Lalemant, in New France, in the Country of the Hurons, by the Iroquois, Enemies of the Faith

FATHER JEAN DE BREBEUF and Father Gabriel Lalemant had set out from our cabin, to go to a small village, called St. Ignace, distant from our cabin about a short quarter of a league, to instruct the savages and the new Christians of that village. It was on the 16th Day of March, in the morning, that we perceived a great fire at the place to which these two good Fathers had gone. This fire made us very uneasy; we did not know whether it were enemies, or if the fire had caught in some of the huts of the village. The Reverend Father Paul Raguenau, our Superior, immediately resolved to send some one to learn what might be the cause. But no sooner had we formed the design of going there to see, than we perceived several savages on the road, coming straight toward us. We all thought it was the Iroquois who were coming to attack us; but, having considered them more closely, we perceived that they were Hurons who were fleeing from the fight, and who had escaped from the combat. These poor savages caused great pity in us. They were all covered with wounds. One had his head fractured; another his arm broken; another had an arrow in his eye; another had his hand cut off by a blow from a hatchet. In fine, the day was passed in receiving into our cabins all these poor wounded people, and in looking with compassion toward the fire, and the place where were those two good Fathers. We saw the fire and the barbarians, but we could not see anything of the two Fathers.

This is what these savages told us of the taking of the village of St. Ignace and about Fathers Jean de Brébeuf and Gabriel Lalemant:

"The Iroquois came, to the number of twelve hundred men; took our village, and seized Father Brébeuf and his companion; and set fire to all the huts. They proceeded to vent their rage on those two Fathers; for they took them both and stripped them entirely naked, and fastened each to a post. They tied both of their hands together. They tore the nails from their fingers. They beat them with a shower of blows from cudgels, on the shoulders, the loins, the belly, the legs, and the face, – there being no part of their body which did not endure this torment." The savages told us further, that, although Father de Brébeuf was overwhelmed under the weight of these blows, he did not cease continually to speak of God, and to encourage all the new Christians who were captives like himself to suffer well, that they might die well, in order to go in company with him to Paradise. While the good Father was thus encouraging these good people, a wretched Huron renegade, – who had remained a captive with the Iroquois, and whom Father de Brébeuf had formerly instructed and baptized, – hearing him speak of Paradise and Holy Baptism, was irritated, and said to him, "Echon," that is Father de Brébeuf's name in Huron, "thou sayest that Baptism and the sufferings of this life lead straight to Paradise; thou wilt go soon, for I am going to baptize thee, and to make thee suffer well, in order to go the sooner to thy Paradise." The barbarian, having said that, took a kettle full of boiling water, which he poured over his body three different times, in derision of Holy Baptism. And, each time that he baptized him in this manner, the barbarian said to him, with bitter sarcasm, "Go to Heaven, for thou art well baptized." After that, they made him suffer several other torments. The 1st was to make hatchets red-hot, and to apply them to the loins and under the armpits. They made a collar of these red-hot hatchets, and put it on the neck of this good Father. This is the fashion in which I have seen the collar made for other prisoners: They make six hatchets red-hot, take a large withe of green wood, pass the 6 hatchets over the large end of the withe, take the two ends together, and then put it over the neck of the sufferer. I have seen no torment which more moved me to compassion than that. For you see a man, bound naked to a post, who, having this collar on his neck, cannot tell what posture to take. For, if he lean forward, those above his shoulders weigh the more on him; if he lean back, those on his stomach make him suffer the same torment; if he keep erect, without leaning to one side or other, the burning hatchets, applied equally on both sides, give him a double torture.

After that they put on him a belt of bark, full of pitch and resin, and set fire to it, which roasted his whole body. During all these torments, Father de Brébeuf endured like a rock, insensible to fire and flames, which astonished all the bloodthirsty wretches who tormented him. His zeal was so great that he preached continually to these infidels, to try to convert them. His executioners were enraged against him for constantly speaking to them of God and of their conversion. To prevent him from speaking more, they cut off his tongue, and both his upper and lower lips. After that, they set themselves to strip the flesh from his legs, thighs, and arms, to the very bone; and then put it to roast before his eyes, in order to eat it.

While they tormented him in this manner, those wretches derided him, saying: "Thou seest plainly that we treat thee as a friend, since we shall be the cause of thy eternal happiness; thank us, then, for these good offices which we render thee, – for, the more thou shalt suffer, the more will thy God reward thee."

Those butchers, seeing that the good Father began to grow weak, made him sit down on the ground; and, one of them, taking a knife, cut off the skin covering his skull. Another one of those barbarians, seeing that the good Father would soon die, made an opening in the upper part of his chest, and tore out his heart, which he roasted and ate. Others came to drink his blood, still warm, which they drank with both hands, – saying that Father de Brébeuf had been very courageous to endure so much pain as they had given him, and that, by drinking his blood, they would become courageous like him.

This is what we learned of the Martyrdom and blessed death of Father Jean de Brébeuf, by several Christian savages worthy of belief, who had been constantly present from the time the good Father was taken until his death. These good Christians were prisoners to the Iroquois, who were taking them into their country to be put to death. But our good God granted them the favor of enabling them to escape by the way; and they came to us to recount all that I have set down in writing.

Father de Brébeuf was captured on the 16th day of March, in the morning, with Father Lalemant, in the year 1649. Father de Brébeuf died the same day as his capture, about 4 o'clock in the afternoon.

Those barbarians threw the remains of his body into the fire; but the fat which still remained on his body extinguished the fire, and he was not consumed.

I do not doubt that all which I have just related is true, and I would seal it with my blood; for I have seen the same treatment given to Iroquois prisoners whom the Huron savages had taken in war, with the exception of the boiling water, which I have not seen poured on any one.

I am about to describe to you truly what I saw of the martyrdom and of the blessed deaths of Father Jean de Brébeuf and of Father Gabriel Lalemant. On the next morning, when we had assurance of the departure of the enemy, we went to the spot to seek for the remains of their bodies, to the place where their lives had been taken. We found them both, but a little apart from each other. They were brought to our cabin, and laid uncovered upon the bark of trees, – where I examined them at leisure, for more than two hours, to see if what the savages had told us of their martyrdom and death were true. I examined first the body of Father de Brébeuf, which was pitiful to see, as well as that of Father Lalemant. Father de Brébeuf had his legs, thighs, and arms stripped of flesh to the very bone; I saw and touched a large number of great blisters, which he had on several places on his body, from the boiling water which these barbarians had poured over him in mockery of Holy Baptism. I saw and touched the wound from a belt of bark, full of pitch and resin, which roasted his whole body. I saw and touched the marks of burns from the collar of hatchets placed on his shoulders and stomach. I saw and touched his two lips, which they had cut off because he constantly spoke of God while they made him suffer.

I saw and touched all parts of his body, which had received more than two hundred blows from a stick. I saw and touched the top of his scalped head; I saw and touched the opening which these barbarians had made to tear out his heart.

In fine, I saw and touched all the wounds of his body, as the savages had told and declared to us; we buried these precious relics on Sunday, the 21st day of March, 1649, with much consolation.

I had the happiness of carrying them to the grave, and of burying them with those of Father Gabriel Lalement. When we left the country of the Hurons, we raised both bodies out of the ground, and set them to boil in strong lye. All the bones were well scraped, and the care of drying them was given to me. I put them every day into a little oven which we had, made of clay, after having heated it slightly; and, when in a state to be packed, they were separately enveloped in silk stuff. Then they were put into two small chests, and we brought them to Quebec, where they are held in great veneration.

It is not a Doctor of the Sorbonne who has composed this, as you may easily see; it is a relic from the Iroquois, and a person who has lived more than thought, – who is, and shall ever be,

     Sir,

Your Very Humble and very obedient servant,

CHRISTOPHE REGNAUT.

(1678)   (1901)

John Gyles
c. 1680-1755

BORN IN MAINE, John Gyles was taken captive by Malecite Indians during a raid on his home in 1689. He was taken to a location on the St. John River near Woodstock, New Brunswick, where he was a slave of the Malecites for six years. In 1695 he was sold to a French seigneur whom he served until he was allowed to sail for Boston in 1698. In 1736, Gyles published *Memoirs of Odd Adventures, Strange Deliverances, etc., in the Captivity of John Gyles.* With its descriptions of physical suffering, the customs of a little-known culture and the workings of providence, this narrative displays many of the elements which made the captivity experience a popular literary subject.

From
Memoirs of Odd Adventures, Strange Deliverances, etc., in the Captivity of John Gyles

[The First Year]

ON THE SECOND day of August, 1689, in the morning, my honored father, THOMAS GYLES, Esq., went with some laborers, my two elder brothers and myself, to one of his farms, which laid upon the river about three miles above fort Charles, adjoining Pemmaquid falls, there to gather in his English harvest, and we labored securely till noon. After we had dined, our people went to their labor, some in one field to their English hay, the others to another field of English corn. My father, the youngest of my two brothers, and myself, tarried near the farm-house in which we had dined till about one of the clock; at which time we heard the report of several great guns at the fort. Upon which my father said he hoped it was a signal of good news, and that the great council had sent back the soldiers, to cover the inhabitants; (for on report of the revolution they had deserted.) But to our great surprise, about thirty or forty Indians, at that moment, discharged a volley of shot at us, from behind a rising ground, near our barn. The yelling of the Indians, the whistling of their shot, and the voice of my father, whom I heard cry out, "What now! what now!" so terrified me, (though he seemed to be handling a gun,) that I endeavored to make my escape. My brother ran one way and I another, and looking over my shoulder, I saw a stout fellow, painted, pursuing me with a gun, and a cutlass glittering in his hand, which I expected every moment in my brains. I soon fell down, and the Indian seized me by the left hand. He offered me no abuse, but tied my arms, then lifted me up, and pointed to the place where the people were at work about the hay, and led me that way. As we went, we crossed where my father was, who looked very pale and bloody, and walked very slowly. When we came to the place, I saw two men shot down on the flats, and one or two more knocked on their heads with hatchets, crying out, "O Lord," &c. There the Indians brought two captives, one a man, and my brother James, who, with me, had endeavored to escape by running from the house, when we were first attacked. This brother was about fourteen years of age. My oldest brother, whose name was Thomas, wonderfully escaped by land to the Barbican, a point of land on the west side of the river, opposite the fort, where several fishing vessels lay. He got on board one of them and sailed that night.

After doing what mischief they could, they sat down, and made us sit with them. After some time we arose, and the Indians pointed for us to go eastward. We marched about a quarter of a mile, and then made a halt. Here they brought my father to us. They made proposals to him, by old Moxus, who told him that those were strange Indians who shot him, and that he was sorry for it. My father replied that he was a dying man, and wanted no favor of them, but to pray with his children. This being granted him, he recommended us to the protection and blessing of God Almighty; then gave us the best advice, and took his leave for this life, hoping in God that we should meet in a better. He parted with a cheerful voice, but looked very pale, by reason of his great loss of blood, which now gushed out of his shoes. The Indians led him aside! – I heard the blows of the hatchet, but neither shriek nor groan! I afterwards heard that he had five or seven shotholes through his waistcoast or jacket, and that he was covered with some boughs.

The Indians led us, their captives, on the east side of the river, towards the fort, and when we came within a mile and a half of the fort and town, and could see the fort, we saw firing and smoke on all sides. Here we made a short stop, and then moved within or near the distance of three quarters of a mile from the fort, into a thick swamp. There I saw my mother and my two little sisters, and many other captives who were taken from the town. My mother asked me about my father. I told her he was killed, but could say no more for grief. She burst into tears, and the Indians moved me a little farther off, and seized me with cords to a tree.

The Indians came to New Harbor, and sent spies several days to observe how and where the people were employed, &c., who found the men were generally at work at noon, and left about their houses only women and children. Therefore the Indians divided themselves into several parties, some ambushing the way between the fort and the houses, as likewise between them and the distant fields; and then alarming the farthest off first, they killed and took the people, as they moved towards the town and fort, at their pleasure, and very few escaped to it. Mr. Pateshall was taken and killed, as he lay with his sloop near the Barbican.

On the first stir about the fort, my youngest brother was at play near it, and running in, was by God's goodness thus preserved. Captain Weems, with great courage and resolution, defended the weak old fort two days; when, being much wounded, and the best of his men killed, he beat for a parley, which eventuated in these conditions:

1. That they, the Indians, should give him Mr. Pateshall's sloop. 2. That they should not molest him in carrying off the few people that had got into the fort, and three captives that they had taken. 3. That the English should carry off in their hands what they could from the fort.

On these conditions the fort was surrendered, and Captain Weems went off; and soon after, the Indians set on fire the fort and houses, which made a terrible blast, and was a melancholy sight to us poor captives, who were sad spectators!

After the Indians had thus laid waste Pemmaquid, they moved us to New Harbor, about two miles east of Pemmaquid, a cove much frequented by fishermen. At this place, there were, before the war, about twelve houses. These the inhabitants deserted as soon as the rumor of war reached the place. When we turned our backs on the town, my heart was ready to break! I saw my mother. She spoke to me, but I could not answer her. That night we tarried at New Harbor, and the next day went in their canoes for Penobscot. About noon, the canoe in which my mother was, and that in which I was, came side by side; whether accidentally or by my mother's desire I cannot say. She asked me how I did. I think I said "pretty well," but my heart was so full of grief I scarcely knew whether audible to her. Then she said, "O, my child! how joyful and pleasant it would be, if we were going to old England, to see your uncle Chalker, and other friends there! Poor babe, we are going into the wilderness, the Lord knows where!" Then bursting into tears, the canoes parted. That night following, the Indians with their captives lodged on an island.

A few days after, we arrived at Penobscot fort, where I again saw my mother, my brother and sisters, and many other captives. I think we tarried here eight days. In that time, the Jesuit of the place had a great mind to buy me. My Indian master made a visit to the Jesuit, and carried me with him. And here I will note, that the Indian who takes a captive is accounted his master, and has a perfect right to him, until he gives or sells him to another. I saw the Jesuit show my master pieces of gold, and understood afterwards that he was tendering them for my ransom. He gave me a biscuit, which I put into my pocket, and not daring to eat it, buried it under a log, fearing he had put something into it to make me love him. Being very young, and having heard much of the Papists torturing the Protestants, caused me to act thus; and I hated the sight of a Jesuit. When my mother heard the talk of my being sold to a Jesuit, she said to me, "Oh, my dear child, if it were God's will, I had rather follow you to your grave, or never see you more in this world, than you should be sold to a Jesuit; for a Jesuit will ruin you, body and soul!" It pleased God to grant her request, for she never saw me more! Yet she and my two little sisters were, after several years' captivity, redeemed, but she died before I returned. My brother who was taken with me, was, after several years' captivity, most barbarously tortured to death by the Indians.

My Indian master carried me up Penobscot river, to a village called *Madawamkee,* which stands on a point of land between the main river and a branch which heads to the east of it. At home I had ever seen strangers treated with the utmost civility, and being a stranger, I expected some kind of treatment here; but I soon found myself deceived, for I presently saw a number of squaws, who had got together in a circle, dancing and yelling. An old grim-looking one took me by the hand, and leading me into the ring, some seized me by my hair, and others by my hands and feet, like so many furies; but my master presently laying down a pledge, they released me.

A captive among the Indians is exposed to all manner of abuses, and to the extremest tortures, unless their master, or some of their master's relations, lay down a ransom; such as a bag of corn, a blanket, or the like, which redeems them from their cruelty for that dance. The next day we went up that eastern branch of Penobscot river many leagues; carried over land to a large pond, and from one pond to another, till, in a few days, we went down a river, called Medocktack, which vents itself into St. John's river. But before we came to the mouth of this river, we passed over a long carrying place, to Medocktack fort, which stands on a bank of St. John's river. My master went before, and left me with an old Indian, and two or three squaws. The old man often said, (which was all the English he could speak,) "By and by come to a great town and fort." I now comforted myself in thinking how finely I should be refreshed when I came to this great town.

After some miles' travel we came in sight of a large cornfield, and soon after of the fort, to my great surprise. Two or three squaws met us, took off my pack, and led me to a large hut or wigwam, where thirty or forty Indians were dancing and yelling round five or six poor captives, who had been taken some months before from Quochech, at the time Major Waldron was so barbarously butchered by them.

* * *

I was whirled in among this circle of Indians, and we prisoners looked on each other with a sorrowful countenance. Presently one of them was seized by each hand and foot, by four Indians, who, swinging him up, let his back fall on the ground with full force. This they repeated, till they had danced, as they called it, round the whole wigwam, which was thirty or forty feet in length. But when they torture a boy they take him up between two. This is one of their customs of torturing captives. Another is to take up a person by the middle, with his head hanging downwards, and jolt him round till one would think his bowels would shake out of his mouth. Sometimes they will take a captive by the hair of the head, and stooping him forward, strike him on the back and shoulder, till the blood gushes out of his mouth and nose. Sometimes an old shrivelled squaw will take up a shovel of hot embers and throw them into a captive's bosom. If he cry out, the Indians will laugh and shout, and say, "What a brave action our old grandmother has done." Sometimes they torture them with whips, &c.

The Indians looked on me with a fierce countenance, as much as to say, it will be your turn next. They champed cornstalks, which they threw into my hat, as I held it in my hand. I smiled on them, though my heart ached. I looked on one, and another, but could not perceive that any eye pitied me. Presently came a squaw and a little girl, and laid down a bag of corn in the ring. The little girl took me by the hand, making signs for me to go out of the circle with them. Not knowing their custom, I supposed they designed to kill me, and refused to go. Then a grave Indian came and gave me a short pipe, and said in English, "Smoke it;" then he took me by the hand and led me out. My heart ached, thinking myself near my end. But he carried me to a French hut, about a mile from the Indian fort. The Frenchman was not at home, but his wife, who was a squaw, had some discourse with my Indian friend, which I did not understand. We tarried about two hours, then returned to the Indian village, where they gave me some victuals. Not long after this I saw one of my fellow-captives, who gave me a melancholy account of their sufferings after I left them.

After some weeks had passed, we left this village and went up St. John's river about ten miles, to a branch called *Medockscenecasis,* where there was one wigwam. At our arrival an old squaw saluted me with a yell, taking me by the hair and one hand, but I was so rude as to break her hold and free myself. She gave me a filthy grin, and the Indians set up a laugh, and so it passed over. Here we lived upon fish, wild grapes, roots, &c., which was hard living to me.

When the winter came on we went up the river, till the ice came down, running thick in the river, when, according to the Indian custom, we laid up our canoes till spring. Then we travelled sometimes on the ice, and sometimes on the land, till we came to a river that was open, but not fordable, where we made a raft, and passed over, bag and baggage. I met with no abuse from them in this winter's hunting, though I was put to great hardships in carrying burdens and for want of food. But they underwent the same difficulty, and would often encourage me, saying, in broken English, *"By and by great deal moose."* Yet they could not answer any question I asked them. And knowing little of their customs and way of life, I thought it tedious to be constantly moving from place to place, though it might be in some respects an advantage; for it ran still in my mind that we were travelling to some settlement; and when my burden was over-heavy, and the Indians left me behind, and the still evening coming on, I fancied I could see through the bushes, and hear the people of some great town; which hope, though some support to me in the day, yet I found not the town at night.

Thus we were hunting three hundred miles from the sea, and knew no man within fifty or sixty miles of us. We were eight or ten in number, and had but two guns, on which we wholly depended for food. If any disaster had happened, we must all have perished. Sometimes we had no manner of sustenance for three or four days; but God wonderfully provides for all creatures. In one of these fasts, God's providence was remarkable. Our two Indian men, who had guns, in hunting started a moose, but there being a shallow crusted snow on the ground, and the moose discovering them, ran with great force into a swamp. The Indians went round the swamp, and finding no track, returned at night to the wigwam, and told what had happened. The next morning they followed him on the track, and soon found him lying on the snow. He had, in crossing the roots of a large tree, that had been blown down, broken through the ice made over the water in the hole occasioned by the roots of the tree taking up the ground, and hitched one of his hind legs among the roots, so fast that by striving to get it out he pulled his thigh bone out of its socket at the hip; and thus extraordinarily were we provided for in our great strait. Sometimes they would take a bear, which go into dens in the fall of the year, without any sort of food, and lie there four or five months without food, never going out till spring; in which time they neither lose nor gain in flesh. If they went into their dens fat they came out so, and if they went in lean they came out lean. I have seen some which have come out with four whelps, and both very fat, and then we feasted. An old squaw and a captive, if any present, must stand without the wigwam, shaking their hands and bodies as in a dance, and singing, "WEGAGE OH NELO WOH," which in English is, "Fat is my eating." This is to signify their thankfulness in feasting times. When one supply was spent we fasted till further success.

The way they preserve meat is by taking the flesh from the bones and drying it in smoke, by which it is kept sound months or years without salt. We moved still further up the country after moose when our store was out, so that by the spring we had got to the northward of the Lady mountains. When the spring came and the rivers broke up, we moved back to the head of St. John's river, and there made canoes of moose hides, sewing three or four together and pitching the seams with balsam mixed with charcoal. Then we went down the river to a place called Madawescook. There an old man lived and kept a sort of trading house, where we tarried several days; then went farther down the river till we came to the greatest falls in these parts, called Checanekepeag, where we carried a little way over the land, and putting off our canoes we went down-stream still. And as we passed down by the mouths of any large branches, we saw Indians; but when any dance was proposed, I was bought off. At length we arrived at the place where we left our birch canoes in the fall, and putting our baggage into them, went down to the fort.

There we planted corn, and after planting went a fishing, and to look for and dig roots, till the corn was fit to weed. After weeding we took a second tour on the same errand, then returned to hill our corn. After hilling we went some distance from the fort and field, up the river, to take salmon and other fish, which we dried for food, where we con-tinued till corn was filled with milk; some of it we dried then, the other as it ripened. To dry corn when in the milk, they gather it in large kettles and boil it on the ears, till it is pretty hard, then shell it from the cob with clam-shells, and dry it on bark in the sun. When it is thoroughly dry, a kernel is no bigger than a pea, and would keep years, and when it is boiled again it swells as large as when on the ear, and tastes incomparably sweeter than other corn. When we had gathered our corn and dried it in the way already described, we put some into Indian barns, that is, into holes in the ground, lined and covered with bark, and then with dirt. The rest we carried up the river upon our next winter's hunting. Thus God wonderfully favored me, and carried me through the first year of my captivity.

(1736)   (1841)

Frances Brooke
1724-1789

———◆———

FRANCES (MOORE) BROOKE was born in Lincolnshire, England, and was an active participant in a coterie of London writers which included Samuel Richardson and Dr. Johnson. As early as 1756 she was the editor of *The Old Maid,* a London periodical, and in the years that followed she wrote essays, plays, poetry, translations and novels. Mrs. Brooke came to Canada soon after her husband, the Reverend John Brooke, was appointed chaplain of the British garrison at Quebec in 1763. Although she returned to England with her husband in 1768, her responses to the landscape and culture of Quebec formed an integral part of the work which is generally regarded as the first Canadian novel, *The History of Emily Montague* (1769).

From
The History of Emily Montague

LETTER XLV

To Miss Rivers, Clarges Street

Silleri, Nov. 23

I HAVE BEEN seeing the last ship go out of the port, Lucy; you have no notion what a melancholy sight it is: we are now left to ourselves, and shut up from all the world for the winter: somehow we seem so forsaken, so cut off from the rest of human kind, I cannot bear the idea: I sent a thousand sighs and a thousand tender wishes to dear England, which I never loved so much as at this moment.

Do you know, my dear, I could cry if I was not ashamed? I shall not absolutely be in spirits again this week.

'Tis the first time I have felt any thing like bad spirits in Canada: I followed the ship with my eyes till it turned Point Levi, and, when I lost sight of it, felt as if I had lost every thing dear to me on earth. I am not particular: I see a gloom on every countenance; I have been at church, and think I never saw so many dejected faces in my life.

29

Adieu! for the present: it will be a fortnight before I can send this letter; another agreeable circumstance that: would to Heaven I were in England, though I changed the bright sun of Canada for a fog!

Dec. 1

We have had a week's snow without intermission: happily for us, your brother and the Fitz* have been weatherbound all the time at Silleri, and cannot possible get away.

We have amused ourselves within doors, for there is no stirring abroad, with playing at cards, playing at shuttlecock, playing the fool, making love, and making moral reflexions: upon the whole, the week has not been very disagreeable.

The snow is when we wake constantly up to our chamber windows; we are literally dug out of it every morning.

As to Quebec, I give up all hopes of ever seeing it again: but my comfort is, that the people there cannot possibly get to their neighbours; and I flatter myself very few of them have been half so well entertained at home.

We shall be abused, I know, for (what is really the fault of the weather) keeping these two creatures here this week; the ladies hate us for engrossing two such fine fellows as your brother and Fitzgerald, as well as for having vastly more than our share of all the men: we generally go out attended by at least a dozen, without any other woman but a lively old French lady, who is a flirt of my father's, and will certainly be my mamma.

We sweep into the general's assembly on Thursdays with such a train of beaux as draws every eye upon us: the rest of the fellows crowd round us; the misses draw up, blush, and flutter their fans; and your little Bell sits down with such a fancy impertinent consciousness in her countenance as is really provoking: Emily on the contrary looks mild and humble, and seems by her civil decent air to apologize to them for being so much more agreeable than themselves, which is a fault I for my part am not in the least inclined to be ashamed of.

Your idea of Quebec, my dear, is perfectly just; it is like a third or fourth rate country town in England; much hospitality, little society; cards, scandal, dancing, and good cheer; all excellent things to pass away a winter evening, and peculiarly adapted to what I am told, and what I begin to feel, of the severity of this climate.

I am told they abuse me, which I can easily believe, because my impertinence to them deserves it: but what care I, you know, Lucy, so long as I please myself, and am at Silleri out of the sound?

---

*Captain J. Fitzgerald, suitor to Arabella Fermor.

They are squabbling at Quebec, I hear, about I cannot tell what, therefore shall not attempt to explain: some dregs of old disputes, it seems, which have had not time to settle: however, we new comers have certainly nothing to do with these matters: you can't think how comfortable we feel at Silleri, out of the way.

My father says, the politics of Canada are as complex and as difficult to be understood as those of the Germanic system.

For my part, I think no politics worth attending to but those of the little commonwealth of woman: if I can maintain my empire over hearts, I leave the men to quarrel for every thing else.

I observe a strict neutrality, that I may have a chance for admirers amongst both parties. Adieu! the post is just going out.

Your faithful
A. FERMOR

LETTER LXXX

To Miss Rivers, Clarges Street

Silleri, Feb. 25

THOSE WHO HAVE heard no more of a Canadian winter than what regards the intenseness of its cold, must suppose it a very joyless season: 'tis, I assure you, quite otherwise; there are indeed some days here of the severity of which those who were never out of England can form no conception; but those days seldom exceed a dozen in a whole winter; nor do they come in succession, but at intermediate periods, as the winds set in from the North-West; which, coming some hundred leagues, from frozen lakes and rivers, over woods and mountains covered with snow, would be insupportable, were it not for the furs with which the country abounds, in such variety and plenty as to be within the reach of all its inhabitants.

Thus defended, the British belles set the winter of Canada at defiance; and the season of which you seem to entertain such terrible ideas, is that of the utmost cheerfulness and festivity.

But what particularly pleases me is, there is no place where women are of such importance: not one of the sex, who has the least share of attractions, is without a levee of beaux interceding for the honor of attending her on some party, of which every day produces three or four.

I am just returned from one of the most agreeable jaunts imagination can paint, to the island of Orleans, by the falls of Montmorenci; the latter is almost nine miles distant, across the great basin of Quebec; but as we are obliged to reach it in winter by the waving line, our direct road being intercepted by the inequalities of the ice, it is now perhaps a third more. You will possibly suppose a ride of this kind must want one of the greatest essentials to entertainment, that of variety, and imagine it only one dull whirl over an unvaried plain of snow: on the contrary, my dear, we pass hills and mountains of ice in the trifling space of these few miles. The basin of Quebec is formed by the conflux of the rivers St. Charles and Montmorenci with the great river St. Lawrence, the rapidity of whose flood-tide, as these rivers are gradually seized by the frost, breaks up the ice, and drives it back in heaps, till it forms ridges of transparent rock to an height that is astonishing, and of a strength which bids defiance to the utmost rage of the most furiously rushing tide.

This circumstance makes this little journey more pleasing than you can possibly conceive: the serene blue sky above, the dazzling brightness of the sun, and the colors from the refraction of its rays on the transparent part of these ridges of ice, the winding course these oblige you to make, the sudden disappearing of a train of fifteen or twenty carrioles, as these ridges intervene, which again discover themselves on your rising to the top of the frozen mount, the tremendous appearance both of the ascent and descent, which however are not attended with the least danger; all together give a grandeur and variety to the scene, which almost rise to enchantment.

Your dull foggy climate affords nothing that can give you the least idea of our frost pieces in Canada; nor can you form any notion of our amusements, of the agreeableness of a covered carriole, with a sprightly fellow, rendered more sprightly by the keen air and romantic scene about him; to say nothing of the fair lady at his side.

Even an overturning has nothing alarming in it; you are laid gently down on a soft bed of snow, without the least danger of any kind; and an accident of this sort only gives a pretty fellow occasion to vary the style of his civilities, and shew a greater degree of attention.

But it is almost time to come to Montmorenci; to avoid, however, fatiguing you or myself, I shall refer the rest of our tour to another letter, which will probably accompany this: my meaning is, that two moderate letters are vastly better than one long one; in which sentiment I know you agree with

Yours,

A. FERMOR.

LETTER CL

To the Earl of ——

Silleri, June 6, 1767

IT IS VERY true, my Lord, that the Jesuit missionaries still continue in the Indian villages in Canada; and I am afraid it is no less true, that they use every art to instill into those people an aversion to the English; at least I have been told this by the Indians themselves, who seem equally surprised and piqued that we do not send missionaries amongst them.

Their ideas of Christianity are extremely circumscribed, and they give no preference to one mode of our faith above another; they regard a missionary of any nation as a kind father, who comes to instruct them in the best way of worshipping the Deity, whom they suppose more propitious to the Europeans than to themselves; and as an ambassador from the prince whose subject he is: they therefore think it a mark of honour, and a proof of esteem, to receive missionaries; and to our remissness, and the French wise attention on this head, is owing the extreme attachment the greater part of the savage nations have ever had to the latter.

The French missionaries, by studying their language, their manners, their tempers, their dispositions; by conforming to their way of life, and using every art to gain their esteem, have acquired an influence over them which is scarce to be conceived; nor would it be difficult for ours to do the same, were they judiciously chose, and properly encouraged.

I believe I have said, that there is a striking resemblance between the manners of the Canadians and the savages; I should have explained it, by adding, that this resemblance has been brought about, not by the French having won the savages to receive European manners, but by the very contrary; the peasants having acquired the savage indolence in peace, their activity and ferocity in war; their fondness for field sports, their hatred of labour; their love of a wandering life, and of liberty; in the latter of which they have been in some degree indulged, the laws here being much milder, and more favourable to the people, than in France.

Many of the officers also, and those of rank in the colony troops, have been adopted into the savage tribes; and there is stronger evidence than, for the honour of humanity, I would wish there was, that some of them have led the death dance at the execution of English captives, have even partook the horrid repast, and imitated them in all their cruelties; cruelties, which, to the eternal disgrace, not only of our holy religion, but even of our nature, these poor people, whose ignorance is their excuse, have been instigated to, both by the French and English colonies, who, with a fury truly diabolical, have offered rewards to those who brought in the scalps of their enemies. Rousseau has taken great pains to prove that the most uncultivated nations are the most virtuous: I have all due respect for this philosopher, of whose writings I am an enthusiastic admirer; but I have a still greater respect for truth, which I believe is not in this instance on his side.

There is little reason to boast of the virtues of a people, who are such brutal slaves to their appetites as to be unable to avoid drinking brandy to an excess scarce to be conceived, whenever it falls in their way, though eternally lamenting the murders and other atrocious crimes of which they are so perpetually guilty when under its influence.

It is unjust to say we have corrupted them, that we have taught them a vice to which we are ourselves not addicted; both French and English are in general sober: we have indeed given them the means of intoxication, which they had not before their intercourse with us; but he must be indeed fond of praising them, who makes a virtue of their having been sober, when water was the only liquor with which they were acquainted.

From all that I have observed, and heard of these people, it appears to me an undoubted fact, that the most civilized Indian nations are the most virtuous; a fact which makes directly against Rousseau's ideal system.

Indeed all systems make against, instead of leading to, the discovery of truth.

Père Lafitau* has, for this reason, in his very learned comparison of the manners of the savages with those of the first ages, given a very imperfect account of Indian manners; he is even so candid as to own, he tells you nothing but what makes for the system he is endeavouring to establish.

My wish, on the contrary, is not to make truth subservient to any favourite sentiment or idea, any child of my fancy; but to discover it, whether agreeable or not to my own opinion.

My accounts may therefore be false or imperfect from mistake or misinformation, but will never be designedly warped from truth.

That the savages have virtues, candour must own; but only a love of paradox can make any man assert they have more than polished nations.

Your Lordship asks me what is the general moral character of the

---

*Père Joseph-François Lafitau, Jesuit missionary in North America and author of *Moeurs des Sauvages Amériquains* (1724).

Canadians; they are simple and hospitable, yet extremely attentive to interest, where it does not interfere with that laziness which is their governing passion.

They are rather devout than virtuous; have religion without morality, and a sense of honour without very strict honesty.

Indeed I believe wherever superstition reigns, the moral sense is greatly weakened; the strongest inducement to the practice of morality is removed, when people are brought to believe that a few outward ceremonies will compensate for the want of virtue.

I myself heard a man, who had raised a large fortune by very indirect means, confess his life had been contrary to every precept of the Gospel; but that he hoped the pardon of Heaven for all his sins, as he intended to devote one of his daughters to a conventual life as an expiation.

This way of being virtuous by proxy, is certainly very easy and convenient to such sinners as have children to sacrifice.

By Colonel Rivers, who leaves us in a few days, I intend myself the honour of addressing your Lordship again.

I have the honour to be

Your Lordship's, etc.

WM. FERMOR

(1769)   (1769)

Jacob Bailey
1731-1808

BORN IN MASSACHUSETTS, Jacob Bailey studied at Harvard University before going to England where he entered the Anglican ministry in 1760. Under the sponsorship of the Society for Promoting the Gospel in Foreign Parts, Bailey subsequently returned to North America as a missionary to the settlers of Pownalboro, Maine. He remained there until 1779 when his continuing opposition to the American Revolution forced him to emigrate to Nova Scotia. From 1780 until his death he served as minister of the Church of England at Annapolis. Selections from Bailey's memoirs were first published in 1853 in W. S. Bartlett's biography, *The Frontier Missionary*.

From
Journal of a Voyage from Pownalboro' to Halifax with Notices of Some Events in the Latter Place

JUNE 7TH, 1779.   We arose this morning before the sun and began to prepare for our expulsion, our hearts replete with apprehension, anxiety and distress.

As the rising sun tinged the various objects around us, I beheld the once delightful scenes with bitter emotions of grief. This, in a word, was the silent language of our faces as we looked upon each other, and it was agreeable to the inward impulse. Must we, after all the trouble, harrassment and cruel persecution we have endured for the cause of truth and virtue, must we leave these pleasing scenes of nature, these friendly shades, these rising plants, these opening flowers, these trees swelling with fruit, and yonder winding river, which appears through the umbrageous avenue, to revive and elevate the mind? We must no longer behold the splendid orb of day peeping over the eastern hills to dissipate the fog, and to brighten the field and the forest. We must hear no more the sweet music of the tuneful tribe, amidst the trembling grove, to gladden, charm and animate the desponding heart.

* * *

June 18th. Towards morning the wind shifted into the N.E., then east, and afterwards into the S.E., when it began to blow and rain, with most threatening appearances of a storm. This unexpected continuance of bad weather had a very malignant influence upon our whole company. The hands, with Dr. Mayer, the old bachelor, swore bitterly; the captain, notwithstanding his moderation, lost all patience, and loudly complained of the unpropitious season, while we began to imagine that we should never be able to reach our intended port, so many impediments arising to retard our progress. We, however, found some consolation when we perceived that the wind rather abated, and in the afternoon it blew in our favor, so that we rediscovered the land towards evening. But the fog continued to hover over the surface of the water in such a manner that it became wholly unsafe to aim at any harbour. In bearing away from the shore we discovered, through the surrounding fog, several little islands, interspersed with rugged rocks, against which the waves, dashing with violence, occasioned a frightful roaring. We had the good fortune, however, to escape without damage.

After keeping almost two days between decks, as it was now more calm and moderate, I ventured out of my confinement to contemplate the striking prospect around us. Nothing appeared but a waste of waters in perpetual motion, with a surface rugged and unshapen beyond imagination, for the seas in this Bay of Fundy do not roll with regular succession as in other oceans, with gradual swellings, which rise in extensive order, one behind another, as far as the eye can reach, but here we perceive waves of a thousand various figures and dimensions, resembling a multitude of rocks and broken fragments of nature, torn by some violent explosion, and rudely scattered over an immense desert or barren plain. While we were sitting upon deck and diverting ourselves as well as our situation would admit, one of our hens escaped from her confinement in the salt room and flew about the vessel from one quarter to another, seemingly exulting in her liberty. But alas! this freedom proved the destruction of the volatile and noisy animal, for one of our company attempted to secure her, upon which she immediately flew overboard into the sea, and sat struggling and cackling upon the waves till we could see her no longer. I must confess that in my present circumstances this accident affected me, and I was moved with compassion for the foolish flutterer, when I observed her exposed to inevitable destruction, striving to regain the vessel, and, as it were, calling aloud for assistance, when we were unable to afford the wretched being any relief. How often do we behold animals who fondly boast of reason, hurrying themselves with almost the same giddy precipitation into ruin. How common is it for men, when impatient of legal restraint, and ardent to acquire unbounded freedom,— how frequent is it for people in these circumstances, when they have escaped from every confinement and gained their wished for liberty, to plunge headlong into destruction, and when they become sensible too late of their unbounded rashness and folly, they are desirous from their hearts to reënter that condition they once called slavery and bondage. In short, I am convinced that no animal in nature makes so pernicious an improvement of liberty as man; for notwithstanding all his boasted pretences to wisdom, if you place him in a situation of unrestrained license, it is a thousand to one if he do not ruin both himself and all his intimate connections. But enough of liberty for the present, since I had a sufficient surfeit from it in New England, and have seen from that abused principle all the miseries of licentiousness, anarchy, and tyranny, flowing like so many torrents to deluge that unhappy and devoted land. Just about sunset we were favored with another flattering prospect of fine weather; a glim from the western hemisphere inspired us with pleasure, but upon the rising of the fog we were alarmed to find ourselves almost contiguous to a dangerous rock, called the Gurnet, which rose with perpendicular sides, like a large building, above the water. The wind was now beginning to blow gently from the S.W., which, when we had cleared the land as we imagined, was extremely favourable to our purpose. But alas! when we had been running, as we fondly conceived, along the coast to the eastward of Cape Sable, to our great surprise we heard a terrible roaring on every hand. In this scene of apprehension and danger Captain Smith brought to, and upon sounding, perceived ourselves amidst shoals and breakers, in about two fathoms of water, and, as he concluded, just upon that terrible ledge or range of rocks, called the Devil's Limb. To extricate ourselves from this alarming situation, the captain put instantly about, and we stood till daylight across this vexatious Bay of Fundy.

* * *

June 21st.   No sooner did the morning light begin to soften the horrors of darkness, than I arose and took possession of the deck to observe the weather and to survey the adjacent country. I found that we were overtaken by a dead calm, and the heavens were covered with rolling volumes of black and dismal clouds which shed a dark and dejecting gloom over all the surrounding scenes of nature. But if I was inspired with melancholy sentiments at this dusky prospect, I was perfectly shocked when I turned my eyes towards the land which stretched along the western quarter. The shore which now engages my attention is the famous Jebucto Head, a most enormous congress of rocky ledges running with a lofty and impregnable front into the sea, while the surface is inexpressibly rugged and broken, covered with shrubby spruce, fir and hemlock, which by their starving and misshapen appearance sufficiently indicate the severity of the climate and the barrenness of the soil. But notwithstanding the unpleasing aspect of this strange region, I could not forbear the returns of gratitude to Providence for safely conducting me and my family to this retreat of freedom and security from the rage of tyranny and the cruelty of oppression. The wind beginning to blow softly as the light increased, we weighed anchor, displayed the canvas and got under way. The sun being risen we perceived that the land on the eastern side of the harbour was in comparison extremely agreeable; the beach was covered with small pebbles, the banks, which were moderately high, resembled the colour of deep burnt bricks, and the trees of various species, tall and well shaped. And what added to the beauty and cheerfulness of the prospect, the forest was in many cases discontinued and finely interspersed with patches of cleared ground, adorned with a lively verdure.

But we were again sadly disappointed in our expectations, for we fondly imagined that upon our entrance into the harbour we should have the whole metropolis in open view, and a number of lofty buildings rising in conspicuous glory, with a respectable part of the Royal Navy lying at anchor before the town. Instead of which flattering instances of power, grandeur and magnificence, we could observe no edifices except the citadel and two or three scattered habitations; and as to shipping we saw only two sail of armed vessels and three or four sail at Major's Beach, for we were ignorant that both the town and the proper harbour were concealed by the interposition of St. George's Island and certain aspiring eminences to the northward. As we sailed slowly up the harbour, the next object which invited our attention, was a large fleet of Indian canoes, coasting along the Jebucto shore and filled with multitudes of the native Micmacs, and at the same time we espied several of these copper-faced sons of liberty either landing on the margin of a little bay, or climbing up the stupendous precipices. We took notice upon this occasion, that artificial ways were formed up these steepy cliffs for the convenience of ascending or conveying down timber, which is frequently cut on the summit of these ridges for the public works at Halifax. As we advanced still further from the ocean, the town began gradually to open, and we had in prospect several strong fortifications, as the Eastern Battery, George's Fort, and strong ramparts upon the neighbouring heights, with all their terrible apparatus of cannon and mortars. When we arrived near the above-mentioned Island of St. George's, we had a most advantageous, striking view of this northern capital, stretching a mile and an half upon the eastern ascent of an extensive hill, while a large collection of shipping lay either contiguous to the wharves, or else were riding, with the Brittanic colours flying, in the channel, a sight which instantly inspired us with the most pleasing sensations. We expected to be hailed as we passed St. George's Fort, but the people, conceiving our vessel to be some coaster from Malagash, we were suffered to proceed without any inquiry.

(1853)

Jonathan Odell
1737-1818

———◆———

JONATHAN ODELL, ONE of the most accomplished of the Loyalist poets, was born in Newark, New Jersey, and served as a surgeon in the British army before resigning his commission to study theology. Ordained in the Church of England in 1767, Odell was the rector of a church in Burlington, New Jersey, when the American Revolution began. Because of his outspoken opposition to the American insurrection, he was forced to seek refuge in the British garrison at New York where he wrote many patriotic and satiric poems before sailing for England in 1783. The following year Odell settled in New Brunswick where he lived until his death. In 1860 many of Odell's poems were collected by Winthrop Sargent in *The Loyal Verses of Joseph Stansbury and Dr. Jonathan Odell.*

Song

For a fishing party near Burlington, on the Delaware, in 1776

How sweet is the season, the sky how serene;
On Delaware's banks how delightful the scene;
The Prince of the Rivers, his waves all asleep,
In silence majestic glides on to the Deep.

Away from the noise of the Fife and the Drum,
And all the rude din of Bellona we come;
And a plentiful store of good humor we bring
To season our feast in the shade of Cold Spring.

A truce then to all whig and tory debate;
True lovers of Freedom, contention we hate: 10
For the Demon of discord in vain tries his art
To possess or inflame a true *Protestant* heart.

41

True Protestant friends to fair Liberty's cause,
To decorum, good order, religion and laws,
From avarice, jealousy, perfidy, free;
We wish all the world were as happy as we.

We have wants, we confess, but are free from the care
Of those that abound, yet have nothing to spare:
Serene as the sky, as the river serene,
We are happy to want envy, malice, and spleen.   20

While thousands around us, misled by a few,
The Phantoms of pride and ambition pursue,
With pity their fatal delusion we see;
And wish all the world were as happy as we!

(1860)   (1860)

Ode for the New Year

When rival Nations first descried,
Emerging from the boundless Main
This Land by Tyrants yet untried,
On high was sung this lofty strain:
Rise Britannia beaming far!
Rise bright Freedom's morning star!

To distant Regions unexplor'd
Extend the blessings of thy sway;
To your benighted World afford
The light of thy all-cheering ray;   10
Rise Britannia, rise bright star!
Spread thy radiance wide and far!

The shoots of Science rich and fair,
Transplanted from thy fostering Isle
And by thy Genius nurtur'd there,
Shall teach the Wilderness to smile.
Shine, Britannia, rise and shine!
To bless Mankind the task be thine!

Nor shall the Muses now disdain
To find a new Asylum there;   20
And ripe for harvest see the plain,
Where lately rov'd the prowling Bear,
Plume Britannia, plume thy wing!
Teach the savage Wild to sing!

From thee descended there the Swain
Shall arm the Port and spread the Sail,
And speed his traffick o'er the Main
With skill to brave the sweeping Gale;
Skill, Britannia, taught by thee,
Unrivall'd Empress of the Sea!   30

This high and holy strain how true
Had now from age to age been shown;
And to the World's admiring view
Rose Freedom's transatlantic throne:
Here, Britannia, here thy fame
Long did we with joy proclaim.

But ah! what frenzy breaks a band
Of love and union held so dear!
Rebellion madly shakes the land,
And love is turn'd to hate and fear.   40
Here, Britannia, here at last
We feel Contagion's deadly blast.

Thus blind, alas! when all is well,
Thus blind are Mortals here below:
As when apostate Angels fell,
Ambition turns our bliss to woe.
Now, Britannia, now beware:
For other conflicts now prepare!

By thee controlled for ages past,
See now half Europe in array;   50
For wild Ambition hopes at last
To fix her long projected sway.
Rise, Britannia, rise again
The scourge of haughty France and Spain!

The howling tempest fiercely blows,
And Ocean rages in the storm:
'Tis then the fearless Pilot shows
What British courage can perform.
Rule, Britannia, rule the waves
And ruin all intruding slaves!   60

(1860)   (1860)

Alexander Henry
1739-1824

———◆———

BORN IN NEW Jersey, Alexander Henry came to Canada in 1760 and in the following year became one of the first English fur traders to enter the previously French territory on the Western Great Lakes. While at Fort Michilimackinac in 1763, he survived the attack on the fort by Pontiac's forces. His description of this event is included in *Travels and Adventures in Canada and the Indian Territories Between the Years 1760 and 1776* (1809).

From
Travels and Adventures in Canada and the Indian Territories

[Massacre at Fort Michilimackinac]

THE MORNING WAS sultry. A Chipeway came to tell me that his nation was going to play at *bag'gat'iway*, with the Sacs or Saakies, another Indian nation, for a high wager. He invited me to witness the sport, adding that the commandant was to be there, and would bet on the side of the Chipeways. In consequence of this information, I went to the commandant, and expostulated with him a little, representing that the Indians might possibly have some sinister end in view; but, the commandant only smiled at my suspicions.

Baggatiway, called by the Canadians, *le jeu de la crosse*, is played with a bat and ball. The bat is about four feet in length, curved, and terminating in a sort of racket. Two posts are planted in the ground, at a considerable distance from each other, as a mile, or more. Each party has its post, and the game consists in throwing the ball up to the post of the adversary. The ball, at the beginning, is placed in the middle of the course, and each party endeavours as well to throw the ball out of the direction of its own post, as into that of the adversary's.

I did not go myself to see the match which was now to be played without the fort, because, there being a canoe prepared to depart, on

45

the following day, for Montréal, I employed myself in writing letters to my friends; and even when a fellow-trader, Mr. Tracy, happened to call upon me, saying that another canoe had just arrived from Detroit, and proposing that I should go with him to the beach, to inquire the news, it so happened that I still remained, to finish my letters; promising to follow Mr. Tracy, in the course of a few minutes. Mr. Tracy had not gone more than twenty paces from my door, when I heard an Indian war-cry, and a noise of general confusion.

Going instantly to my window, I saw a crowd of Indians, within the fort, furiously cutting down and scalping every Englishman they found. In particular, I witnessed the fate of Lieutenant Jemette.

I had, in the room in which I was, a fowling-piece, loaded with swan-shot. This I immediately seized, and held it for a few minutes, waiting to hear the drum beat to arms. In this dreadful interval, I saw several of my countrymen fall, and more than one struggling between the knees of an Indian, who, holding him in this manner, scalped him, while yet living.

At length, disappointed in the hope of seeing resistance made to the enemy, and sensible, of course, that no effort, of my own unassisted arm, could avail against four hundred Indians, I thought only of seeking shelter. Amid the slaughter which was raging, I observed many of the Canadian inhabitants of the fort, calmly looking on, neither opposing the Indians, nor suffering injury; and, from this circumstance, I conceived a hope of finding security in their houses.

Between the yard-door of my own house, and that of M. Langlade, my next neighbour, there was only a low fence, over which I easily climbed. At my entrance, I found the whole family at the windows, gazing at the scene of blood before them. I addressed myself immediately to M. Langlade, begging that he would put me into some place of safety, until the heat of the affair should be over; an act of charity by which he might perhaps preserve me from the general massacre; but, while I uttered my petition, M. Langlade, who had looked for a moment at me, turned again to the window, shrugging his shoulders, and intimating, that he could do nothing for me: − *"Que voudriez-vous que j'en ferais?"*

This was a moment for despair; but, the next, a Pani woman, a slave of M. Langlade's, beckoned to me to follow her. She brought me to a door, which she opened, desiring me to enter, and telling me that it led to the garret, where I must go and conceal myself. I joyfully obeyed her directions; and she, having followed me up to the garret-door, locked it after me, and with great presence of mind took away the key.

This shelter obtained, if shelter I could hope to find it, I was naturally anxious to know what might still be passing without. Through an aperture, which afforded me a view of the area of the fort, I beheld, in shapes the foulest and most terrible, the ferocious triumphs of barbarian conquerors. The dead were scalped and mangled; the dying were writhing and shrieking, under the unsatiated knife and tomahawk; and, from the bodies of some ripped open, their butchers were drinking the blood, scooped up in the hollow of joined hands, and quaffed amid shouts of rage and victory. I was shaken, not only with horror, but with fear. The sufferings which I witnessed, I seemed on the point of experiencing. No long time elasped, before every one being destroyed, who could be found, there was a general cry, of "All is finished!" At the same instant, I heard some of the Indians enter the house in which I was.

The garret was separated from the room below, only by a layer of single boards, at once the flooring of the one and the ceiling of the other. I could therefore hear every thing that passed; and, the Indians, no sooner in, than they inquired, whether or not any Englishman were in the house? M. Langlade replied, that "He could not say – he did not know of any;" – answers in which he did not exceed the truth; for the Pani woman had not only hidden me by stealth, but kept my secret, and her own, M. Langlade was therefore, as I presume, as far from a wish to destroy me, as he was careless about saving me, when he added to these answers, that "They might examine for themselves, and would soon be satisfied, as to the object of their question." Saying this, he brought them to the garret-door.

The state of my mind will be imagined. Arrived at the door, some delay was occasioned by the absence of the key, and a few moments were thus allowed me, in which to look around for a hiding place. In one corner of the garret was a heap of those vessels of birch-bark, used in maple-sugar making, as I have recently described.

The door was unlocked, and opening, and the Indians ascending the stairs before I had completely crept into a small opening which presented itself, at one end of the heap. An instant after, four Indians entered the room, all armed with tomahawks, and all besmeared with blood, upon every part of their bodies.

The die appeared to be cast. I could scarcely breathe; but I thought that the throbbing of my heart occasioned a noise loud enough to betray me. The Indians walked in every direction about the garret, and one of them approached me so closely that at a particular moment, had he put out his hand, he must have touched me. Still, I remained undiscovered; a circumstance to which the dark colour of my clothes, and the corner in which I was must have contributed. In a word, after taking several turns in the room, during want of light, in a room which had no window, and in which they told M. Langlade how many they had killed, and how many scalps they had taken, they returned down stairs, and I, with sensations not to be expressed, heard the door, which was the barrier between me and my fate, locked for the second time.

There was a feather-bed on the floor; and, on this, exhausted as I was, by the agitation of my mind, I threw myself down and fell asleep. In this state I remained till the dusk of the evening, when I was awakened by a second opening of the door. The person, that now entered, was M. Langlade's wife, who was much surprised at finding me, but advised me not to be uneasy, observing, that the Indians had killed most of the English, but that she hoped I might myself escape. – A shower of rain having begun to fall, she had come to stop a hole in the roof. On her going away, I begged her to send me a little water, to drink; which she did.

As night was now advancing, I continued to lie on the bed, ruminating on my condition, but unable to discover a resource, from which I could hope for life. A flight, to Détroit, had no probable chance of success. The distance, from Michilimackinac, was four hundred miles; I was without provisions; and the whole length of the road lay through Indian countries, countries of an enemy in arms, where the first man whom I should meet would kill me. To stay where I was, threatened nearly the same issue. As before, fatigue of mind, and not tranquility, suspended my cares, and procured me further sleep.

(1809)   (1809)

Joseph Stansbury
1740-1809

BORN IN ENGLAND, Joseph Stansbury emigrated to Philadelphia in
1767; during the American Revolution he remained loyal to the Crown
and in 1783 he was banished for his British sympathies. Until he was
allowed to return to the United States two years later, he lived rather
unhappily in Nova Scotia. In 1860 many of his poems were collected
together with those of Jonathan Odell by Winthrop Sargent in *The
Loyal Verses of Joseph Stansbury and Dr. Jonathan Odell.*

Ode

For the Year 1778

When rival nations, great in arms,
Great in power, in glory great,
Fill the world with loud alarms,
And breathe a temporary hate:
The hostile storms but rage awhile,
And the tir'd contest ends.
But ah! how hard to reconcile
The foes who once were friends.

Each hasty word, each look unkind,
Each distant hint, that seems to mean   10
A something lurking in the mind
That almost longs to lurk unseen;
Each shadow of a shade offends
Th' embittered foes who once were friends.

That Pow'r alone, who fram'd the Soul,
And bade the springs of passion play,
Can all their jarring strings control;
And form, on discord, concord's sway.
'Tis He alone, whose breath of love

Did o'er the world of waters move –   20
Whose touch the mountain bends –
Whose word from darkness call'd forth light;
'Tis He alone can reunite
The foes who once were friends.

To Him, O Britain! bow the knee,
His awful, his august decree,
Ye rebel tribes adore!
Forgive at once and be forgiven:
Ope' in each breast a little heaven;
And discord is no more!   30

(1860)   (1860)

God Save the King

Time was, in defence of his King and the Right,
We applauded brave Washington foremost in fight:
On the banks of Ohio he shouted lustily
      God save the King!
Disappointed ambition his feet has misled;
Corrupted his heart and perverted his head:
Loyal no longer, no more he cries faithfully
      Glory and Joy crown the King!

With Envy inflam'd 'tis in Britain the same;
Where leaders, despairing of virtuous fame,   10
Have push'd from their seats those whose watchword was constantly
      God save the King!
The helm of the State they have clutched in their grasp
When American Treason is at its last gasp:
When Firmness and Loyalty soon should sing valiantly
      Glory and Joy crown the King!

But Britain, with Glory and Conquest in view,
When nothing was wanted, but just to pursue –
To yield – while her Heroes chanted triumphantly
      God save the King!   20

With curses consign to the Furies his Name,
Whose Counsels thus cover'd his Country with shame!
Loyalists still will chant, tho' heavily,
      Glory and Joy crown the King!

Tho' ruin'd so deeply no Angel can save:
The Empire dismember'd: our King made a Slave:
Still loving, revering, we shout forth honestly
      God save the King!
Tho' fated to Banishment, Poverty, Death,
Our Hearts are unalter'd, and with our last breath   30
Loyal to George, we'll pray most fervently
      Glory and Joy crown the King!

(1860)   (1860)

To Cordelia

Believe me, Love, this vagrant life
   O'er Nova Scotia's wilds to roam,
While far from children, friends, or wife,
   Or place that I can call a home
Delights not me; – another way
My treasures, pleasures, wishes lay.

In piercing, wet, and wintry skies,
   Where man would seem in vain to toil,
I see, where'er I turn my eyes,
   Luxuriant pasture, trees, and soil.   10
Uncharm'd I see: – another way
My fondest hopes and wishes lay.

Oh could I through the future see
   Enough to form a settled plan,
To feed my infant train and thee
   And fill the rank and style of man:
I'd cheerful be the livelong day;
Since all my wishes point that way.

But when I see a sordid shed
   Of birchen bark, procured with care,   20
Design'd to shield the aged head
   Which British mercy placed there –
'Tis too, too much: I cannot stay,
But turn with streaming eyes away.

Oh! how your heart would bleed to view
   Six pretty prattlers like your own,
Expos'd to every wind that blew;
   Condemn'd in such a hut to moan.
Could this be borne, Cordelia, say?
Contented in your cottage stay.   30

'Tis true, that in this climate rude,
   The mind resolv'd may happy be;
And may, with toil and solitude,
   Live independent and be free.
So the lone hermit yields to slow decay:
Unfriended lives – unheeded glides away.

If so far humbled that no pride remains,
   But moot indifference which way flows the stream;
Resign'd to penury, its cares and pains;
   And hope has left you like a painted dream;   40
Then here, Cordelia, bend your pensive way,
And close the evening of Life's wretched day.

(1860)   (1860)

Samuel Hearne
1745-1792

———◆———

BORN IN LONDON, England, Samuel Hearne joined the Hudson's Bay Company in 1766 and was posted to Fort Prince of Wales on the Churchill River. There he led three expeditions into the interior of the Northwest in search of copper and the mouth of the Coppermine River on the Arctic coast. His account of these expeditions and of his success in becoming the first European to reach the Arctic Ocean overland from Hudson's Bay was published posthumously as *A Journey from Prince of Wales's Fort, in Hudson's Bay, to the Northern Ocean, Undertaken by Order of the Hudson's Bay Company, for the Discovery of Copper Mines, a North West Passage, etc. in the Years 1769, 1770, 1771, & 1772* (1795).

From
A Journey from Prince of Wales's Fort in Hudson's Bay to the Northern Ocean

[The Coppermine Massacre]

[*July 16, 1771*]

EARLY IN THE morning of the sixteenth, the weather being fine and pleasant, I again proceeded with my survey, and continued it for ten miles farther down the river; but still found it the same as before, being everywhere full of falls and shoals. At this time (it being about noon) the three men who had been sent as spies met us on their return, and informed my companions that five tents of Esquimaux were on the west side of the river. The situation, they said, was very convenient for surprising them; and, according to their account, I judged it to be about twelve miles from the place we met the spies. When the Indians received this intelligence, no farther attendance or attention was paid to my survey, but their whole thoughts were immediately engaged in planning the best method of attack, and how they might steal on the poor Esquimaux the ensuing night, and kill them all while asleep. To accomplish this bloody design more effectually, the Indians thought it necessary to cross the river as soon as possible; and, by the account of the spies, it appeared that no part was more convenient for the purpose than that where we had met them, it being there very smooth, and at a considerable distance from any fall. Accordingly, after the Indians had put all their guns, spears, targets, etc. in good order, we crossed the river, which took up some time.

When we arrived on the West side of the river, each painted the front of his target or shield; some with the figure of the Sun, others with that of the Moon, several with different kinds of birds and beasts of prey, and many with the images of imaginary beings, which, according to their silly notions, are the inhabitants of the different elements, Earth, Sea, Air, etc.

On enquiring the reason of their doing so, I learned that each man painted his shield with the image of that being on which he relied most for success in the intended engagement. Some were contented with a single representation; while others, doubtful, as I suppose, of the quality and power of any single being, had their shields covered to the very margin with a group of hieroglyphics, quite unintelligible to every one except the painter. Indeed, from the hurry in which this business was necessarily done, the want of every colour but red and black, and the deficiency of skill in the artist, most of those paintings had more the appearance of a number of accidental blotches, than "of any thing that is on the earth, or in the water under the earth"; and though some few of them conveyed a tolerable idea of the thing intended, yet even these were many degrees worse than our country sign-paintings in England.

When this piece of superstition was completed, we began to advance toward the Esquimaux tents; but were very careful to avoid crossing any hills, or talking loud, for fear of being seen or overheard by the inhabitants; by which means the distance was not only much greater than it otherwise would have been, but, for the sake of keeping in the lowest grounds, we were obliged to walk through entire swamps of stiff marly clay, sometimes up to the knees. Our course, however, on this occasion, though very serpentine, was not altogether so remote from the river as entirely to exclude me from a view of it the whole way: on the contrary, several times (according to the situation of the ground) we advanced so near it, as to give me an opportunity of convincing myself that it was as unnavigable as it was in those parts which I had surveyed before, and which entirely corresponded with the accounts given of it by the spies.

It is perhaps worth remarking, that my crew, though an undisciplined rabble, and by no means accustomed to war or command, seemingly acted on this horrid occasion with the utmost uniformity of sentiment. There was not among them the least altercation or separate opinion; all were united in the general cause, and as ready to follow where Matonabbee* led, as he appeared to be ready to lead, according to the advice of an old Copper Indian, who had joined us on our first arrival at the river where this bloody business was first proposed.

Never was reciprocity of interest more generally regarded among a number of people, than it was on the present occasion by my crew, for not one was a moment in want of any thing that another could spare; and if ever the spirit of disinterested friendship expanded the heart of a Northern Indian, it was here exhibited in the most extensive meaning of the word. Property of every kind that could be of general use now ceased to be private, and every one who had any thing which came under that description, seemed proud of an opportunity of giving it, or lending it to those who had none, or were most in want of it.

The number of my crew was so much greater than that which five tents could contain, and the warlike manner in which they were equipped so greatly superior to what could be expected of the poor Esquimaux, that no less than a total massacre of every one of them was likely to be the case, unless Providence should work a miracle for their deliverance.

The land was so situated that we walked under cover of the rocks and hills till we were within two hundred yards of the tents. There we lay in ambush for some time, watching the motions of the Esquimaux; and here the Indians would have advised me to stay till the fight was over, but to this I could by no means consent; for I considered that when the Esquimaux came to be surprised, they would try every way to escape, and if they found me alone, not knowing me from an enemy, they would probably proceed to violence against me when no person was near to assist. For this reason I determined to accompany them, telling them at the same time, that I would not have any hand in the murder they were about to commit, unless I found it necessary for my own safety. The Indians were not displeased at this proposal; one of them immediately fixed me a spear, and another lent me a broad bayonet for my protection, but at that time I could not be provided with a target; nor did I want to be encumbered with such an unnecessary piece of lumber.

While we lay in ambush, the Indians performed the last ceremonies

*Matonabee (1736-1782), Hearne's Chipewyan guide.

which were thought necessary before the engagement. These chiefly consisted in painting their faces; some all black, some all red, and others with a mixture of the two; and to prevent their hair from blowing into their eyes, it was either tied before and behind, and on both sides, or else cut short all round. The next thing they considered was to make themselves as light as possible for running: which they did, by pulling off their stockings, and either cutting off the sleeves of their jackets, or rolling them up close to their armpits; and though the mosquitoes at that time were so numerous as to surpass all credibility, yet some of the Indians actually pulled off their jackets and entered the lists quite naked, except their breech-cloths and shoes. Fearing I might have occasion to run with the rest, I thought it also advisable to pull off my stockings and cap, and to tie my hair as close up as possible.

By the time the Indians had made themselves thus completely frightful, it was near one o'clock in the morning of the seventeenth; when finding all the Esquimaux quiet in their tents, they rushed forth from their ambuscade, and fell on the poor unsuspecting creatures, unperceived till close at the very eaves of their tents, when they soon began the bloody massacre, while I stood neuter in the rear.

In a few seconds the horrible scene commenced; it was shocking beyond description; the poor unhappy victims were surprised in the midst of their sleep, and had neither time nor power to make any resistance; men, women, and children, in all upward of twenty, ran out of their tents stark naked, and endeavoured to make their escape; but the Indians having possession of all the landside, to no place could they fly for shelter. One alternative only remained, that of jumping into the river; but, as none of them attempted it, they all fell a sacrifice to Indian barbarity!

The shrieks and groans of the poor expiring wretches were truly dreadful; and my horror was much increased at seeing a young girl, seemingly about eighteen years of age, killed so near me, that when the first spear was stuck into her side she fell down at my feet, and twisted round my legs, so that it was with difficulty that I could disengage myself from her dying grasps. As two Indian men pursued this unfortunate victim, I solicited very hard for her life; but the murderers made no reply till they had stuck both their spears through her body, and transfixed her to the ground. They then looked me sternly in the face, and began to ridicule me, by asking if I wanted an Esquimaux wife; and paid not the smallest regard to the shrieks and agony of the poor wretch, who was twining round their spears like an eel! Indeed, after receiving much abusive language from them on the occasion, I was at length obliged to desire that they would be more expeditious in dispatching their victim out of her misery, otherwise I should be obliged, out of pity, to assist in the friendly office of putting an end to the existence of a fellow-creature who was so cruelly wounded. On this request being made, one of the Indians hastily drew his spear from the place where it was first lodged, and pierced it through her breast near the heart. The love of life, however, even in this most miserable state, was so predominant, that though this might justly be called the most merciful act that could be done for the poor creature, it seemed to be unwelcome, for though much exhausted by pain and loss of blood, she made several efforts to ward off the friendly blow. My situation and the terror of my mind at beholding this butchery, cannot easily be conceived, much less described; though I summed up all the fortitude I was master of on the occasion, it was with difficulty that I could refrain from tears; and I am confident that my features must have feelingly expressed how sincerely I was affected at the barbarous scene I then witnessed; even at this hour I cannot reflect on the transactions of that horrid day without shedding tears.

(1795)   (1795)

Henry Alline
1748-1784

———◆———

BORN IN NEWPORT, Rhode Island, Henry Alline accompanied his parents when they moved to a farm near Falmouth, Nova Scotia, in 1760. He became an itinerant evangelist in 1776, preaching throughout the Maritimes and inspiring the religious revival known as the New-Light movement. Alline's fervent religious beliefs are forcefully expressed in his *Hymns and Spiritual Songs* (1786) and in his autobiography, *The Life and Journal of the Rev. Mr. Henry Alline* (1806).

HYMN VIII
Against Carnal Mirth

How vain the wretch that dares employ
His mind in quest of sensual joy,
And for an hour of carnal mirth
Chains down his soul to endless death!

Why will you waste your days in vain,
Expos'd to everlasting pain?
Your hours are short, your moments fly,
O think, vain man, you're born to die.

When death arrests, how will you bear
To close your eyes in black despair?   10
How will you bear eternal pain
Where horrors, woes and darkness reign?

Ah! could you now one moment know
The horrors of that gulf below,
You would not hug your sensual joys,
Nor sell your souls for empty toys.

(1786)   (1802)

HYMN IX

A Sinner Awakened

Lord, what a wretched soul am I!
In midnight shades I dwell;
Laden with guilt, and born to die,
And rushing down to hell.

Hell yawns for my unhappy soul,
And threatens ev'ry breath;
While swift as fleeting moments roll,
I'm hurried down to death.

No hand but thine, O God of love,
My wretched soul can save;   10
O come, dear Jesus, and remove
This load of guilt I have.

My wounded soul can never rest
A stranger, Lord, to thee;
O grant me, grant me my request,
And set the pris'ner free.

Thy blood can wash my guilt away;
Thy love my heart can cheer;
O turn my midnight into day,
And banish all my fear.   20

(1786)   (1802)

HYMN XIII

On Death

Death reign'd with vigour since the Fall,
And rides with fury still;
Nor rich nor poor, nor great nor small,
Can e'er resist his will.

He ravages both night and day,
Through all our mortal stage;
And ev'ry creature falls a prey
To his resistless rage.

Nations and empires he has slain,
And laid whole cities waste,   10
And doth his cruel siege maintain
To sweep the world in haste.

Ride forth, O mighty Prince of Peace,
And take away his sting,
Then shall his cruel kingdom cease,
And saints his triumph sing.

(1786)   (1802)

HYMN LII
The Conduct of Most Sailors

While sailors blest with wind and tide,
Do safely o'er the ocean ride,
Cheerful they spend their hours in mirth:
But when the raging tempests blow,
And yawning graves invade below,
They tremble on the verge of death.

Then to their knees the wretches fly
To seek a friend, they mourn and cry,
Confess their sins and help implore;
And while distress'd to heav'n they vow   10
If God will help, and save them now
They'll tread their sinful ways no more.

But when he stills the foaming main,
And calms the furious winds again,
Soon they forget the vows they made;
"Come on, they say, ye merry souls,
We'll drown our grief with jolly bowls;
Good luck has all our fears allay'd."

O poor returns for grace so great
To wretches on the brink of fate!   20
Good Lord forgive th' unhappy crew;
O may they now by grace reform,
Before the great and dreadful storm
Prove their eternal overthrow.

(1786)   (1802)

Adam Allan
1757-1823

ADAM ALLAN WAS born in Dumfries, Scotland, and emigrated to New Brunswick where he served as a lieutenant in the King's New Brunswick Regiment. In 1798 Allan published *The New Gentle Shepherd*, a translation of Allan Ramsay's dialect poem, *The Gentle Shepherd* (1725), together with an original work, "A Description of the Great Falls of the River St. John, in the Province of New Brunswick."

A Description of the Great Falls, of the River Saint John, in the Province of New Brunswick.

Yes, "the commanding muse my chariot guides,
Which o'er the dubious cliff securely rides:
And pleas'd I am no beaten road to take,
But first the way to new discov'ries make."

DRYDEN.

A placid river, gliding easy on
To its dire Fall, o'er a huge bed of stone;
Into an abyss, – dreadful! even to thought,
Where caves immense by whirlpools are wrought;
And where huge trees, by annual freshes brought,
Are by incessant motion ground to nought.
See, where obstruction checks the torrent's way,
The part's announc'd by a vast mount of spray;
Where, as the sun its daily course pursues,
Reflects an arch of the most beauteous hues;   10
Combining elegance with scenes of horror,
Delight, and wonder, with most awful terror.
From this dread gulf of never-ending noise,
Resembling that where devils but rejoice,
The waters rush, like lava from the pits

Of fam'd Vesuvius, and Mount Etna's lips;
Foaming with rage, it forward presses on
From fall to fall, o'er variegated stone;
'Tween banks stupendous! seeming to the eye
An eagle's flight, when tow'ring to the sky.   20
This wond'rous chasm takes the crescent form,
The better its rude majesty to 'dorn;
So that, where'er you ramble for a view,
Each change of station shows you something new;
Verse colours faintly when strain'd from fiction,
Truth, here alone, has govern'd this description.

Now on the wings of fancy let me rove,
To paint the Fall, and margin of the grove,
In depth of winter, – when the river's bound,
And op'nings rarely but at falls are found.   30
How chang'd the scene! – each horror now is fled,
And frost's chill hand enchanting prospects made:
Now ev'ry tree with ice is spangled o'er,
And ev'ry rock is crystall'd on the shore:
The Fall, too, now most gorgeously appears,
Since purer waters aid its bold career;
Strong banks of ice contract its former bounds,
And under ice it echoes hollow sounds:
Around the verge what curious objects rise
To feed the fancy, and to feast the eyes!   40
Pilasters, arches, pyramids, and cones,
Turrets enrich'd with porticos and domes;
In artless order, – form'd by surge and spray,
And crystalline-garnet hues their rich array;
A dazzling cascade ground throughout the whole
Strikes deep with pleasure the enraptur'd soul.

(1798)   (1798)

George Vancouver
1757-1798

BORN IN KING'S Lynn, Norfolk, England, George Vancouver entered the navy at the age of fifteen and served under Captain James Cook on his second and third voyages to the Pacific in 1772 and 1776. He was promoted to the rank of commander in 1790 and in the following year was commissioned to sail to the Pacific coast of North America in order to take over territory from the Spaniards in the Nootka Sound area and to make an accurate survey of the coast. Vancouver returned to England in 1795 and spent the rest of his life preparing his journals for publication. A few months after his death these accounts were published as *Voyage of Discovery to the North Pacific Ocean and Round the World in the Years 1790-1795* (1798).

From
Voyage of Discovery to the North Pacific Ocean

[Burrard Inlet]

[June 13, 1792]

ABOUT FIVE ON Wednesday morning, we again directed our course to the eastern shore, and landed about noon, on the above-mentioned low bluff point. This, as was suspected, formed the south point of a very extensive sound, with a small arm leading to the eastward: the space, which seemed to be its main direction, and appeared very extensive, took a northerly course. The observed latitude here was 49° 19', longitude 237° 6', making this point (which, in compliment to my friend Captain George Grey of the navy, was called POINT GREY) 7 leagues from point Roberts. The intermediate space is occupied by very low land, apparently a swampy flat, that retires several miles, before the country rises to meet the rugged snowy mountains, which we found still continuing in a direction nearly along the coast. This low flat being very much inundated, and extending behind point Roberts, to join the low land in the bay to the eastward of that point; gives it high land, when seen at a distance, the appearance of an island: this, however, is not the case, notwithstanding there are two openings between

64

this point and point Grey. These can only be navigable for canoes, as the shoal continues along the coast to the distance of seven or eight miles from the shore, on which were lodged, and especially before these openings, logs of wood, and stumps of trees innumerable.

From point Grey we proceeded first up the eastern branch of the sound, where, about a league within its entrance, we passed to the northward of an island which nearly terminated its extent, forming a passage from 10 to 7 fathoms deep, not more than a cable's length in width. This island lying exactly across the canal, appeared to form a similar passage to the south of it, with a smaller island lying before it. From these islands, the canal, in width about half a mile, continued its direction about east. Here we were met by about fifty Indians, in their canoes, who conducted themselves with the greatest decorum, and civility, presenting us with several fish cooked, and undressed, of the sort already mentioned as resembling the smelt. These good people finding we were inclined to make some return for their hospitality, shewed much understanding in preferring iron to copper.

For the sake of the company of our new friends, we stood on under an easy sail, which encouraged them to attend us some little distance up the arm. The major part of the canoes twice paddled forward, assembled before us, and each time a conference was held. Our visit and appearance were most likely the object of their consultation, as our motions on these occasions seemed to engage the whole of their attention. The subject matter, which remained a profound secret to us, did not appear of an unfriendly nature to us, as they soon returned, and if possible, expressed additional cordiality and respect. This sort of conduct always creates a degree of suspicion, and should ever be regarded with a watchful eye. In our short intercourse with the people of this country we have generally found these consultations take place, whether their numbers were great or small; and though I have ever considered it prudent to be cautiously attentive on such occasions, they ought by no means to be considered as indicating at all times a positive intention of concerting hostile measures; having witnessed many of these conferences, without our experiencing afterwards any alteration in their friendly disposition. This was now the case with our numerous attendants, who gradually dispersed as we advanced from the station where we had first met them, and three of four canoes only accompanied us up a navigation which, in some places, does not exceed a hundred and fifty yards in width.

We landed for the night about half a league from the head of the inlet, and about 3 leagues from its entrance. Our Indian visitors remained with us until by signs we gave them to understand we were going to rest, and after receiving some acceptable articles they retired, and by means of the same language, promised an abundant supply of fish the next day; our seine having been tried in their presence with very little success. A great desire was manifested by these people to imitate our actions, especially in the firing of a musket, which one of them performed, though with much fear and trembling. They minutely attended to all our transactions, and examined the colour of our skins with infinite curiosity. In other respects they differed little from the generality of the natives we had seen: they possessed no European commodities, or trinkets, except some rude ornaments apparently made from sheet copper; this circumstance, and the general tenor of their behaviour, gave us reason to conclude that we were the first people from a civilized country they had yet seen. Nor did it appear that they were nearly connected, or had much intercourse with other Indians, who traded with the European or American adventurers.

The shores in this situation were formed by steep rocky cliffs, that afforded no convenient space for pitching our tent, which compelled us to sleep in the boats. Some of the young gentlemen however preferring the stony beach for their couch, without duly considering the line of high water mark, found themselves incommoded by the flood tide, of which they were not apprised until they were nearly afloat; and one of them slept so sound, that I believe he might have been conveyed to some distance, had he not been awakened by his companions.

Perfectly satisfied with our researches in this branch of the sound, at four the next morning we retraced our passage in; leaving on the northern shore, a small opening extending to the northward with two little islets before it of little importance, whilst we had a grander object in contemplation; and more particularly so, as this arm or canal could not be deemed navigable for shipping. The tide caused no stream; the colour of its water after we had passed the island the day before, was perfectly clear, whereas that in the main branch of the sound, extending nearly half over the gulf, and accompanied by a rapid tide, was nearly colourless, which gave us some reason to suppose that the northern branch of the sound might possibly be discovered to terminate in a river of considerable extent.

As we passed the situation from whence the Indians had first visited us the preceding day, which is a small border of low marshy land on the northern shore, intersected by several creeks of fresh water, we were in expectation of their company, but were disappointed, owing to our travelling so soon in the morning. Most of their canoes were hauled up into the creeks, and two or three only of the natives were seen straggling about on the beach. None of their habitations could be discovered, whence we concluded that their village was within the forest.

Two canoes came off as we passed the island, but our boats being under sail, with a fresh favourable breeze, I was not inclined to halt, and they almost immediately returned.

The shores of this canal, which after Sir Harry Burrard of the navy I have distinguished by the name of BURRARD'S CANAL, may be considered, on the southern side, of a moderate height, and though rocky, well covered with trees of large growth, principally of the pine tribe. On the northern side, the rugged snowy barrier, whose base we had now nearly approached, rose very abruptly, and was only protected from the wash of the sea by a very narrow border of low land. By seven o'clock we had reached the N.W. point of the canal, which forms also the south point of the main branch of the sound: this also, after another particular friend, I called POINT ATKINSON, situated north from point Grey, about a league-distant. Here the opposite point of entrance into the sound bore by compass west, at the distance of about 3 miles; and nearly in the center between these two points, is a low rocky island producing some trees, to which the name of PASSAGE ISLAND was given. We passed in an uninterrupted channel to the east of it, with the appearance of an equally good one on the other side.

Quitting point Atkinson, and proceeding up the sound, we passed on the western shore some detached rocks, with some sunken ones amongst them, that extend about two miles, but are not so far from the shore as to impede the navigation of the sound; up which we made a rapid progress, by the assistance of a fresh southerly gale, attended with dark gloomy weather, that greatly added to the dreary prospect of the surrounding country. The low fertile shores we had been accustomed to see, though lately with some interruption, here no longer existed; their place was now occupied by the base of the stupendous snowy barrier, thinly wooded, and rising from the sea abruptly to the clouds; from whose frigid summit, the dissolving snow in foaming torrents rushed down the sides and chasms of its rugged surface, exhibiting altogether a sublime, though gloomy spectacle, which animated nature seemed to have deserted. Not a bird, nor living creature was to be seen, and the roaring of the falling cataracts in every direction precluded their being heard, had any been in our neighborhood.

(1798)   (1798)

J. MacKay

LITTLE IS KNOWN about J. MacKay except that in 1797 he published *Quebec Hill; or, Canadian Scenery: A Poem in Two Parts* in Lindon. Mac-Kay's Preface reveals that "the greatest part of the Poem was written in Canada where the Writer has spent a considerable portion of his time." The poem, a narrative of almost six hundred lines, includes descriptions of Niagara Falls, Quebec and the scenery of the St. Lawrence River as well as an account of the death of Wolfe and commentary on the Indians and French Canadians. *Quebec Hill* is included in *Three Early Poems From Lower Canada* (1969), edited by Michael Gnarowski.

Quebec Hill

From
PART I
Summer

> Ye who, in stanzas, celebrate the Po,
> Or teach the Tyber in your strains to flow,
> How would you toil for numbers to proclaim
> The liquid grandeur of St. Lawrence' Stream?
> Offspring of lakes that like to seas extend,
> Where floods, unknown, their willing tribute send;
> Adorn'd by isles, that, crown'd with trees, arise,
> And hemm'd by lofty groves of various dyes:
> On their expanse the vent'rous trader bears
> The downy furs exchang'd for Britain's wares: 10
> Here, as on Ocean's breast, the tempests roar,
> And, round the bark, impetuous billows pour:
> Nor safe the task to tread their winding shores,
> Or range those wilds the Indian explores;
> Where danger's hue in divers forms prevails,
> And ev'ry grove a hidden foe conceals.

Here, prowling wolves their struggling captives tear,
And rattling snakes advise of perils near:
Whene'er the stranger hears the warning sound,
He starts, he flies to shun the baleful wound: 20
So fly the few to higher joys inclin'd,
From those gay snares would wound their peace of mind:
Here fiery tygers darting on their prey,
In comely forms, insatiate rage display;
The surly bear emerging from his den,
In awkward prance explores the wood amain;
With circling paws, and high-erected crest,
He folds the gasping victim to his breast:
On ev'ry side the speckled adder roves,
And brutal warfare fills the chequer'd groves.   30
Thus, worldly pleasures fair in outward show,
Conceal the stings that ever lurk below.

Here, deep involv'd in woods, the Indians range
In quest of prey, or panting for revenge;
With fixt resolve, and nerves inur'd to toil,
The roe to vanquish, or the foe to foil:
With steady aim they hurl their darts from far,
And bleeding victims own the pointed war.

Here, dread diseases rise from fœtid fens,
Spread thro' the woods, and hover o'er the plains;   40
Cramps, fevers, agues, vent'rous traders seize,
Who, seeking wealth, relinquish health and ease;
A sad exchange! how dearly won that wealth,
Acquir'd by loss of happiness and health?

Between where Erie his wide tribute pours,
And where extend Ontario's swelling shores,
High soar Niagara's renowned Falls,
Whose dreadful grandeur passengers appalls:
With force collected, down the waters roll
Condensed, spread, impatient of control: 50
Now, o'er the tallest cliff in chaos bright,
The sparkling volumn wings its giddy flight;
In one wide wave the bounding torrent pours,
And echo swells responsive to its roars;

Thro' pendant surges gasping fishes fly,
And in the circling eddies lifeless lie;
The rising mist obscures the face of day,
Faint seems the sun, and feeble gleams his ray;
Out from the scene the lofty banks retire,
And shun the foaming torrent's mighty ire.   60
Oft, savage beasts, descending from the wood,
To lave their sides, or cross the ample flood,
Become involv'd within the Rapids' verge,
And downward urg'd, hard struggle to emerge;
A vain attempt, ev'n birds partake their fate,
And scream and spread their feeble wings too late;
For as 'gainst speed augmenting they contend,
Adown the steep terrific they descend.

So careless, roving men, devoid of thought,
Are in the rapids of their passions caught;   70
At times, alarm'd, they strive the shore to gain,
But, deep involv'd, their efforts oft are vain;
And soon o'erwhelm'd by excess' baleful breath,
In bloom of youth they prove the pangs of death.

Unsettled still the river pours along,
Thro' sloping glades, unknown to classic song;
Or boils chaotic round each jutting rock,
That, stubborn, shrinks not from its sounding shock:
At length, more calm, it murm'ring glides away,
While sportive fishes on its surface play.   80
Great are the treasures of your ample woods,
And large your tribute, wide-extending floods:
Slow parts the river from its final source,
And various winding prosecutes its course;
While, with majestic dignity, it claims
The humble tribute of the lesser streams.
Great is the wealth its fruitful waves enclose,
These brightly gleam, and gold bespangles those;
The finny race its mighty current crowd,
And yield the natives salutary food: 90
As some choice swain, bless'd in a feeling mind,
Intent on aiding each poor famish'd hind;
His noble bent with ample means are crown'd,
Not to amass, but distribute around.

Long rolls the stream, or rapid, or serene,
Now o'er the steep, and now along the plain;
When, gentler gliding, it forgets to brawl,
As still it laves the shores of Montreal:
That verdant isle, where we with commerce find
The precious gifts of Nature amply join'd;   100
Enrich'd with culture, bloom its fertile grounds,
And scenes romantic circumvent its bounds.
As down it flows how pleasant is the scene,
The shade, the lawn, the burnish'd cot is seen:
Hills, dales, and forests on each border smile,
And rural plenty smooths the trav'ller's toil:
Yet, here neglected droops the human mind,
Or, bred in error, scrupulously blind.

Be brief, my strain, see where each placid wave
Quebec's firm front with gentle murmurs lave;   110
The frozen fetters that their course delay'd,
In glowing Summer's ardent sunshine fled,
Upon its waves the navies gently ride,
And lo! a fleet approaching on the tide.
The sons of Britain hasten to the strand,
See, where, beneath, in swelling crowds they stand!
The eager groups with expectation glow,
As to the shore the slender barges row;
The gay and busy have their various views,
These pant for merchandise, and those for news.   120

The stream, with lazy motion, pours along,
While, in the sun-beam, gleams the finny throng;
Its heaving banks with rip'ning increase clad,
And, interspersed, the cottages are spread:
Higher, the flocks are skipping with their brood,
How close behind appears th'entangled wood!
The distant hills, with arbor richly clad,
Afford the wild inhabitants a shade.

From
PART II

Winter

The northern winds now sweep along the woods,
Fraught with the ardour of the frozen floods,
That stretch along the pole, keen as the gales,
That spread athwart Siberia's cheerless vales.
Out from the arctic pole the potent blasts,
Swift wing their flight, and o'er the dreary wastes.
Both land and sea, that form the utmost north,
Now link'd together, howling, they rush forth
To where, as yet, the agitated main
Disowns the bonds that Greenland's shores enchain: 10
A while, the ocean, mindful on defence,
With shifting billows blunts the cold intense:
Its surface thicken'd by the chill around,
More heavy, sinks into the depth profound;
And, as the billows from the wind recede,
Still warmer draughts the empty space pervade:
But when, in course, the waters all ascend,
And all confess the action of the wind,
More slow the surface from the blast recedes,
The cold the action of the tide impedes,   20
The restless floods become a solid plain,
And frigid fetters bind the torpid main.

What wonder is it that this potent gale,
Which o'er the mighty ocean can prevail,
To which the hardy son of Greenland yields,
And binds our navies in its frozen fields!
What wonder, tho' it here pervade each scene,
And o'er those wilds, and o'er these rivers reign!

How heedless he, in scanty vestments clad
That, careless, ventures on the ice to tread,   30
When, o'er these regions, piercing Boreas blows,
Howls thro' the woods, and drifts the new-laid snows.
If far he stray, the keen ethereal flood,
Pervades his skin, and thickens all his blood;
His frigid limbs forego their native hue,

Then livid red gives way to deep'ning blue;
The sanguine current stagnates in his veins,
And cold, intense, his active pow'rs enchains.
Happy, at length, if some obsequious door,
To his maim'd limbs a shelter may procure: 40
But if the wand'rer finds no like resource,
Behold the sequel in the frozen corse,
That lies, perhaps, unheeded in the snows,
Till weeping thaws the hidden spot disclose.

    Nor in the fields alone the cold prevails,
Nor only there pervade the frigid gales;
The shelter'd domes confess their searching breath,
Which pierces walls, and issues from beneath.
The shiv'ring stranger sees with new surprize,
As in the morn his chamber he surveys,   50
That fields of ice the solid mass pervade,
And on the wall like pendant charts are spread.

    No more the merchant climbs the hoary height,
Foremost to spy the navies come in sight;
Or should his eye, accustom'd to explore
The utmost verges of the neighb'ring shore,
Unmindful, glance along the frozen stream,
Soon he recovers from his waking dream,
Perhaps, to count the months that shall recede,
Ere drooping Commerce rears her languid head.   60

    Full many a Briton has deplor'd the day,
That to these regions he resolv'd to stray,
Where commerce varies like the ether stream,
And Winter passes not unlike a dream.
How wide a field for those who love to err,
And make their pleasures their peculiar care!
Some, void of thought, with mien fantastic rove,
And shake the dice, or breath th'ideal love;
While, crowds combin'd, their mental pow'rs impair,
By scorching draughts, that short-liv'd joys confer: 70
Alas! how few adhere to virtue true,
Or stamp their conduct with its heav'nly hue!
How very few the right from wrong can scan,
Or, knowing, prize this privilege of man!

Does Winter, then, no soothing charms display?
Are all departed with th'autumnal ray?
No — here we still some local pleasures find,
Some mental joys are to no clime confin'd:
Now, wrapp'd in furs, the wealthy mount their cars,
Each, smoothly gliding, like a barge appears;   80
Now study courts whoever will but dare
Spurn sensual joys, and each ignoble care.
Now, soothing Hope fresh offers to the view,
Those rural charms that Summer's flight withdrew,
Again to bloom when some short months revolve,
And vernal thaws the Winter's weight dissolve;
When parting Spring's more ardent warmth begins,
Ere radiant Phœbus quits th'aerial twins.
Then shall the dreary woods again look gay,
And fleecy flocks on flow'ry meadows play;   90
Then, shall the groves their balmy odours send,
Upon the pinions of the whispering wind:
Then Philomela shall resume her lays,
And flutt'ring warblers strains melodious raise;
Then, shall the navies on our shores appear,
And Trade, again, resume his full career.
Thus, busy Hope the active mind employs,
By still alluding to untasted joys.

So, when his days with wintry clouds are spread,
And howling tempests gather round his head: 100
The wise man soars on Hope's celestial wing,
Towards the regions of eternal spring.

Now, having sung Canadian woods and vales,
Its Summer's heat, and Winter's frigid gales,
Let me remark, as climates I compare,
And manners note, 'tis Britain I prefer.
Dear isle! where temp'rate years their empire hold,
Free from extremes of ardent heat or cold;
Thy spacious fields, tho'generous the soil,
Exertion claim, and urge thy sons to toil: 110
Compleatly bounded by the mighty main,
No neighb'ring state intrudes on thy domain:
Thy commerce, trade, and industry surpass,
What Europe shows, or Carthage could amass:

Ah then, beware thro' luxury to fall,
And selfish pride, the common foes of all.
Delightful isle! injur'd by artful men,
Fomenting broils, in hopes of private gain;
Not gain, but loss, when on such terms procur'd,
And, by base arts, from indigence secur'd.   120
Yet, lo where western climes their forests spread,
Disorders spring, and faction rears its head:
For, in each state, are restless sons of strife,
Who, still unhappy, still molest thro' life.

    Britain, to thee my vent'rous course I bend,
From realms remote, where beasts with men contend;
Where cultur'd fields but narrow tracts display,
Hemm'd in by wilds, where savage nations stray.
The novelty of lonely wilds and woods,
And desert hills, and wide expanding floods,   130
Full soon subsides: and then we long again,
For gayer scenes, the smiling haunts of men:
Yet, small delight in local views we find,
Compar'd to that arising from the mind:
The chasten'd mind, where purer pleasure glows,
And joy receiving as it joy bestows.
In ev'ry region habitable made,
Are local comforts still commix'd with shade;
Fair fragrant flow'rs the lurid heath adorn,
And tender roses ripen on the thorn.   140
If there's a spot you prize above the rest,
And there to live conceive is to be blest:
Your wish attain'd, and this lov'd spot your share,
New wants disturb, new wishes claim your care.
Ev'n in the bosom of domestic joy,
We ever trace a mixture of alloy.
More proofs unite, in teaching, chequer'd bliss,
From aught below, is all we can possess:
And, thus, invoke our higher hopes to rise,
Beyond the world, and centre in the skies.   150

(1797)   (1797)

David Thomson
1770-1857

————◆————

BORN IN LONDON, England, David Thompson was apprenticed to the Hudson's Bay Company and sent to Fort Prince of Wales in 1784. He spent thirteen years with the company as a clerk, trader and surveyor of uncharted areas in the interior before resigning to become a partner in the North West Company in 1797. He continued his work as a trader and explorer in western Canada until 1812 when he moved to Terrebonne, Quebec. A detailed description of many of his map-making expeditions, *David Thompson's Narrative of His Explorations in Western America, 1784-1812*, edited by J. B. Tyrrell, was first published in 1916. A new edition with additional material was edited by Richard Glover in 1962.

From
David Thompson's Narrative of His Explorations in Western America 1784-1812

[Swan River Country]

[*October, 1797*]

FROM THIS LONG digression, I return to my travels in the Nut Hill; on a fine afternoon in October, the leaves beginning to fall with every breeze, a season to me of pleasing melancholy from the reflections it brings to the mind, my guide informed me that we would have to pass over a long beaver dam. I naturally expected we should have to load our horses carefully over it; when we came to it, we found it a narrow strip of apparently old, solid ground with short grass, and wide enough for two horses to walk abreast. We passed on; the lower side showed a descent of seven feet, and steep, with a rill of water from beneath it. The side of the dam next to the water was a gentle slope. To the southward was a sheet of water of about one mile and a half square of area, surrounded by moderate, low grassy banks, the forests mostly of aspen and poplar but very numerous stumps of the trees cut down and partly carried away by the beavers. In two places of this pond were a cluster of beaver houses, like miniature villages. When we had proceeded over more than half way of the dam, which was a full mile in length, we came to an aged Indian, his arms folded across his breast, with a pensive countenance, looking at the beavers swimming in the water, and carrying their winter's provisions to their houses, his form tall and erect, his hair almost white, which was almost the only effect that age appeared to have on him, though we concluded he must be about eighty years of age, and in this opinion we were afterwards confirmed by the ease and readiness with which he spoke of times long past. I enquired of him how many beaver houses there were in the pond before us; he said, "There are now fifty-two; we have taken several of their houses; they are difficult to take, and those we have taken were by means of the noise of the water on their houses from a strong wind which enabled us to stake them in; otherwise they would have retired to their burrows, which are very many." He invited us to pass the night at his tent which was close by; the sun was low, and we accepted the offer.

In the tent was an old man, almost his equal in age with women and children; we preferred the open air, and made a good fire to which both of the old men came, and after smoking a while conversation came on. I had always conversed with the natives as one Indian with another, and been attentive to learn their traditions on the animals, on mankind, and on other matter in ancient times, and the present occasion appeared favorable for this purpose. Setting aside questions and answers which would be tiresome, they said, by ancient tradition of which they did not know the origin the beavers had been an ancient people, and then lived on the dry land; they were always beavers, not men; they were wise and powerful, and neither man, nor any animal made war on them.

"They were well clothed as at present, and as they did not eat meat they made no use of fire, and did not want it. How long they lived this way we cannot tell, but we must suppose they did not live well, for the Great Spirit became angry with them, and ordered Weesaukejauk to drive them all into the water and there let them live, still to be wise, but without power, to be food and clothing for man, and the prey of other animals, against all which his defence shall be his dams, his house and his burrows. You see how strong he makes his dams; those that we make for fishing weirs are often destroyed by the water, but his always stands. His house is not made of sand, or loose stones, but of strong earth with wood and sometimes small stones; and he makes burrows to escape from his enemies, and he always has his winter stock of provisions secured in good time. When he cuts down a tree, you see how he watches it, and takes care that it shall not fall on him." "But if so wise, for what purpose does the beaver cut down large trees of which he makes no use whatever?" "We do not know, perhaps an itching of his teeth and gums."

The old Indian paused, became silent, and then in a low tone [they] talked with each other; after which he continued his discourse. "I have told you that we believe in years long passed away, the Great Spirit was angry with the beaver, and ordered Weesaukejauk (the Flatterer) to drive them all from the dry land into the water; and they became and continued very numerous; but the Great Spirit has been, and now is, very angry with them and they are now all to be destroyed. About two winters ago Weesaukejauk showed to our brethren, the Nepissings and Algonquins, the secret of their destruction; that all of them were infatuated with the love of the castorum of their own species, and more fond of it than we are of fire water. We are now killing the beaver without any labor; we are now rich, but [shall] soon be poor; for when the beaver are destroyed we have nothing to depend on to purchase what we want for our families, strangers now overrun our country with their iron traps, and we and they will soon be poor."

The Indian is not a materialist, nor does he believe in instinct, a word of civilized man, which accounts for great part of the actions of mankind, and of all those of animated nature; the Indian believes that every animal has a soul which directs all its motions, and governs all its actions; even a tree, he conceives must somehow be animated, though it cannot stir from its place. Some three years ago (1797) the Indians of Canada and New Brunswick, on seeing the steel traps so successful in catching foxes and other animals, thought of applying it to the beaver, instead of [using] the awkward traps they made, which often failed. At first they were set in the landing paths of the beaver, with about four inches of water on them, and a piece of green aspen for a bait, and in this manner more were caught than by the common way; but the beaver paths made their use too limited and their ingenuity was employed to find a bait that would allure the beaver to the place of the trap; various things and mixtures of ingredients were tried without success; but chance made some try if the male could not be caught by adding the castorum of the female; a mixture of this castorum beat up with the green buds of the aspen was made. A piece of dry willow of about eight inches in length beat and bruised fine was dipped in the mixture; it was placed at the water edge about a foot from the steel trap, so that the beaver should pass direct over it and be caught; this bait proved successful, but to the surprise of the Indians, the females were caught as well as the males. The secret of this bait was soon spread, every Indian procured from the traders four to six steel traps, the weight of one was about six to eight pounds; all labor was now at an end; the hunter moved about at pleasure with his traps and infallible bait of castorum. Of the infatuation of this animal for castorum I saw several instances. A trap was negligently fastened by its small chain to the stake to prevent the beaver taking away the trap when caught; it slipped, and the beaver swam away with the trap, and it was looked upon as lost. Two nights after, he was taken in a trap with the other trap fast to his thigh. Another time, a beaver passing over a trap to get the castorum, had his hind leg broke; with his teeth he cut his broken leg off, and went away; we concluded he would not come again, but two nights afterwards, he was found fast in a trap. In every case the castorum is taken away. The stick with this, was always licked, or sucked clean, and seemed to act as a soporific, as they remained more than a day, without coming out of their houses.

The Nepissings, the Algonquins and Iroquois Indians having exhausted their own countries, now spread themselves over these countries, and as they destroyed the beaver, moved forwards to the northward and westward; the natives, the Nahathaways, did not in the least molest them; the Chippaways and other tribes made use of traps of steel, and of the castorum. For several years all these Indians were rich, the women and children, as well as the men, were covered with silver brooches, ear rings, wampum, beads and other trinkets. Their mantles were of fine scarlet cloth, and all was finery and dress. The canoes of the fur traders were loaded with packs of beaver, the abundance of the article lowered the London prices. Every intelligent man saw the poverty that would follow the destruction of the beaver, but there were no Chiefs to control it; all was perfect liberty and equality. Four years afterwards almost the whole of these extensive countries were denuded of beaver, the natives became poor, and with difficulty procured the first necessaries of life, and in this state they remain, and probably for ever. A worn out field may be manured, and again made fertile; but the beaver, once destroyed, cannot be replaced; they were the gold coin of the country, with which the necessaries of life were purchased.

It would be worth while for some gentleman who has nothing to do to look at the sales by auction, the number of skins by private sale and otherwise disposed of, to count the number of beavers that have been killed, and procured from the northern part of this continent.

Thomas McCulloch
1776-1843

———◆———

A GRADUATE OF the University of Glasgow and the Secession Divinity
School at Whitburn, Thomas McCulloch emigrated to Pictou, Nova
Scotia, in 1803 and became the first president of Dalhousie College in
1838. In addition to religious works, editorials, essays and two novellas,
McCulloch wrote a series of satiric sketches, *The Letters of Mephibosheth
Stepsure*. These sketches first appeared in the *Acadian Recorder* between
December 22, 1821 and May 11, 1822 and were published as a book in
1862.

From
The Letters of Mephibosheth Stepsure

LETTER IX

GENTLEMEN, – I formerly stated, that, with a lot of land, a few acres
chopped and a pair of lame legs, I began the world. In the subsequent
part of my life none of your readers must expect a relation of surprising events. I was not, like Robinson Crusoe, cast upon a desolate island,
and forced to try shifts which nobody had ever tried before me. On the
contrary, I was in a Christian country; and in the midst of neighbours
who kindly spent a great part of their time, in preventing one another
from being lonely. Not much of the visiting, it is true, came to my share;
for in those days I was lame Meph, and of not much consideration
among our great folks. Besides, when I was out of bed, I was generally
doing something; and, on this account, as well as because in those days I
neither smoked nor kept grog in my house, it was supposed that I did
not need to be visited. My only visitors were a few young people, who
would lay their hands together to go to Meph's in the evening, and have
a little fun. But when I understood their drift, I used to read to them a
sermon. Of my gift in preaching I can say very little. It has been often
said, read sermons rarely do much good; and, sure enough, though I
read good sermons, and very distinctly too, the young people profited

so little under my ministry, that none of them ever came back a second time.

Before I proceed to the history of my life, I must remind your readers of the apprenticeship which I had served to my lame legs. As I formerly stated necessity kept me at home; and there the same necessity forced me to keep every thing in its own place, and to do every thing well and at the proper time. By pursuing this course, though I was seldom hurried, I had not much spare time in working hours; so that, at last, I contracted such a habit of doing some thing or other, that, when I had nothing to do, I felt myself uneasy. – The only additional particulars in which I differed from the rest of the youngsters, were the habits of reading in the evening and going pretty often to Widow Scant's, for whom I had contracted the same affection as my master's family.

When I was about to clear up my few chopped acres in the spring, a number of young people proposed to make a frolic of the business, and do it for me. This would have been a great help in the mean time; and at first I was very much inclined to accept the offer. But a little consideration showed me that the profit of a frolic would be dearly purchased. At a business of this kind a number attend principally for amusement. In return, I would owe each of them a day when his frolic came round; and, in order to pay my debt, it would be necessary for my lame legs to travel to every part of the town; perhaps too at the very time when I might be most needed at home. Besides, young people, upon such occasions, expect something better than ordinary eating and drinking; and feasting I could not afford without running into debt. Mr. Ledger, it is true, had told me to come to his store for whatever I wanted; but a conversation which I had with my old master a few days before, convinced me that applying to that gentleman in a strait, was, as Saunders Scantocreesh says, like going down to Egypt for help; instead of finding myself better off, I might be drowned in the Red Sea.

The Squire had stopped over to see how I was getting on; and, when about to leave me, he said that he was going to give me a very serious advice. The evening before I had been to see widow Scant, and thought that he intended to speak about the daughter, but he had a different subject in view. "Never," says he, "Mephibosheth, allow yourself to get into a merchant's books. Debt hangs about the neck of an honest man like a millstone; and, in this country, it requires no ordinary uprightness and activity, to prevent him from sinking under the load. Running into debt and long credits, have been the destruction of both property and religion among us. The person who has credit in a store, is apt to feel wants which his circumstances do not warrant him to gratify; and to gratify these wants, he involves himself in debts, which, perhaps, never leave him till he has lost his little property and his character too. There is Puff, who has credit with Mr. Ledger; and he is living, not by his labour, but by sinking his farm. And there is old Guess, who, for these thirty years, has been telling his creditors when he would pay them; and, you know, he has nothing left him but the name of a notorious liar. Merchants are very useful, and we cannot do without them; but they live altogether by the labours of other people; and they usually live well. Those, therefore, who employ them, must support them; and, hence, a merchant cannot live, unless he lay the loss of bad pay, upon the purchases of good customers. In short, according to the way in which business is carried on in the country, a merchant could not live, unless the one half of us could afford to pay the debts of the whole. If, therefore, a farmer wish to thrive, he must take care to have much credit but little debt." The old gentleman's advice was not lost; and from that day to this, though I have often rejected Mr. Ledger's counsels as obstinately as Jack Scorem, my greybeard was never sent away empty from the store.

About the time that my farming commenced, the suits which had been long pending between Mr. Bullock and young Quirk were decided. Quirk was what our townsfolk call a 'cute young man. Indeed, he was a smart chap; but somehow or other he was very poor, and not much respected. When he began the world by settling on a farm like the rest of us, he happened to be made a constable. This led him to acquire a great knowledge of the law, which was at times useful to him in the way of his profession: for, as he had the counting of other people's money, he often found it much easier to tell how the cash came into his hands, than how it got out of them. He was also very helpful to the neighbours by giving them advice. This, as it saved them a guinea at the commencement of a suit, was very acceptable. But, though I speak to the shame of our town, I must say, that those who followed Quirk's cheap counsels, when their suits were decided, were always very ungrateful, and abused him without mercy.

Quirk, by his new occupation, made a great deal of money. On this account, his little clearing was not in good order; and one day when he was from home, serving an ejectment, Mr. Bullock's oxen came along, and seeing something very inviting within a little brush, they stepped over it, and took peaceable possession of his grain. When Quirk returned, he was in a great rage, beat the oxen unmercifully, and then drove them to the pound. The case had now become complicated. Mr. Bullock, who is one of our great people, spoke big; and Quirk, who thought that the beating of the cattle could not be proved, answered him with law in abundance. Suits were entered; and, as the lawyers said, on account of the intricacy of the business, protracted from term to term; till, at last, Quirk had justice done to him, and then sold his farm to cover the expenses. To me this was a useful lesson. Before planting I put a good fence around my few acres; and I must say, that, though both Mr. Bullock's cattle and neighbour Snout's pigs were often about, I always found them civil. Since that time I have had much experience of both beasts and fences; and I have always found that good fences make good friends and safe crops. Many persons believe that cattle break down fences because they have no sense. But, I assure you, that they are more sensible animals than those who try to keep them out. As far as my experience goes, no ordinary beast tries to get into a field, after a farmer has fairly convinced it that he intends to keep it on the outside of the fence; and I have never seen a farmer who proceeds upon this principle, either quarrel with his neighbors about trespasses, or protect himself against them by selling his farm.

My clearing was small, and, therefore easily managed; and, as I was always at home to do everything about my little crop in the proper time and way, it throve wonderfully well. At that time, I recollect, the satisfaction of viewing it, was greater than the pleasure which I derived from considering its value. My old master, too, was so well pleased with my success, that he brought a number of the neighbours to see what industry would do. They all agreed that everything was excellent, and in excellent order; but to account for appearances each had a different reason. When Deacon Sharp saw how my potatoes were hoed, he was sure I must have wrought upon Sunday. Old Pumpkin, who has a large farm and expends his labour chiefly in hunting away cattle from his fields, remarked, that lame people are lucky; and Mrs Grumble, who had come out of curiosity with the rest, complained, that there had always been a crook in Job's lot and hers; and that, if Providence had been as kind to them as to Meph, they would have had a very different life of it. My old master, I could see, was very much displeased. After hearing them out, he told them, that, though they had seen Mephibosheth's fields, they had never yet taken a proper view of himself. Every person's eyes were now directed to my lame feet: which, the Squire perceiving, told them that that was not what he meant; and observing Mrs. Grumble feeling for her spectacles, he asked them if they did not see about Mephibosheth, good sense directing labour and care to their proper ends. Here my visitors left me displeased, and all speaking loudly that I might hear them. Deacon Sharp declared that he and Deacon Scruple would see into the business; for such doings must not be permitted in the town. Old Pumpkin wondered that the Squire was not ashamed to hint that they had less sense than a lame creature; and, that when Meph was so careful to fence out other people's cattle, he had better take care not to send his own about his farm. And Mrs. Grumble said that she wished me no ill; but it was a hard case that lame Meph should be so well off, when her Job and other decent men had such bad crops. This little pet, however, did not last long; for next spring I sold my spare wheat to Pumpkin, whose family live chiefly upon pies; and Job, who is obliged to live very meanly, bought all the spare potatoes which I had raised.

For myself, I was so pleased with my success, and so encouraged by my master's commendations, that I resolved to get on as I had done; and, during the whole of my life, I have never had the least reason to complain of my returns. Many of my neighbours, it is true, have not been so successful. Still they are in general very good people, and very helpful to one another. Indeed, if they did not help each other, their life would be very miserable. I am always at home, looking after my affairs, and never fail to have good crops; but my neighbours so often meet with bad land, hard labour, and poor returns, that they are obliged to spend much of their time in mutual visits, for the purpose of unburthening their minds, condoling, and keeping each other in heart.

The man who settles upon a wood lot, has a good deal to do the first year; and if he be not disposed to get into debt, he must take care to lose no time. Yet if he employ himself with ordinary judgment and steadiness, it is wonderful how much he will do, without doing great days work. After getting in my seed, I began to think about my house and barn. By the help of the squire's team I had got the logs upon the spot; (for I could not, like Jack Scorem, venture upon two frames,) and just when I was considering who would help me put them up, young Loopy came up. Loopy lived then, as he does now, in a little log hut, covered with spruce bark. Neither the outside or inside of it, I recollect, presented any inducement to visit it twice. His door was always beset by a couple of starved pigs, which occupied this station for the double purpose of enjoying the benefit of the puddle, and of being at hand to make their entrance good when the door happened to be opened. Loopy and his wife were good-looking, flashy, young people; and, on Sundays and other public occasions, few dressed better, or carried their heads higher. But, in speaking of them, our old parson used to say, that if you trace a butterfly to its shell, you will find it a maggot; and, sure enough, if there was any comfort or cleanliness about Loopy's house, the pigs had got them. His whole furniture was a large looking-glass, a cross-legged table, a few broken chairs, a number of nails driven into the walls; and for a bed, a couple of blankets laid upon a little straw. As his articles were few, they were of course pretty much used. Mrs. Loopy was frequently from home, and required to be dressed. On this account the eating apparatus was not much looked after. They usually stood upon the table, amidst scraps of pork or fish and piles of potatoe skins; of which, also, the chairs had usually a proportion. The nails were very useful for keeping their clothes out of the pigs' way; and for showing how many gowns, petticoats, trowsers, and other finery, the young people had got. As for the bed, it was in constant use; and served the whole family. In Loopy's it was a standing order, that the dog jumped out, and Loopy and his wife jumped in. When he was finely dressed, I remember, he had a particular way of twisting his shoulders. Not that he carried any of his stock about with him; for I never knew him have more than one cow and the two pigs; except when he happened to be in the horse trade. But some people's clothes, you know, do not sit easily upon them; and then they are fidgety. I make this remark, because many flashy young people may think that I am pointing at them; when I am only describing Loopy, who came past at the time that I was thinking how I should get up my log house and barn.

Loopy, stopping a little for the purpose of offering me a great bargain of a horse, gave me a very discouraging view of the farming life. "I'll tell you," says he, "Meph, what it is; you have got a world of hard work before you. Upon my word, the farmer has a laborious life of it. I do assure you, it takes a great deal of toiling to maintain a family by a farm; and after all, it won't do." But, as Loopy had never been guilty of working hard, he could know the toil of it only by tradition, which is not a very sure guide. I was not, therefore, discouraged completely, though I refused the horse; and, when he left me to call upon his aunt, Mrs. Grumble, I began the preparation for getting up my house and barn.

A log house is easily managed; and where its owner has any taste, it is susceptible of a degree of neatness and comfort, which comparatively few farmers of this country can afford to display in a larger building. For example, my neighbour Pumpkin, whose ideas were always large, in order that his building might correspond with his farm, raised a huge frame; and really, when the outside was finished, had an imposing appearance. Travellers admired it very much, and Pumpkin himself, from the praise bestowed upon his good taste, began to look big. But, in building the outside to please travellers, he forgot that he had the inside to build for the comfort of his family. As I formerly stated, much of his farming labour is expended in hunting the cattle from his large fields, on this account he was never very forehanded; and, when passengers were admiring Mr. Pumpkin's fine house, he and his family were living in a corner of it, which had been partitioned off by a few loose boards. The rest of the building was found very handy for holding odd things. Now, about a farm house, this is a discovery which the owner cannot keep to himself. Pigs, dogs, carts, and fowls, all make it and make use of it too; and my neighbour's house, besides the finery of the young ladies, suspended upon nails and pegs around the walls, generally contained a great variety of articles and smells, very useful to a farmer. Pumpkin had resolved to finish by degrees; but fighting against time, is a hard battle. The other day I had occasion to pass by his house, and came home very thankful to Providence, as I have often been, for my lame legs. I found the family, emptying the windows of the old hats and trowsers; and one of his sons, who was tearing the clapboards from the end of the house, told me, that had I been anything else than a lame old rascal, he would have given me a beating. By the bye, since I wrote you about Jack Scorem's house, there has been sad havoc among the clapboards in our town. Some of the youngsters have got wooden spouts erected; which you will see standing out from the houses, when you come up the country. How the rest intend to conduct the distillation in future, I have not yet learned. But, with the exception of Jack's house, and those of old Stot, Ehud Slush, and one or two more, the buildings of the town are very much altered.

Where every thing is done in a hurry, according to the old farming, there are a great many little things omitted, because they can be done at any time. For example, when a new settler builds a log house, he often leaves the ground about his door in a state of nature; and the chimney top, or roof, or the corners, remain unfinished. This part of the old system, my master could never endure; and, indeed, I have generally seen, that, where these things are without, there is a corresponding want of comfort within. The farmer who does not finish his jobs, has either too many of them for his profit, or wants that industry which ensures comfort. I therefore, finished my house as it ought to be; and, by doing so, found myself a gainer. The additional labour was trifling. In return for this trifling labour, I was relieved equally from smoke and puddle; and when my neighbours, in their large open houses, were shivering before huge fires in winter; my little hut well stuffed with moss, rendered me snug with a small quantity of fuel.

After finishing my house, I began to think about a garden and orchard. In visiting widow Scant, who derived a great part of her living from a little garden kept in excellent order, I had seen its importance to a family. In my master's, too, whose house was surrounded with fruit trees, we never went to the door in summer without being delighted;

and, upon his table, I have often seen a dinner, derived from his own premises, which would have gratified a prince.

With respect to my garden and orchard, however, as I was in no hurry, I did not proceed according to the old farming. The most of my neighbours had tried to raise an orchard; but had given it up in despair. Either the trees would not grow at all or, if they did grow, it was only for a year or two; and then they died, or were destroyed by the cattle. But upon these points, I never found any difficulty. Pigs and fruit trees I have found to be much alike; starvation brings leanness; and good feed, a flourishing appearance and profit. As for my cattle, after looking at the fence of my orchard, they always went away abusing the trees for being as sour as crabs; and now, the only difference between many of my neighbours and me, is, that they have not been able to raise orchards, and I sell them fruit.

When my garden and orchard were put in good order, with the addition of a few flourishing polls of hops, rose bushes, and honeysuckles, planted about my house, my premises looked very well. My good old master, I remember, who took an interest in my success, was so pleased, that, when any of the great folks from Halifax, came about, he never failed to bring them, as he said, to see industry rewarded with prosperity and comfort. Those gentlemen, too, would sit down in my house or at the door, with as much cheerfulness and familiarity as any of the neighbours; and, in conversing with the squire would draw a great many comparisons between my little hut and her Pumpkin's large white castle, surrounded by fields ill cultivated and as wretchedly fenced.

Many of your readers may not believe that a stout, active person, and much less a lame lad, could get on so well. I will, therefore, explain the business to their satisfaction, in a very few words. I was no visitor myself, and few came to see me. Here was a large saving of time and expense. I was neither a great man nor a great man's son: I was Mephibosheth Stepsure, whose highest ambition was, to be a plain, decent farmer. Here, the whole habiliments and expenses of a gentleman were saved; and, being a gentleman, I assure you, is a trade which requires costly tools. But, though I was lame Mephibosheth, I had a good stout back and good hard hands, and a disposition to keep them both out of mischief, by giving them something useful to do. I was always at home to do everything properly, and at the proper time. On this account, though I was rarely in a hurry, and seldom needed to work hard, I was able to do a great deal; and I must here observe, that I never accounted any kind of labour too mean or slavish, if I saw it to be useful. Besides, though I was farmer, I was lumberer too. I did not, indeed, like Jack Scorem, make great lots of timber. But knowing that I owned trees, as well as land, I judged that I had the right to turn them to my advantage; and, therefore, rarely entered the woods without laying them under contribution. It was easy to arrange matters so as to carry home a companion; and whether it was a junk for shingles, staves, axe handles, or any other use, my shoulders never grumbled. All these I deposited at home; and, during the long winter nights, when my neighbors were at Tipple's, or visiting each other, some little article was added to my stock. These, according to my usual custom, I always made well; and, as my neighbours generally found it cheaper to buy than to make, my articles met with a ready sale, and brought ready money too. At first, also, I lived hardly; for what right had I to live otherwise? But the time slipped past, and I soon found myself surrounded with every comfort which a farmer ought to desire.

MEPHIBOSHETH STEPSURE.

(1862)   (1862)

Philippe Aubert de Gaspé
1786-1871

———————◆———————

BORN IN QUEBEC, Philippe-Joseph Aubert de Gaspé studied law and was called to the bar in 1813. He served as sheriff of the district of Quebec from 1816 to 1822 when he was forced by financial problems to retire with his family to the ancestral estate at Saint-Jean-Port-Joli. Here, Aubert de Gaspé, now more than seventy years of age, wrote the historical romance, *Les Anciens Canadiens* (1863). This work, which combines the customs and folklore of Quebec with a conventional romantic narrative, quickly became a classic of French-Canadian literature. In 1890 Charles G. D. Roberts published a translation of Aubert de Gaspé's volume under the title *The Canadians of Old*.

From
The Canadians of Old

[La Corriveau]

AS SOON AS our young travellers, crossing the St. Lawrence opposite Quebec, have reached Point Lévis, José makes haste to harness a splendid Norman horse into one of those low sledges which furnish the only means of transport at this season, when the roads are only covered here and there with snow or ice, and when overflowing streams intercept the way at intervals. When they come to one of these obstacles José unharnesses the horse, all three mount, and the brook is speedily forded. It is true that Jules, who clasps José around the waist, tries every now and then to throw him off, at the risk of partaking with him the luxury of a bath at a little above zero. He might as well have tried to throw Cape Tourmente into the St. Lawrence. José, who, in spite of his comparatively small stature, is as strong as an elephant, laughs in his sleeve and pretends not to notice it. The brook forded, José goes back for the sledge, reharnesses the horse, climbs into the sledge with the baggage in front of him lest he should get it wet, and speedily overtakes his fellow-travellers, who have not halted a moment in their march.

Thanks to Jules, the conversation never flags during the journey.

Archie does nothing but laugh over the witticisms that Jules perpet-
rates at his expense. He has long given up attempting any retort.

* * *

"Now," said Archie, "since you seem to have emptied your budget of
all the absurdities that a hair-brained French head can contain, try and
speak seriously, and tell me why the Isle of Orleans is called the Isle of
the Sorcerers."

"For the very simple reason," answered Jules, "that a great many
sorcerers live there."

"There you begin again with your nonsense," said Lochiel.

"I am in earnest," said Jules. "These Scotch are unbearably conceited. They can't acknowledge any excellence in other nations. Do you
think, my dear fellow, that Scotland has the monopoly of witches and
wizards? I would beg you to know that we too have our sorcerers; and
that two hours ago, between Point Lévis and Beaumont, I might as
easily as not have introduced you to a very respectable sorceress. I
would have you know, moreover, that on the estate of my illustrious
father you shall see a witch of the most remarkable skill. The difference
is, my dear boy, that in Scotland you burn them, while here we treat
them in a manner fitting their power and social influence. Ask José if I
am not telling the truth?"

José did not fail to confirm all he said. In his eyes the witches of
Beaumont and St. Jean Port Joli were genuine and mighty sorceresses.

"But to speak seriously," continued Jules, "since you would make a
reasonable man of me, *nolens volens*, as my sixth-form master used to
say when he gave me a dose of the strap, I believe the fable takes its rise
from the fact that the *habitants* on the north and south shores of the
river, seeing the islanders on dark nights go out fishing with torches,
mistake their lights for will-o'-the-wisps. Then, you know that our
country folk regard the will-o'-the-wisps as witches, or as evil spirits
who endeavor to lure the wandering wretch to his death. They even
profess to hear them laugh when the deluded traveller falls into the
quagmire. The truth is, that there is an inflammable gas continually
escaping from our bogs and swampy places, from which to the hobgoblins and sorcerers is but a single step."

"Impossible," said Archie; "your logic is at fault, as the professor so
often had to tell you. You see the inhabitants of the north and south
shores themselves go fishing with torches, whence, according to your
reasoning, the islanders should have called them sorcerers; which is
not the case."

While Jules was shaking his head, with no answer ready, José took up
the word.

"If you would let me speak, gentlemen, I might explain your difficulty by telling you what happened to my late father who is now dead."

"Oh, by all means, tell us that; tell us what happened to your late father who is now dead," cried Jules, with a marked emphasis on the last four words.

"Yes, my dear José, do us the favor of telling us about it," added Lochiel.

"I can't half tell the story," answered José, "for, you see, I have neither the fine accent nor the splended voice of my lamented parent. When he used to tell us what happened to him in his vigil, our bodies would shake so, as if with ague, as would do you good to see. But I'll do my best to satisfy you:

"It happened one day that my late father, who is now dead, had left the city for home somewhat late. He had even diverted himself a little, so to speak, with his acquaintances in Point Lévis. Like an honest man, he loved his drop; and on his journeys he always carried a flask of brandy in his dogfish-skin satchel. They say the liquor is the milk for old men."

"*Lac dulce*," interjected Archie, sententiously.

"Begging your pardon, Mr. Archie," answered José, with some warmth, "it was neither *sweet water* (*de l'eau douce*) nor *lake-water* (*eau de lac*), but very good, unadulterated brandy which my late father, now dead, was carrying in his satchel."

"Capital, upon my word!" cried Jules. "It serves you right for your perpetual Latin quotations!"

"I beg your pardon, José" said Lochiel, very seriously. "I intended not the shadow of disrespect to your late father."

"You are excused, sir," said José, entirely mollified. "It happened that it was quite dark when my father at last got under way. His friends did their best to keep him all night, telling him that he would have to pass, all by himself, the iron cage wherein *La Corriveau* did penance for having killed her husband.

"You saw it yourselves, gentlemen, when leaving Point Lévis at one o'clock. She was quiet then in her cage, the wicked creature, with her eyeless skull. But never you trust to her being blind. She is a cunning one, you had better believe! If she can't see in the daytime, she knows well enough how to find her way to torment poor folks at night. Well, as for my late father, who was as brave as his captain's sword, he told his friends that he didn't care – that he didn't owe *La Corriveau* a farthing – with a heap more reasons which I can not remember now. He put the whip to his horse, a fine brute that could travel like the wind, and was gone in a second.

"As he was passing the skeleton, he thought he heard a noise, a sort of wailing; but, as a heavy southwest wind was blowing, he made up his mind it was only the gale whistling through the bones of the corpse. It gave him a kind of a start, nevertheless, and he took a good pull at the flask to brace himself up. All things considered, however, as he said to himself, Christians should be ready to help each other; perhaps the poor creature was wanting his prayers. He took off his cap and devoutly recited a *de profundis* for her benefit, thinking that, if it didn't do her any good, it could at least do her no harm, and that he himself would be the better for it. Well, then he kept on as fast as he could; but, for all that, he heard a queer sound behind him – tic-tac, tic-tac, like a piece of iron striking on the stones. He thought it was the tire of his wheel, or some piece of the wagon, that had come unfastened. He got out to see, but found everything snug. He touched the horse to make up for lost time, but after a little he heard again that tic-tac, tic-tac, on the stones. Being brave, he didn't pay much attention.

"When he got to the high ground of St. Michel, which we passed a little way back, he grew very drowsy. 'After all,' said my late father, 'a man is not a dog! let us take a little nap; we'll both be the better for it, my horse and I.' Well, he unharnessed his horse, tied his legs so he would not wander too far, and said: 'There, my pet, there's good grass, and you can hear the brook yonder. Good-night.'

"As my late father crawled himself into the wagon to keep out of the dew, it struck hin to wonder what time it was. After studying the 'Three Kings' to the south'ard and the 'Wagon' to the north'ard, he made up his mind it must be midnight. 'It is time,' said he, 'for honest men to be in bed.'

"Suddenly, however, it seemed to him as if Isle d'Orléans was on fire. He sprang over the ditch, leaned on the fence, opened his eyes wide, and stared with all his might. He saw at last that the flames were dancing up and down the shore, as if all the will-o'-the-wisps, all the damned souls of Canada, were gathered there to hold the witches' sabbath. He stared so hard that his eyes which had grown a little dim grew very clear again, and he saw a curious sight; you would have said they were a kind of men, a queer breed altogether. They had a head big as a peck measure, topped off with a pointed cap a yard long; then they had arms, legs, feet, and hands armed with long claws, but no body to speak of. Their crotch, begging your pardon, gentlemen, was split right up to their ears. They had scarcely anything in the way of flesh; they were kind of all bone, like skeletons. Every one of these pretty fellows had his upper lip split like a rabbit's, and through the split stuck out a rhinoceros tusk a foot long, like you see, Mr. Archie, in your book of unnatural history. As for the nose, it was nothing more nor less, begging your pardon, than a long pig's snout, which they would rub first on one side and then on the other of their great tusk, perhaps to sharpen it. I almost forgot to say that they had a long tail, twice as long as a cow's, which they used, I suppose, to keep off the flies.

"The funniest thing of all was that there were but three eyes to every couple of imps. Those that had but one eye, in the middle of the forehead, like those Cyclopes that your uncle, who is a learned man, Mr. Jules, used to read to us about out of that big book of his, all Latin, like the priest's prayer-book, which he called his Virgil – those that had but one eye held each by the claw two novices with the proper number of eyes. Out of all these eyes spurted the flames which lit up Isle d'Orléans like broad day. The novices seemed very respectful to their companions, who were, as one might say, half blind; they bowed down to them, they fawned upon them, they fluttered their arms and legs, just like good Christians dancing the minuet.

"The eyes of my late father were fairly starting out of his head. It was worse and worse when they began to jump and dance without moving from their places, and to chant in a voice as hoarse as that of a choking cow, this song:

> "Hoary Frisker, Goblin gay,
> Long-nosed Neighbor, come away!
> Come my Grumbler in the mud,
> Brother Frog of tainted blood!
> Come, and on this juicy Christian
> Let us feast it while we may!"

" 'Ah! the accursed heathens,' exclaimed my late father, 'an honest man can not be sure of his property for a moment! Not satisfied with having stolen my favorite song, which I always keep to wind up with at weddings and feasts, just see how they've played the devil with it! One would hardly recognize it. It is Christians instead of good wine that they are going to treat themselves to, the scoundrels!'

"Then the imps went on with their hellish song, glaring at my late father, and curling their long snouts around their great rhinoceros tusks:

> "Come, my tricksy Traveler's Guide,
> Devil's Minion true and tried,
> Come, my Sucking-Pig, my Simple,
> Brother Wart and Brother Pimple;
> Here's a fat and juicy Frenchman
> To be pickled, to be fried!"

" 'All that I can say to you just now, my darlings,' cried my late father, 'is that if you get no more fat to eat than what I'm going to bring you on my lean carcass you'll hardly need to skim your broth.'

"The goblins, however, seemed to be expecting something, for they kept turning their heads every moment. My late father looked in the same direction. What was that he saw on the hill-side? A mighty devil, built like the rest, but as long as the steeple St. Michel, which we passed awhile back. Instead of the pointed bonnet, he wore a three-horned hat, topped with a big thorn bush in place of a feather. He had but one eye, blackguard that he was, but that was as good as a dozen. He was doubtless the drum-major of the regiment, for he held in his hand a saucepan twice as big as our maple-sugar kettles, which hold twenty gallons, and in the other hand a bell-clapper, which no doubt the dog of a heretic had stolen from some church before its consecration. He pounded on his saucepan, and all the scoundrels began to laugh, to jump, to flutter, nodding to my late father as if inviting him to come and amuse himself with them.

"'You'll wait a long time, my lambs,' thought my late father to himself, his teeth chattering in his head as if he had the shaking fever – 'you will wait a long time, my gentle lambs. I'm not in any hurry to quit the good Lord's earth to live with the goblins!'

"Suddenly the tall devil began to sing a hellish round, accompanying himself on the saucepan, which he beat furiously, and all the goblins darted away like lightning – so fast, indeed, that it took them less than a minute to go all the way around the island. My poor late father was so stupefied by the hubbub that he could not remember more than three verses of the song, which ran like this:

> "Here's the spot that suits us well
> When it gets too hot in hell –
> Toura-loura;
> Here we go all round,
> Hands all round,
> Here we go all round.

> "Come along and stir your sticks,
> You jolly dogs of heretics –
> Toura-loura;

* * *

"Well," said José, "it happened that my late father, brave as he was, was in such a devil of a funk that the sweat was hanging from the end of his nose like a head of oats. There he was, the dear man, with his eyes bigger than his head, never daring to budge. Presently he thought he heard behind him the 'tic tac,' 'tic tac,' which he had already heard several times on the journey; but he had too much to occupy his attention in front of him to pay much heed to what might pass behind. Suddenly, when he was least expecting it, he felt two great bony hands, like the claws of a bear, grip him by the shoulders. He turned around horrified, and found himself face to face with La Corriveau, who was climbing on his back. She had thrust her hands through the bars of her cage and succeeded in clutching him; but the cage was heavy, and at every leap she fell back again to the ground with a hoarse cry, without losing her hold, however, on the shoulders of my late father, who bent under the burden. If he had not held tight to the fence with both hands, he would have been crushed under the weight. My poor late father was so overwhelmed with horror that one might have heard the sweat that rolled off his forehead dropping down on the fence like grains of duck-shot.

"'My dear Francis,' said La Corriveau, 'do me the pleasure of taking me to dance with my friends of Isle d'Orléans?'

"'Oh, you devil's wench!' cried my late father. That was the only oath the good man ever used, and that only when very much tried."

"The deuce!" exclaimed Jules, "it seems to me that the occasion was a very suitable one. For my own part, I should have been swearing like a heathen."

"And I," said Archie, "like an Englishman."

"Isn't that much the same thing," answered D'Haberville.

"You are wrong, my dear Jules. I must acknowledge that the heathen acquit themselves very well; but the English? Oh, my! Le Roux who, soon as he got out of college, made a point of reading all the bad books he could get hold of, told us, if you remember, that that blackguard of a Voltaire, as my uncle the Jesuit used to call him, had declared in a book of his, treating of what happened in France in the reign of Charles VII, when that prince was hunting the islanders out of his kingdom – Le Roux told us that Voltaire had put it on record that 'every Englishman swears.' Well, my boy, those events took place about the year 1445 – let us say, three hundred years ago. Judge, then, what dreadful oaths that ill-tempered nation must have invented in the course of three centuries!"

"I surrender," said Jules. "But go on, my dear José."

"'Devil's wench!' exclaimed my late father, 'is that your gratitude for my *de profundis* and all my other prayers? You'd drag *me* into the orgy, would you? I was thinking you must have been in for at least three or four thousand years of purgatory for your pranks; and you had only killed two husbands – which was a mere nothing. So having always a tender heart for everything, I felt sorry for you, and said to myself we must give you a helping hand. And this is the way you thank me, that you want to straddle my shoulders and ride me to hell like a heretic!'

"'My dear Francis,' said La Corriveau, 'take me over to dance with my dear friends;' and she knocked her head against that of my late father till her skull rattled like a dry bladder filled with pebbles.

"'You may be sure,' said my late father, 'You hellish wench of Judas Iscariot, I'm not going to be your jackass to carry you over to dance with those pretty darlings!'

"'My dear Francis,' answered the witch, 'I can not cross the St. Lawrence, which is a consecrated stream, except with the help of a Christian.'

"'Get over as best you can, you devilish gallows bird,' said my late father. 'Get over as best you can; every one to his own business. Oh, yes, a likely thing that I'll carry you over to dance with your dear friends; but that will be a devil of a journey you have come, the Lord knows how, dragging that fine cage of yours, which must have torn up all the stones on the king's highway! A nice row there'll be when the inspector passes this way one of these days and finds the road in such a condition! And then, who but the poor *habitant* will have to suffer for your frolics, getting fined for not having kept the road properly!'

"The drum-major suddenly stopped beating on his great sauce-pan. All the goblins halted and gave three yells, three frightful whoops, like the Indians give when they have danced that war-dance with which they always begin their bloody expeditions. The island was shaken to its foundation, the wolves, the bears, all the other wild beasts, and the demons of the northern mountains took up the cry, and the echoes repeated it till it was lost in the forests of the far-off Saguenay.

"My poor, late father thought that the end of the world had come, and the Day of Judgment.

"The tall devil with the sauce-pan struck three blows; and a silence most profound succeeded the hellish hubbub. He stretched out his arm toward my late father, and cried with a voice of thunder: 'Will you make haste, you lazy dog? will you make haste, you cur of a Christian, and ferry our friend across? We have only fourteen thousand four hundred times more to prance around the island before cock-crow. Are you going to make her lose the best of the fun?'

"'Go to the devil, where you all belong,' answered my late father, losing all patience.

"'Come, my dear Francis,' said La Corriveau, 'be a little more obliging. You are acting like a child about a mere trifle. Moreover, see how the time is flying. Come, now, one little effort!'

"'No, no, my wench of Satan,' said my late father. 'Would to Heaven you still had on the fine collar which the hangman put around your neck two years ago. You wouldn't have so clear a wind-pipe.'

"During this dialogue the goblins on the island resumed their chorus:

> "'Here we go all round,
> Hands all round,
> Here we go all round.'

"'My dear Francis,' said the witch, 'if your body and bones won't carry me over, I'm going to strangle you. I will straddle your soul and ride over to the festival.' With these words, she seized him by the throat and strangled him."

"What," exclaimed the young men, "she strangled your poor, late father, now dead?"

"When I said strangled, it was very little better than that," answered José," for the dear man lost his consciousness.

"When he came to himself he heard a little bird, which cried *Qué-tu?* (Who art thou?)

"'Oh, ho!' said my late father, 'it's plain I'm not in hell, since I hear the dear Lord's birds!" He opened first one eye, then the other, and saw that it was broad daylight. The sun was shining right in his face; the little bird, perched on a neighboring branch, kept crying *qué-tu?*'

"'My dear child,' said my late father, 'it is not very easy to answer your question, for I'm not very certain this morning just who I am. Only yesterday I believed myself to be a brave, honest, and God-fearing man; but I have had such an experience this night that I can hardly be sure that it is I, Francis Dubé, here present in body and soul. Then the dear man began to sing:

> "'Here we go all round,
> Hands all round,
> Here we go all round.'

"In fact, he was half bewitched. At last, however, he perceived that he was lying full length in a ditch where, happily, there was more mud than water; but for that my poor, late father, who now sleeps with the saints, surrounded by all his relations and friends, and fortified by all the holy sacraments, would have died without absolution, like a monkey in his old tree, begging your pardon for the comparison, young gentlemen. When he had got his face clear from the mud of the ditch, in which he was stuck fast as in a vise, the first thing he saw was his flask on the bank above him. At this he plucked up his courage and stretched out his hand to take a drink. But no such luck! The flask was empty! The witch had drained every drop."

"My dear José," said Lochiel, "I think I am about as brave as the next one. Nevertheless, if such an adventure had happened to me, never again would I have traveled alone at night."

"Nor I either," said D'Haberville.

"To tell you the truth, gentlemen," said José, "since you are so discriminating, I will confess that my late father, who before this adventure would not have turned a hair in the graveyard at midnight, was never afterward so bold; he dared not even go alone after sunset to do his chores in the stable."

"And very sensible he was; but finish your story," said Jules.

"It is finished," said José. "My late father harnessed his horse, who appeared, poor brute, to have noticed nothing unusual, and made his way home fast as possible. It was not till a fortnight later that he told us his adventure."

"What do you say to all that, my self-satisfied skeptic who would refuse to Canada the luxury of witches and wizards?" inquired D'Haberville.

"I say," answered Archie, "that our Highland witches are mere infants compared with those of New France, and, what's more, if ever I get back to my Scottish hills, I'm going to imprison all our hobgoblins in bottles, as Le Sage did with his wooden-legged devil, Asmodeus."

"Hum-m-m!" said José. "It would serve them just right, accursed blackguards; but where would you get bottles big enough? There'd be the difficulty."

(1863)   (1890)

Oliver Goldsmith
1794-1861

———◆———

BORN IN ST. ANDREWS, New Brunswick, Oliver Goldsmith was the son of a Loyalist who fought in the American Revolution and the grand-nephew of the Anglo-Irish poet, playwright and novelist, Oliver Goldsmith. In 1810 he entered the Commissariat, the civilian supply branch of the British army, and remained there until his retirement to England forty-five years later. Goldsmith's most important poem, *The Rising Village* (1825), was modelled on his great-uncle's work, *The Deserted Village* (1770), and is among the most successful examples of the pre-Confederation narrative poem. A revised edition of the poem appeared in *The Rising Village, with Other Poems* (1834).

The Rising Village

Thou dear companion of my early years,
Partner of all my boyish hopes and fears,
To whom I oft addressed the youthful strain,
And sought no other praise than thine to gain;
Who oft hast bid me emulate his fame
Whose genius formed the glory of our name;
Say, when thou canst, in manhood's ripened age,
With judgment scan the more aspiring page,
Wilt thou accept this tribute of my lay,
By far too small thy fondness to repay?   10
Say, dearest Brother, wilt thou now excuse
This bolder flight of my adventurous muse?
        If, then, adown your cheek a tear should flow
For Auburn's village, and its speechless woe:
If, while you weep, you think the "lowly train"
Their early joys can never more regain,
Come, turn with me where happier prospects rise,
Beneath the sternness of Acadian skies.
And thou, dear spirit! whose harmonious lay

Didst lovely Auburn's piercing woes display,   20
Do thou to thy fond relative impart
Some portion of thy sweet poetic art;
Like thine, Oh! let my verse as gently flow,
While truth and virtue in my numbers glow:
And guide my pen with thy bewitching hand,
To paint the Rising Village of the land.
    How chaste and splendid are the scenes that lie
Beneath the circle of Britannia's sky!
What charming prospects there arrest the view,
How bright, how varied, and how boundless too!   30
Cities and plains extending far and wide,
The merchant's glory, and the farmer's pride.
Majestic palaces in pomp display
The wealth and splendour of the regal sway;
While the low hamlet and the shepherd's cot,
In peace and freedom mark the peasant's lot.
There nature's vernal bloom adorns the field,
And autumn's fruits their rich luxuriance yield.
There men, in busy crowds, with men combine,
That arts may flourish, and fair science shine;   40
And thence, to distant climes their labours send,
As o'er the world their widening views extend.
Compar'd with scenes like these, how lone and drear
Did once Acadia's woods and wilds appear;
Where wandering savages, and beasts of prey,
Displayed, by turns, the fury of their sway.
What noble courage must their hearts have fired,
How great the ardour which their souls inspired,
Who leaving far behind their native plain,
Have sought a home beyond the Western main;   50
And braved the perils of the stormy seas,
In search of wealth, of freedom, and of ease!
Oh! none can tell but they who sadly share
The bosom's anguish, and its wild despair,
What dire distress awaits the hardy bands,
That venture first on bleak and desert lands.
How great the pain, the danger, and the toil,
Which mark the first rude culture of the soil.
When, looking round, the lonely settler sees
His home amid a wilderness of trees;   60
How sinks his heart in those deep solitudes,
Where not a voice upon his ear intrudes;

Where solemn silence all the waste pervades,
Heightening the horror of its gloomy shades;
Save where the sturdy woodman's strokes resound,
That strew the fallen forest on the ground.
See! from their heights the lofty pines descend,
And crackling, down their pond'rous lengths extend.
Soon from their boughs the curling flames arise,
Mount into air, and redden all the skies;   70
And where the forest once its foliage spread,
The golden corn triumphant waves its head.
    How blest, did nature's ruggedness appear
The only source of trouble or of fear;
How happy, did no hardship meet his view,
No other care his anxious steps pursue;
But, while his labour gains a short repose,
And hope presents a solace for his woes,
New ills arise, new fears his peace annoy,
And other dangers all his hopes destroy.   80
Behold the savage tribes in wildest strain,
Approach with death and terror in their train;
No longer silence o'er the forest reigns,
No longer stillness now her power retains;
But hideous yells announce the murderous band,
Whose bloody footsteps desolate the land;
He hears them oft in sternest mood maintain,
Their right to rule the mountain and the plain;
He hears them doom the *white man's* instant death,
Shrinks from the sentence, while he gasps for breath,   90
Then, rousing with one effort all his might,
Darts from his hut, and saves himself by flight.
Yet, what a refuge! Here a host of foes,
On every side, his trembling steps oppose;
Here savage beasts around his cottage howl,
As through the gloomy wood they nightly prowl,
Till morning comes, and then is heard no more
The shouts of man, or beast's appalling roar;
The wandering Indian turns another way,
And brutes avoid the first approach of day.   100
    Yet, tho' these threat'ning dangers round him roll,
Perplex his thoughts, and agitate his soul,
By patient firmness and industrious toil,
He still retains possession of the soil;
Around his dwelling scattered huts extend,

Whilst every hut affords another friend.
And now, behold! his bold aggressors fly,
To seek their prey beneath some other sky;
Resign the haunts they can maintain no more,
And safety in far distant wilds explore.   110
His perils vanished, and his fears o'ercome,
Sweet hope portrays a happy peaceful home.
On every side fair prospects charm his eyes,
And future joys in every thought arise.
His humble cot, built from the neighbouring trees,
Affords protection from each chilling breeze;
His rising crops, with rich luxuriance crowned,
In waving softness shed their freshness round;
By nature nourished, by her bounty blest,
He looks to Heaven, and lulls his cares to rest.   120
    The arts of culture now extend their sway,
And many a charm of rural life display.
Where once the pine upreared its lofty head,
The settlers' humble cottages are spread;
Where the broad firs once sheltered from the storm,
By slow degrees a neighbourhood they form;
And, as it bounds, each circling year, increase
In social life, prosperity, and peace,
New prospects rise, new objects too appear,
To add more comfort to its lowly sphere.   130
Where some rude sign or post the spot betrays,
The tavern first its useful front displays.
Here, oft the weary traveller at the close
Of evening, finds a snug and safe repose.
The passing stranger here, a welcome guest,
From all his toil enjoys a peaceful rest;
Unless the host, solicitous to please,
With care officious mar his hope of ease,
With flippant questions to no end confined,
Exhaust his patience, and perplex his mind.   140
    Yet, let no one condemn with thoughtless haste,
The hardy settler of the dreary waste,
Who, far removed from every busy throng,
And social pleasures that to life belong,
Whene'er a stranger comes within his reach,
Will sigh to learn whatever he can teach.
To this, must be ascribed in great degree,
That ceaseless, idle curiosity,

Which over all the Western world prevails,
And every breast, or more or less, assails; 150
Till, by indulgence, so o'erpowering grown,
It seeks to know all business but its own.
Here, oft when winter's dreary terrors reign,
And cold, and snow, and storm, pervade the plain,
Around the birch-wood blaze the settlers draw,
"To tell of all they felt, and all they saw."
When, thus in peace are met a happy few,
Sweet are the social pleasures that ensue.
What lively joy each honest bosom feels,
As o'er the past events his memory steals, 160
And to the listeners paints the dire distress,
That marked his progress in the wilderness;
The danger, trouble, hardship, toil, and strife,
Which chased each effort of his struggling life.
  In some lone spot of consecrated ground,
Whose silence spreads a holy gloom around,
The village church in unadorned array,
Now lifts its turret to the opening day.
How sweet to see the villagers repair
In groups to pay their adoration there; 170
To view, in homespun dress, each sacred morn,
The old and young its hallowed seats adorn,
While, grateful for each blessing God has given,
In pious strains, they waft their thanks to Heaven.
  Oh, heaven-born faith! sure solace of our woes,
How lost is he who ne'er thy influence knows,
How cold the heart thy charity ne'er fires,
How dead the soul thy spirit ne'er inspires!
When troubles vex and agitate the mind,
By gracious Heaven for wisest ends designed, 180
When dangers threaten, or when fears invade,
Man flies to thee for comfort and for aid;
The soul, impelled by thy all-powerful laws,
Seeks safety, only, in a Great First Cause!
If, then, amid the busy scene of life,
Its joy and pleasure, care, distrust, and strife;
Man, to his God for help and succour fly,
And on his mighty power to save, rely;
If, then, his thoughts can force him to confess
His errors, wants, and utter helplessness; 190
How strong must be those feelings which impart

A sense of all his weakness to the heart,
Where not a friend in solitude is nigh,
His home the wild, his canopy the sky;
And, far removed from every human arm,
His God alone can shelter him from harm.
    While now the Rising Village claims a name,
Its limits still increase, and still its fame.
The wandering Pedlar, who undaunted traced
His lonely footsteps o'er the silent waste;   200
Who traversed once the cold and snow-clad plain,
Reckless of danger, trouble, or of pain,
To find a market for his little wares,
The source of all his hopes, and all his cares,
Established here, his settled home maintains,
And soon a merchant's higher title gains.
Around his store, on spacious shelves arrayed,
Behold his great and various stock in trade.
Here, nails and blankets, side by side, are seen,
There, horses' collars, and a large tureen;   210
Buttons and tumblers, fish-hooks, spoons and knives,
Shawls for young damsels, flannel for old wives;
Woolcards and stockings, hats for men and boys,
Mill-saws and fenders, silks, and children's toys;
All useful things, and joined with many more,
Compose the well-assorted country store.
    The half-bred Doctor next then settles down,
And hopes the village soon will prove a town.
No rival here disputes his doubtful skill,
He cures, by chance, or ends each human ill;   220
By turn he physics, or his patient bleeds,
Uncertain in what case each best succeeds.
And if, from friends untimely snatched away,
Some beauty fall a victim to decay;
If some fine youth, his parents' fond delight,
Be early hurried to the shades of night,
Death bears the blame, 'tis his envenomed dart
That strikes the suffering mortal to the heart.
    Beneath the shelter of a log-built shed
The country school-house next erects its head.   230
No "man severe," with learning's bright display,
Here leads the opening blossoms into day;
No master here, in every art refined,
Through fields of science guides the aspiring mind;

But some poor wanderer of the human race,
Unequal to the task, supplies his place,
Whose greatest source of knowledge or of skill
Consists in reading, and in writing ill;
Whose efforts can no higher merit claim,
Than spreading Dilworth's* great scholastic fame.   240
No modest youths surround his awful chair,
His frowns to deprecate, or smiles to share,
But all the terrors of his lawful sway
The proud despise, the fearless disobey;
The rugged urchins spurn at all control,
Which cramps the movements of the free-born soul,
Till, in their own conceit so wise they've grown,
They think their knowledge far exceeds his own.
     As thus the village each successive year
Presents new prospects, and extends its sphere,   250
While all around its smiling charms expand,
And rural beauties decorate the land.
The humble tenants, who were taught to know,
By years of suffering, all the weight of woe;
Who felt each hardship nature could endure,
Such pains as time alone could ease or cure,
Relieved from want, in sportive pleasures find
A balm to soften and relax the mind;
And now, forgetful of their former care,
Enjoy each sport, and every pastime share.   260
Beneath some spreading tree's expanded shade
Here many a manly youth and gentle maid,
With festive dances or with sprightly song
The summer's evening hours in joy prolong,
And as the young their simple sports renew,
The aged witness, and approve them too.
And when the Summer's bloomy charms are fled,
When Autumn's fallen leaves around are spread,
When Winter rules the sad inverted year,
And ice and snow alternately appear,   270
Sports not less welcome lightly they essay,
To chase the long and tedious hours away.
Here, ranged in joyous groups around the fire,
Gambols and freaks each honest heart inspire;
And if some venturous youth obtain a kiss,

*Thomas Dilworth, author of *The Schoolmaster's Assistant* (1784).

The game's reward, and summit of its bliss,
Applauding shouts the victor's prize proclaim,
And every tongue augments his well-earned fame;
While all the modest fair one's blushes tell
Success had crowned his fondest hopes too well.   280
Dear humble sports, Oh! long may you impart
A guileless pleasure to the youthful heart,
Still may your joys from year to year increase,
And fill each breast with happiness and peace.
    Yet, tho' these simple pleasures crown the year,
Relieve its cares, and every bosom cheer,
As life's gay scenes in quick succession rise,
To lure the heart and captivate the eyes;
Soon vice steals on, in thoughtless pleasure's train,
And spreads her miseries o'er the village plain.   290
Her baneful arts some happy home invade,
Some bashful lover, or some tender maid;
Until, at length, repressed by no control,
They sink, debase, and overwhelm the soul.
How many aching breasts now live to know
The shame, the anguish, misery and woe,
That heedless passions, by no laws confined,
Entail forever on the human mind.
Oh, Virtue! that thy powerful charms could bind
Each rising impulse of thy erring mind.   300
That every heart might own thy sovereign sway,
And every bosom fear to disobey;
No father's heart would then in anguish trace
The sad remembrance of a son's disgrace;
No mother's tears for some dear child undone
Would then in streams of poignant sorrow run,
Nor could my verse the hapless story tell
Of one poor maid who loved — and loved too well.
    Among the youths that graced their native plain,
Albert was foremost of the village train;   310
The hand of nature had profusely shed
Her choicest blessings on his youthful head;
His heart seemed generous, noble, kind and free,
Just bursting into manhood's energy.
Flora was fair, and blooming as that flower
Which spreads its blossom to the April shower;
Her gentle manners and unstudied grace
Still added lustre to her beaming face,

While every look, by purity refined,
Displayed the lovelier beauties of her mind.   320
    Sweet was the hour, and peaceful was the scene
When Albert first met Flora on the green;
Her modest looks, in youthful bloom displayed,
Then touched his heart, and there a conquest made
Nor long he sighed, by love and rapture fired,
He soon declared the passion she inspired.
In silence, blushing sweetly, Flora heard
His vows of love and constancy preferred;
And, as his soft and tender suit he pressed,
The maid, at length, a mutual flame confessed.   330
    Love now had shed, with visions light as air,
His golden prospects on this happy pair;
Those moments soon rolled rapidly away,
Those hours of joy and bliss that gently play
Around young hearts, ere yet they learn to know
Life's care or trouble, or to feel its woe.
The day was fixed, the bridal dress was made,
And time alone their happiness delayed,
The anxious moment that, in joy begun,
Would join their fond and faithful hearts in one.   340
'Twas now at evening's hour, about the time
When in Acadia's cold and northern clime
The setting sun, with pale and cheerless glow,
Extends his beams o'er trackless fields of snow,
That Flora felt her throbbing heart oppressed
By thoughts, till then, a stranger to her breast.
Albert had promised that his bosom's pride
That very morning should become his bride;
Yet morn had come and passed; and not one vow
Of his had e'er been broken until now.   350
But, hark! a hurried step advances near,
'Tis Albert's breaks upon her listening ear;
Albert's, ah, no! a ruder footstep bore,
With eager haste, a letter to the door;
Flora received it, and could scarce conceal
Her rapture, as she kissed her lover's seal.
Yet, anxious tears were gathered in her eye,
As on the note it rested wistfully;
Her trembling hands unclosed the folded page,
That soon she hoped would every fear assuage,   360
And while intently o'er the lines she ran,

In broken half breathed tones she thus began:
    "Dear Flora, I have left my native plain,
And fate forbids that we shall meet again:
'Twere vain to tell, nor can I now impart
The sudden motive to this change of heart.
The vows so oft repeated to thine ear
As tales of cruel falsehood must appear.
Forgive the hand that deals this treacherous blow,
Forget the heart that can afflict this woe;   370
Farewell! and think no more of Albert's name,
His weakness pity, now involved in shame."
        Ah! who can paint her features as, amazed,
In breathless agony, she stood and gazed!
"Oh, Albert, cruel Albert!" she exclaimed,
Albert was all her faltering accents named.
A deadly feeling seized upon her frame,
Her pulse throbb'd quick, her colour went and came;
A darting pain shot through her frenzied head,
And from that fatal hour her reason fled!   380
        The sun had set; his lingering beams of light
From western hills had vanished into night.
The northern blast along the valley rolled,
Keen was that blast, and piercing was the cold,
When, urged by frenzy, and by love inspired,
For what but madness could her breast have fired!
Flora, with one slight mantle round her waved,
Forsook her home, and all the tempest braved.
Her lover's falsehood wrung her gentle breast,
His broken vows her tortured mind possessed;   390
Heedless of danger, on she bent her way
Through drifts of snow, where Albert's dwelling lay,
With frantic haste her tottering steps pursued
Amid the long night's darkness unsubdued;
Until, benumbed, her fair and fragile form
Yielded beneath the fury of the storm;
Exhausted nature could no further go,
And, senseless, down she sank amid the snow.
        Now as the morn had streaked the eastern sky
With dawning light, a passing stranger's eye,   400
By chance directed, glanced upon the spot
Where lay the lovely sufferer: To his cot
The peasant bore her, and with anxious care
Tried every art, till hope became despair.

With kind solicitude his tender wife
Long vainly strove to call her back to life;
At length her gentle bosom throbs again,
Her torpid limbs their wonted power obtain;
The loitering current now begins to flow,
And hapless Flora wakes once more to woe: 410
But all their friendly efforts could not find
A balm to heal the anguish of her mind.
     Come hither, wretch, and see what thou hast done,
Behold the heart thou hast so falsely won,
Behold it, wounded, broken, crushed and riven,
By thy unmanly arts to ruin driven;
Hear Flora calling on thy much loved name,
Which, e'en in madness, she forbears to blame.
Not all thy sighs and tears can now restore
One hour of pleasure that she knew before;   420
Not all thy prayers can now remove the pain,
That floats and revels o'er her maddened brain.
Oh, shame of manhood! that could thus betray
A maiden's hopes, and lead her heart away;
Oh, shame of manhood! that could blast her joy,
And one so fair, so lovely, could destroy.
     Yet, think not oft such tales of real woe
Degrade the land, and round the village flow.
Here virtue's charms appear in bright array,
And all their pleasing influence display;   430
Here modest youths, impressed in beauty's train,
Or captive led by love's endearing chain,
And fairest girls whom vows have ne'er betrayed,
Vows that are broken oft as soon as made,
Unite their hopes, and join their lives in one,
In bliss pursue them, as at first begun.
Then, as life's current onward gently flows,
With scarce one fault to ruffle its repose,
With minds prepared, they sink in peace to rest,
To meet on high the spirits of the blest.   440
     While time thus rolls his rapid years away,
The Village rises gently into day.
How sweet it is, at first approach of morn,
Before the silvery dew has left the lawn,
When warring winds are sleeping yet on high,
Or breathe as softly as the bosom's sigh,
To gain some easy hill's ascending height,

Where all the landscape brightens with delight,
And boundless prospects stretched on every side,
Proclaim the country's industry and pride.   45c
Here the broad marsh extends its open plain,
Until its limits touch the distant main;
There verdant meads along the uplands spring,
And grateful odours to the breezes fling;
Here crops of grain in rich luxuriance rise,
And wave their golden riches to the skies;
There smiling orchards interrupt the scene,
Or gardens bounded by some fence of green;
The farmer's cottage, bosomed 'mong the trees,
Whose spreading branches shelter from the breeze;   46c
The winding stream that turns the busy mill,
Whose clacking echos o'er the distant hill;
The neat white church, beside whose walls are spread
The grass-clod hillocks of the sacred dead,
Where rude cut stones or painted tablets tell,
In laboured verse, how youth and beauty fell;
How worth and hope were hurried to the grave,
And torn from those who had no power to save.
    Or, when the Summer's dry and sultry sun
Adown the West his fiery course has run;   47c
When o'er the vale his parting rays of light
Just linger, ere they vanish into night,
How sweet to wander round the wood-bound lake,
Whose glassy stillness scarce the zephyrs wake;
How sweet to hear the murmuring of the rill,
As down it gurgles from the distant hill;
The note of Whip-poor-Will how sweet to hear,
When sadly slow it breaks upon the ear,
And tells each night, to all the silent vale,
The hopeless sorrows of its mournful tale.   48c
Dear lovely spot! Oh may such charms as these,
Sweet tranquil charms, that cannot fail to please,
Forever reign around thee, and impart
Joy, peace, and comfort to each native heart.
    Happy Acadia! though around thy shore
Is heard the stormy wind's terrific roar;
Though round thee Winter binds his icy chain,
And his rude tempests sweep along thy plain,
Still Summer comes, and decorates thy land
With fruits and flowers from her luxuriant hand;   49c

Still Autumn's gifts repay the labourer's toil
With richest products from thy fertile soil;
With bounteous store his varied wants supply,
And scarce the plants of other suns deny.
How pleasing, and how glowing with delight
Are now thy budding hopes! How sweetly bright
They rise to view! How full of joy appear
The expectations of each future year!
Not fifty Summers yet have blessed thy clime,
How short a period in the page of time!   500
Since savage tribes, with terror in their train,
Rushed o'er thy fields, and ravaged all thy plain.
But some few years have rolled in haste away
Since, through thy vales, the fearless beast of prey,
With dismal yell and loud appalling cry,
Proclaimed his midnight reign of terror nigh.
And now how changed the scene! the first, afar,
Have fled to wilds beneath the northern star;
The last has learned to shun man's dreaded eye,
And, in his turn, to distant regions fly.   510
While the poor peasant, whose laborious care
Scarce from the soil could wring his scanty fare;
Now in the peaceful arts of culture skilled,
Sees his wide barn with ample treasures filled;
Now finds his dwelling, as the year goes round,
Beyond his hopes, with joy and plenty crowned.

    Nor culture's arts, a nation's noblest friend,
Alone o'er Scotia's fields their power extend;
From all her shores, with every gentle gale,
Commerce expands her free and swelling sail;   520
And all the land, luxuriant, rich, and gay,
Exulting owns the splendour of their sway.
These are thy blessings, Scotia, and for these,
For wealth, for freedom, happiness, and ease,
Thy grateful thanks to Britain's care are due,
Her power protects, her smiles past hopes renew,
Her valour guards thee, and her councils guide,
Then, may thy parent ever be thy pride!

    Happy Britannia! though thy history's page
In darkest ignorance shrouds thine infant age,   530
Though long thy childhood's years in error strayed,
And long in superstition's bands delayed;
Matur'd and strong, thou shin'st in manhood's prime,

The first and brightest star of Europe's clime.
The nurse of science, and the seat of arts,
The home of fairest forms and gentlest hearts;
The land of heroes, generous, free, and brave,
The noblest conquerors of the field and wave;
Thy flag, on every sea and shore unfurled,
Has spread thy glory, and thy thunder hurled.   540
When, o'er the earth, a tyrant would have thrown
His iron chain, and called the world his own,
Thine arm preserved it, in its darkest hour,
Destroyed his hopes, and crushed his dreaded power,
To sinking nations life and freedom gave,
'Twas thine to conquer, as 'twas thine to save.
    Then blest Acadia! ever may thy name,
Like hers, be graven on the rolls of fame;
May all thy sons, like hers, be brave and free,
Possessors of her laws and liberty;   550
Heirs of her splendour, science, power, and skill,
And through succeeding years her children still.
And as the sun, with gentle dawning ray,
From night's dull bosom wakes, and leads the day,
His course majestic keeps, till in the height
He glows one blaze of pure exhaustless light;
So may thy years increase, thy glories rise,
To be the wonder of the Western skies;
And bliss and peace encircle all thy shore,
Till empires rise and sink, on earth, no more.   560

(1825)   (1834)

Anna Jameson
1794-1860

———◆———

THE DAUGHTER OF an Irish painter, Anna (Murphy) Jameson was already a recognized author in London before she travelled to Upper Canada in 1836 to join her estranged husband. She spent less than a year in Canada but her account of her experiences, *Winter Studies and Summer Rambles* (1838), is one of the best of the many travel books dealing with nineteenth-century Canada.

From
Winter Studies and Summer Rambles in Canada

[Upper Canada]

THIS LAND OF Upper Canada is in truth the very paradise of hope. In spite of all I see and hear, which might well move to censure, to regret, to pity, – how much there is in which the trustful spirit may reasonably rejoice! It would be possible, looking at things under one aspect, to draw such a picture of the mistakes of the government, the corruption of its petty agents, the social backwardness and moral destitution of the people, as would shock you, and tempt you to regard Canada as a place of exile for convicts. On the other hand, I could, without deviating from the sober and literal truth, give you such vivid pictures of the beauty and fertility of this land of the west, of its glorious capabilities for agriculture and commerce, of the goodness and kindliness and resources of poor, much-abused human nature, as developed amid all the crushing influences of oppression, ignorance, and prejudice; and of the gratitude and self-complacency of those who have exchanged want, servitude, and hopeless toil at home, for plenty and independence and liberty here, – as would transport you in fancy into an earthly elysium. Thus, as I travel on, I am disgusted, or I am enchanted; I despair or I exult by turns; and these inconsistent and apparently contradictory emotions and impressions I set down as they arise, leaving you to reconcile them as well as you can, and make out the result for yourself.

It is seldom that in this country the mind is ever carried backward by associations or recollections of any kind. Horace Walpole said of Italy, that it was "a land in which the memory saw more than the eye," and in Canada hope must play the part of memory. It is all the difference between seed-time and harvest. We are rich in anticipation, but poor in possession – more poor in memorials. Some vague and general traditions, of no interest whatever to the ignorant settlers, do indeed exist, of horrid conflicts between the Hurons and the Iroquois, all along these shores, in the time and before the time of the French dominion; of the enterprise and daring of the early fur traders; above all, of the unrequited labours and sacrifices of the missionaries, whether Jesuits or Moravians, or Methodists, some of whom perished in tortures; others devoted themselves to the most horrible privations – each for what he believed to be the cause of truth, and for the diffusion of the light of salvation; none near to applaud the fortitude with which they died, or to gain hope and courage from their example. During the last war between Great Britain and the United States – that war, in its commencement dishonourable to the Americans, in its conclusion shameful to the British, and in its progress disgraceful and demoralising to both; – that war, which began and was continued in the worst passions of our nature, cupidity and vengeance; – which brought no advantage to any one human being – not even the foolish noise and empty glory which wait oftentimes on human conflicts; a war scarce heard of in Europe, even by the mother country, who paid its cost in millions, and in the blood of some of her best subjects; a war obscure, fratricidal, and barbarous, which has left behind no effect but a mutual exasperation and distress along the frontiers of both nations; and a hatred which, like hatred between near kinsmen, is more bitter and irreconcilable than any hostility between the mercenary armies of rival nations; for here, not only the two governments quarrelled – but the people, their institutions, feelings, opinions, prejudices, local and personal interests, were brought into collision; – during this vile, profitless, and unnatural war, a battle was fought near Chatham, called by some the battle of the Thames, and by others the battle of the Moravian towns, in which the Americans, under General Harrison, beat General Proctor with considerable loss. But it is chiefly worthy of notice, as the last scene of the life of Tecumseh, a Shawanee chief, of whom it is possible you may not have heard, but who is the historical hero of these wild regions. Some American writers call him the "Indian Napoleon;" both began their plans of policy and conquest about the same time, and both about the same time terminated their career, the one by captivity, the other by death. But the genius of the Indian warrior and his exploits were limited to a narrow field along the confines of civilisation, and their record is necessarily imperfect. It is clear that he had entertained the daring and really magnificent plan formerly embraced by Pontiac – that of uniting all the Indian tribes and nations in a league against the whites. That he became the ally of the British was not from friendship to us, but hatred to the Americans, whom it was his first object to repel from any further encroachments on the rights and territories of the Red men – in vain! These attempts of a noble and a fated race, to oppose, or even to delay for a time, the rolling westward of the great tide of civilisation, are like efforts to dam up the rapids of Niagara. The moral world has its laws, fixed as those of physical nature. The hunter must make way before the agriculturist, and the Indian must learn to take the bit between his teeth, and set his hand to the ploughshare, or *perish.* As yet I am inclined to think that the idea of the Indians becoming what *we* call a civilised people seems quite hopeless; those who entertain such benevolent anticipations should come here, and behold the effect which three centuries of contact with the whites have produced on the nature and habits of the Indian. The benevolent theorists in England should come and see with their own eyes that there is a bar to the civilisation of the Indians, and the increase or even preservation of their numbers, which no power can overleap. Their own principle, that "the Great Spirit did indeed create both the red man and the white man, but created them essentially different in nature and manners," is not perhaps far from the truth.

There is a large settlement of Moravian Indians located above Chatham, on the river Thames. They are a tribe of Delawares, and have been for a number of years congregated under the care of Moravian Missionaries, and living on the lands reserved for them by the British government; a fertile and beautiful region, comprehending about one hundred thousand acres of the richest soil of the province. Part of this district has been purchased from them by the present Lieutenant-governor; a measure for which he has been severely censured, for the tribe were by no means unanimous in consenting to part with their possessions. About one hundred and fifty refused to agree, but they were in the minority, and twenty-five thousand acres of rich land have been ceded to the government, and are already lotted out in townships.

The Moravian missionary from whom I had these particulars, seemed an honest, commonplace man, pious, conscientious, but very simple, and very ignorant on every subject but that of his mission. He told me further, that the Moravians had resided among these Dela-wares from generation to generation, since the first establishment of the mission in the Southern States, in 1735; from that period to 1772, seven hundred and twenty Indians had been baptized. The War of the Revolution, in all its results, had fallen heavily on them; they had been driven northwards from one settlement to another, from the banks of the Delaware to that of the Ohio – from the Ohio beyond the lakes – and now they were driven from this last refuge. His assistant, Brother Vogler, was about to emigrate west with the one hundred and fifty families who objected to the sale of their lands. They were going to join a remnant of their nation beyond the Missouri, and he added that he himself would probably soon follow with the rest, for he did not expect that they would be able to retain the residue of their lands; no doubt they would be required for the use of the white settlers, and if government urged on the purchase, they had no means of resisting. He admitted that only a small portion of the tribe under his care and tuition could be called Christians; there were about two hundred and thirty baptized out of seven hundred, principally women and children, and yet the mission has been established and supported for more than a century. Their only chance, he said, was with the children; and on my putting the question to him in a direct form, he replied decidedly, that he considered the civilisation and conversion of the Indians, *to any great extent,* a hopeless task.

He admitted the reasonableness and the truth of those motives and facts, which had induced the Lieutenant-governor to purchase so large a portion of the Delaware hunting-grounds: that they lay in the midst of the white settlements, and were continually exposed to the illegal encroachments as well as the contagious example of the whites: that numbers of the tribe were half-cast – that nearly the whole were in a frightful state of degeneration, addicted to the use of ardent spirits, which they found it easy to procure; and, from the gradual diminution of the wild animals, and their own depravity and indolence, miserably poor and wretched; and that such was the diminution of their numbers from year to year, there seemed no hope for them but in removing them as far as possible from the influence of the whites. All this he allowed, and it certainly excuses the Governor, if you consider only the expediency and the benevolence, independent of the justice, of the measure.

God forbid that I should attempt to make light of the zeal and the labours of the missionaries in this land. *They* only stand between the Indian and his oppressors, and by their generous self-devotion in some measure atone for the injuries and soften the mischiefs which have been inflicted by their countrymen and fellow Christians; but while speaking with this worthy, simple-minded man, I could not help wishing that he had united more knowledge and judgment with his conscientious piety – more ability with good-will – more discretion with faith and zeal. The spirit was willing, but it was weak. The ignorance and intolerance of some of these enthusiastic, well-meaning men, have done as much injury to the good cause for which they suffered and preached, as their devotion and self-sacrifices have done honour to the same cause and to human nature. Take, for instance, the following scene, as described with great naïveté by one of these very Moravians. After a conference with some of the Delaware chief men, in which they were informed that the missionaries had come to teach them a better and purer religion, of which the one fundamental principle, leading to eternal salvation, was belief in the Redeemer, and atonement through his blood for the sins of all mankind – all which was contained in the book which he held in his hand, – "Wangoman, a great chief and medicine-man among them, rose to reply. He began by tracing two lines on the ground, and endeavoured to explain that there were two ways which led alike to God and to happiness, the way of the Red man, and the way of the White man, but the way of the Red man, he said, was the straighter and the shorter of the two."

The missionary here interposed, and represented that God himself had descended on earth to teach men the *true* way. Wangoman declared that "he had been intimately acquainted with God for many years, and had never heard that God became a man and shed his blood, and therefore the God of whom Brother Zeisberger preached could not be the true God, or he, Wangoman, would have been made acquainted with the circumstance."

The missionary then declared, "in the power of the spirit, that the God in whom Wangoman and his Indians believed was no other than the devil, the father of lies." Wangoman replied in a very moderate tone, "I cannot understand your doctrine; it is quite new and strange to me. If it be true," he added, "that the Great Spirit came down into the world, became a man and suffered so much, I assure you the Indians are not in fault, but the white men alone. God has given us the beasts of the forest for food, and our employment is to hunt them. We know nothing of your book – we cannot learn it; it is much too difficult for an Indian to comprehend."

Brother Zeisberger replied, "I will tell you the reason of it. Satan is the prince of darkness: where he reigns all is dark, and he dwells in you – therefore you can comprehend nothing of God and his word; but when you return from the evil of your ways, and come as a wretched lost sinner to Jesus Christ, it may be that he will have mercy upon you. Do not delay therefore; make haste and save your poor souls!" &c.

I forbear to repeat the rest, because it would seem as if I intended to turn it into ridicule, which Heavens knows I do not; for it is of far too serious import. But if it be in this style that the simple and sublime precepts of Christianity are first presented to the understanding of the Indians, can we wonder at the little progress hitherto made in converting them to the truth? And with regard to all attempts to civilise them, what should the red man see in the civilisation of the white man which should move him to envy or emulation, or raise in his mind a wish to exchange his "own unshackled life, and his innate capacities of soul," for our artificial social habits, our morals, which are contradicted by our opinions, and our religion, which is violated both in our laws and our lives? When the good missionary said, with emphasis, that there was no hope for the conversion of the Indians but in removing them as far as possible from all intercourse with Europeans, he spoke a terrible truth, confirmed by all I see and hear – by the opinion of every one I have spoken to, who has ever had any intercourse with these people. It will be said, as it has often been said, that *here* it is the selfishness of the white man which speaks; that it is for his interest, and for his worldly advantage, that the red man should be removed out of his way, and be thrust back from the extending limits of civilisation – even like these forests, which fall before us, and vanish from the earth, leaving for a while some decaying stumps and roots over which the plough goes in time, and no vestige remains to say that here they *have been*. True; it *is* for the advantage of the European agriculturist or artisan, that the hunter of the woods, who requires the range of many hundred square miles of land for the adequate support of a single family, should make way for populous towns, and fields teeming with the means of subsistence for thousands. There is no denying this; and if there be those who think that in the present state of things the interests of the red man and the white man can ever be blended, and their natures and habits brought to harmonise, then I repeat, let them come here, and behold and see the heathen and the so-called Christian placed in near neighbourhood and comparison, and judge what are the chances for both! Wherever the Christian comes, he brings the Bible in one hand, disease, corruption, and the accursed fire-water, in the other; or flinging down the book of peace, he boldly and openly proclaims that might gives right, and substitutes the sabre and the rifle for the slower desolation of starvation and whisky.

(1838)   (1838)

[Alexander Henry]

I HAVE ALSO another book to which I must introduce you more particularly – "The Travels and Adventures of Alexander Henry." Did you every hear of such a man? No. Listen then, and perpend.

This Mr. Henry was a fur-trader who journeyed over these lake regions about seventy years ago, and is quoted as first-rate authority in more recent books of travels. His book, which was lent to me at Toronto, struck me so much as to have had some influence in directing the course of my present tour. Plain, unaffected, telling what he has to tell in few and simple words, and without comment – the internal evidence of truth – the natural sensibility and power of fancy, betrayed rather than displayed – render not only the narrative, but the man himself, his personal character, unspeakably interesting. Wild as are the tales of his hairbreadth escapes, I never heard the slightest impeachment of his veracity. He was living at Montreal so late as 1810 or 1811, when a friend of mine saw him, and described him to me as a very old man past eighty, with white hair, and still hale-looking and cheerful, so that his hard and adventurous life, and the horrors he had witnessed and suffered had in no respect impaired his spirits or his constitution. His book has been long out of print. I had the greatest difficulty in procuring the loan of a copy, after sending to Montreal, Quebec, and New York, in vain. Mr. Henry is to be my travelling companion, or rather *our* travelling companion, for I always fancy *you* of the party. I do not know how he might have figured as a squire of dames when living, but I assure you that being dead he makes a very respectable hero of epic or romance. He is the Ulysses of these parts, and to cruise among the shores, rocks, and islands of Lake Huron without Henry's travels, were like coasting Calabria and Sicily without the Odyssey in your head or hand, – only here you have the island of Mackinaw instead of the island of Circe; the land of the Ottawas instead of the shores of the Lotophagi; cannibal Chippewas, instead of man-eating Læstrygons; Pontiac figures as Polypheme; and Wa,wa,tam plays the part of good king Alcinous. I can find no type for the women, as Henry does not tell us his adventures among the squaws, but no doubt he might have found both Calypsos and Nausicaas, and even a Penelope, among them.

(1838)   (1838)

William Lyon Mackenzie
1795-1861

BORN NEAR DUNDEE, Scotland, William Lyon Mackenzie emigrated to Upper Canada in 1820. Four years later he founded a newspaper, the *Colonial Advocate*, near York and soon began his career as a reform journalist and a leading critic of the Family Compact. Elected to the House of Assembly in 1828, Mackenzie was expelled from and re-elected to the Assembly on several occasions and in 1837 he led an abortive rebellion against the government of Upper Canada. When the revolt failed, Mackenzie fled to the United States and remained there until 1849 when he returned to Canada and became active in politics once more. His account of the rebellion was intended as a rejoinder to "a very incorrect narrative of the insurrection" which Mackenzie had found in an Upper Canadian newspaper; his own version first appeared in 1838 in the *Jeffersonian*, a newspaper published in Watertown, New York.

From
Mackenzie's Own Narrative of the Rebellion

MY CHIEF HOPE lay in this, that if we were not attacked till Thursday night, vast reinforcements would join us from the outer townships, and that reformers at a distance would march to our aid, the moment they heard that we had struck for self-government. With this view, I sought to confine the attention of the enemy to the defence of the city, and on Thursday morning selected 40 riflemen and 20 others to go down and burn the Don bridge, the eastern approach to Toronto, and the house at its end, to take the Montreal mail stage and mails, and to draw out the forces in that quarter if possible. I also proposed that the rest of our men who had arms, should take the direction of the city, and be ready to move to the right or left, or to retreat to a strong position as prudence might dictate. At this moment Colonel Van Egmond, a native of Holland, owning 13,000 acres of land in the Huron Tract, a tried patriot, and of great military experience under Napoleon, joined us, and one of the Captains desired a council to be held, which was done. Col. V. approved of my plan, a party went off, set fire to the bridge, burnt the house, took the mails, and went through a part of the city unmolested. But the councilling and discussing of my project occasioned a delay of two hours, which proved our ruin, for the enemy having obtained large reinforcements by the steamers from Cobourg, Niagara and Hamilton, resolved to attack us in three divisions, one of them to march up Yonge street, and the others by ways about a mile to the right and left of that road. Had our forces started in the morning, the party at the bridge would have interfered with and broken up the enemy's plan of attack, and we would have been in motion near To-ronto, ready to retreat to some one of the commanding positions in its rear, or to join the riflemen below and there enter the city.

We were still at the hotel, discussing what was best to be done, when one of the guards told us that the enemy was marching up with music and artillery, and within a mile of us. Our people immediately pre-pared for battle, I rode down towards the enemy, doubting the intelli-gence, until when within a short distance I saw them with my own eyes. I rode quickly back, asked our men if they were ready to fight a greatly superior force, well armed, and with artillery well served. They were ready, and I bade them go to the woods and do their best. – They did so, and never did men fight more courageously. In the face of a heavy fire of grape and canister, with broadside following broadside of mus-ketry in steady and rapid succession, they stood their ground firmly, and killed & wounded a large number of the enemy, but were at length compelled to retreat. In a more favorable position, I have no doubt but that they would have beaten off their assailants with immense loss. As it was they had only three killed and three or four wounded. I felt anxious to go to Montgomery's for my portfolio and paper, which were important, but it was out of the question, so they fell into the hands of Sir Francis. All my papers previous to the events of that week I had destroyed, except a number of business letters, and these it took my family upwards of an hour and a quarter to burn. But with all my caution, some letters fell into their hands to the injury of others.

The manly courage with which two hundred farmers, miserably armed, withstood the formidable attack of an enemy 1200 strong, and who had plenty of ammunition, with new muskets and bayonets, artil-lery, first rate European officers, and the choice of a position of attack, convinces me that discipline, order, obedience and subordination, under competent leaders, would enable them speedily to attain a confidence sufficient to foil even the regulars from Europe. About 200 of our friends stood at the tavern during the battle, being unarmed.

Mr. Fletcher, Col. Van Egmond, myself, and others, held a consultation near Hogg's Hollow, and concluded that it would be useless to reassemble our scattered forces, for that without arms, success would be doubtful. I instantly determined to pass over to the United States, and accomplished my purpose in three days, travelled 125 miles, was seen by 2000 persons at least, and with a reward of 4000 dollars advertised for my head, speedily reached Buffalo.

It is said we were cruel to our prisoners, 54 in number, but nothing could be farther from the truth. They had the largest and best rooms in the hotel, twelve bed chambers were appropriated to their especial use, and bedding, while our volunteers lay in their wearing clothes on the floor of the bar and other apartments – they fared as we fared; and for their amusement I sent them up European, American and Canadian papers, often without reading them myself. Mr. McDonald wrote to his family that he was kindly treated, and it is unjust for any British officer to allow such slanders as have appeared in the newspapers to go uncontradicted.

As to Sir Francis Head's story of 10,000 men instantly making to the capital to support him, it is a sheer fabrication. If that were true, why has a law become necessary since to suspend the trial by jury? Why were his family confined for two days on board a steamboat? Why did he send us a flag of truce on Tuesday, when all the force he could muster was 150 men and boys, out of a population of 20,000 in and near to Toronto? The truth is, that thousands were on their way to join us on Thursday evening, that being the regular time for which the towns had been summoned; and they, on learning that we were dispersed, made a virtue of necessity, and professed that they had come to aid the torics! Sir Francis, in his Speech, says they were "generally speaking, without arms;" and in fact most of them had none to bring. That was the grand difficulty; and would have been remedied had our movement been delayed till Thursday, as agreed on. – Very few Militia men in Upper Canada had been entrusted with arms, and of these few the Government had endeavored, through Captain Magrath and others, to deprive them previous to the outbreak.

The burning of Mr. Gibson's house, stables, and outhouses, by the order and in the presence of Governor Head, was highly disgraceful to him, and is a stain upon his reputation. Dr. Horne's premises was head quarters to the spies and traitors who invested our camp, and used for the purpose of the enemy, but this was not the case with those of Mr. Gibson. Yet Government destroyed them, and carried off his cattle, horses, grain, and property, and used or sold it, and kept the money. The moveables of hundreds of others were taken in the same way. Sir

Francis' advisers may live to see this example followed more extensively than they desire. When the reformers destroyed the house of Dr. Horne, they did not carry off to the value of one farthing of his effects. As to Sheriff Jarvis' premises, they would have been burnt but for two reasons – 1st, we had no proof that the Sheriff's house was used as a rendezvous for our enemies; and, 2ndly, there were sick people in it, whom we did not wish to make war upon.

About 3,500 persons joined us during the three days on which we were behind Totonto.

My large and extensive Book Store, the newest and most valuable Printing Establishment in Upper Canada, and my Bindery, were entered by Alderman Powell, and others, on the Tuesday, the types upset, the work destroyed, and every thing on the premises either rendered useless or carried off.

The American people will understand the state of society in the Canadas, when informed, that martial law obtains at Montreal, and that the Habeas Corpus Act is suspended at Toronto – that the opposition presses are all destroyed or silenced, and their Editors expatriated – and that the liberty of speech, and of the press, is enjoined in an equal degree in conquered Poland and in conquered Canada.

There may be errors in the preceding narrative, and if so, I shall be thankful for their correction. My motives having been impeached by some, I cheerfully refer to those of all parties who have had the best means of observing my public and private conduct for many years past, whether I am deserving of blame, as one who recommended a movement which has not been successful, or for lack of discretion, or energy, so far as concerned in its execution, are questions which, if worth while, the public have the facts before them to determine. – Being of opinion that a vast majority of the people of Upper Canada earnestly desire independence, and firmly persuaded that with perseverance they will attain it, I intend to continue to devote my very humble efforts towards hastening the happy time when Colonial vassalage will be exchanged for freedom and peace.

The Canadian people owe to their American brethren a large debt of gratitude, and will, I trust, ever remember the kindness and sympathy extended towards them. The freemen of this frontier have lost sight of the political and party divisions of the hour, and enthusiastically cheered our aspirants for liberty, indulging a lively hope that heaven would speedily bless their efforts, and hasten the day in which they will be enabled to burst the bonds of ages of tyranny, attain liberal political institutions, and become prosperous and free.

(1838)   (1937)

Thomas Chandler Haliburton
1796-1865

BORN AND EDUCATED in Windsor, Nova Scotia, Thomas Chandler Haliburton practised law in Annapolis Royal and was elected to Nova Scotia's House of Assembly in 1826. Later he became a judge of the Court of Common Pleas, a position he held until his appointment as judge of the Supreme Court of Nova Scotia in 1841. He remained in this post until 1856 when he moved permanently to England where he spent his last years as a member of the British House of Commons. Among the first native-born Canadian writers to achieve an international reputation, Haliburton's success was largely the result of a single character, Sam Slick, a Yankee clockmaker who first appeared in a series of sketches published in Joseph Howe's newspaper, the *Nova-scotian*, in 1835. Sam Slick's adventures were expanded in seven subsequent volumes, *The Clockmaker; or, The Sayings and Doings of Samuel Slick of Slickville* (1836, 1838 and 1840), *The Attaché; or, Sam Slick in England* (1843 and 1844), *Sam Slick's Wise Saws and Modern Instances; or, What He Said, Did, or Invented* (1853) and *Nature and Human Nature* (1855).

The Clockmaker

I HAD HEARD of Yankee clock pedlars, tin pedlars, and bible pedlars, expecially of him who sold Polyglot Bibles (*all in English*) to the amount of sixteen thousand pounds. The house of every substantial farmer had three substantial ornaments, a wooden clock, a tin reflector, and a Polyglot Bible. How is it that an American can sell his wares, at whatever price he pleases, where a blue-nose would fail to make a sale at all? I will enquire of the Clockmaker the secret of his success.

"What a pity it is, Mr. *Slick*," (for such was his name) "what a pity it is," said I, "that you, who are so successful in teaching these people the value of *clocks*, could not also teach them the value of *time."* "I guess," said he, "they have got that ring to grow on their horns yet, which every four year old has in our country. We reckon hours and minutes to be dollars and cents. They do nothin' in these parts, but eat, drink, smoke, sleep, ride about, lounge at taverns, make speeches at temperance meetings, and talk about '*House of Assembly.*' If a man don't hoe his corn, and he don't get a crop, he says it is all owin' to the Bank; and if he runs into debt and is sued, why he says lawyers are a cuss to the country. They are a most idle set of folks, I tell *you.*"

"But how is it," said I, "that you manage to sell such an immense number of clocks, (which certainly cannot be called necessary articles) among a people with whom there seems to be so great a scarcity of money?"

Mr. Slick paused, as if considering the propriety of answering the question, and looking me in the face, said, in a confidential tone, "Why, I don't care if I do tell you, for the market is glutted, and I shall quit this circuit. It is done by a knowledge of *soft sawder* and *human natur'*. But here is Deacon Flint's," said he, "I have but one clock left, and I guess I will sell it to him."

At the gate of a most comfortable looking farm house stood Deacon Flint, a respectable old man, who had understood the value of time better than most of his neighbours, if one might judge from the appearance of every thing about him. After the usual salutation, an invitation to "alight" was accepted by Mr. Slick, who said, he wished to take leave of Mrs. Flint before he left Colchester.

We had hardly entered the house, before the Clockmaker pointed to the view from the window, and addressing himself to me, said, "if I was to tell them in Connecticut, there was such a farm as this away down east here in Nova Scotia, they wouldn't believe me – why there ain't such a location in all New England. The deacon has a hundred acres of dyke – " "Seventy," said the deacon, "only seventy." "Well, seventy; but then there is your fine deep bottom, why I could run a ramrod into it – " "Interval, we call it," said the Deacon, who, though evidently pleased at this eulogium, seemed to wish the experiment of the ramrod to be tried in the right place – "Well, interval if you please, (though Professor Eleazer Cumstick, in his work on Ohio, calls them bottoms,) is just as good as dyke. Then there is that water privilege, worth 3,000 or 4,000 dollars, twice as good as what Governor Cass paid 15,000 dollars for. I wonder, Deacon, you don't put up a carding mill on it: the same works would carry a turning lathe, a shingle machine, a circular saw, grind bark, and – " "Too old," said the Deacon, "too old for all those speculations" – "Old," repeated the Clockmaker, "not you; why you are worth half a dozen of the young men we see, now a-days, you are young enough to have —" here he said something in a lower tone of voice, which I did not distinctly hear; but whatever it was, the Deacon was pleased, he smiled and said he did not think of such things now.

"But your beasts, dear me, your beasts must be put in and have a feed;" saying which, he went out to order them to be taken to the stable.

As the old gentleman closed the door after him, Mr. Slick drew near to me, and said in an under tone, "now that is what I call *soft sawder*. An Englishman would pass that man as a sheep passes a hog in a pastur', without lookin' at him; or," said he, looking rather archly, "if he was mounted on a pretty smart horse, I guess he'd trot away, *if he could*. Now I find —" Here his lecture on *soft sawder* was cut short by the entrance of Mrs. Flint. "Jist come to say good bye, Mrs. Flint." "What, have you sold all your clocks?" "yes, and very low, too, for money is scarce, and I wished to close the concarn; no, I am wrong in saying all, for I have jist one left. Neighbour Steel's wife asked to have the refusal of it, but I guess I won't sell it; I had but two of them, this one and the feller of it that I sold Governor Lincoln. General Green, the Secretary of State for Maine, said he'd give me 50 dollars for this here one – it has composition wheels and patent axles, it is a beautiful article – a real first chop – no mistake, genuine superfine, but I guess I'll take it back; and beside, Squire Hawk might think kinder harder that I didn't give him the offer." "Dear me," said Mrs. Flint, "I should like to see it; where is it?" "It is in a chist of mine over the way, at Tom Tape's store. I guess he can ship it on to Eastport." "That's a good man," said Mrs. Flint, "jist let's look at it."

Mr. Slick, willing to oblige, yielded to these entreaties, and soon produced the clock – a gawdy, highly varnished, trumpery looking affair. He placed it on the chimney-piece where its beauties were pointed out and duly appreciated by Mrs. Flint, whose admiration was about ending in a proposal, when Mr. Flint returned from giving his directions about the care of the horses. The Deacon praised the clock, he too thought it a handsome one; but the Deacon was a prudent man, he had a watch – he was sorry, but he had no occasion for a clock. "I guess you're in the wrong furrow this time, Deacon, it an't for sale," said Mr. Slick; "and if it was, I reckon neighbour Steel's wife would have it, for she gives me no peace about it." Mrs. Flint said, that Mr. Steel had enough to do, poor man, to pay his interest, without buying clocks for his wife. "It's no concarn of mine," said Mr. Slick, "so long as he pays me, what he has to do, but I guess I don't want to sell it, and besides it comes too high; that clock can't be made at Rhode Island under 40 dollars. Why it ain't possible," said the Clockmaker, in apparent surprise, looking at his watch, "why as I'm alive it is 4 o'clock, and if I hav'nt been two blessed hours here – how on airth shall I reach River

Philip to-night? I'll tell you what, Mrs. Flint, I'll leave the clock in your care till I return on my way to the States – I'll set it a goin and put it to the right time."

As soon as this operation was performed, he delivered the key to the Deacon with a sort of serio-comic injunction to wind up the clock every Saturday night, which Mrs. Flint said she would take care should be done, and promised to remind her husband of it, in case he should chance to forget it.

"That," said the Clockmaker, as soon as we were mounted, "that I call *'human natur'!* Now that clock is sold for 40 dollars – it cost me jist 6 dollars and 50 cents. Mrs. Flint will never let Mrs. Steel have the refusal – nor will the Deacon larn until I call for the clock that having once indulged in the use of a superfluity, how difficult it is to give it up. We can do without any article of luxury we have never had, but when once obtained, it isn't 'in *human natur'* to surrender it voluntarily. Of fifteen thousand sold by myself and partners in this Province, twelve thousand were left in this manner, and only ten clocks were ever returned – when we called for them they invariably bought them. We trust to *'soft sawder'* to get them into the house, and to *'human natur'* that they never come out of it."

(1836)   (1838)

The Silent Girls

"DO YOU SEE them are swallers," said the Clockmaker, "how low they fly? Well, I presume, we shall have rain right away, and them noisy critturs, them gulls, how close they keep to the water down there in the Shubenacadie; well that's a sure sign. If we study natur', we don't wont no thermometer. But I guess we shall be in time to get under cover in a shingle-maker's shed, about three miles ahead on us."

We had just reached the deserted hovel when the rain fell in torrents.

"I reckon," said the Clock-maker, as he sat himself down on a bundle of shingles, "I reckon they are bad off for inns in this country. When a feller is too lazy to work here he paints his name over his door, and calls it a tavern, and as like as not he makes the whole neighbourhood as lazy as himself – it is about as easy to find a good inn in Halifax, as it is to find wool on a goat's back. An inn, to be a good concarn must be built a purpose, you can no more make a good tavern out of a common dwelling-house, I expect, than a good coat out of an old pair of trowsers. They are etarnal lazy, you may depend – now there might be a grand spec made there, in building a good Inn and a good Church." "What a sacrilegious and unnatural union," said I, with most unaffected surprise. "Not at all," said Mr. Slick, "we build both on spekilation in the States, and make a good deal of profit out of 'em too, I tell you. We look out a good sightly place, in a town like Halifax, that is pretty considerably well peopled with folks that are good marks; and if there is no rael right down good preacher among them, we build a handsome Church, touched off like a New-York liner, a rael takin', lookin' thing – and then we look out for a preacher, a crack man, a regular ten-horse-power chap – well, we hire him, and we have to give pretty high wages too, say twelve hundred or sixteen hundred dollars a year. We take him at first on trial for a Sabbath or two, to try his paces, and if he takes with the folks, if he goes down well we clinch the bargain, and let and sell the pews; and I tell you it pays well and makes a rael good investment. There were few better specs among us than Inns and Churches, until the Railroads came on the carpet – as soon as the novelty of the new preacher wears off, we hire another, and that keeps up the steam." "I trust it will be long, very long, my friend," said I, "ere the rage for speculation introduces 'the money-changers into the temple,' with us."

Mr. Slick looked at me with a most ineffable expression of pity and surprise. "Depend on it, sir," said he, with a most philosophical air, "this Province is much behind the intelligence of the age. But if it is behind us in that respect, it is a long chalk ahead on us in others. I never seed or heard tell of a country that had so many nateral privileges as this. Why there are twice as many harbours and water powers here, as we have all the way from Eastport to New Or*leens*. They have all they can ax, and more than they desarve. They have iron, coal, slate, grindstone, lime, firestone, gypsum, freestone, and a list as long as an auctioneer's catalogue. But they are either asleep, or stone blind to them. Their shores are crowded with fish, and their lands covered with wood. A government that lays as light on 'em as a down counterpin, and no taxes. Then look at their dykes. The Lord seems to have made 'em on purpose for such lazy folks. If you were to tell the citizens of our country that these dykes had been cropped for a hundred years without manure, they'd say, they guessed you had seen Col. Crockett, the greatest hand at a flam in our nation. You have heerd tell of a man who couldn't see London for the houses, I tell you, if we had this country, you couldn't see the harbours for the shippin'. There'd be a rush of folks to it, as there is in one of our inns, to the dinner table, when they sometimes get jammed together in the door-way, and a man has to take a running leap over their heads, afore he can get in. A little nigger boy in New York found a diamond worth 2,000 dollars; well, he sold it to a watchmaker for 50 cents – the little critter didn't know no better. *Your people are just like the nigger boy, they don't know the valy of their diamond.*"

"Do you know the reason monkeys are no good? because they chatter all day long – so do the niggers – and so do the blue-noses of Nova Scotia – it's all talk and no work; now, with us it's all work and no talk – in our shipyards, our factories, our mills, and even in our vessels, there's no talk – a man can't work and talk too. I guess if you were to the factories to Lowel we'd show you a wonder – *five hundred galls at work together all in silence.* I don't think our great country has such a rael nateral curosity as that – I expect the world don't contain the beat of that; for a woman's tongue goes so slick of itself, without water power or steam, and moves so easy on its hinges, that it's no easy matter to put a spring stop on it, I tell you – it comes as natural as drinkin mint julip."

"I don't pretend to say the galls don't nullify the rule, sometimes at intermission and arter hours, but when they do, if they don't let go, then it's a pity. You have heerd a school come out, of little boys, Lord it's no touch to it; or a flock of geese at it, they are no more a match for 'em than a pony is for a coach-horse. But when they are to work, all's as still as sleep and no snoring. I guess we have a right to brag o' that invention – we trained the dear critters, so they don't think of striking the minutes and seconds no longer."

"Now the folks to Halifax take it all out in talkin' – they talk of steam-boats, whalers, and rail-roads – but they all end where they begin – in talk. I don't think I'd be out in my latitude, if I was to say they beat the women kind at that. One feller says, I talk of going to England – another says, I talk of going to the Country – while a third says, I talk of goin to sleep. If we happen to speak of such things, we say, 'I'm right off down East; or I'm away off South,' and away we go jist like a streak of lightnin."

"When we want folks to talk, we pay 'em for it, such as ministers, lawyers, and members of congress; but then we expect the use of their tongues, and not their hands; and when we pay folks to work, we expect the use of their hands, and not their tongues. I guess work don't come kind o' nateral to the people of this province, no more than it does to a full bred horse. I expect they think they have a little *too much blood* in 'em for work, for they are near about as proud as they are lazy."

"Now the bees know how to sarve out such chaps, for they have their drones too. Well, they reckon it's no fun, a making of honey all summer, for these idle critters to eat all winter – so they give 'em Lynch Law. They have a regilar built mob of citizens, and string up the drones like the Vixburg gamblers. Their maxim is, and not a bad one neither, I guess, 'no work no honey.'"

(1836)   (1838)

Aiming High

"WHAT DO YOU intend to do, Squire, with your two youngest boys?" said Mr. Slick to me to-day, as we were walking in the Park.

"I design them," I said, "for professions. One I shall educate for a lawyer, and the other for a clergyman."

"Where?"

"In Nova Scotia."

"Exactly," says he. "It shews your sense; it's the very place for 'em. It's a fine field for a young man; I don't know no better one no where in the whole univarsal world. When I was a boy larnin' to shoot, sais father to me, one day, 'Sam,' sais he, 'I'll give you a lesson in gunnin' that's worth knowin'. *Aim high,* my boy; your gun naterally settles down a little takin' sight, cause your arm gets tired, and wabbles, and the ball settles a little while it's a travellin', accordin' to a law of natur, called Franklin's law; and I observe you always hit below the mark. Now, make allowances for these things in gunnin', and "aim high," for your life, always. And, Sam,' sais he, 'I've seed a great deal of the world, all mili*tary* men do. I was to Bunker's Hill durin' the engagement, and I saw Washington the day he was made President, and in course must know more nor most men of my age; and I'll give you another bit of advice, "Aim high" in life, and if you don't hit the bull's eye, you'll hit the "fust circles," and that ain't a bad shot nother.'"

"'Father,' sais I, 'I guess I've seed more of the world than you have, arter all.'"

"'How so, Sam?' sais he."

"'Why,' sais I, 'father, you've only been to Bunker's Hill, and that's nothin'; no part of it ain't too steep to plough; it's only a sizeable hillock, arter all. But I've been to the Notch on the White Mountain, so high up, that the snow don't melt there, and seed five States all to once, and half way over to England, and then I've seed Jim Crow dance. So there now?' He jist up with the flat of his hand, and gave me a wipe with it on the side of my face, that knocked me over; and as I fell, he lent me a kick on my musn't-mention-it, that sent me a rod or so afore I took ground on all fours."

"'Take that, you young scoundrel!' said he, 'and larn to speak respectful next time to an old man, a mili*tary* man, and your father, too.'"

"It hurt me properly, you may depend. 'Why,' sais I, as I picked myself up, 'didn't you tell me to "aim high," father? So I thought I'd do it, and beat your brag, that's all.'"

"Truth is, Squire, I never could let a joke pass all my life, without havin' a lark with it. I was fond of one, ever since I was knee high to a goose, or could recollect any thin' amost; I have got into a horrid sight of scrapes by 'em, that's a fact. I never forgot that lesson though, it was kicked into me: and lessons that are larnt on the right eend, ain't never forgot amost. I *have* "aimed high" ever since, and see where I be now. Here I am an Attaché, made out of a wooden clock pedlar. Tell you what, I shall be "embassador" yet, made out of nothin' but an "Attaché," and I'll be President of our great Republic, and almighty nation in the eend, made out of an embassador, see if I don't. That comes of "aimin' high." What do you call that water near your coach-house?"

"A pond."

"Is there any brook runnin' in, or any stream runnin' out?"

"No."

"Well, that's the difference between a lake and a pond. Now, set that down for a traveller's fact. Now, where do you go to fish?"

"To the lakes, of course; there are no fish in the ponds."

"Exactly," said Mr. Slick, "that is what I want to bring you to; there is no fish in a pond, there is nothin' but frogs. Nova Scotia is only a pond, and so is New Brunswick, and such outlandish, out o' the way, little crampt up, stagnant places. There is no 'big fish' there, nor never can be; there ain't no food for 'em. A colony frog!! Heavens and airth, what an odd fish that is? A colony pollywog! do, for gracious sake, catch one, put him into a glass bottle full of spirits, and send him to the Museum as a curiosity in natur. So you are a goin' to make your two nice pretty little smart boys a pair of colony frogs, eh? Oh! do, by all means."

"You'll have great comfort in 'em, Squire. Monstrous comfort. It will do your old heart good to go down to the edge of the pond on the fust of May, or thereabouts, accordin' to the season, jist at sun down, and hear 'em sing. You'll see the little fellers swell out their cheeks, and roar away like young suckin' thunders. For the frogs beat all natur there for noise; they have no notion of it here at all. I've seed Englishmen that couldn't sleep all night, for the everlastin' noise these critters made. Their frogs have somethin' else to do here besides singin'. Ain't it a splendid prospect that, havin' these young frogs settled all round you in the same mudhole, all gathered in a nice little musical family party. All fine fun this, till some fine day we Yankee storks will come down and gobble them all up, and make clear work of it."

"No, Squire, take my advice now, for once; jist go to your colony minister when he is alone. Don't set down, but stand up as if you was in airnest, and didn't come to gossip, and tell him, 'Turn these ponds into a lake,' sais you, 'my lord minister, give them an inlet and outlet. Let them be kept pure, and sweet, and wholesome, by a stream runnin' through. Fish will live there then if you put them in, and they will breed there, and keep up the stock. At present they die; it ain't big enough; there ain't room. If he sais he hante time to hear you, and asks you to put it into writin', do you jist walk over to his table, take up his lignum vitæ ruler into your fist, put your back to the door, and say 'By the 'tarnal empire, you *shall* hear me; you don't go out of this, till I give you the butt eend of my mind, I can tell you. I am an old bull frog now; the Nova Scotia pond is big enough for me; I'll get drowned if I get into a bigger one, for I hante got no fins, nothin' but legs and arms to swim with, and deep water wouldn't suit me, I ain't fit for it, and I must live and die there, that's my fate as sure as rates.' If he gets tired, and goes to get up or to move, do you shake the big ruler at him, as fierce as a painter, and say, 'Don't you stir for your life; I don't want to lay nothin *on* your head, I only want to put somethin' *in* it. I am a father and have got youngsters. I am a native, and have got countrymen. Enlarge our sphere, give us a chance in the world.' 'Let me out,' he'll say, 'this minute, Sir, or I'll put you in charge of a policeman.' 'Let you out is it,' sais you. 'Oh! you feel bein' pent up, do you? I am glad of it. The tables are turned now, that's what we complain of. You've stood at the door, and kept us in; now I'll keep you in awhile. I want to talk to you, that's more than you ever did to us. How do you like bein' shut in? Does it feel good? Does it make your dander rise?' 'Let me out,' he'll say agin, 'this moment, Sir, how dare you.' 'Oh! you are in a hurry, are you?' sais you. 'You've kept me in all my life; don't be oneasy if I keep you in five minutes.'"

"'Well, what do you want then?' he'll say, kinder peevish; 'what do you want?' 'I don't want nothin' for myself,' sais you. 'I've got all I can get in that pond; and I got that from the Whigs, fellers I've been abusin' all my life; and I'm glad to make amends by acknowledging this good turn they did me; for I am a tory, and no mistake. I don't want nothin'; but I want to be an *Englishman.* I don't want to be an English *subject;* do you understand that now? If you don't, this is the meanin', that there is no fun in bein' a fag, if you are never to have a fag yourself. Give us all fair play. Don't move now,' sais you, 'for I'm gettin' warm; I'm gettin' spotty on the back, my bristles is up, and I might hurt you with this ruler; it's a tender pint this, for I've rubbed the skin off of a sore place; but I'll tell you a gospel truth, and mind what I tell you, for nobody else has sense enough, and if they had, they hante courage enough. If you don't make *Englishmen of us,* the force of circumstances will *make Yankees* of us, as sure as you are born.' He'll stare at that. He is a clever man, and aint wantin' in gumption. He is no fool, that's a fact. 'Is it no compliment to you and your institutions this?' sais you. 'Don't it make you feel proud that even independence won't tempt us to dissolve the connexion? Ain't it a noble proof of your good qualities that, instead of agitatin' for Repeal of the Union, we want a closer union? But have we no pride too? We would be onworthy of the name of Englishmen, if we hadn't it, and we won't stand beggin' for ever I tell *you*. Here's our hands, give us yourn; let's be all Englishmen together. Give us a chance, and if us, young English boys, don't astonish you old English, my name ain't Tom Poker, that's all.' 'Sit down,' he'll say, 'Mr. Poker; there is a great deal in that; sit down; I am interested.'"

"The instant he sais that, take your ruler, lay it down on the table, pick up your hat, make a scrape with your hind leg, and say, 'I regret I have detained you so long, Sir. I am most peskily afraid my warmth has kinder betrayed me into rudeness. I really beg pardon, I do upon my soul. I feel I have smashed down all decency, I am horrid ashamed of myself.' Well, he won't say you hante rode the high hoss, and done the unhandsum thing, because it wouldn't be true if he did; but he'll say, 'Pray be seated. I can make allowances, Sir, even for intemperate zeal. And this is a very important subject, very indeed. There is a monstrous deal in what you say, though you have, I must say, rather a peculiar, an unusual way of puttin' it.' Don't you stay another minit though, nor say another word, for your life; but bow, beg pardon, hold in your breath, that your face may look red, as if you was blushin', and back out, starn fust. Whenever you make an impression on a man, stop; your reasonin' and details may ruin you. Like a feller who sais a good thing, he'd better shove off, and leave every one larfin' at his wit, than stop and tire them out, till they say what a great screw augur that is. Well, if you find he opens the colonies, and patronises the smart folks, leave your sons there if you like, and let 'em work up, and work out of it, if they are fit, and time and opportunity offers. But one thing is sartain, *the very openin' of the door will open their minds,* as a matter of course. If he don't do it, and I can tell you before hand he won't – for they actilly hante got time here, to think of these things – send your boys here into the great world. Sais you to the young Lawyer, 'Bob,' sais you, '"aim high." If you don't get to be Lord Chancellor, I shall never die in peace. I've set my heart on it. It's within your reach, if you are good for anything. Let me see the great seal – let me handle it before I die – do, that's a dear; if not, go back to your Colony pond, and sing with your provincial frogs, and I hope to Heaven the fust long-legged bittern that comes there will make a supper of you.'"

"Then sais you to the young parson, 'Arthur,' sais you 'Natur' jist made you for a clergyman. Now, do you jist make yourself 'Archbishop of Canterbury.' My death-bed scene will be an awful one, if I don't see you 'the Primate'; for my affections, my hopes, my heart, is fixed on it. I shall be willin' to die then, I shall depart in peace, and leave this world happy. And, Arthur,' sais you, 'they talk and brag here till one is sick of the sound a'most about "Addison's death-bed." Good people refer to it as an example, authors as a theatrical scene and hypocrites as a grand illustration for them to turn up the whites of their cold cantin' eyes at. Lord love you, my son,' sais you, 'let them brag of it; but what would it be to mine; you congratulatin' me on goin' to a better world, and me congratulatin' you on bein' "Archbishop." Then,' sais you, in a starn voice like a boatsan's trumpet – for if you want things to be remembered, give 'em effect, "Aim high," Sir,' sais you. Then like my old father, fetch him a kick on his western eend, that will lift him clean over the table, and say 'that's the way to rise in the world, you young sucking parson you. "Aim high," Sir.'"

"Neither of them will ever forget it as long as they live. The hit does that; for a kick is a very *striking* thing, that's a fact. There has been *no good scholars since birch rods went out o' school, and sentiment went in.*"

"But you know," I said, "Mr. Slick, that those high prizes in the lottery of life, can, in the nature of things, be drawn but by few people, and how many blanks are there to one prize in this world."

"Well, what's to prevent your boys gettin' those prizes, if colonists was made Christians of, instead of outlawed, exiled, transported, onsarcumcised heathen Indgean niggers, as they be. If people don't put into a lottery, how the devil can they get prizes? will you tell me that. Look at the critters here, look at the publicans, taylors, barbers, and porters' sons, how the've rose here, 'in this big lake,' to be chancellors and archbishops; how did they get them? They 'aimed high,' and besides, all that, like father's story of the gun, by 'aiming high,' though they may miss the mark, they will be sure to hit the upper circles. Oh, Squire, there is nothing like 'aiming high,' in this world."

"I quite agree with you, Sam," said Mr. Hopewell. "I never heard you speak so sensibly before. Nothing can be better for young men than "Aiming high." Though they may not attain to the highest honours, they may, as you say, reach to a most respectable station. But surely, Squire, you will never so far forget the respect that is due to so high an officer as a Secretary of State, or, indeed, so far forget yourself as to adopt a course, which from its eccentricity, violence, and impropriety, must leave the impression that your intellects are disordered. Surely you will never be tempted to make the experiment?"

"I should think not, indeed," I said. "I have no desire to become an inmate of a lunatic asylum."

"Good," said he; "I am satisfied. I quite agree with Sam, though.

Indeed, I go further. I do not think he has advised you to recommend your boys to 'aim high enough.'"

"Creation!" said Mr. Slick, "how much higher do you want provincial frogs to go, than to be 'Chancellor' and 'Primate'?"

"I'll tell you, Sam; I'd advise them to 'aim higher' than earthly honours. I would advise them to do their duty, in any station of life in which it shall please Providence to place them; and instead of striving after unattainable objects here, to be unceasing in their endeavours to obtain that which, on certain conditions, is promised to all hereafter. In their worldly pursuits, as men, it is right for them to *'aim high;'* but as Christians, it is also their duty to *'aim higher.'*"

(1843)   (1843)

Valedictory Address

GENTLE READER, HAVING taken my leave of Mr. Slick, it is now fit I should take my leave of you. But first, let me entreat you to join with me in the wish that the Attaché may arrive safely at home, and live to enjoy the reputation he has acquired. It would be ungracious, indeed, in me not to express the greatest gratitude to him for the many favours he has conferred upon me, and for the numerous benefits I have incidentally derived from his acquaintance. When he offered his services to accompany me to England, to make me well known to the public, and to give me numerous introductions to persons of distinction, that as a colonist I could not otherwise obtain, I could scarcely restrain a smile at the complacent self-sufficiency of his benevolence; but I am bound to say that he has more than fulfilled his promise. In all cases but two he has exceeded his own anticipations of advancing me. He has not procured for me the situation of Governor-General of Canada, which as an ambitious man, it was natural he should desire, whilst as a friend it was equally natural that he should overlook my entire unfitness for the office; nor has he procured for me a peerage, which, as an American, it is surprising he should prize so highly, or as a man of good, sound judgment, and common sense, not perceive to be more likely to cover an humble man, like me, with ridicule than anything else. For both these disappointments, however, he has one common solution, – English monopoly, English arrogance, and English pride on the one hand, and provincial dependence and colonial helotism on the other.

For myself, I am at a loss to know which to feel most grateful for, that which he has done, or that which he has left undone. To have attained all his objects, where success would have neutralized the effect of all, would, indeed, have been unfortunate; but to succeed in all that was desirable, and to fail only where failure was to be preferred, was the height of good fortune. I am happy to say that on the whole he is no less gratified himself, and that he thinks, at least, I have been of equal service to him. "It tante every one, Squire," he would often say, "that's as lucky as Johnston and me. He had his Boswell, and I have had my Squire; and if you two hante immortalized both us fellers for ever and a day, it's a pity, that's all. Fact is, I have made you known, and you have made me known, and it's some comfort too, ain't it, not to be obliged to keep a dog and do your own barkin'. It tante pleasant to be your own trumpeter always, as Kissinkirk, the Prince's bugler found, is it?"

It must not be supposed that I have recorded, like Boswell, all Mr. Slick's conversations. I have selected only such parts as suited my object. Neither the "Clockmaker" nor the "Attaché" were ever designed as books of travels, but to portray character – to give practical lessons in morals, and politics – to expose hypocrisy – to uphold the connection betweeen the parent country and the colonies, to develop the resources of the province, and to enforce the just claims of my countrymen – to discountenance agitation – to strengthen the union between Church and State – and to foster and excite a love for our own form of government, and a preference of it over all others. So many objects necessarily required several continuations of the work, and although seven volumes warn me not to trespass too long on the patience of the public, yet many excluded topics make me feel, with regret, that I have been either too diffuse, or too presumptuous. Prolixity was unavoidable from another cause. In order to attain my objects, I found it expedient so to intermingle humour with the several topics, so as to render subjects attractive that in themselves are generally considered as too deep and dry for general reading. All these matters, however, high and difficult as they are to discuss properly, are exhausted and hackneyed enough. But little that is new can now be said upon them. The only attraction they are susceptible of is the novelty of a new dress. That I have succeeded in rendering them popular by clothing them in the natural language, and illustrating them by the humour of a shrewd and droll man like Mr. Slick, their unprecedented circulation on both sides of the Atlantic, leaves me no room to doubt, while I am daily receiving the most gratifying testimony of the beneficial effects they have produced, and are still producing in the colonies, for whose use they were principally designed. Much as I value the popularity of these works, I value their utility much higher, and of the many benefits that have accrued to myself as the author, and they have been most numerous, none have been so grateful as that of knowing that "they have done good." Under these circumstances I cannot but feel in parting with Mr. Slick that I am separating from a most serviceable friend, and as the public have so often expressed their approbation of him both as a Clockmaker and an Attaché, I am not without hopes, gentle reader, that this regret is mutual. He has often pressed upon me, and at parting renewed in a most urgent manner, his request that I would not yet lay aside my pen. He was pleased to say it was both a popular and a useful one, and that as the greater part of my life had been spent in a colony, it could not be better employed than in recording *"Provincial Recollections,* or *Sketches of Colonial Life."*

In his opinion the harvest is most abundant, and needs only a reaper accustomed to the work, to garner up its riches. I think so too, but am not so confident of my ability to execute the task as he is, and still less certain of having the health or the leisure requisite for it.

I indulge the hope, however, at some future day, of at least making the attempt, and if other avocations permit me to complete it, I shall then, gentle reader, have the pleasure of again inviting your attention to my native land, by presenting you with "Sketches of Colonial Life."

(1844)   (1844)

John Richardson
1796-1852

———◆———

BORN IN QUEENSTON, Upper Canada, Major John Richardson fought in
the War of 1812 at the age of sixteen and was a career soldier in the
West Indies and Europe until 1837. Returning to Canada in 1838, he
was dogged by financial problems which in 1850 finally drove him to
emigrate to New York where he died two years later. Richardson
published many works set in North America including *Wacousta*
(1832), a frontier romance dealing with the Indian uprising led by
Pontiac in 1763, *The Canadian Brothers* (1840), a sequel to *Wacousta*, and
several volumes of poetry, history and autobiography.

From
Wacousta

[Fort Michilimackinac]

AT THE WESTERN extremity of the lake Huron, and almost washed by
the waters of that pigmy ocean, stands the fort of Michilimackinac.
Constructed on a smaller scale, and garrisoned by a less numerical
force, the defences of this post, although less formidable than those of
the Detroit, were nearly similar, at the period embraced by our story,
both in matter and in manner. Unlike the latter fortress, however, it
boasted none of the advantages afforded by culture; neither, indeed,
was there a single spot in the immediate vicinity that was not clad in the
eternal forest of these regions. It is true, that art and laborious exertion
had so far supplied the deficiencies of nature as to isolate the fort, and
throw it under the protecting sweep of its cannon; but, while this
afforded security, it failed to produce any thing like a pleasing effect to
the eye. The very site on which the fortress now stood had at one period
been a portion of the wilderness that every where around was only
terminated by the sands on the lake shore; and, although time and the
axe of the pioneer had in some degree changed its features, still there

was no trace of that blended natural scenery that so pleasingly diversified the vicinity of the sister fort. Here and there, along the imperfect clearing, and amid the dark and thickly studded stumps of the felled trees, which in themselves were sufficient to give the most lugubrious character to the scene, rose the rude log cabin of the settler; but, beyond this, cultivation appeared to have lost her power in proportion with the difficulties she had to encounter. Even the two Indian villages, L'Arbre-Croche and Chabouiga, situate about a mile from the fort, with which they formed nearly an equilateral triangle, were hid from the view of the garrison by the dark dense forest, in the heart of which they were embedded.

Lakeward the view was scarcely less monotonous; but it was not, as in the rear, that monotony which is never occasionally broken in upon by some occurrence of interest. If the eye gazed long and anxiously for the white sail of the well known armed vessel, charged at stated intervals with letters and tidings of those whom time, and distance, and danger, far from estranging, rendered more dear to the memory, and bound more closely to the heart, it was sure of being rewarded at last; and then there was no picture on which it could love to linger as well as that of the silver waves bearing that valued vessel in safety to its wonted anchorage in the offing. Moreover, the light swift bark canoes of the natives often danced joyously on its surface; and while the sight was offended at the savage, skulking among the trees of the forest, like some dark spirit moving cautiously in its course of secret destruction, and watching the moment when he might pounce unnoticed upon his unprepared victim, it followed with momentary pleasure and excitement, the activity and skill displayed by the harmless paddler, in the swift and meteor-like race that set the troubled surface of the Huron in a sheet of hissing foam. Nor was this all. When the eye turned woodward, it fell heavily, and without interest, upon a dim and dusky point, known to enter upon savage scenes and unexplored countries; whereas whenever it reposed upon the lake, it was with an eagerness and energy that embraced the most vivid recollections of the past, and led the imagination buoyantly over every well-remembered scene that had previously been traversed, and which must be traversed again before the land of the European could be pressed once more. The forest, in a word, formed, as it were, the gloomy and impenetrable walls of the prison-house, and the bright lake that lay before it the only portal through which happiness and liberty could be again secured.

The principal entrance into the fort, which presented four equal sides of a square, was from the forest; but immediately opposite to this, and behind the apartments of the commanding officer, there was another small gate that opened upon the lake shore; but which, since the investment of the place, had been kept bolted and locked, with a precaution befitting the danger to which the garrison was exposed. Still, there were periods, even now, when its sullen hinges were to be heard moaning on the midnight breeze; for it served as a medium of communication between the besieged and others who were no less critically circumstanced than themselves.

The very day before the Indians commenced their simultaneous attack on the several posts of the English, the only armed vessel that had been constructed on these upper lakes, serving chiefly as a medium of communication between Detroit and Michilimackinac, had arrived with despatches and letters from the former fort. A well-concerted plan of the savages to seize her in her passage through the narrow waters of the river St. Clair had only been defeated by the vigilance of her commander; but ever since the breaking out of the war, she had been imprisoned within the limits of the Huron. Laborious indeed was the duty of the devoted crew. Several attempts had been renewed by the Indians to surprise them; but, although their little fleets stole cautiously and noiselessly, at the still hour of midnight, to the spot where, at the last expiring rays of twilight, they had beheld her carelessly anchored and apparently lulled into security, the subject of their search was never to be met with. No sooner were objects on the shore rendered indistinct to the eye than the anchor was silently weighed, and gliding wherever the breeze might choose to carry her, the light bark was made to traverse the lake, with every sail set, until dawn. None, however, were suffered to slumber in the presumed security afforded by this judicious flight. Every man was at his post; and, while a silence so profound was preserved that the noise of a falling pin might have been heard upon her decks, everything was in readiness to repel an attack of their enemies, should the vessel in her course, come accidentally in collision with their pigmy fleets. When morning broke, and no sign of their treacherous foes was visible, the vessel was again anchored, and the majority of the crew suffered to retire to their hammocks, while the few whose turn of duty it chanced to be, kept a vigilant look-out that, on the slightest appearance of alarm, their slumbering comrades might again be aroused to energy and action.

Severe and harassing as had been the duty on board this vessel for many months, — at one moment exposed to the assaults of savages, at another assailed by hurricanes that are so prevalent and so dangerous on the American lakes, — the situation of the crew was even less enviable than that of the garrison itself. What chiefly contributed to their disquietude, was the dreadful consciousness that, however their present efforts might secure a temporary safety, the period of their fall was only protracted. A few months more must bring with them all the severity of the winter of those climes, and then, blocked up in a sea of ice, – exposed to all the rigor of cold, – all the miseries of hunger, – what effectual resistance could they oppose to the many bands of Indians who, availing themselves of the defenceless position of their enemies, would rush from every quarter to their destruction.

At the outset of these disheartening circumstances, the officer had summoned his faithful crew together, and pointing out the danger and uncertainty of their position, stated that two chances of escape still remained to them. The first was by an attempt to accomplish the passage of the river St. Clair during some dark and boisterous night, when the Indians would be least likely to suspect such an intention: it was at this point that the efforts of their enemies were principally to be apprehended; but if, under cover of storm and darkness, they could accomplish this difficult passage, they would easily gain the Detroit, and thence pass into Lake Erie, at the further extremity of which they might, favored by Providence, effect a landing, and penetrate to the inhabited parts of the colony of New York. The other alternative was, – and he left it to themselves to determine, – to sink the vessel on the approach of winter, and throw themselves into the fort before them, there to await and share the destiny of its gallant defenders.

With the generous enthusiasm of their profession, the noble fellows had determined on the latter course. With their officer they fully coincided in opinion, that their ultimate hopes of life depended on the safe passage of the St. Clair; for it was but too obvious, that soon or late unless some very extraordinary revolution should be effected in the intentions of the Indians, the fortress must be starved into submission. Still, as it was tolerably well supplied with provisions, this gloomy prospect was remote, and they were willing to run all chances with their friends on shore, rather than desert them in their extremity. The determination expressed by them, therefore, was that when they could no longer keep the lake in safety, they would, if the officer permitted it, scuttle the vessel, and attempt an entrance into the fort, where they would share the fate of the troops, whatever it might chance to be.

No sooner was this resolution made known, than their young commander sought an opportunity of communicating with the garrison. This, however, was no very easy task; for, so closely was the fort hemmed in by the savages, it was impossible to introduce a messenger within its walls; and so sudden had been the cutting off of all communication between the vessel and the shore, that the thought had not even occurred to either commander to establish the most ordinary intelligence by signal. In this dilemma, recourse was had to an ingenious expedient. The despatches of the officer were enclosed in one of the long tin tubes in which were generally deposited the maps and charts of the schooner, and to this, after having been carefully soldered, was attached an inch rope of several hundred fathoms in length: the case was then put into one of the ship's guns, so placed as to give it the elevation of a mortar; thus prepared, advantage was taken of a temporary absence of the Indians to bring the vessel within half a mile of the shore, and when the attention of the garrison, naturally attracted by this unusual movement, was sufficiently awakened, that opportunity was chosen for the discharge of the gun; and as the quantity of powder had been proportionably reduced for the limited range, the tube was soon safely deposited within the rampart. The same means were adopted in replying; and one end of the rope remaining attached to the schooner, all that was necessary was to solder up the tube as before, and throw it over the ramparts upon the sands, whence it was immediately pulled over her side by the watchful mariners.

As the despatch conveyed to the garrison, among other subjects of interest, bore the unwelcome intelligence that the supplies of the crew were nearly expended, an arrangement was proposed by which, at stated intervals, a more immediate communication with the former might be effected. Whenever, therefore, the wind permitted, the vessel was kept hovering in sight during the day beneath the eyes of the savages, and on the approach of evening an unshotted gun was discharged, with a view of drawing their attention more immediately to her movements; every sail was then set, and under a cloud of canvas the course of the schooner was directed towards the source of the St. Clair, as if an attempt to accomplish that passage was to be made during the night. No sooner, however had the darkness fairly set in, than the vessel was put about, and beating against the wind, generally contrived to reach the offing at a stated hour, when a boat, provided with muffled oars, was sent off to the shore. This ruse had several times deceived the Indians, and it was on these occasions that the small gate to which we have alluded was opened, for the purpose of conveying the necessary supplies.

The buildings of the fort consisted chiefly of block-houses, the internal accommodations of which were fully in keeping with their rude exterior, being but indifferently provided with the most ordinary articles of comfort, and fitted up as the limited resources of that wild and remote district could supply. The best and most agreeably situated of these, if a choice could be made, was that of the commanding officer. This building rose considerably above the others, and overhanging that part of the rampart which skirted the shores of the Huron, commanded a full view of the lake, even to its extremity of frowning and belting forest.

To this block-house there were two staircases; the principal leading to the front entrance from the barrack-square, the other opening in the rear, close under the rampart, and communicating by a few rude steps with the small gate that led upon the sands. In the lower part of this building, appropriated by the commanding officer to that exclusive purpose, the official duties of his situation were usually performed; and on the ground-floor a large room, that extended from front to rear of the block-house on one side of the passage, had formerly been used as a hall of council with the Indian chiefs. The floor above this comprised both his own private apartments and those set apart for the general use of the family; but, above all, and preferable from their cheerful view over the lake, were others, which had been reserved for the exclusive accommodation of Miss de Haldimar. The upper floor consisted of two sleeping apartments, with a sitting-room, the latter extending the whole length of the block-house, and opening immediately upon the lake from the only two windows with which that side of the building was provided. The principal staircase led into one of the bed-rooms, and both of the latter communicated immediately with the sitting room, which again, in its turn, opened, at the opposite extremity on the narrow staircase that led to the rear of the block-house.

The furniture of the apartment, which might be taken as a fair sample of the best the country could afford, was wild, yet simple, in the extreme. Neat rush mats, of an oblong square, and fantastically put together, so as to exhibit in the weaving of the several colored reeds both figures that were known to exist in the creation, and those which could have no being save in the imagination of their framers, served as excellent substitutes for carpets; while rush bottomed chairs, the product of Indian ingenuity also, occupied those intervals around the room that were unsupplied by the matting. Upon the walls were hung numerous specimens both of the dress and of the equipments of the savages, and mingled with these were many natural curiosities, the gifts of Indian chiefs to the commandant at various times before the war.

Nothing could be more unlike the embellishments of a modern European boudoir than those of this apartment, which had, in some degree, been made the sanctum of its present occupants. Here was to be seen the scaly carcase of some huge serpent, extending its now harmless length from the ceiling to the floor – there an alligator, stuffed after the same fashion; and in various directions the skins of the beaver, the marten, the otter, and an infinitude of others of that genus, filled up spaces that were left unsupplied by the more ingenious specimens of Indian art. Head dresses tastefully wrought in the shape of the crowning bays of the ancients, and composed of the gorgeous feathers of the most splendid of the forest birds — bows and quivers, handsomely and even elegantly ornamented with that most tasteful of Indian decorations, the stained quill of the porcupine; war clubs of massive iron wood, their handles covered with stained horsehair and feathers, curiously mingled together — machecotis, hunting coats, moccasins, and leggings all worked in porcupine quill, and fancifully arranged, — these, with many others, had been called into requisition to bedeck and relieve the otherwise rude and naked walls of the apartment.

Nor did the walls alone reflect back the picture of savage ingenuity; for on the various tables, the rude polish of which was hid from view by the simple covering of green baize, which moreover constituted the garniture of the windows, were to be seen other products of their art. Here stood upon an elevated stand a model of a bark canoe, filled with its complement of paddlers carved in wood and dressed in full costume; the latter executed with such singular fidelity of feature, that although the speaking figures sprung not from the experienced and classic chisel of the sculptor, but from the rude scalping knife of the savage, the very tribe to which they belonged could be discovered at a glance by the European who was conversant with the features of each; then there were handsomely ornamented vessels made of the birch bark, and filled with the delicate sugars which the natives extract from the maple tree in early spring; these of all sizes, even to the most tiny that could well be imagined, were valuable rather as exquisite specimens of the neatness with which those slight vessels could be put together, sewn as they were merely with strips of the same bark, than from any intrinsic value they possessed. Covered over with fantastic figures, done either in paint, or in quill work artfully interwoven into the fibres of the bark, they presented, in their smooth and polished surface, strong evidence of the address of the savages in their preparation of this most useful and abundant produce of the country. Interspersed with these, too, were numerous stands filled with stuffed birds, some of which combined in themselves every variety and shade of dazzling plumage; and numerous rude cases contained the rarest specimens of the American butterfly, most of which were of sizes and tints that are no where equalled in Europe. One solitary table alone was appropriated to whatever wore a transatlantic character in this wild and museum-like apartment. On this lay a Spanish guitar, a few pieces of old music, a collection of English and French books, a couple of writing desks, and, scattered over the whole, several articles of unfinished needle-work.

Such was the apartment in which Madeline and Clara de Haldimar were met at the moment we have selected for their introduction to our readers. It was the morning of that day on which the second council of the chiefs, the result of which has already been seen, was held at Detroit. The sun had risen bright and gorgeously above the adjacent forest, throwing his golden beams upon the calm glassy waters of the lake; and now, approaching rapidly towards the meridian, gradually diminished the tall bold shadows of the block-houses upon the shore. At the distance of about a mile lay the armed vessel so often alluded to; her light low hull, dimly seen in the hazy atmosphere that danced upon the waters, and her attenuated masts and sloping yards, with their slight tracery cordage, recalling rather the complex and delicate ramifications of the spider's web, than the elastic yet solid machinery to which the lives of those within had so often been committed in sea and tempest. Upon the strand, and close opposite to the small gate which now stood ajar, lay one of her boats, the crew of which had abandoned her with the exception only of a single individual, apparently her cockswain, who, with the tiller under his arm, lay half extended in the stern sheets, his naked chest exposed, and his tarpaulin hat shielding his eyes from the sun while he indulged in profound repose. These were the only objects that told of human life. Every where beyond the eye rested on the faint outline of forest, that appeared like the softened tracing of a pencil at the distinct junction of the waters with the horizon.

(1832)   (1868)

Catharine Parr Traill
1802-1899

———————◆———————

A SISTER OF Susanna Moodie, Catharine Parr (Strickland) Traill was born in London, England, and in 1832 emigrated with her husband, Thomas Traill, to the Peterborough region of Upper Canada. Here she wrote children's stories, studies of plants and flowers, a practical handbook on pioneering, and *The Backwoods of Canada* (1836), a series of letters written to her mother giving a realistic account of settlers' lives in Upper Canada.

From
The Backwoods of Canada

LETTER VIII

November the 20th, 1832.

OUR LOG-HOUSE is not yet finished, though it is in a state of forwardness. We are still indebted to the hospitable kindness of S——— and his wife for a home. This being their first settlement on their land they have as yet many difficulties, in common with all residents in the backwoods, to put up with this year. They have a fine block of land, well situated; and S——— laughs at the present privations, to which he opposes a spirit of cheerfulness and energy that is admirably calculated to effect their conquest. They are now about to remove to a larger and more commodious house that has been put up this fall, leaving us the use of the old one till our own is ready.

We begin to get reconciled to our Robinson Crusoe sort of life, and the consideration that the present evils are but temporary, goes a great way towards reconciling us to them.

One of our greatest inconveniences arises from the badness of our roads, and the distance at which we are placed from any village or town where provisions are to be procured.

Till we raise our own grain and fatten our own hogs, sheep, and poultry, we must be dependent upon the stores for food of every kind. These supplies have to be brought up at considerable expense and loss of time, through our beautiful bush roads; which, to use the words of a poor Irish woman, "can't be no worser." "Och, darlint," she said, "but they are just bad enough, and can't be no worser. Och, but they arn't like to our iligant roads in Ireland."

You may send down a list of groceries to be forwarded when a team comes up, and when we examine our stores, behold rice, sugar, currants, pepper, and mustard all jumbled into one mess. What think you of a rice-pudding seasoned plentifully with pepper, mustard, and, may be, a little rappee or prince's mixture added by way of sauce. I think the recipe would cut quite a figure in the Cook's Oracle or Mrs. Dalgairn's Practice of Cookery, under the original title of a "bush pudding."

And then woe and destruction to the brittle ware that may chance to travel through our roads. Lucky, indeed, are we if, through the superior carefulness of the person who packs them, more than one-half happens to arrive in safety. For such mishaps we have no redress. The storekeeper lays the accident upon the teamster, and the teamster upon the bad roads, wondering that he himself escapes with whole bones after a journey through the bush.

This is now the worst season of the year; – this, and just after the breaking up of the snow. Nothing hardly but an ox-cart can travel along the roads, and even that with difficulty, occupying two days to perform the journey; and the worst of the matter is, that there are times when the most necessary articles of provisions are not to be procured at any price. You see, then, that a settler in the bush requires to hold himself pretty independent, not only of the luxuries and delicacies of the table, but not unfrequently even of the very necessaries.

One time no pork is to be procured; another time there is a scarcity of flour, owing to some accident that has happened to the mill, or for the want of proper supplies of wheat for grinding; or perhaps the weather and bad roads at the same time prevent a team coming up, or people from going down. Then you must have recourse to a neighbour, if you have the good fortune to be near one, or fare the best you can on potatoes. The potato is indeed a great blessing here; new settlers would otherwise be often greatly distressed, and the poor man and his family who are without resources, without the potato must starve.

Once our stock of tea was exhausted, and we were unable to procure more. In this dilemma milk would have been an excellent substitute, or coffee, if we had possessed it; but we had neither the one nor the other, so we agreed to try the Yankee tea – hemlock sprigs boiled. This proved, to my taste, a vile decoction; though I recognized some herb in the tea that was sold in London at five shillings a pound, which I am certain was nothing better than dried hemlock leaves reduced to a coarse powder.

S——— laughed at our wry faces, declaring the potation was excellent; and he set us all an example by drinking six cups of this truly sylvan beverage. His eloquence failed in gaining a single convert; we could not believe it was only second to young hyson. To his assurance that to its other good qualities it united medicinal virtues, we replied that, like all other physic, it was very unpalatable.

"After all," said S———, with a thoughtful air, "the blessings and the evils of this life owe their chief effect to the force of contrast, and are to be estimated by that principally. We should not appreciate the comforts we enjoy half so much did we not occasionally feel the want of them. How we shall value the conveniences of a cleared farm after a few years, when we can realize all the necessaries and many of the luxuries of life."

"And how we shall enjoy green tea after this odious decoction of hemlock," said I.

"Very true; and a comfortable frame-house, and nice garden, and pleasant pastures, after these dark forests, log-houses, and no garden at all."

"And the absence of horrid black stumps," rejoined I. "Yes, and the absence of horrid stumps. Depend upon it, my dear, your Canadian farm will seem to you a perfect paradise by the time it is all under cultivation; and you will look upon it with the more pleasure and pride from the consciousness that it was once a forest wild, which, by the effects of industry and well-applied means, has changed to fruitful fields. Every fresh comfort you realize around you will add to your happiness; every improvement within-doors or without will raise a sensation of gratitude and delight in your mind, to which those that revel in the habitual enjoyment of luxury, and even of the commonest advantages of civilization, must in a great degree be strangers. My pass-words are, 'Hope! Resolution! and Perseverence!'"

"This," said my husband, "is true philosophy; and the more forcible, because you not only recommend the maxim but practise it also."

I had reckoned much on the Indian summer, of which I had read such delightful descriptions, but I must say it has fallen far below my expectations. Just at the commencement of this month (November) we experienced three or four warm hazy days, that proved rather close and oppressive. The sun looked red through the misty atmosphere, tinging the fantastic clouds that hung in smoky volumes, with saffron and pale crimson light, much as I have seen the clouds above London look on a warm, sultry spring morning.

Not a breeze ruffled the waters, not a leaf (for the leaves had not entirely fallen) moved. This perfect stagnation of the air was suddenly changed by a hurricane of wind and snow that came on without any previous warning. I was standing near a group of tall pines that had been left in the middle of the clearing, collecting some beautiful crimson lichens, S———— not being many paces distant, with his oxen drawing fire-wood. Suddenly we heard a distant hollow rushing sound that momentarily increased, the air around us being yet perfectly calm. I looked up, and beheld the clouds, hitherto so motionless, moving with amazing rapidity in several different directions. A dense gloom overspread the heavens. S————, who had been busily engaged with the cattle, had not noticed my being so near, and now called to me to use all the speed I could to gain the house, or an open part of the clearing, distant from the pine-trees. Instinctively I turned towards the house, while the thundering shock of trees falling in all directions at the edge of the forest, the rending of the branches from the pines I had just quitted, and the rush of the whirlwind sweeping down the lake, made me sensible of the danger with which I had been threatened.

The scattered boughs of the pines darkened the air as they whirled above me; then came the blinding snow-storm: but I could behold the progress of the tempest in safety, having gained the threshold of our house. The driver of the oxen had thrown himself on the ground, while the poor beasts held down their meek heads, patiently abiding "the pelting of the pitiless storm." S————, my husband, and the rest of the household, collected in a group, watched with anxiety the wild havoc of the warring elements. Not a leaf remained on the trees when the hurricane was over; they were bare and desolate. Thus ended the short reign of the Indian summer.

I think the notion entertained by some travellers, that the Indian summer is caused by the annual conflagration of forests by those Indians inhabiting the unexplored regions beyond the larger lakes is absurd. Imagine for an instant what immense tracts of woods must be yearly consumed to affect nearly the whole of the continent of North America: besides, it takes place at that season of the year when the fire is least likely to run freely, owing to the humidity of the ground from the autumnal rains. I should rather attribute the peculiar warmth and hazy appearance of the air that marks this season, to the fermentation going on of so great a mass of vegetable matter that is undergoing a state of decomposition during the latter part of October and beginning of November. It has been supposed by some persons that a great alteration will be effected in this season, as the process of clearing the land continues to decrease the quantity of decaying vegetation. Nay, I have heard the difference is already observable by those long acquainted with the American continent.

Hitherto my experience of the climate is favourable. The autumn has been very fine, though the frosts are felt early in the month of September; at first slightly, of a morning, but towards October more severely. Still, though the first part of the day is cold, the middle of it is warm and cheerful.

We already see the stern advances of winter. It commenced very decidedly from the breaking up of the Indian summer. November is not at all like the same month at home. The early part was soft and warm, the latter cold, with keen frosts and occasional falls of snow; but it does not seem to possess the dark, gloomy, damp character of our British Novembers. However, it is not one season's acquaintance with the climate that enables a person to form any correct judgment of its general character, but a close observance of its peculiarities and vicissitudes during many years' residence in the country.

I must now tell you what my husband is doing on our land. He has let out ten acres to some Irish choppers who have established themselves in the shanty for the winter. They are to receive fourteen dollars per acre for chopping, burning, and fencing in that quantity. The ground is to be perfectly cleared of every thing but the stumps: these will take from seven to nine or ten years to decay; the pine, hemlock, and fir remain much longer. The process of clearing away the stumps is too expensive for new beginners to venture upon, labour being so high that it cannot be appropriated to any but indispensable work. The working season is very short on account of the length of time the frost remains on the ground. With the exception of chopping trees, very little can be done. Those that understand the proper management of uncleared land, usually underbrush (that is, cut down all the small timbers and brushwood), while the leaf is yet on them; this is piled in heaps, and the windfallen trees are chopped through in lengths, to be logged up in the spring with the winter's chopping. The latter end of the summer and the autumn are the best seasons for this work. The leaves then become quite dry and sear, and greatly assist in the important business of burning off the heavy timbers. Another reason is, that when the snow has fallen to some depth, the light timbers cannot be cut close to the ground, or the dead branches and other incumbrances collected and thrown in heaps.

We shall have about three acres ready for spring-crops, provided we get a good burning of that which is already chopped near the site of the house, – this will be sown with oats, pumpkins, Indian corn, and potatoes: the other ten acres will be ready for putting in a crop of wheat. So you see it will be a long time before we reap a harvest. We could not even get in spring-wheat early enough to come to perfection this year.

We shall try to get two cows in the spring, as they are little expense during the spring, summer, and autumn; and by the winter we shall have pumpkins and oat-straw for them.

(1836)   (1836)

Susanna Moodie
1803-1885

A SISTER OF Catharine Parr Traill, Susanna (Strickland) Moodie was born in Suffolk, England. In 1832, a year after her marriage to J. W. Dunbar Moodie, a half-pay officer in the British army, she emigrated with him to a farm near Cobourg in Upper Canada. Two years later, they moved to the backwoods near Peterborough where they struggled to establish a farm until 1839 when they moved to Belleville. Mrs. Moodie contributed poems, stories, serial novels and sketches to several Canadian periodicals; however, her best known works are *Roughing It in the Bush* (1852), an account of the Moodies' struggles on the Upper Canadian frontier, and *Life in the Clearings* (1853), a description of their experiences following the move to Belleville.

From
Roughing It in the Bush

Introduction

IN MOST INSTANCES, emigration is a matter of necessity, not of choice; and this is more especially true of the emigration of persons of respectable connections, or of any station or position in the world. Few educated persons, accustomed to the refinements and luxuries of European society, ever willingly relinquish those advantages, and place themselves beyond the protective influence of the wise and revered institutions of their native land, without the pressure of some urgent cause. Emigration may, indeed, generally be regarded as an act of severe duty, performed at the expense of personal enjoyment, and accompanied by the sacrifice of those local attachments which stamp the scenes amid which our childhood grew, in imperishable characters upon the heart. Nor is it until adversity has pressed sorely upon the proud and wounded spirit of the well-educated sons and daughters of old but impoverished families, that they gird up the loins of the mind, and arm themselves with fortitude to meet and dare the heart-breaking conflict.

The ordinary motives for the emigration of such persons may be summed up in a few brief words; – the emigrant's hope of bettering his condition, and of escaping from the vulgar sarcasms too often hurled at the less wealthy by the purse-proud, commonplace people of the world. But there is a higher motive still, which has its origin in that love of independence which springs up spontaneously in the breasts of the high-souled children of a glorious land. They cannot labour in a menial capacity in the country where they were born and educated to command. They can trace no difference between themselves and the more fortunate individuals of a race whose blood warms their veins, and whose name they bear. The want of wealth alone places an impassable barrier between them and the more favoured offspring of the same parent stock; and they go forth to make for themselves a new name and to find another country, to forget the past and to live in the future, to exult in the prospect of their children being free and the land of their adoption great.

The choice of the country to which they devote their talents and energies depends less upon their pecuniary means than upon the fancy of the emigrant or the popularity of a name. From the year 1826 to 1829, Australia and the Swan River were all the rage. No other portions of the habitable globe were deemed worthy of notice. These were the *El Dorados* and lands of Goshen to which all respectable emigrants eagerly flocked. Disappointment, as a matter of course, followed their high-raised expectations. Many of the most sanguine of these adventurers returned to their native shores in a worse condition than when they left them. In 1830, the great tide of emigration flowed westward. Canada became the great land-mark for the rich in hope and poor in purse. Public newspapers and private letters teemed with the unheard-of advantages to be derived from a settlement in this highly-favoured region.

Its salubrious climate, its fertile soil, commerical advantages, great water privileges, its proximity to the mother country, and last, not least, its almost total exemption from taxation – that bugbear which keeps honest John Bull in a state of constant ferment – were the theme of every tongue, and lauded beyond all praise. The general interest, once excited, was industriously kept alive by pamphlets, published by interested parties, which prominently set forth all the *good* to be derived from a settlement in the Backwoods of Canada; while they carefully concealed the toil and hardship to be endured in order to secure these advantages. They told of lands yielding forty bushels to the acre, but they said nothing of the years when these lands, with the most careful cultivation, would barely return fifteen; when rust and smut, engendered by the vicinity of damp over-hanging woods, would blast the fruits of the poor emigrant's labour, and almost deprive him of bread. They talked of log houses to be raised in a single day, by the generous exertions of friends and neighbours, but they never ventured upon a picture of the disgusting scenes of riot and low debauchery exhibited during the raising, or upon a description of the dwellings when raised – dens of dirt and misery, which would, in many instances, be shamed by an English pig-sty. The necessaries of life were described as inestimably cheap; but they forgot to add that in remote bush settlements, often twenty miles from a market town, and some of them even that distance from the nearest dwelling, the necessaries of life, which would be deemed indispensable to the European, could not be procured at all, or, if obtained, could only be so by sending a man and team through a blazed forest road, – a process far too expensive for frequent repetition.

Oh, ye dealers in wild lands – ye speculators in the folly and credulity of your fellow men – what a mass of misery, and of misrepresentation productive of that misery, have ye not to answer for! You had your acres to sell, and what to you were the worn-down frames and broken hearts of the infatuated purchasers? The public believed the plausible statements you made with such earnestness, and men of all grades rushed to hear your hired orators declaim upon the blessings to be obtained by the clearers of the wilderness.

Men who had been hopeless of supporting their families in comfort and independence at home thought that they had only to come out to Canada to make their fortunes; almost even to realise the story told in the nursery, of the sheep and oxen that ran about the streets, ready roasted, and with knives and forks upon their backs. They were made to believe that if it did not actually rain gold, that precious metal could be obtained, as is now stated of California and Australia, by stooping to pick it up.

The infection became general. A Canada mania pervaded the middle ranks of British society; thousands and tens of thousands, for the space of three or four years landed upon these shores. A large majority of the higher class were officers of the army and navy, with their families – a class perfectly unfitted by their previous habits and education for contending with the stern realities of emigrant life. The hand that has long held the sword, and been accustomed to receive implicit obedience from those under its control, is seldom adapted to wield the spade and guide the plough, or try its strength against the stubborn trees of the forest. Nor will such persons submit cheerfully to the saucy familiarity of servants, who, republicans in spirit, think themselves as good as their employers. Too many of these brave and honourable men were easy dupes to the designing land-speculators. Not having counted the cost, but only looked upon the bright side of the picture held up to their admiring gaze, they fell easily into the snares of their artful seducers.

To prove their zeal as colonists, they were induced to purchase large tracts of wild land in remote and unfavourable situations. This, while it impoverished and often proved the ruin of the unfortunate immigrant, possessed a double advantage to the seller. He obtained an exorbitant price for the land which he actually sold, while the residence of a respectable settler upon the spot greatly enhanced the value and price of all other lands in the neighbourhood.

It is not by such instruments as those I have just mentioned, that Providence works when it would reclaim the waste places of the earth, and make them subservient to the wants and happiness of its creatures. The Great Father of the souls and bodies of men knows the arm which wholesome labour from infancy has made strong, the nerves which have become iron by patient endurance, by exposure to weather, coarse fare, and rude shelter; and he chooses such, to send forth into the forest to hew out the rough paths for the advance of civilisation. These men become wealthy and prosperous, and form the bones and sinews of a great and rising country. Their labour is wealth, not exhaustion; its produce independence and content, not home-sickness and despair. What the Backwoods of Canada are to the industrious and ever-to-be-honoured sons of honest poverty, and what they are to the refined and accomplished gentleman, these simple sketches will endeavour to portray. They are drawn principally from my own experience, during a sojourn of nineteen years in the colony.

In order to diversify my subject, and make it as amusing as possible, I have between the sketches introduced a few small poems, all written during my residence in Canada, and descriptive of the country.

In this pleasing task I have been assisted by my husband, J. W. Dunbar Moodie, author of "Ten Years in South Africa."

A Visit to Grosse Isle

Alas! that man's stern spirit e'er should mar
A scene so pure – so exquisite as this.

THE DREADFUL CHOLERA was depopulating Quebec and Montreal, when our ship cast anchor off Grosse Isle, on the 30th of August, 1832, and we were boarded a few minutes after by the health-officers. One of these gentlemen – a little, shrivelled-up Frenchman – from his solemn aspect and attenuated figure, would have made no bad representative of him who sat upon the pale horse. He was the only grave Frenchman I had ever seen, and I naturally enough regarded him as a phenomenon. His companion – a fine-looking fair-haired Scotchman – though a little consequential in his manners, looked like one who in his own person could combat and vanquish all the evils which flesh is heir to. Such was the contrast between these doctors, that they would have formed very good emblems – one, of vigorous health; the other, of hopeless decay.

Our captain, a rude, blunt north-country sailor, possessing certainly not more politeness than might be expected in a bear, received his sprucely dressed visitors on the deck, and, with very little courtesy, abruptly bade them follow him down into the cabin.

The officials were no sooner seated, than glancing hastily round the place, they commenced the following dialogue: –

"From what port, captain?"

Now, the captain had a peculiar language of his own, from which he commonly expunged all the connecting links. Small words, such as "and" and "the," he contrived to dispense with altogether.

"Scotland – sailed from port o'Leith, bound for Quebec, Montreal – general cargo – seventy-two steerage, four cabin passengers – brig, ninety-two tons burden, crew eight hands." Here he produced his credentials, and handed them to the strangers. The Scotchman just glanced over the documents, and laid them on the table.

"Had you a good passage out?"

"Tedious, baffling winds, heavy fogs, detained three weeks on Banks – foul weather making Gulf – short of water, people out of provisions, steerage passengers starving."

"Any case of sickness or death on board?"

"All sound as crickets."

"Any births?" lisped the little Frenchman.

The captain screwed up his mouth, and after a moment's reflection he replied, "Births? Why, yes; now I think on't, gentlemen, we had one female on board, who produced three at a birth."

"That's uncommon," said the Scotch doctor, with an air of lively curiosity. "Are the children alive and well? I should like much to see them." He started up, and knocked his head, for he was very tall, against the ceiling. "Confound your low cribs! I have nearly dashed out my brains."

"A hard task, that," looked the captain to me. He did not speak, but I knew by his sarcastic grin what was uppermost in his thoughts. "The young ones are all males – fine thriving fellows. Step upon deck, Sam Frazer," turning to his steward; "bring them down for doctors to see." Sam vanished, with a knowing wink to his superior, and quickly returned, bearing in his arms three fat, chuckle-headed bull-terriers; the sagacious mother following close at his heels, and looked ready to give and take offence on the slightest provocation.

"Here, gentlemen, are the babies," said Frazer, depositing his burden on the floor. "They do credit to the nursing of the brindled slut."

The old tar laughed, chuckled and rubbed his hands in an ecstasy of delight at the indignation and disappointment visible in the countenance of the Scotch Esculapius, who, angry as he was, wisely held his tongue. Not so the Frenchman; his rage scarcely knew bounds, – he danced in a state of most ludicrous excitement, – he shook his fist at our rough captain, and screamed at the top of his voice,

"Sacré, you bête! You tink us dog, ven you try to pass your puppies on us for babies?"

"Hout, man, don't be angry," said the Scotchman, stifling a laugh; "you see 'tis only a joke!"

"Joke! me no understand such joke. Bête!" returned the angry Frenchman, bestowing a savage kick on one of the unoffending pups which was frisking about his feet. The pup yelped; the slut barked and leaped furiously at the offender, and was only kept from biting him by Sam, who could scarcely hold her back for laughing; the captain was uproarious; the offended Frenchman alone maintained a severe and dignified aspect. The dogs were at length dismissed, and peace restored.

After some further questioning from the officials, a bible was required for the captain to take an oath. Mine was mislaid, and there was none at hand.

"Confound it!" muttered the old sailor, tossing over the papers in his desk; "that scoundrel, Sam, always stows my traps out of the way." Then taking up from the table a book which I had been reading, which happened to be *Voltaire's History of Charles XII.*, he presented it, with as grave an air as he could assume, to the Frenchman. Taking for granted that it was the volume required, the little doctor was too polite to open the book, the captain was duly sworn, and the party returned to the deck.

Here a new difficulty occurred, which nearly ended in a serious quarrel. The gentlemen requested the old sailor to give them a few feet of old planking, to repair some damage which their boat had sustained the day before. This the captain could not do. They seemed to think his refusal intentional, and took it as a personal affront. In no very gentle tones, they ordered him instantly to prepare his boats, and put his passengers on shore.

"Stiff breeze – short sea," returned the bluff old seaman; "great risk in making land – boats heavily laden with women and children will be swamped. Not a soul goes on shore this night."

"If you refuse to comply with our orders, we will report you to the authorities."

"I know my duty – you stick to yours. When the wind falls off, I'll see to it. Not a life shall be risked to please you or your authorities."

He turned upon his heel, and the medical men left the vessel in great disdain. We had every reason to be thankful for the firmness displayed by our rough commander. That same evening we saw eleven persons drowned, from another vessel close beside us, while attempting to make the shore.

By daybreak all was hurry and confusion on board the *Anne.* I watched boat after boat depart for the island, full of people and goods, and envied them the glorious privilege of once more standing firmly on the earth, after two long months of rocking and rolling at sea. How ardently we anticipate pleasure, which often ends in positive pain! Such was my case when at last indulged in the gratification so eagerly desired. As cabin passengers, we were not included in the general order of purification, but were only obliged to send our servant, with the clothes and bedding we had used during the voyage, on shore, to be washed.

The ship was soon emptied of all her live cargo. My husband went off with the boats, to reconnoitre the island, and I was left alone with my baby, in the otherwise empty vessel. Even Oscar, the Captain's Scotch terrier, who had formed a devoted attachment to me during the voyage, forgot his allegiance, became possessed of the land mania, and was away with the rest. With the most intense desire to go on shore, I was doomed to look and long and envy every boatful of emigrants that glided past. Nor was this all; the ship was out of provisions, and I was condemned to undergo a rigid fast until the return of the boat, when the captain had promised a supply of fresh butter and bread. The vessel had been nine weeks at sea; the poor steerage passengers for the two last weeks had been out of food, and the captain had been obliged to feed them from the ship's stores. The promised bread was to be obtained from a small steam-boat, which plied daily between Quebec and the island, transporting convalescent emigrants and their goods in her upward trip, and provisions for the sick on her return.

How I reckoned on once more tasting bread and butter! The very thought of the treat in store served to sharpen my appetite, and render the long fast more irksome. I could now fully realise all Mrs. Bowdich's longings for English bread and butter, after her three years' travel through the burning African deserts, with her talented husband.

"When we arrived at the hotel at Plymouth," said she, "and were asked what refreshment we chose – 'Tea, and home-made bread and butter,' was my instant reply. 'Brown bread, if you please, and plenty of it.' I never enjoyed any luxury like it. I was positively ashamed of asking the waiter to refill the plate. After the execrable messes, and the hard ship-biscuit, imagine the luxury of a good slice of English bread and butter!"

At home, I laughed heartily at the lively energy with which that charming woman of genius related this little incident in her eventful history, – but off Grosse Isle, I realised it all.

As the sun rose above the horizon, all these matter-of-fact circumstances were gradually forgotten, and merged in the surpassing grandeur of the scene that rose majestically before me. The previous day had been dark and stormy; and a heavy fog had concealed the mountain chain, which forms the stupendous background to this sublime view, entirely from our sight. As the clouds rolled away from their grey, bald brows, and cast into denser shadow the vast forest belt that girdled them round, they loomed out like mighty giants – Titans of the earth, in all their rugged and awful beauty – a thrill of wonder and delight pervaded my mind. The spectacle floated dimly on my sight – my eyes were blinded with tears – blinded with the excess of beauty. I turned to the right and to the left, I looked up and down the glorious river; never had I beheld so many striking objects blended into one mighty whole! Nature had lavished all her noblest features in producing that enchanting scene.

The rocky isle in front, with its neat farm-houses at the eastern point, and its high bluff at the western extremity, crowned with the telegraph – the middle space occupied by tents and sheds for the cholera patients, and its wooded shores dotted over with motley groups – added greatly to the picturesque effect of the land scene. Then the broad, glittering river, covered with boats darting to and fro, conveying passengers from twenty-five vessels, of various size and tonnage, which rode at anchor, with their flags flying from the mast-head, gave an air of life and interest to the whole. Turning to the south side of the St. Lawrence, I was not less struck with its low fertile shores, white houses, and neat churches, whose slender spires and bright tin roofs shone like silver as they caught the first rays of the sun. As far as the eye could reach, a line of white buildings extended along the bank; their background formed by the purple hue of the dense, interminable forest. It was a scene unlike any I had ever beheld, and to which Britain contains no parallel. Mackenzie, an old Scotch dragoon, who was one of our passengers, when he rose in the morning, and saw the parish of St. Thomas for the first time, exclaimed – "Weel, it beats a'! Can thae white clouts be a' houses? They look like claes hung out to drie!" There was some truth in this odd comparison, and for some minutes, I could scarcely convince myself that the white patches scattered so thickly over the opposite shore could be the dwellings of a busy, lively population.

"What sublime views of the north side of the river those *habitans* of St. Thomas must enjoy," thought I. Perhaps familiarity with the scene has rendered them indifferent to its astonishing beauty.

Eastward, the view down the St. Lawrence towards the Gulf, is the finest of all, scarcely surpassed by anything in the world. Your eye follows the long range of lofty mountains until their blue summits are blended and lost in the blue of the sky. Some of these, partially cleared round the base, are sprinkled over with neat cottages; and the green slopes that spread around them are covered with flocks and herds. The surface of the splendid river is diversified with islands of every size and shape, some in wood, others partially cleared, and adorned with orchards and white farm-houses. As the early sun streamed upon the most prominent of these, leaving the others in deep shade, the effect was strangely novel and imposing. In more remote regions, where the forest has never yet echoed to the woodman's axe, or received the impress of civilisation, the first approach to the shore inspires a melancholy awe, which becomes painful in its intensity.

> Land of vast hills and mighty streams,
> The lofty sun that o'er thee beams
> On fairer clime sheds not his ray,
> When basking in the noon of day
> Thy waters dance in silver light,
> And o'er them frowning, dark as night,
> Thy shadowy forests, soaring high,
> Stretch forth beyond the aching eye,
> And blend in distance with the sky.
>
> And silence –awful silence broods
> Profoundly o'er these solitudes;
> Nought but the lapsing of the floods
> Breaks the deep stillness of the woods;
> A sense of desolation reigns
> O'er these unpeopled forest plains.
> Where sounds of life ne'er wake a tone
> Of cheerful praise round Nature's throne,
> Man finds himself with God – alone.

My day-dreams were dispelled by the return of the boat, which brought my husband and the captain from the island.

"No bread," said the latter, shaking his head; "you must be content to starve a little longer. Provision-ship not in till four o'clock." My husband smiled at the look of blank disappointment with which I received these unwelcome tidings. "Never mind, I have news which will comfort you. The officer who commands the station sent a note to me by an orderly, inviting us to spend the afternoon with him. He promises to show us everything worthy of notice on the island. Captain———— claims acquaintance with me; but I have not the least recollection of him. Would you like to go?"

"Oh, by all means. I long to see the lovely island. It looks a perfect paradise at this distance."

The rough sailor-captain screwed his mouth on one side, and gave me one of his comical looks, but he said nothing until he assisted in placing me and the baby in the boat.

"Don't be too sanguine, Mrs. Moodie; many things look well at a distance which are bad enough when near."

I scarcely regarded the old sailor's warning, so eager was I to go on shore –to put my foot upon the soil of the new world for the first time. I was in no humour to listen to any depreciation of what seemed so beautiful.

It was four o'clock when we landed on the rocks, which the rays of an intensely scorching sun had rendered so hot that I could scarcely place my foot upon them. How the people without shoes bore it, I cannot imagine. Never shall I forget the extraordinary spectacle that met our sight the moment we passed the low range of bushes which formed a screen in front of the river. A crowd of many hundred Irish emigrants had been landed during the present and former day; and all this motley crew – men, women, and children, who were not confined by sickness to the sheds (which greatly resembled cattle-pens) – were employed in washing clothes, or spreading them out on the rocks and bushes to dry.

The men and boys were *in* the water, while the women, with their scanty garments tucked above their knees, were trampling their bedding in tubs, or in holes in the rocks, which the retiring tide had left half full of water. Those who did not possess washing-tubs, pails, or iron pots, or could not obtain access to a hole in the rocks, were running to and fro, screaming and scolding in no measured terms. The confusion of Babel was among them. All talkers and no hearers – each shouting and yelling in his or her uncouth dialect, and all accompanying their vociferations with violent and extraordinary gestures, quite incomprehensible to the uninitiated. We were literally stunned by the strife of tongues. I shrank, with feelings almost akin to fear, from the hard-featured, sun-burnt harpies, as they elbowed rudely past me.

I had heard and read much of savages, and have since seen, during my long residence in the bush, somewhat of uncivilised life; but the Indian is one of Nature's gentlemen – he never says or does a rude or vulgar thing. The vicious, uneducated barbarians who form the surplus of over-populous European countries, are far behind the wild man in delicacy of feeling or natural courtesy. The people who covered the island appeared perfectly destitute of shame, or even of a sense of common decency. Many were almost naked, still more but partially clothed. We turned in disgust from the revolting scene, but were unable to leave the spot until the captain had satisfied a noisy group of his own people, who were demanding a supply of stores.

And here I must observe that our passengers, who were chiefly honest Scotch labourers and mechanics from the vicinity of Edinburgh, and who while on board ship had conducted themselves with the greatest propriety, and appeared the most quiet, orderly set of people in the world, no sooner set foot upon the island than they became infected by the same spirit of insubordination and misrule, and were just as insolent and noisy as the rest.

While our captain was vainly endeavouring to satisfy the unreasonable demands of his rebellious people, Moodie had discovered a woodland path that led to the back of the island. Sheltered by some hazel-bushes from the intense heat of the sun, we sat down by the cool, gushing river, out of sight, but, alas! not out of hearing of the noisy, riotous crowd. Could we have shut out the profane sounds which came to us on every breeze, how deeply should we have enjoyed an hour amid the tranquil beauties of that retired and lovely spot!

The rocky banks of the island were adorned with beautiful evergreens, which sprang up spontaneously in every nook and crevice. I remarked many of our favourite garden shrubs among these wildings of nature. The fillagree, with its narrow, dark glossy-green leaves; the privet, with its modest white blossoms and purple berries; the lignum-vitæ, with its strong resinous odour, the burnet-rose, and a great variety of elegant unknowns.

Here, the shores of the island and mainland, receding from each other, formed a small cove, overhung with lofty trees, clothed from the base to the summit with wild vines, that hung in graceful festoons from the topmost branches to the water's edge. The dark shadows of the mountains, thrown upon the water, as they towered to the height of some thousand feet above us, gave to the surface of the river an ebon hue. The sunbeams, dancing through the thick, quivering foliage, fell in stars of gold, or long lines of dazzling brightness, upon the deep black waters, producing the most novel and beautiful effects. It was a scene over which the spirit of peace might brood in silent adoration; but how spoiled by the discordant yells of the filthy beings who were sullying the purity of the air and water with contaminating sights and sounds!

We were now joined by the sergeant, who very kindly brought us his capful of ripe plums and hazel-nuts, the growth of the island; a joyful present, but marred by a note from Captain————, who had found that he had been mistaken in his supposed knowledge of us, and politely aplogised for not being allowed by the health-officers to receive any emigrant beyond the bounds appointed for the performance of quarantine.

I was deeply disappointed, but my husband laughingly told me that I had seen enough of the island; and turning to the good-natured soldier, remarked, that "it could be no easy task to keep such wild savages in order."

"You may well say that, sir – but our night scenes far exceed those of the day. You would think they were incarnate devils; singing, drinking, dancing, shouting, and cutting antics that would surprise the leader of a circus. They have no shame –are under no restraint –nobody knows them here, and they think they can speak and act as they please; and they are such thieves that they rob one another of the little they possess. The healthy actually run the risk of taking the cholera by robbing the sick. If you have not hired one or two stout, honest fellows from among your fellow-passengers to guard your clothes while they are drying, you will never see half of them again. They are a sad set, sir, a sad set. We could, perhaps, manage the men; but the women, sir! –the women! Oh, sir!"

Anxious as we were to return to the ship, we were obliged to remain until sun-down in our retired nook. We were hungry, tired, and out of spirits; the mosquitoes swarmed in myriads around us, tormenting the poor baby, who, not at all pleased with her first visit to the new world, filled the air with cries. When the captain came to tell us that the boat was ready, it was a welcome sound. Forcing our way once more through the still squabbling crowd, we gained the landing place. Here we encountered a boat, just landing a fresh cargo of lively savages from the Emerald Isle. One fellow, of gigantic proportions, whose long, tattered great-coat just reached below the middle of his bare red legs, and like charity, hid the defects of his other garments, or perhaps concealed his want of them, leaped upon the rocks, and flourishing aloft his shilelagh, bounded and capered like a wild goat from his native mountains. "Whurrah! my boys!" he cried, "Shure we'll all be jontlemen!"

"Pull away, my lads!" exclaimed our captain, and in a few moments we were again on board. Thus ended my first day's experience of the land of all our hopes.

Oh! Can You Leave Your Native Land?

A CANADIAN SONG

Oh! can you leave your native land
  An exile's bride to be;
Your mother's home, and cheerful hearth,
  To tempt the main with me;

Across the wide and storm sea
  To trace our foaming track,
And know the wave that bears us on
  Will ne'er convey us back?

And can you in Canadian woods
  With me the harvest bind,
Nor feel one lingering, sad regret
  For all you leave behind?
Can those dear hands, unused to toil,
  The woodman's wants supply,
Nor shrink beneath the chilly blast
  When wintry storms are nigh?

Amid the shades of forests dark,
  Our loved isle will appear
An Eden, whose delicious bloom
  Will make the wild more drear.
And you in solitude will weep
  O'er scenes beloved in vain,
And pine away your life to view
  Once more your native plain.

Then pause, dear girl! ere those fond lips
  Your wanderer's fate decide;
My spirit spurns the selfish wish –
  You must not be my bride.
But oh, that smile –those tearful eyes,
  My firmer purpose move –
Our hearts are one, and we will dare
  All perils thus to love!

(1852)   (1852)

Joseph Howe
1804-1873

———◆———

THE SON OF a Loyalist journalist, Joseph Howe was born in Halifax and pursued careers as a newspaper editor and a politician. He purchased the Halifax *Novascotian* in 1827 and under his editorship this newspaper became not only an important vehicle in the fight for responsible government but also an important literary journal which published writers such as Thomas Haliburton. Howe himself contributed two series of sketches, "Western Rambles" (1828) and "Eastern Rambles" (1829-31), dealing with the landscape and people of Nova Scotia. These sketches were collected in *Western and Eastern Rambles,* edited by M. G. Parks in 1973. A collection of Howe's poems and essays was published posthumously in 1874.

From
Western Rambles

[Cornwallis Township]

28 August 1828

THE FIRST REFLECTION we make, after a full survey of Cornwallis, is, that the great mass of its population may live, and live well, by working three days a week. Some, of course, work more, but others do not even give this portion of their time to assiduous and persevering exertion. In all countries and all ages it has ever been recorded, that man has a natural antipathy to labor; it seems as if the few days of idleness which our first Parents spent in the Garden of Eden had so bewitched them – had hung round their memories so long, that at length their children, who heard of Paradise but never saw it, finding it difficult to fix any more definite idea in their minds, imagined that it was a place where plenty of comforts and luxuries were provided, and where *there was nothing to do.* Hence, I believe, has arisen the disinclination of the bipeds to constant and unremitting industry. They have resolved the whole thing into a very consoling syllogism –'Adam', say they, 'did not work in

Eden – Adam was very happy while he staid there – ergo, if we do not work we shall be very happy too.' This kind of reasoning has at all times been more or less pernicious. When driven by stern necessity, Adam toiled; his children follow his footsteps, and taking them en masse, necessity is a task-master that gets more labor done than either Ambition or Industry. When overloaded by taxes, with a heavy rent to pay and few comforts to hope, the farmer works like a beaver – the early cock is disturbed by his footstep – night closes on him while his hand is still upon the plough, and his mind, quickened to a shrewd and constant activity, is employed during the evening in reflecting or resolving on something which can put one potatoe more into each hill, or hang an additional grain on every spire of wheat. Habit at length renders that a pleasure, which was at first a burthen; he soon finds that it is no great hardship to labour, and that thought, which at first seemed irksome, brings its own pleasures with it, and eke its profits too. But take the same man – give him 100 acres of soil which requires little or no manure, and for which he shall pay no rent – take from him no taxes, and give him a fair market for his produce, and I am not prepared to swear, but think I may venture to affirm, on a review of more than fifty cases in the Township of Cornwallis, that in a few years he will be just where he started; with this difference, that his house and barn will be getting older, while the stock of neither (children always excepted) will be much improved, nor the general appearance and intrinsic value of his farm heightened but in a very trifling degree. But happy is he if things are no worse than this; but there is too much reason to fear that his farm will be mortgaged to some griping old curmudgeon, who, if he does not foreclose, and arrest the indolent possessor, will sit on his future prospects with the specific gravity and cool taciturnity of an incubus. All this 'seems strange – seems passing strange', and when assured of its truth, how sinks our estimate of the order to which we belong. The brutes labour while the rein is in their mouths, and the whip on their withers – and let but necessity slacken the ribbons, and lay aside the scourge of poverty and want, and what becomes of man's superiority over the beast he drives?

But to leave general reasoning, and come to the practice rather than the theory of idleness, perhaps in no part of the province are its effects more injurious than in that Township which has been justly styled the garden of Nova Scotia. – More Mortgages are held on property in King's and Annapolis, than in any other counties of the Province, and the theory aforesaid is the only explanation I can give. The soil of both is highly fertile and productive – yielding, with less than ordinary labor, almost all of the necessaries of life in abundance; surrounded by water in every direction, export and import of bulky articles are easily made; and with regular habits of industry, frugal living, and common foresight, every farmer within their limits ought at least to be independent, and most of them comparatively rich. If this may be affirmed of the two Counties generally, it is applicable in a more especial manner to Cornwallis, where thousands of acres require no other labour than a little dyking, and the gathering of their bountiful and spontaneous crops; and where, with but few exceptions, every *necessary* article of use may be brought within the means, and created by the industry of a frugal family. But, unfortunately, the soil is too productive, and many, from finding that a living may be made with so little labour, think of course it can be made with less. And instead of running a race with fortune, trying by every effort of body and mind to tread upon its heels –what do they do? Run it with poverty, and so long as they can keep one length ahead, never think how close Sparebones is upon their rear. Nor is indolence the only evil –a cursed fondness for dress, and tea parties, and gossipings, which not only lead to the squandering of money, but to the squandering of time, which is the parent of wealth, all serve to make Mortgages grey headed, and if they do not saddle a farm with new incumbrances, are sure to perpetuate the old ones.

Musing on these things, as I gazed from an eminence down on this beautiful Township –the calm serenity of the view –

> The silent breathing of the flowers,
> The melting light that beamed above,

and the whispery waving of an oak that rose over my head, hushed me into a gentle slumber. God forbid that the noonday sun should ever again find my eyelids closed; and, were it not for the vision that blessed my sleep, and which I would fain describe, I should be ashamed to tell of my drowsiness. Methought that the Genius of Nova Scotia rose before my sight, as did the image of Coila to the inspired Burns. She was tall as the Pine, of a firm but not ungraceful frame; and though her features, on a first view, seemed rude and forbidding, yet when you gazed more intently upon them, new beauties struck the eye at every glance; her countenance was frank and open, and though its expression was various, there was a redeeming quality, even in the least benign. At one season she frowned, and a chill came over the plains, and the pleasant rivers were congealed, and rude blasts tore their verdure from the trees, and withered each blossom and flower; but the frost quickened the spirit and braced the nerves, and the germs of future plenty were scattered far and wide, beneath the white shroud in which the glories of spring and summer lay entombed. Then again she burst into tears, and her sighs stole on the ear with a sad sound, like the March wind – but anon, beautiful flowers sprung up where her tears fell, and the Forest was clothed with blossom and leaf, and a sweet smile mantled over her face, shedding life, and animation, and glory on every inanimate and every living thing. Her head was crowned with a sheaf of wheat – mingled with Barley, Oats and Rye, and round her neck was thrown a string of berries and Fruits; while a broad zone, in which many of the vegetable tribe were mingled, circled her waist, and sustained the dignity of her demeanour. Her right hand rested on the Plough, to which she seemed to look for a steady support – and in her left she held an Oar, which at times she waved around the coast, and the deep sent forth its treasures, and the white wings of commerce expanded to the gale. And as she gazed around upon her offspring, she seemed to address them in the following words, to which her every feature lent force and expression. Children, I have spread before you all that your necessities require – Timber waves upon my hills – and fertility enriches my vallies, my coasts and rivers are swarming with fish, and minerals abound within my bosom, and all that I ask of you is active and persevering toil, industrious and frugal habits, untiring and diligent enquiry, and in return, you shall be rich, intelligent and happy.

I awoke, and the vision was gone – but there is many a drone in the Province, that I wish it would sometimes appear to, and rouse him from his lethargic slumber – and fright from his back and his board the miserable trappings which his pride substitutes for the lasting and substantial elements of independence. Idleness cannot be charged on our whole population – this would be unjust, but certain it is that in our western counties, it is by far too general. Men own farms – or at all events hold them, and expend a certain portion of labour on their cultivation, and gather a corresponding portion of increase – but few labour as assiduously as they could, or derive from their land as much as it might be made to yield. And then, with some few exceptions, almost all expend more for importations, either for personal and household decoration, or to administer to the profusion of their tables, than is consistent with the dignity and character of the Farmer. I say dignity – for of all employments on the face of the earth, there is none which lifts a man above the industrious and independent cultivator of the soil. There he is at his plough tail – turning up the earth which his own exertions have redeemed from the wilderness – his well-fed cattle repaying his care by steady and quiet toil, and the free air of Heaven fanning his cheek and the sun, smiling on his path. Only look at the brawny vigor of his limbs – the fearlessness of his stride, the elevated expansion of his brow –the whole man seems sentient with the feeling which Smollett so well expressed:

> Thy spirit, independence, let me share
> Lord of the lion heart and eagle eye.

Let me see the Sheriff, or Sheriff's Deputy – or money lender, or lawyer's clerk, that would venture into that field, to profane the earth by his footstep. By the fist of a farmer, there is no merit in whip cord, if he would not fly away from that fellow faster than he ever flew after one –why the very flash of the Ploughman's eye would wither him, as did the glance of Marius the murderous gladiator. With whom would he change situations? Can he envy the pale cheeks of Tinkers, Tailors, Lawyers, Parsons, Cordwainers and Editors – God forbid that he should – would he change the free air for some close cell, where sedentary labor might perhaps make him richer but could never make him so happy or healthy as he is now? which would cramp his free spirit, and change his firm stride into the mincing hobble of a rickety woman? No! he would not descend to be either.

But see where the sun sinks in the west –and the Ploughman unyokes his cattle, and returns to his home; and just for the sake of variety let us go with him, and partake of his evening meal. It is as it should be – simple but substantial, the produce of his own farm. Not one article of his food has helped to swell the Balance of Trade against the Province, or has paid a farthing of duty into the Provincial Chest. There, take a bowl, man, and help yourself to milk, warm and rich from the cow; none of your slops of Bohea and Hyson, –or if you must have tea, go and gather some leaves from the hill side and the good woman will make some for you; but as to bringing a weed from China to fatten a Ploughman in Nova Scotia, there never was a more confounded humbug. The Bread, Sir, was grown in that field, and ground in that mill, and though perhaps not so white as Howard Street, it is a great deal sweeter; and it is not saddled with half a dozen profits to Brother Jonathan for sowing, grinding, shipping, &c., nor has it paid a crown of British silver into the Custom House –so fall to, man, and do it justice, for when did such butter and cheese tickle your palate before, or a finer plate of raspberries gladden your epicurean spirit?

Only look at the fat and happy faces around you; Plenty has set its broad arrow on every member of the family; and why? Because Industry and Frugality preside over all –Because they scorn to be indebted to other lands for food and clothes that can be created at home. Think you the moulding of that Stripling's neck is not as well displayed in flax of his own growing, as though his shirt collar was bleached in the Emerald Isle? Has not his breast as fair an expansion beneath that homespun jacket, as though it was cased in broad cloth? and take him altogether, with his keen eye and florid cheek, if you were a girl of 18, and wanted a fellow to cheer you by night and to toil for and guard you by day, would you not rather give your heart to his keeping than to any dandified imitator of city fashion and extravagance, who would range a black coat of the first cut along side of his home manufacture? If you would not, may you never have a sound nap on an honest bosom, nor march forth of a Sabbath, followed by your eighteen children.

The poisoned shirt of Dejanira was not more pernicious to Hercules, than are the frippery trappings of affected gentility to our Agricultural population; who, with a virtuous reliance on their own character and importance, should be too proud to wear them. Would they not laugh to see the Eagle, casting off the plumage on which he had cloven the air and gazed on the sun, to array himself in the gaudy feathers of the Peacock, when such a change would sink the brave Bird to earth, never again to rise? And how can they covet what lowers them from the elevation of independent yeomen to the galling servitude of country Traders, and the long train of legal cormorants, who live by the extravagance of the Farmer? But in this cottage there is none of it; the thrifty wife by whom we sit would not change the sweet scene before her – the sight of her own healthy and happy household collected round her evening meal, for the ominous gatherings of village gossips, with their ribbons, and caps, and tawdry ornaments; who ride five miles to waste five hours, and exhibit finery worth as many pounds, and for which their husband's names are standing on the wrong side of some merchant's Ledger, who understands the whole mystery of cent per cent. What is it to her if Mrs. Turnip's cow has calved, or Mrs. Withrod has had twins, or Miss Broomstick has spoiled her new Bombazine with currant stains, and all the other items of important intelligence which take women away from their own firesides; which break in on these hours of sweet repose which labor claims for his reward, and wastes time which should be devoted to the cultivation and improvement of the adult and the infant mind, in the trivial idleness and dissipation which destroy them.

(1973)

(1973)

Song for the 8th June

Hail to the day when the Briton came o'er
   And planted his flag where the Mayflower blows,
And gathered the blossoms, unheeded before,
   To entwine with the Shamrock, the Thistle, and Rose.

Let us never forget, while our revels we keep
   'Neath the shade of the green woods that hang overhead,
The labors of those in our churchyards who sleep,
   But fill up a bumper to honor the Dead.

Oh! dear to our hearts is the land they bequeathed,
   And the standard they reared proudly waves o'er us yet;   10
While we gather and cherish the flowers they wreathed,
   Let us never the graves of our fathers forget.

They vanquished the forest to make us a home,
   Though the knife of the savage defended each grove;
And, while ocean's proud waves round our headlands shall foam,
   This day must be honored where'ever we rove.

The valleys their garments of emerald wear,
   The flocks on the mountains unharried repose,
And the songs of our maidens rise mirthful and clear
   By the side of each stream in the starlight that flows.   20

The Cities are growing with wealth in their train,
   The Hamlet securely expands in the glen;
And our white sails are glancing far over the main,
   To the islands that nourish'd those stout hearted men.

Then fill up a bumper, uncovered, we'll name,
   And drink to THE DEAD, and the day they've endeared;
May the spirit they left, like a circle of flame,
   Guard forever the homes and the standard they rear'd.

(1874)   (1874)

The Micmac

Though o'er Acadia's hills and plains
   The wand'ring Micmac listless strays,
While scarce a single trace remains
   Of what he was in other days.

And though he now an outcast seems
   Upon the lands his Fathers trod,
And his dark eye no longer beams
   With pride which bent but to his God, –

Though the fire-water's deadly wave
   Which even pride could not control,   10
Has drown'd each feeling high that gave
   Such innate grandeur to his soul; –

There was a time when Nature's child
   With nobler port and manner bore him,
And ranged with joy his native wild,
   Or slept with Heaven's blue curtain o'er him.

Long ere the white man's axe was heard
   Resounding in the forest shade,
Long ere the rifle's voice had stirr'd
   The stillness of the Sylvan glade, –   20

Ere Science, with her plastic hand,
   And Labor, with his patient toil,
Had changed the features of the land,
   And dispossess'd him of the soil.

Then let fair Fancy change the scene,
   While gazing on the Micmac's brow,
And showing what he once has been,
   Make us forget what he is now.

(1874)   (1874)

Coming Home

Mantled in snow, my native land,
   I hail thee from the sea;
Cheerless to others looks the strand,
   But oh! how dear to me.

My fellow-voyagers gaze and shrink,
   As blows the breeze from shore,
With raptured pulse the air I drink –
   The Northern breeze once more.

They, thinking of their Southern homes,
   And of the trellised vine;   10
Wonder from icy shores there comes
   Excited thought like mine.

As landmarks, they, thy headlands view,
   Right glad to pass them by;
To me they're pictures, stern, but true,
   That charm and cheer the eye.

They cannot see the scenes beyond,
   Of happy household mirth,
The skaters on the glittering pond,
   The children round the hearth.   20

They cannot hear the merry cheer
   Of coasters on the steep;
They do not know how soundly here,
   The free and happy sleep.

They cannot hear the peasant's axe
   Sharp ringing through the groves,
Nor see the blazing fire he piles
   To gladden those he loves.

The sleighs go through the crowded street,
   Like swallows on the wing;   30
Beneath the furs warm fingers meet,
   Hark! how the sleigh-bells ring.

There's not a sound that cleaves the air
   But music has for me;
Nightly the warm hearts beating there,
   Have blest me on the sea.

The stately piles of old renown
   With reverent thought I've trod,
Where noble hearts have laid them down
   With History and with God.

The crowded mart, the busy throng,
   The gay and brilliant halls;
The tramp of steeds, the voice of song,
   The many-pictured walls,

Are all behind; but, all before,
   My native land I view;
A blessing on her sea-girt shore,
   Where toil the good and true.

January 25, 1862

(1874)   (1874)

Charles Heavysege
1816-1876

BORN IN YORKSHIRE, England, Charles Heavysege was largely self-educated. Before his immigration to Montreal in 1853, Heavysege had become an accomplished woodcarver and he continued his work as a cabinetmaker and carpenter after his arrival in Canada. In 1860 he became a reporter for the *Montreal Transcript* and a short time later joined the *Montreal Daily Witness* where he worked until his retirement in 1874. Heavysege's work includes verse dramas, *The Revolt of Tartarus* (1852) and *Saul: A Drama in Three Parts* (1857), a novel, *The Advocate* (1865), and several poems including *Jephthah's Daughter* (1865).

From
Jephthah's Daughter

SONNETS

IV

Childhood alone is glad. With it time flees
In constant mimes and bright festivities.
It, like the ever-restless butterfly,
Or seeks or settles on some flower of joy.
Youth chases pleasure, but oft starteth pain;
And love, youth's birthright, oft is love in vain;
While manhood follows wealth, or woos ambition,
That are but courted cares; and, with transition
Insensible, he enters upon age;
Thence, gliding like a spectre from life's stage,   10
E'en through the door of dotage. So he passes
To second childhood; but, as quickening gases,
Being fled, leave zestless a once cheering draught,
We grow not merry though the Dotard laughed.

(1865)

(1865)

IX

To spend dull evenings when dull day is done,
To be distressed until the couch be won;
In food, and sleep, and labour to sum life,
And die ignobly in the last grim strife,
Without eternity's great hope or dread,
Behold a being multitudes have led.
To start each morn afresh for life and fame,
As lamps new trimmed project a brighter flame;
Along day's hours conduct the noble care,
And for eve's leisure the crude thought prepare;   10
To shorten night, and to forestall the day,
The part ordained for some, though few, to play.
Men start remote, and still diverging wend;
At length how distant if they never end!

(1865)   (1865)

XIV

The stars are glittering in the frosty sky,
Frequent as pebbles on a broad sea-coast;
And o'er the vault the cloud-like galaxy
Has marshalled its innumerable host.
Alive all heaven seems! with wondrous glow
Ten fold refulgent every star appears,
As if some wide celestial gale did blow,
And thrice illume the ever-kindled spheres.
Orbs, with glad orbs rejoicing, burning, beam,
Ray-crowned, with lambent lustre in their zones,   10
Till o'er the blue, bespangled spaces seem
Angels and great archangels on their thrones;
A host divine, whose eyes are sparkling gems,
And forms more bright than diamond diadems.

(1865)   (1865)

XVIII

How great unto the living seem the dead!
How sacred, solemn; how heroic grown;
How vast and vague, as they obscurely tread
The shadowy confines of the dim unknown! —
For they have met the monster that we dread,
Have learned the secret not to mortal shown.
E'en as gigantic shadows on the wall
The spirit of the daunted child amaze,
So on us thoughts of the departed fall,
And with phantasma fill our gloomy gaze.   10
Awe and deep wonder lend the living lines,
And hope and ecstasy the borrowed beams;
While fitful fancy the full form divines,
And all is what imagination dreams.

(1865)   (1865)

William Kirby
1817-1906

———◆———

AFTER EMIGRATING WITH his family from England to the United States at the age of fifteen, William Kirby moved to Canada in 1839 where he became a newspaper editor and subsequently a collector of customs in Niagara-on-the-Lake. His major works include *The U.E.: A Tale of Upper Canada* (1859), a narrative poem of immigration and settlement, *The Golden Dog* (1877), a historical romance of the ancien régime of Quebec, and *Canadian Idylls* (1884), a collection of lyric and narrative poems which in a second edition of 1894 included "The Hungry Year" (1878).

The Hungry Year

Part I

The war was over. Seven red years of blood
Had scourged the land from mountain-top to sea:
(So long it took to rend the mighty frame
Of England's empire in the western world).
With help of foreign arms and foreign gold,
Base faction and the Bourbon's mad revenge,
Rebellion won at last; and they who loved
The cause that had been lost, and kept their faith
To England's crown, and scorned an alien name,
Passed into exile; leaving all behind   10
Except their honour and the conscious pride
Of duty done to country and to king.
Broad lands, ancestral homes, the gathered wealth
Of patient toil and self-denying years
Were confiscate and lost; for they had been
The salt and savor of the land; trained up
In honour, loyalty, and fear of God.
The wine upon the lees, decanted when
They left their native soil, with sword-belts drawn

The tighter; while the women only, wept   20
At thought of old firesides no longer theirs;
At household treasures reft, and all the land
Upset, and ruled by rebels to the King.

Not drooping like poor fugitives, they came
In exodus to our Canadian wilds;
But full of heart and hope, with heads erect
And fearless eyes, victorious in defeat.
With thousand toils they forced their devious way
Through the great wilderness of silent woods
That gloomed o'er lake and stream; till higher rose   30
The northern star above the broad domain
Of half a continent, still theirs to hold,
Defend, and keep forever as their own;
Their own and England's, to the end of time.

The virgin forests, carpeted with leaves
Of many autumns fallen, crisp and sear,
Put on their woodland state; while overhead
Green seas of foliage roared a welcome home
To the proud exiles, who for empire fought,
And kept, though losing much, this northern land   40
A refuge and defence for all who love
The broader freedom of a commonwealth,
Which wears upon its head a kingly crown.

Our great Canadian woods of mighty trees,
Proud oaks and pines, that grew for centuries –
King's gifts upon the exiles were bestowed.
Ten thousand homes were planted; and each one,
With axe, and fire, and mutual help, made war
Against the wilderness, and smote it down.
Into the open glades, unlit before,   50
Since forests grew or rivers ran, there leaped
The sun's bright rays, creative heat and light,
Waking to life the buried seeds that slept
Since Time's beginning, in the earth's dark womb.

The tender grass sprang up, no man knew how;
The daisies' eyes unclosed; wild strawberries
Lay white as hoar-frost on the slopes –and sweet
The violets perfumed the evening air;
The nodding clover grew up everwhere, –

The trailing rasp, the trefoil's yellow cup   60
Sparkled with dew drops; while the humming bees
And birds and butterflies, unseen before,
Found out the sunny spots and came in throngs.

But earth is man's own shadow, say the wise,
As wisdom's secrets are two-fold; and each
Responds to other, both in good and ill –
A crescent thought will one day orb to full.
The ground, uncovered by the woodman's axe,
Burst into bloom; but with the tender grass
And pretty violets, came up the dock,   70
The thistle, fennel, mullen, and a crowd
Of noisome weeds, that with the gentle flowers
Struggled for mastery, till the ploughman trod
Them down beneath his feet, and sowed the ground
With seed of corn for daily use and food.

But long and arduous were their labours ere
The rugged fields produced enough for all –
(For thousands came ere hundreds could be fed)
The scanty harvests, gleaned to their last ear,
Sufficed not yet. Men hungered for their bread   80
Before it grew, yet cheerful bore the hard,
Coarse fare and russet garb of pioneers; –
In the great woods content to build a home
And commonwealth, where they could live secure
A life of honour, loyalty, and peace.

The century's last decade came with signs
Foreboding evil to the forest land.
The sun and moon alternate rose and set,
Red, dry, and fiery, in a rainless sky;
And month succeeded month of parching drouth,   90
That ushered in the gaunt and hungry year, –
The hungry year whose name still haunts the land
With memories of famine and of death!

Corn failed, and fruit and herb. The tender grass
Fell into dust. Trees died like sentient things,
And stood wrapped in their shrouds of withered leaves,
That rustled weirdly round them, sear and dead.
From springs and brooks no morning mist arose;
The water vanished; and a brazen sky

Glowed hot and sullen through the pall of smoke   100
That rose from burning forests, far and near.
The starving cattle died, looking at man
With dumb reproach, as if the blame were his, –
Perhaps it was; but man looked up to heaven
In stern-lipped silence, or in earnest prayer
Besought relief of God, or, in despair,
Invoked the fiercest storms from tropic seas
To quench the earth with rain, and loose the claws
And teeth of famine from the scorching land.
Slowly the months rolled round on fiery wheels;   110
The savage year relented not, nor shut
Its glaring eye, till all things perished, –food
For present, seed for future use were gone.
"All swallowed up," the starving Indians said,
"By the great serpent of the Chenonda
That underlies the ground and sucks it dry."

While equally perplexed at such distress,
Despite his better knowledge, –"Why is this?"
The white man asked and pondered; but in vain.
There came no quick response. Nature is deaf   120
And voiceless both, to satisfy the heart
That needs a deeper answer than she gives.
And till we seek for light of God alone,
Putting ourselves aside and all we know, –
Learning the truth in His way, not in ours,
The mystery of mysteries remains.
Sin, sorrow, death; enexplicable! were
There not beyond the vail a power of love:
God in the human, infinitely like,
Who bore our pains himself, as if to show   130
He cannot, without suffering, pluck away
The rooted sin that tangles in the heart,
Like tares with wheat. Permissive love, that lets
Them grow together for a troubled space,
Till ripe for harvest. Love triumphant, when
The Reaper comes, and life is winnowed clean
Of its base weeds, and all that's good and true
In human souls is garnered up by Him,
Till His vast purposes are all fulfilled.

(1878)   (1894)

Alexander McLachlan
1818-1896

———◆———

BORN NEAR GLASGOW, Scotland, Alexander McLachlan emigrated to Upper Canada in 1840. Following several unsuccessful attempts at farming, he moved to Erin Township near Guelph, Ontario, where he worked as a tailor. In 1877 he settled on a farm near Orangeville and remained there until a few months before his death. McLachlan published his first volume in poems, *The Spirit of Love, and Other Poems,* in 1846; his collected poems were published posthumously in 1900.

We Lean on One Another

Oh, come and listen while I sing
    A song of human nature;
For, high or low, we're all akin
    To ev'ry human creature:
We're all the children of the same,
    The great, the "mighty mother,"
And from the cradle to the grave
    We lean on one another.

It matters little what we wear,
    How high or low our station,   10
We're all alike the slaves of sin
    And sons of tribulation.
No matter what may be the coat
    With which our breasts we cover,
Our hearts within are of one stuff,
    And link'd to one another.

The earth beneath's our common home,
    The heavens bending o'er us,
And wheresoever we may turn
    Eternity's before us.   20

Thro' pride and envy we have been
   But strangers to each other,
But Nature meant that we should lean
   In love on one another.

With Adam from the bow'r of bliss
   We all alike were driven,
And king and cadger at the last
   Must square accounts with heaven.
We're all in need of sympathy –
   Tho' pride the fact would smother –   30
And it's as little 's we can do
   To comfort one another.

A fool's a fool, the wide world o'er,
   Whate'er may be his station;
A snob's a snob, tho' he may hold
   The sceptre of the nation
And Wisdom was ordained to rule –
   (Tho' knaves that truth would smother) –
That all the human race might live
   In love with one another.   40

A king may need our sympathy,
   For all his great attendance;
Among all men ther's no such thing
   As perfect independence.
Tho' great is mighty England's heir,
   Poor Paddy is his brother,
And from the cabin to the throne
   We lean on one another.

(1861)   (1900)

We Live in a Rickety House

We live in a rickety house,
   In a dirty dismal street,
Where the naked hide from day,
   And thieves and drunkards meet.

And pious folks with their tracts,
    When our dens they enter in,
They point to our shirtless backs,
    As the fruits of beer and gin.

And they quote us texts, to prove
    That our hearts are hard as stone;   10
And they feed us with the fact,
    That the fault is all our own.

And the parson comes and prays –
    He's very concerned 'bout our souls;
But he never asks, in the coldest days,
    How we may be off for coals.

It will be long ere the poor
    Will learn their grog to shun;
While it's raiment, food and fire,
    And religion all in one.   20

I wonder some pious folks
    Can look us straight in the face,
For our ignorance and crime
    Are the Church's shame and disgrace.

We live in a rickety house,
    In a dirty dismal street,
Where the naked hide from day,
    And thieves and drunkards meet.

(1861)   (1900)

From
The Emigrant

The Greenwood Shade

Oh, seek the greenwood shade,
    Away from the city din,
From heartless strife of trade,

From fumes of beer and gin;
Where Commerce spreads her fleets,
   Where bloated Luxury lies,
Where lean Want prowls the streets,
   And stares with wolfish eyes.

Flee from the city's sin,
   Its many-color'd code,   10
Its palaces raised to sin,
   Its temples rear'd to God;
Its cellars dark and dank,
   Where ne'er a sunbeam falls,
'Mid faces lean and lank
   As the hungry-looking walls;

Its fest'ring pits of woe,
   Its teeming earthly hells,
Whose surges ever flow
   In sound of Sabbath bells.   20
O God! I'd rather be
   An Indian in the wood,
To range through forest free
   In search of daily food.

Oh! rather I'd pursue
   The wolf and grizzly bear,
Than toil for the thankless few
   In seething pits of care.
Here Winter's breath is rude,
   His fingers cold and wan;   30
But what's his wildest mood
   To the tyranny of man?

To trackless forest wild,
   To loneliest abode,
The heart is reconciled
   That's felt Oppression's load.
The desert place is bright,
   The wilderness is fair,
If Hope but shed her light –
   If Freedom be but there.   40

(1861)   (1900)

Cartha Again

Oh! why did I leave thee? Oh! why did I part
Frae thee, lovely Cartha, thou stream o' my heart?
Oh, why did I leave thee and wander awa'
Frae the hame o' my childhood, Gleniffer an' a'?
The thocht o' thee aye mak's my bosom o'erflow
Wi' a langing that nane save the weary can know;
And a' fortune's favors are empty and vain,
If I'm ne'er to return to thee, Cartha, again.

When I hear the soft tone o' my ain Lowlan' tongue,
Ance mair I'm a laddie the gowans among: 10
I see thee still winding thy green valley through,
And the Highland hills tow'ring afar in the blue;
But the lintie, the lav'rock, the blackbird, an' a',
Aye singing, "My laddie, ye've lang been awa'."
Nae wonder I sit down an' mak' my sad mane —
Am I ne'er to behold thee, sweet Cartha, again?

When I hear the sweet lilt o' some auld Scottish sang,
Oh, how my bluid leaps as it coorses alang!
The thumps o' my heart gar my bosom a' stoun',
My heid it grows dizzy and rins roun' an' roun';   20
My very heartstrings tug as gin they would crack,
And burst a' the bonds that are keepin' me back;
But then comes the thocht, here I'm doom'd to remain,
And ne'er to return to thee, Cartha, again!

In a grave o' the forest, when life's journey's past,
Unknown and unhonor'd they'll lay me at last;
Abune me nae bluebell nor gowan shall wave,
And nae robin come to sing over my grave.
But, surely! ah, surely! the love o' this heart
For thee, lovely Cartha, can never depart;   30
But free frae a' sorrow, a' sadness and pain,
My spirit shall haunt thee, dear Cartha, again.

(1874)   (1900)

Young Canada

Or, Jack's as Good's his Master

I love this land of forest grand,
    The land where labor's free;
Let others roam away from home,
    Be this the land for me!
Where no one moils and strains and toils
    That snobs may thrive the faster,
But all are free as men should be,
    And Jack's as good's his master!

Where none are slaves that lordly knaves
    May idle all the year;   10
For rank and caste are of the past –
    They'll never flourish here!
And Jew or Turk, if he'll but work,
    Need never fear disaster;
He reaps the crop he sowed in hope,
    For Jack's as good's his master.

Our aristocracy of toil
    Have made us what you see,
The nobles of the forge and soil,
    With ne'er a pedigree.   20
It makes one feel himself a man,
    His very blood leaps faster,
Where wit or worth's preferr'd to birth,
    And Jack's as good's his master.

Here's to the land of forests grand,
    The land where labor's free;
Let others roam away from home,
    Be this the land for me!
For here 'tis plain the heart and brain,
    The very soul, grow vaster,   30
Where men are free as they should be,
    And Jack's as good's his master.

(1874)   (1900)

Charles Sangster
1822-1893

———◆———

CHARLES SANGSTER WAS born in Kingston, Upper Canada, and worked there and in Amherstburg as a journalist before moving to Ottawa in 1868. After spending eighteen years as a clerk in the Post Office Department, he returned to Kingston where he spent the rest of his life working on four volumes of manuscript poems. One of these volumes was published in a limited edition as *Our Norland* (1893) but Sangster's reputation rests on two earlier collections: *The St. Lawrence and the Saguenay, and Other Poems* (1856) and *Hesperus, and Other Poems and Lyrics* (1860).

From
The St. Lawrence and the Saguenay

LXXIX
In golden volumes rolls the blessed light
Along the sterile mountains. Pile on Pile
The granite masses rise to left and right:
Bald, stately bluffs that never wear a smile;
Where vegetation fails to reconcile
The parchèd shrubbery and stunted trees
To the stern mercies of the flinty soil.
And we must pass a thousand bluffs like these,
Within whose breasts are locked a myriad mysteries.

LXXX
Here is a barren crag, at whose brown feet
Patiently sits the church and gleams the spire.
Commerce has found this a deserved retreat:
Here groan the mills, and there, the household fire
Sends up its smoke above the struggling briar
And dwarfish evergreens that grow between
The stubborn rocks – that grow but to expire.
Not here the thrifty farmer's face serene –
The lumberer alone lends life to the grim scene.

10

LXXXI

No further evidence of life, save where
The young whales bask their broad backs in the sun,   20
Or the gay grampus, sportive as a hare,
Leaps and rejoices, playfully as one
In youth who sees some holiday begun.
Perhaps a crowded steamer, passing by,
Lights up the scene a moment. Trebly dun
The shades of sullen loneliness that lie
On rugged L'Ance l'eau when no living thing is nigh.

LXXXII

Over the darkening waters! on through scenes
Whose unimaginable wildness fills
The mind with joy insatiate, and weans   30
The soul from earth, to Him whose Presence thrills
All Beauty as all Truth. These iron Hills!
In what profusion did He pile them here,
Thick as the flowers that blossom where the rills
Chant to the primal woods. Year after year
In solitude eternal, rapt in contemplation drear.

LXXXIII

Dreaming of the old years before they rose
Triumphant from the deep, whose waters roll'd
Above their solemn and unknown repose;
Dreaming of that bright morning, when, of old,   40
Beyond the Red Man's memory, they told
The Secrets of the Ages to the sun,
That smiled upon them from his throne of gold;
Dreaming of the bright stars and loving moon,
That first shone on them from the Night's impressive noon:

LXXXIV

Dreaming of the long ages that have passed
Since then, and with them that diminished race
Whose birchen fleets these inky waters glassed,
As they swept o'er them with the wind's swift pace.
Of their wild legends scarce remains a trace;   50
Thou hold'st the myriad secrets in thy brain,
Oh! stately bluffs! As well seek to efface
The light of the bless'd stars, as to obtain
From thy sealed, granite lips, tradition or refrain!

LXXXV

But they are there, though man may never know
Their number or their beauty. Pass the eye
Along the ever-looming scene, where'er we go,
Through these long corridors of rock and sky —
What startling barriers, rising sullenly
From the dark deeps, like giants, seem to place   60
An adamantine gateway, close and high,
To bar our progress; meet them face to face,
The magic doors fly open, and the rocks recede apace.

(1856)   (1856)

From
Sonnets Written in the Orillia Woods
August, 1859

V

Blest Spirit of Calm that dwellest in these woods!
Thou art a part of that serene repose
That ofttimes lingers in the solitudes
Of my lone heart, when the tumultuous throes
Of some vast Grief have borne me to the earth.
For I have fought with Sorrow face to face;
Have tasted of the cup that brings to some
A frantic madness and delirious mirth,
But prayed and trusted for the light to come,
To break the gloom and darkness of the place.
Through the dim aisles the sunlight penetrates,
And nature's self rejoices; heaven's light
Comes down into my heart, and in its might
My soul stands up and knocks at God's own temple-gates.

(1860)   (1860)

VIII

Above where I am sitting, o'er these stones,
The ocean waves once heaved their mighty forms;
And vengeful tempests and appalling storms
Wrung from the stricken sea portentous moans,
That rent stupendous icebergs, whose huge heights
Crashed down in fragments through the startled nights.
Change, change, eternal change in all but God!
Mysterious nature! thrice mysterious state
Of body, soul, and spirit! Man is awed,
But triumphs in his littleness. A mote,   10
He specks the eye of the age and turns to dust,
And is the sport of centuries. We note
More surely nature's ever-changing fate;
  Her fossil records tell how she performs her trust.

(1860)   (1860)

XVI

My footsteps press where, centuries ago,
The Red Men fought and conquered; lost and won.
Whole tribes and races, gone like last year's snow,
Have found the Eternal Hunting-Grounds, and run
The fiery gauntlet of their active days,
Till few are left to tell the mournful tale:
And these inspire us with such wild amaze
They seem like spectres passing down a vale
Steeped in uncertain moonlight, on their way
Towards some bourn where darkness blinds the day,   10
And night is wrapped in mystery profound.
We cannot lift the mantle of the past:
We seem to wander over hallowed ground:
  We scan the trail of Thought, but all is overcast.

(1860)   (1860)

XXII

Dark, dismal day – the first of many such!
The wind is sighing through the plaintive trees,
In fitful gusts of a half-frenzied woe;
Affrighted clouds the hand might almost touch,
Their black wings bend so mournfully and low,
Sweep through the skies like night-winds o'er the seas.
There is no chirp of bird through all the grove,
Save that of the young fledgeling rudely flung
From its warm nest; and like the clouds above
My soul is dark, and restless as the breeze   10
That leaps and dances over Couchiching.
Soon will the last duet be sweetly sung;
But through the years to come our hearts will ring
With memories, as dear as time and love can bring.

(1860)   (1860)

Brock

October 13th, 1859.*

One voice, one people, one in heart
        And soul, and feeling, and desire!
        Re-light the smouldering martial fire,
        Sound the mute trumpet, strike the lyre,
        The hero deed can not expire,
                The dead still play their part.

Raise high the monumental stone!
        A nation's fealty is theirs,
        And we are the rejoicing heirs,
        The honored sons of sires whose cares   10
        We take upon us unawares,
                As freely as our own.

*The date of the dedication of the Brock Monument on Queenston Heights.

We boast not of the victory,
    But render homage, deep and just,
    To his – to their – immortal dust,
    Who proved so worthy of their trust
    No lofty pile nor sculptured bust
        Can herald their degree.

No tongue need blazon forth their fame –
    The cheers that stir the sacred hill   20
    Are but mere promptings of the will
    That conquered then, that conquers still;
    And generations yet shall thrill
        At Brock's remembered name.

Some souls are the Hesperides
    Heaven sends to guard the golden age,
    Illuming the historic page
    With records of their pilgrimage;
    True Martyr, Hero, Poet, Sage:
        And he was one of these.   30

Each in his lofty sphere sublime
    Sits crowned above the common throng,
    Wrestling with some Pythonic wrong,
    In prayer, in thunder, thought, or song;
    Briareus-limbed, they sweep along,
        The Typhons of the time.

(1860)   (1860)

Octave Crémazie
1827-1879

———◆———

OCTAVE CRÉMAZIE WAS born in Quebec and completed his studies at the Seminary of Quebec in 1844. Subsequently, he managed a bookstore which became a meeting place for such figures as F.-X. Garneau, Antoine Gérin-Lajoie and Louis Fréchette, and which served as a centre for the group of writers known as L'Ecole de Québec. In 1862, threatened by legal charges of forgery and fraud following the financial collapse of the bookstore, Crémazie fled to France where he remained until his death. Crémazie published no poetry after leaving Quebec but in several of the poems written before 1862, he articulates a nationalistic pride in Quebec's past which was echoed by many of his literary successors in the second half of the nineteenth century. *Oeuvres complètes de Crémazie* was first published in 1882.

The Dead

O dead! within your graves you find repose.
No more you bear the weary weight of woes,
    The world in which we live.
For you the sky's bright stars and storms are gone,
Spring-odours and horizon-clouds are done,
    The sun now has no rays to give.

Deep in your sepulchres, inert and cold,
You ask not if the echoes of the world
    Are sad or happy ones;
The idle chat of men you hear no more,
That withers hearts and makes us what we are,
    Misfortune's evil sons.

10

The bitter wind of grief and envy's sigh,
Tormentors while you lived, no longer dry
      The pith your bones enclose.
For you have found beneath the graveyard sward
The good our whole existence seeks to hoard,
      O you have found repose.

While full of our sad thoughts we take our way
And hold our souls in servitude each day   20
      All alone and silently,
You hear the song the holy voices sing
That come from heaven and pass the earth, a-wing
      To reascend the sky.

You ask for nothing from the human race
That bears but to the tombs it would efface
      Not even tear or sigh;
You ask for nothing from the breeze that throws
Over the silent grave its breath of rose,
      Nothing but memory.   30

All pleasures that our souls are bound to bear
Are naught to you beside this faithful care,
      The heart's true charity,
Returning now to warm your frigid dust
And bear your name that prayers hold in trust
      To the Lord's throne on high.

Alas, that memories which friendships give
Should die in hearts before your bodies leave
      The vestments of the dead,
And in the tomb the fact that men forget   40
Upon your fleshless bones falls heavier yet
      Than any coffin's lid.

The selfish heart engrossed in what is now
Can see but pages of a book in you
      That it has read before:
In joy and sorrow it can only love
The ones where hate and pride go hand in glove;
      The dead are such no more.

O dusty bodies, you are no more than toys
To our ambitions and our feeble joys!   50
       We soon forget your memory.
What means to us this suffering world at all
That moans beyond the vast and dreary wall
       Which death has reared on high?

They say that, pained by our ingratitude,
You sometimes leave the icy solitude
       Where we have laid you down;
And that oft-times at midnight you appear
And drop funereal lamentations drear
       From lips that graves have known.   60

    Sad and weeping shades
    That in the gloomy glades
    Display your ivory weeds
    And grieve with noises drear
    Listened to with fear
    Moaning among the reeds;

    O luminous wanderers,
    Those bright flames of yours
    Are seen throughout the night
    In the humid valley   70
    Where you are silently
    Led by the wind's flight.

    Soft voices of sad presage
    Are heard at the water's edge
    When evening shadows fold
    Their veils to a deep line
    And turn all the star-shine
    To monstrances of gold;

    Voices of mystery
    That the furious sea   80
    Throws in the wind,
    Whose echoes amain
    Will echo again
    In the moving sand;

Voices, flames, shadows,
Are you souls of those
That the tomb holds tight,
Like a faithful guard
Underneath the sward
All the eternal night?   90

As you leave coffins now
Seek you on earth below
Mortal forgiveness?
Or ask you the way
Where prayer can repay
Those who wait heaven's dress?

When the sweet nightingale has left the woods,
When autumn's grey sky, gathering its clouds,
Makes ready the shrouds that winter must pour
On frozen fields, there comes a harsh bleak day   100
When our hearts, putting earth's vain cares away,
Love best to dwell on those who are no more.

There comes a day when the dead leave behind
Their tombs, a flight of glad doves in the wind
Escaping their cold prisons a while;
They do not repel us as they are then seen,
Dreamy of aspect and gentle of mien,
And inside their dark gaze no hints of guile.

When they come thus, and when their vision rolls
On the thronged church which prays that all their souls   110
May have God's grace, a happy spark is lit
Which, like the pure glint some fire-opals house,
Wanders a moment on their calm pale brows
To warm each frozen heart a little bit.

All chosen ones of God, all holy saints
Who bear life's grievous yoke with no complaints
And daily walk beneath the Almighty's gaze
Will have good angels guard their nightly sleep;
Their eyes, untroubled by strange visions deep,
Will not in dreams glimpse hell's fiery haze.   120

All those on earth whose pure hearts only know
Echoes of heaven which sweeten all the woe,
Of doleful paths which men must walk as men,
These good below defeat life's emptiness,
Unrolling virtue like a splendid dress,
And walk on evil without the slightest stain;

As in a dream which Dante's eye had caught,
When all the weeping city's hosts are brought
Before us on one day's solemnity,
It is so for these. Only they can tend   130
The secrets of the tomb, or comprehend
Those pale mendicants who demand the sky.

The holy psalms of Solomon, the bard,
And Job's most lofty griefs are also heard
Sobbing and deep inside the sanctuary,
Where trumpet voices full of dismal blares
Sound funeral knells and ask of us our tears
For wandering ghosts like waves of the sea.

Give then to-day, when all the church in grief
Presents a moving plea on their behalf,   140
To calm your own regrets, perhaps remorse;
Reviving memory's flames, give to the tombs
Your flowers, to the souls your prayers; twin-perfumes
Of heaven to console the dead in course.

Pray for your friends, and for your mother, too,
Who gave glad days in the sad life you knew,
Pray for young hearts asleep in the tombs.
Alas! those objects of young tenderness
Know in their slim graves no other caress
Than worm-kisses that eat up their bones.   150

Pray for the exile who, far from his home,
Dies in a place where no kind word can come,
As lonely then as when he lived alone.
No one will go to pray on his bier,
Alms of a tear dropped for an alien there,
Who thinks of his lying there, the buried unknown?

Pray yet for those whose souls in pain and woe
Have known but dismal thoughts in this world below,
Whose day goes dreary and whose sleep is spilt;
For those who bless existence every night   160
But find instead of hope another plight,
A horrid waking from their dreams' rich gilt.

Ah! for those outcasts from the human race
Who, burdened by the weight of their disgrace,
Have climbed misfortune's ladder to the skies,
O let your heart be moved to give to each
The rich coin of memory and the holy speech
That disclose God's face to their waiting eyes.

Pay them this tribute of both prayer and tears
Before the moment of horrible fears   170
When your life's term is as a dream gone by;
Your name, repeated by the gratitude
Of those whose suffering you have made good,
May not be unknown when you arrive on high.

And, taking that tribute, a white-winged angel
Will pause in his heavenly flight a spell
To set it down above a tombstoned head.
The dying flowers in the graveyard there
Will bloom at once in a sweet wind of prayer
To pour their perfume on the sleeping dead.   180

(1882)   (1977)

FRED COGSWELL (TR.)

Rosanna Leprohon
1829-1879

———◆———

BORN AND EDUCATED in Montreal, Rosanna Eleanor Mullins was married to Dr. Jean-Lukin Leprohon in 1851. Mrs. Leprohon was a prolific writer of both poetry and fiction and was a major contributor to journals such as *The Literary Garland* and *The Canadian Monthly and National Review*. Many of her novels were serialized in journals and "My Visit to Fairview Villa" appeared in three issues of the *Canadian Illustrated News* published in May, 1870. Her poetry was collected and published posthumously as *The Poetical Works of Mrs. Leprohon* in 1881.

My Visit to Fairview Villa

"LOVE! PSHAW! I don't believe in it, and I really think I shall live and die an old maid, lest I should be wooed and married for my money. Men are such selfish, grasping, egotistical creatures!"

Such was the uncompromising judgment I heard pronounced on my sex as I entered the pleasant shady drawing-room of my friend, Stephen Merton, in compliance with a pressing invitation lately received, to spend a few weeks of the hot, dusty summer months at his pleasant residence, Fairview Villa, situated on the beautiful Saint Foy Road, some short distance from picturesque old Quebec.

The moment of my arrival was rather unpropitious, and I think I would have retreated had not my hostess caught sight of my rather embarrassed countenance. Instantly rising, she came forward and kindly welcomed me, introducing me afterwards to her two daughters, Fanny and Charlotte Merton, her niece, Miss Gray, and a young lady guest, Miss Otway.

"Hem!" thought I, when fairly seated, and replying with tolerable composure to the liberally gay small talk addressed me on all sides: "Which of these fair ladies has just proclaimed so unequivocally her contempt for mankind?" and my glance here travelled round the fair circle. "Oh, that is the one," I pronounced, as my gaze rested on Miss

Geraldine Otway, who stood haughtily erect beside the mantlepiece, twisting a piece of honey-suckle round her taper fingers. The scorn was yet lingering in the dark eyes that met mine so fearlessly – in the rosy lip so contemptuously curved, and a yet more femininely beautiful being I had rarely met. Features of childish delicacy, a varying, transparent complexion, and a figure of the most fragile, though graceful proportions, were hers; all forming a striking contrast to the words and manner of this determined hater of mankind.

"Pray, Mr. Saville, did you overhear any part of the discussion we were engaged in when you opportunely entered to prevent its animation degenerating into animosity?" enquired Miss Gray, with a mischievous glance towards Miss Otway.

"Only the concluding sentences," I replied.

"If Mr. Saville wishes, I am ready to repeat what I have already said, and to defend it," exclaimed the lovely occupant of the hearth-rug, nibbling with superb indifference at the spray of honey-suckle in her hand.

"No, Miss Otway," I rejoined with a low bow, "that would be unnecessary, for I acknowledge the justice of your remarks. More than that, I will say you were not half severe enough."

I had flattered myself that my ironical acquiescence in her stern views would have slightly disconcerted this fair Amazon with the tender bloom of eighteen summers still fresh on her cheek, but so far from that, she merely averted her long fringed azure eyes contemptuously from me, as if judging me unworthy of further notice.

"Why, Mr. Saville," interposed little Charlotte Merton, "you should blush for subscribing so unreservedly to such a sweeping, odious accusation against your sex!"

"I beg pardon, Miss Merton, but since you take me up so seriously, I must say that I assent only in part to Miss Otway's opinions."

"And pray what part does Mr. Saville judge fit to dispute?" questioned my fair enemy, pursuing her fragrant repast without deigning to cast a glance in my direction.

The overwhelming contempt for my humble self and judgment, conveyed in the clear cold tones and averted eyes, was something really wonderful in its way, and would have utterly annihilated a more sensitive individual than myself. I contrived, however, with tolerable composure, to rejoin:

"As to the selfishness and rapacity of men, we will leave it an open question; but with regard to Miss Otway's intention of living and dying in single blessedness, holding as she does, so poor an opinion of our sex, I highly applaud her wisdom."

"Oh!" thought I, inwardly elated, "what a magnificent thrust! She'll scarcely get over it!"

Slowly she brought her full clear eyes to bear on mine, and having steadily stared at my hapless countenance a full moment, quietly said:

"It is barely possible I may yet be induced to change my present opinion of the lords of creation for a more favourable one; to commit the egregious folly of trusting in them; but I do not think," and here she came to a pause expressive of the most unutterable scorn; "I do not think that Mr. Saville, or any person at all resembling him, will be the one who shall succeed in making me do so."

I was vanquished, for I could not descend to vulgar retort and tell her she might rest assured that Mr. Saville would never seek her capricious favour, so making her a low bow I retired from the lists, intercepting as I did so a deprecating look from dove-eyed Fanny Merton towards Miss Otway, which that young lady answered by a slight toss of her graceful head. My gentle hostess here compassionately hastened to my assistance, and became suddenly interested in the health of my married sister and her olive branches, till the entrance of Mr. Merton, his two sons, and a couple of gentlemen guests, completely restored my equanimity.

Smarting as I still was under the unsparing onslaught Miss Otway had just made on me, I found my gaze involuntarily following and I fear admiring her every movement, so full of careless grace, of easy elegance. Of course she was surrounded, flattered, courted, for she was an heiress as well as a beauty, not to speak of her being a matchless and most capricious coquette. How bewitchingly she would smile one moment on the suitor from whom she would scornfully turn the next! – how she would overwhelm with contemptuous raillery this hour the unlucky being to whose whispered flatteries she had perhaps silently listened a short time before!

Beautiful, wonderfully beautiful she was, and changeable in her loveliness as an April day; now all smiles, sparkling epigram and repartee, then full of quiet, graceful dignity, a creature formed surely to bewilder, fascinate, utterly bewitch a man, do anything but make him happy. Such were my reflections, despite all efforts to the contrary, as I sat beside pretty, gentle Miss Merton, vainly endeavouring to concentrate my attention on herself. My folly, however, went no farther and I never joined the group paying Miss Otway such assiduous court. I felt instinctively that my nature was capable of conceiving a deep and lasting attachment, one which, if unhappy, would cloud a great part perhaps of my future life, and I knew that Geraldine Otway was one formed to inspire such a feeling, and after winning her aim, to laugh at the sufferings of her victim. Warned in time, I resolved to be prudent, and to keep without the charmed circle surrounding this modern Circe.

After the lapse of a few days, during the course of which we had barely exchanged a few words of commonplace civility, she seemed to become gradually aware of my existence, and then came my fiery ordeal. When she would ask with her bewildering smile, "Mr Saville, please turn my music for me?" how could I say no, and then, when I would make a feeble effort to get away from her side, from the witchery of her sparkling eyes, and she would softly say, "What, tired so soon?" I would struggle like a bird in the grasp of the fowler, and for the time submit, I began to fear it was my destiny to love this beautiful, wayward siren, and well I knew what my reward would be if I weakly allowed myself to do so. I never deceived myself by indulging any illusory hopes. I knew that I was passably good-looking, young, and not a dunce. My family was as good as her own. My income, though likely to appear small in the eyes of an heiress, was a comfortable one, but these advantages never induced me to hope even for one moment that I would have any chance with her. I knew that she had spent a winter in Quebec and another in Montreal, during both of which she had been a reigning *belle*, had discarded men far superior to myself in wealth and position, and would probably yield up her freedom only to some great magnet whose social standing would elevate him, at least in her estimation, above the greater part of his fellow-men.

Life would have been very pleasant to me during my visit at Fairview Villa had it not been for the constant struggle between judgment and inclination. Could I have blindly yielded myself up to her fascinations, living only for the present, careless – oblivious of the future, all would have been sunshine; but I knew that an awakening from the intoxicating trance, bringing with it an hour of reckoning for me, not for her, would come, when she would say "good-bye for ever," and go on her way careless and smiling, leaving me to the misery of shattered hopes and an aching heart. I repeated inwardly, over and over again, that it should never come to this – that I would turn a deaf ear to her soft words, be marble to her wiles. We shall see with what success.

Pic-nics, boating and riding parties; walks by moonlight, sunlight, starlight; croquet on the lawn; billiards in the parlour; music in the drawing-room, succeeded each other with bewildering rapidity, and through all, Geraldine Otway shone, and glittered, and queened it, till I sometimes feared my only chance of safety lay in instant flight. Prudence whispered it would be my surest protection, but weak will found many excuses for avoiding the step. My sudden departure might offend Mrs. Merton; I wanted change of air; I was conscious of danger, and therefore able to take care of myself, and – in short, I stayed.

Pic-nics were a favourite pastime with us, and we often resorted to the beautiful woods that lay about a mile from Fairview Villa, and spent a pleasant time with green foliage and sunbeams overhead, and soft moss and wild flowers beneath our feet.

On one occasion that our wandering had extended into the green depths of the wood farther than usual, a sudden and violent rainstorm set in. I happened to be somewhat behind my companions, intent on gathering a bouquet of wild flowers for Charlotte Merton, a duty she had laughingly charged me with, when the deluge came down, and finding myself in a comparatively open clearing, where my choice summer suit was receiving more than a fair share of the shower, I quickened my steps to a run. On reaching a dense part of the wood I slackened my pace, and casting a glance of satisfaction at the thick roof of verdure overhead, suddenly perceived Miss Otway standing drenched and draggled (no other word for it, dear reader) under the shelter of a huge maple.

"Why, you are all wet, Miss Otway," I hastily said. "And alone, too!"

"Yes, that stupid Willy Merton worried me into standing here whilst he should go back to the carriages in search of an umbrella and shawls," was her petulant answer. "I do not think I will wait, though. I will try a race through the shower."

I held up my finger warningly as the rain suddenly poured down with renewed violence, whilst a vivid flash of lightning rent the sky, and was succeeded by a sullen peal of thunder.

She turned pale as death, murmuring:

"I do not fear many things, but I certainly stand in awe of lightning and thunder."

What was to be done? The rain pouring down with added force was penetrating the thick foliage, literally drenching my delicate companion. After a moment I removed my light over-coat and, with considerable hesitation, asked might I wrap it around her. She was generally so haughty and independent I made the offer timidly, fearing perhaps a sharp rebuff, but instead, she gratefully thanked me, and nestled her little cheek inside the collar with a child-like satisfaction at the additional shelter it afforded. Wrenching off the little dainty fabric of tulle and rosebuds that had done duty as a bonnet a few minutes before, but which was now a shapeless, gaudy pulp, she flung it away, saying:

"Now, I have an excuse for getting a new one to-morrow. It shall be illusion, trimmed with honeysuckle."

"But you must not let the rain pour down on your uncovered head in this way," I remonstrated.

"Oh, it will do no harm. There are no false tresses embellishing it."

How very lovely she was! Disordered, drenched, still the face looked out so calmly beautiful from amid the shining wet masses of hair on either side. I felt the spell of her rare loveliness stealing over me, and I knew I must strengthen myself against its dangerous influence, doubly insidious in the soft, feminine mood that ruled her at the moment.

Another vivid flash with accompanying sullen rumble, and again the colour left her cheek, and a look of terror crept over her face.

"What are we to do?" she piteously asked, turning to me.

She was so touching, so winning in her girlish tremors and helplessness that a wild impulse to tell her there and then how loveable, how fascinating she was, took possession of me, and afraid of myself, of my own want of self-control, I stood silent at her side. Another flash, another peal, and she convulsively clutched my arm, bowing her head on it to shut out the lightning from her sight. She was trembling in every limb, her very lips white with terror, and I, weak fool, was as unnerved as herself, though from a very different cause. Ah, my fears, my presentiments had all pointed to the truth, and I had learned to love her in spite of prudence, judgment, and common sense. Yes, I had fallen into the snare I had so firmly resolved on avoiding, but she, at least, should never know my folly, never have an opportunity of curling her lip in scorn at my audacity – of trampling on feelings that to me, alas! were only too earnest. Was I not tried – tried almost beyond my strength with her clinging, trembling and helpless to my arm in the recesses of that dim wood? Surely I would betray myself. Ability to act or speak with outward calmness was fast deserting me. Again another terrible flash. The very elements were leagued against me. Closer she clung, whispering:

"Lawrence, Mr. Saville, I shall die with terror."

The sound of my Christian name, which seemed to have escaped her lips involuntarily, the close, but soft pressure of her little fingers as they closed so imploringly on my arm, the graceful head bowed almost on my shoulder, all combined to rout completely my presence of mind – the calmness so necessary to me then, and I felt that unless I made a mighty and immediate effort, my doom was sealed.

"Miss Otway," I quietly said, "there is really no danger. Pray be calm, and allow me to seat you here, under the tree, where you will be more sheltered from the rain."

Whether owing to the struggle going on within me, my voice had assumed a degree of coldness I had not intended it should, or that the words in themselves, containing a sort of implied wish to rid myself of the duty of supporting her, incensed her proud spirit, she instantly raised her head from my arm, and with the look and bearing of an offended queen, flung my coat from her and walked forth in the midst of the deluge coming down still with undiminished violence.

"Miss Otway," I besought, I urged, "for heaven's sake wait a few moments longer. This heavy rain will soon be over!"

She made no reply beyond slightly contracting her dark eyebrows, and pursued her course. It was distressing beyond measure to see that delicate frail creature exposed to such a storm, and I renewed my entreaties for her to return to the shelter of the wood, but received no reply, nothing but contemptuous silence. Again a vivid flash of lightning, a crashing peal of thunder overhead. "Ah, poor girl, she will stop now," thought I. But I was mistaken. Her indomitable pride triumphed over every feeling, and though her cheek became if possible of a still more deathly whiteness, she steadily kept on her way. I came closer to her, proffering my arm, my coat, which were both mutely but disdainfully rejected. Thus, I following her in an ignominious, valet style of companionship, we plashed on through rain and mire till we at length reached our party, the men of which had constructed a temporary shelter for the ladies by drawing the carriages together.

"Why, you are in a shocking plight, Miss Otway. I hope friend Saville has taken good care of you," said Mr. Merton.

"Oh yes," she rejoined with stinging sarcasm; "he is such a very prudent young gentleman."

"Come, Geraldine, don't be cross because your pretty bonnet is among the things that were," interrupted Miss Merton, who always kindly came to my rescue.

"But did you not meet Willy and the shawls?" questioned our host. "He set off some time ago with a sufficient quantity to construct a wigwam if you had desired it, not to mention two umbrellas and a parasol."

"We did not meet him, Mr. Merton. I suppose he has been seeking for a short cut through the wood, which instead has proved a long one."

"Geraldine, quick, step into the carriage. We have plenty of place for you," called out Miss Gray.

"Yes, if you are not afraid of getting your dresses wet or spoiled, or of my fatiguing you otherwise," she replied, darting another withering look towards my hapless self.

"What an unlucky fellow I am," I mournfully thought when, fairly started some time later on our homeward route, I wondered over the events of the day. "I have made myself fairly odious to her; and heavens! what a fire-brand she is!" But, alas, I vainly sought to fortify myself by the latter uncharitable reflection, and I was no sooner in my own room, whither I had instantly retired on arriving at the house, to change my wet clothes, than I found myself kissing like a verdant school boy the silk lining of my coat collar against which her soft cheek had so prettily nestled a short while ago.

"Fool! idiot! mad-man!" I groaned, as the full meaning of this act of folly rose suddenly upon me, revealing that love for this peerless creature had indeed, spite of all my resolutions and efforts, crept into my heart. "All I can do now is to hide my madness from every eye, but from hers above all other. She hates, scorns me now, but, so help me heaven, she shall never laugh at me!"

On entering the drawing-room, there was Miss Otway in a fresh, delicate tinted robe, showing no signs of the late great fatigue and exposure she had undergone beyond a brighter flush on her cheek and a greater brilliancy in her dark eyes. She never noticed me all the evening beyond launching at my devoted head, on one or two occasions, some sarcasms as cutting as they were wholly unprovoked, and from which I sought refuge in the society of Miss Merton. The companionship of the latter really pretty, amiable girl was always agreeable to me, principally for two reasons. First, she was quite in love, I well knew, with the gallant Captain Graham, of the —th, a handsome young officer who had lately joined our party, (and who by the way was hopelessly in love himself with Miss Otway) so I saw no risk of my attentions being misinterpreted; secondly, she was an intimate, or as young ladies call it, a bosom friend of the wilful mistress of my heart, and often chose her for the theme of our long chats together, recounting so many instances of the generosity, kindness and better nature of the latter that my chains after each such dangerous dialogue were more closely riveted than if I had been in company with Miss Otway herself. The conduct of that young lady continued the same for a few days as it had been on the evening of the luckless pic-nic, I, all the time, even whilst smarting under her petulant injustice, finding a gloomy satisfaction in the thought that my secret was safe. Then again her mood changed, and she became friendly and conciliating even to the point of making advances which I certainly did not meet more than half way, even if I went that far.

One beautiful afternoon that several of us had gone on an exploring expedition on horseback to some fine view in the neighbourhood, I found myself by her side with Capt. Graham as we were turning our horses' heads homewards. Suddenly she discovered that "she had forgotten her lace handkerchief, and hoped that Captain Graham would have gallantry enough to go for it." The directions, to say the least, were rather vague, and the accomplished son of Mars departed on his mission, smiles on his lips and weary disgust in his heart. Turning towards me she said with her softest smile:

"Spur up, Mr. Saville. We can ride two abreast here."

Ah! merciless coquette! arch traitress! she was determined on leading me into a confession. How could I resist her? Would that she had been a serf – a peasant girl, anything that I might have hoped to have room for my own, but instead she was the petted heiress, the merciless flirt, and I a miserable captive with nothing to console me under the weight of my chains save the certainty that none knew I wore them. Very calmly I accepted her invitation to ride beside her, and we journeyed on, the golden sunlight quivering through the green branches overhead, the soft summer winds caressing our foreheads, and yet our talk was as dull and prosaic as if we had been a couple of elderly respectable people with the cares of the state, or of a family, on our shoulders. Suddenly she turned full towards me, saying with a charming smile:

"Now for a race, Mr. Saville. If you win, you may name your reward."

With a look of laughing defiance that wonderfully heightened her exquisite beauty, she glanced archly at me and then set off at full speed. Easily I could have overtaken her and she must have known that well, for few horses excelled in speed my own good steed kindly accommodated with a comfortable stall in the stables at Fairview Villa, but I had no intention of jeopardizing my secret which this girl seemed bent on wringing from me, and at a very moderate rate of speed I followed in her wake. After a time she looked sharply round, and either angered by the slowness of my pace, or by my preoccupied look, she struck her spirited little mare angrily across the ears, and the latter catching the fiery mood of her mistress, gave a bound forward and set off at break-neck speed. Anxious beyond measure, I spurred forward, dreading every moment some accident to the frail girlish creature I saw flying before me through the interstices of the wood with such reckless disregard of caution. Now, had I not firmly determined when commencing this humble recital, that it should possess the merit of being at least veracious, even at the expense of dullness, I should here enliven it by a rapid, brilliant account of some deadly peril which would suddenly menace Miss Otway, say for instance, her horse rearing on the brink of a precipice, from which strait she would be delivered entirely by my strength of arm and presence of mind; but resisting manfully the temptation, doubly strong in the present case, as I feel convinced I could make a graphic, indeed splendid sketch of the thing, I will honestly confess that she at length drew rein, safe though flushed and panting, at Fairview Villa.

I hastily dismounted so as to assist her to alight, but without waiting for my help, she sprang to the ground at the risk of a sprained ankle if not of more serious injury, and as I pressed towards her, uttered the one word, "Laggard!" with a look and voice of indignant contempt, striking at the same time her horse another light but angry blow over its neck. From her expression as she swept by me, I knew she would much rather have applied the whip to my own shoulders, but had she done so, I would not only have borne it, but spaniel-like have caressed the hand that struck me, for alas! my desperate struggles were but rivetting my chains the more securely, and I felt I was beginning to love Geraldine Otway with a love almost terrible in its intensity. Surely, surely, I was foolish – mad – to remain longer exposed to the fascinations of this temptress. I must leave without delay, leave before yielding to the impulse of some moment of passion, I should utter words of love which would be answered by smiles of ridicule; before laying bare feelings too sacred and secret to be made the jest of a hollow-hearted coquette and her friends.

How she persecuted, lashed, taunted me that evening! More than once I retorted, sharply if not rudely, for my own character was beginning to suffer from the peculiar irritation engendered by mental suffering. Really this girl was trying me in every way beyond my strength! On my pillow, that night, I made up my mind that the next day should be my last at Fairview Villa and that I should tear myself away from the fascinations of this Eden, the memories of which would embitter many a long hour in the dreary future.

With the sunshine of the following morning, Miss Otway's smiles had returned, and as the day was bright but pleasantly cool, Miss Gray proposed a botanizing excursion to the woods, indignantly protesting against baskets of refreshments which would give our expedition the air of a vulgar, every day pic-nic, instead of a scientific exploration. "Papa" Merton quietly smiled at this, and in despite of the warning, some hampers containing the *materiel* of a very dainty lunch, were slipped into the carriage, proving I may as well say before hand, as welcome to Miss Gray as to the rest of our hungry party when luncheon hour came round.

The members of the coming expedition were already standing in groups on the verandah when I joined them, and Miss Otway, radiant in fresh loveliness, and in the coolest and most becoming of morning toilettes, was standing chatting to Miss Gray who, armed with a basket and some tiny garden implement for transplanting, looked as if she intended business.

"Who knows anything about plants, their classes, orders and genera?" inquired Miss Otway.

As she fixed her eyes on me at the conclusion of the sentence, I muttered something about having forgotten Botany since I had left college. The other gentlemen of the party murmured a similar confession.

"Well, as I do not intend that Miss Gray, who is really well versed in it, shall have all the glory of the expedition to herself, I propose we make it a sort of generally scientific thing. Each member shall pursue the study for which he or she has most aptitude, be it geology, mineralogy, botany, so that all may return learned-looking and triumphant. What do you think Mr. Saville?"

"I have forgotten them all," I pleaded. A general and significant cough of acquiescence, each on his own count, again ran round the gentlemen of the circle, when Miss Otway reported:

"I see Mr. Saville is bent on demoralizing our scientific forces, so to punish his indolence and keep him out of mischief, I shall condemn him to hold my specimens. He will at least be able to do that."

Thus enlisted in her train, and only too happy, if the truth be told, for the circumstance, I approached her side, inwardly thinking that as it was my last day (for her smiles and charms had but strengthened my resolve of leaving her) I might take one more sip of the intoxicating happiness I found in her society ere I renounced it for ever.

Started on our way, she turned to me, saying, "Now, every little weed or wild flower you see, gather it so that in such a number we may chance on getting some verdant treasure with which to astonish and delight the real botanists of the party."

Oh, what a walk that was! Loitering among sunshine and flowers – stooping sometimes to gather some plant or fern.

"It is fortunate for me," thought I, "that this is the last day of temptation, or otherwise I should surely make a fool of myself."

"Come, show me the fruits or rather flowers of your industry, Mr. Saville. What! common clover – dandelion – catnip – why, what are you thinking of? If this is a specimen of your abilities, I fear I will never be able to teach you even the little botany I know myself."

I looked steadily, earnestly at her as she stood beside me, smiling up in my face, and then suddenly said, it seemed in spite of myself:

"You have taught me one lesson too many already – one which I only hope I may be able to speedily forget."

I was unprepared for the crimson tide that so abruptly rushed to her face, flushing even the tiny shell-shaped ears showing so daintily from under her little hat, and I was equally unprepared for the suddenness with which her eyes, abashed and half frightened-looking, sought the ground. A long silence followed, I inwardly ruminating on my rashness and resolving on more circumspection; when at length raising her eyes, but still looking away from me, she hesitatingly said in a low tone, very unlike her usual clear ringing accents,

"Explain your words, Mr. Saville."

Ah, Siren! She had brought me to the very verge of a declaration – another moment and I would have been at her feet, almost kissing the hem of her garments, but summoning all my self-command, my manhood's pride to my aid, I replied with a tone of gay politeness that cost me a mighty effort, for I had to bite my lip till the blood almost started.

"You have taught me, Miss Otway, how charming, how irresistible a pretty woman can render herself."

Her face flushed again, but this time angrily and proudly.

"Good!" thought I, finding even in the midst of my own secret suffering, a satisfaction in the pang I had just inflicted on her vanity.

"Diamond cut diamond, wily coquette! You have robbed me of happiness and hope, but not of self-respect. You shall have one *scalp* the less to hang on to your girdle of feminine triumphs."

Another pause, during which I assiduously commenced gathering another handful of the first weeds that came within reach, to replace the former specimens which she had thrown away. As usual, she first broke silence by carelessly asking,

"Are you going to row for Mrs. Merton's silver arrow in the boat race coming off this week?"

"I won't be here, Miss Otway. I am obliged to leave."

"Yes — when?" she calmly asked, as she carefully shook off a little insect resting on a pretty fern, forming part of her collection.

"To-morrow," was my brief rejoinder.

If I had unconsciously calculated on the sudden announcement of my approaching departure producing any impression on her flinty heart, I had good cause to feel woefully disappointed. There was no regret, no emotion exhibited, not even as much interest as she displayed in getting rid of the tiny beetle on which her eyes were fixed. Chatting freely on different topics, expressing much interest in the forthcoming race in which Captain Graham was to ply an oar, accompanied by a carelessly polite regret that I should miss it, as well as a moonlight drive and some other pleasures in contemplation, we hastened our steps and soon rejoined the party, finding Miss Gray severely lecturing some if its members on the nature of the botanical collections they had made.

"The charity-school children might have known better than to have gathered such trash," she indignantly exclaimed, tossing aside bundles of what she sarcastically suggested might be useful to the cook at Fairview Villa as "greens." Lunch was immediately produced, however, and in the welcome prospect thus afforded to all, Miss Gray's denunciations were borne with considerable philosophy. Our return home was very cheerful, the mineralogists of the party amusing themselves by firing their specimens at each other, or at a given mark.

Miss Otway was in excellent spirits, brilliant, witty, playful, a strong contrast to my own self, wrapped up in moody taciturnity, brooding over the woeful thought that on the morrow I should be far away from

212 / Rosanna Leprohon

the enchantress who, despite prudence, reticence, resolve, had called to life so strong a passion in my aching heart.

After our return the ladies sought their rooms to dress for dinner. She (what other woman than Geraldine Otway did I give a thought to now) came down soon in one of the light, transparent, soft-tinted toilets that became her delicate beauty so well, and looking so childishly lighthearted as she fondled and teazed a pretty King Charles given her by Captain Graham, that I was divided between a wish to strangle the dog on one hand, and on the other to curse the day on which I had first met its radiant mistress. After a time Mr. Merton came in with some papers and letters, one of which he handed to Miss Otway. She opened it and then retired into the embrasure of the window to read it at her leisure behind the lace curtains. Restless and wretched, I strolled out on the lawn. Capt. Graham accosted me – I turned shortly from him. Then Miss Merton, but for once she failed to please. Next I encountered my hostess to whom I had not as yet spoken of my intended departure, but I wanted energy to meet and resist the kind entreaties which I knew would be forthcoming to induce me to change my intention.

After a listless half-hour I re-entered the drawing-room, like the moth returning to the flame that had already singed my heart, I suppose I must say, instead of wings. No one was there except Miss Otway, who was still standing near the window, looking absently from it, and mechanically twisting and creasing the corners of the envelope she held in her hand. Approaching her, I made some slight common-place remark which she as indifferently answered, and then suddenly, without word or warning, she burst into tears. Grieved, shocked, I ventured to hope that Miss Otway had received no painful news from her correspondents.

Springing to her feet, she exclaimed:

"Dolt! Don't you know that nine times out of ten a woman cries without cause?"

Ere I could recover from my astonishment, she was gone, whilst I remained rooted dumbly to the spot, not so much by the unprovoked epithet flung at my head with such a wrathful glance, as by the wondering surmise of what had I done to offend her, to call forth such an exhibition of anger.

What a termagant she was, and yet what would I not have given for the privilege of taking that termagant to my heart for life.

I saw no more of her till evening, when returning from a short stroll with my host, in which I had declared my resolve of starting, notwithstanding his hospitable entreaties, the following morning, I noted

Geraldine's slight figure step forth on the verandah. Anxious for a kindly farewell word, for I knew my departure would take place the following morning ere she should have left her couch, I broke off a sprig of ivy twining round one of the pillars of the porch, and approached her.

"May I offer this as a species of olive branch, Miss Otway? I leave tomorrow."

"But we have not quarrelled," she coldly said, drawing back from me.

"Because I would not quarrel with you," I retorted, with considerable bitterness, for the thought of all she was making me suffer in the present, as well as what I would suffer in the future, awoke angry feelings within me. "Provocation on your part was certainly not wanting. Accept, however, my token, and our parting will at least be friendly. Ignorant as I am of botany, I know this leaf signifies friendship. Pray take it?"

"Why should I?" she asked. "It would be even more utterly worthless than the vegetable phenomena which Miss Gray suggested this morning might answer for greens," and with a scornful look she flung my offering away and turned back into the house. Ah, she had had the best of our singular duel, and she was still heart-free, unfettered, able to heap scorn on me which burned like fire into my very soul. Cruel, merciless flirt! Why had destiny ever permitted us to meet?

But we learn to dissemble through life, and as I sauntered round the grounds later that evening, for the glorious beauty of the moonlight tempted us all into the open air, no one would have suspected from my calm cheerful look and easy playful retorts to friendly witticisms, that I had already entered on what I feared would be to me a life-long, absorbing sorrow. Still I yearned for solitude, for quiet, and on seeing Miss Merton step forth from the library on the lawn, I quietly fell back into the shade of the trees to avoid her. My heart was too sore for even her gentle companionship then; and as soon as chance favoured me, I stole up into the room she had just left. It was as I expected, quite deserted, and lit only by the arrowy beams of moonlight that streamed through the half-drawn curtains. It was a welcome haven, and peering about through the semi-obscurity, I saw a small sofa, deep in shadow, on which I seated myself, and which probably had just been vacated by Miss Merton, for her handkerchief, recognizable by her favourite perfume, Mignionette, lay yet upon it. I took it up and inhaled the fragrance its folds gave forth, thinking all the while how feminine was the gentle owner, how different to the mocking Circe on whom I had so idly lavished the treasured love of an honest heart.

Suddenly a light figure entered from the garden and approached my obscure sofa. "Ah! here comes Miss Merton," I thought. "I will give her a surprise."

But the figure quietly seated itself beside me, saying, "I have kept you waiting, Fanny, dear; but I could not get away from that tiresome Graham before;" and the speaker was not Fanny Merton but Geraldine Otway.

And now had I not so exactly and fearlessly told the plain truth up to this present moment, I should feel tempted here to depart from it, and slur over matters a little, for instead of instantly rising, and saying as any honourable high principled man would have done, "Miss Otway, it is Lawrence Saville, not Miss Merton," I treacherously and silently retained my seat, still keeping the handkerchief to my face.

"I promised you, dear friend, to tell you what I was crying for before I should go to bed to-night," she said in a low, sweet tone, which, alas, was almost unknown to me, so rarely had she employed it in my presence.

"It was not the letter as you thought. No, it is because that wretch, Saville, who does not care one farthing for me, is going away tomorrow, and, God help me, Fanny! I dearly love him."

Here a little soft arm stole round my neck, and with a gasping sob she laid her head upon my breast.

Suddenly, involuntarily, I pressed her to my heart with a rapture beyond the power of words to express. Whether the fervour of my embrace awoke her suspicions; or, that her soft cheek had come in contact with my rough bearded one, she suddenly sprang from my side, and in a voice thrilling in its agonized shame and terror, gasped forth,

"For God's sake, who are you?"

In a moment I was at her feet, telling I was one who loved as no man had ever loved her yet, loved her in silence, in hopeless despair, almost from the moment we had first met.

"What! Lawrence Saville?" she whispered.

I renewed my prayers, my vows; but she recoiled from me in horror.

"False, cruel, treacherous!" she faltered. "How dare you allow me to betray myself thus?"

Almost forgetting in my sympathy with the terrible humiliation of that proud though noble nature, my own boundless joy to know myself beloved by her, I still knelt at her feet, imploring her to forgive – to listen to me.

"Begone from my sight, for ever," she passionately exclaimed.

"I believe not in this story of your new-found love, and even if it be true, I shall go down unwedded to my grave before you shall ever place a ring on my finger."

At this moment the door opened, and Mrs. Merton, bearing a waxen taper, entered. Her look of offended amazement on seeing Miss Otway's terrible agitation, and I kneeling at her feet, was indescribable.

"What is it?" she asked. "Tell me, Geraldine, at once."

"He, that man has insulted me," she answered, with death-pale face and glittering eyes.

My hostess turned majestically towards me, and I rose to my feet.

"How dare you, sir," she angrily questioned. "How dare you insult a young lady under my protection – under my roof. It is fortunate that you intend leaving without delay, or I should be under the necessity of saying to you – go. Mr. Saville, I have been terribly deceived in you. You are one of the very last I would have suspected capable of such conduct!"

I listened in silence to all this, for a firm resolution was taken by me in that moment to never give to man or woman explanation of the present scene; and if she chose to leave me open to obloquy and blame, was it not a cheap price to pay for the knowledge that the priceless treasure of her love was mine?

"Leave me, sir, and never let me see you again under my roof," continued Mrs. Merton, waving me imperiously from the room, whilst Miss Otway, turning to still more marble whiteness, leaned against her for support.

Resolving to make my preparations for departure without delay, I proceeded to my own room, but 'ere I had been long there, a slight tap sounded at my door, and opening it, I found it was Captain Graham.

"Mr. Saville," he said. "We are both men of the world, so a few words will suffice. I happened to be in the hall when Miss Otway made her indignant complaint to Mrs. Merton that you had insulted her. Though having no legal right to defend that young lady, she is very dear to me and without waiting for further formalities, I ask at your hands reparation for the insult she alleges having received from you?"

"At your time and hour, Captain Graham," I stiffly replied.

"Well, if I mistake not, you intend leaving for town, early to-morrow, and I will run down the day after. We can then settle everything, as well as invent a cause for our quarrel, for the young lady's name must not be mixed up in it."

I handed him my card with place of residence on it, inwardly thinking he was a manly and spirited, if not successful wooer, and with a formal interchange of bows, we parted.

Then I sat down to think for my brain was almost giddy. I who had never yet been engaged in a duel, even as a second, was now pledged to one with an adversary who was a practical hand; then again, I, a most peaceful, unoffending man by disposition, found myself lying under the grave charge of having grossly insulted a young lady in a house where I was a guest. But what mattered it all? I was beloved by her whom I had so blindly worshipped in secret, and even though she might never consent to look on me again (a thing possible with that wayward, proud spirit) the blissful consciousness that her love was mine, was amply worth all I had suffered or might suffer.

When my parting arrangements were completed, I sat down and wrote to Geraldine Otway a letter such as a man on the brink of parting from life might write to her who was the chief link that bound him to it. There was no mocking smile to dread now, no scornful taunt to fear; and I poured out my whole soul in the letter I was writing. All was earnest between her and I now. I told her, my proud, beautiful darling, how, from the first, I had struggled against loving her, how when affection for her, despite my efforts had crept into my heart, I had striven to tear it thence, never daring to dream it could be returned, but had been foiled, worsted in the combat, succeeding only in hiding my secret, and finding the only sure means of doing that – flight. I went over it all; my struggle with self in the wood the day of the storm; during our ride; our botanical excursions; and then, when my letter was finished, I sealed, pressed it to my lips for her sake, and rose to my feet.

Day was dawning cold and chill; and I resolved to hasten down to the stables and get out my horse myself, but the bridle was not to be found, and the servants were still in bed. Action was necessary to me, and finding the keen sharp air of early morning welcome to my hot cheek and temples, I decided on a stroll down the road. On my return I saw a sleepy stable boy lounging near the gate, and I gave him the requisite directions. Whilst he was attending to them, I scribbled a line to my host containing farewell thanks and excuses for my early departure, mentioning I should send for my luggage the ensuing day. This note I left on the hall table, then with one long yearning look towards the closely curtained window of Miss Otway's room, one wild agonized wish that we might yet meet again, were it only for a moment, I descended the stairs and took my solitary way.

It was hard, too, loving and loved, to part thus, but earth gives only a certain portion of happiness to each of her children, and I had had probably my share, surely an ample one, when leaning her head on my breast she had avowed her love. Would she ever relent later? Well, it did not matter much, for though no coward, I was also no shot, Graham a sure one, so in all probability, my heart so restless and full of throbbing emotions now, would soon be quiet enough. Suddenly, who should confront me emerging from a side alley but Miss Otway herself. Despite the great agitation of the moment, I noticed she looked very ill, and her eyes were swollen as if with weeping.

Almost as much embarrassed as herself, I was silent for a moment and then entreatingly said:

"Miss Otway, dare I hope that your hand will touch mine in friendly greeting before we part? I am leaving now."

"Ah, so you and that tiresome Captain Graham are really running to town to have a quiet shot at each other. What redoubtable Don Quixotes you both are!"

This was said with a very wretched attempt at her usual careless sarcasm, and then suddenly bursting into tears, she covered her face with her hands, whispering:

"Forgive me, Lawrence, forgive me! Your noble letter (I have already stolen and mean to always keep it) has softened at last my icy, selfish heart, and I can bring myself not only to confess to my follies, but also to plead for your pardon."

My darling! Surely the rapture of that moment was worth a life's ransom! Then we walked to a garden seat near us, and with the soft twittering of birds overhead and the glorious hues of sunrise rolling up in the east, bringing morning's pure fragrant breath to us, she entered on her short tale. I have never witnessed a summer sunrise since that memorable morning without recalling with gratitude to the Giver of all Good the happiness its soft dawning once brought me.

"Well, Lawrence, for so I will henceforth call you," she faltered, her charming colour and frequent pauses betraying an agitation that rendered her so feminine, so doubly dear to me, "after you left us last night, I went at once to my room, and throwing myself on a sofa, sobbed and raved alternately at myself and you, till I was almost exhausted. It was so inexpressibly mortifying to have betrayed myself so utterly to you, who had always recoiled from my advances; as to your avowal of love, I looked on it as a fiction, invented at the moment to meet that which I had so openly declared to yourself. After a time reason regained some little sway, and then Mrs. Merton knocked at my door and entered, full of wrath against you and compassion for myself. Oh, Lawrence, it was decreed that you should be an instrument in cruelly humbling my overweening pride, for there, sitting at her feet, my burning face bowed on her motherly lap, I had to do you justice and tell my tale clearly and plainly. Once finished she gently stroked my head and said: "Noble young man, how generously he bore for your sake unmerited obloquy and reproach!" Whilst Mrs. Merton was yet speaking, her quick ear caught the sound of cautious footsteps in the passage. She carefully peered out and saw Capt. Graham enter your room. The circumstance was unusual, for all the household had retired to rest, and divining some mischief, she lay in wait for him, and on his return pounced on and dragged him into the small sitting-room where we often sew and chat on rainy mornings. When smilingly but abruptly interrogated as to his business with yourself, he hesitated and stammered, upon which Mrs. Merton, who immediately began to suspect the true state of things, subjected him to a most searching cross-examination. He was yet blundering through a confused, equivocating reply, through which, however, a portion of truth penetrated, when she called my trembling self in. Again, Lawrence, you were avenged for all I had made you suffer, as I stammered forth a declaration that not only were you entirely guiltless of having insulted me in any manner, but that, I know not how it came out, you were anything but an object of dislike to me. I found some consolation for my own overwhelming mortification in the knowledge of the pang I inflicted at the same time on my luckless admirer whose officiousness had rendered the explanation necessary.

"This hard task over, Mrs. Merton brought me back to my room, and insisted on my lying down, as all danger of a duel between yourself and Captain Graham was now over. But I could not rest. I still feared some rashness on your part, some treachery on his, and I resolved to have an explanation with yourself in the morning before you should leave, a coldly polite one of course, containing a final farewell, something very different to this; so that anything like mischief should be entirely precluded. Worn out with watching, I fell into a doze on the sofa, a little before day-break.

"Awoke by the sound of a door closing, I sprang to the window, and saw you leaving the house. Oh, in that moment, Lawrence, I first realized how dear you were to me, and, trembling with anxiety, I hurried in the direction of your room, the door of which was open, to gather, if possible, some indication of where or for what you had gone so early. This letter (my darling pressed it to her lips as she spoke) was lying on the table. It was addressed to me, and, breaking the seal, I read it. Need I say its generous devotion touched me even to the inmost core of my wayward heart; need I tell you I sobbed and cried over it, fearing you had left me for ever. Ah, my selfish pride was utterly and completely subdued! Suddenly I heard the front gate unclose, and looking out, saw you enter the grounds. No time for delay, for hesitation now, and with a beating heart I hastened down the side staircase. A few moments of irresolution, a last short, sharp struggle with myself, as I saw you hastening away, and the end is told."

It was my turn now, and at the risk of being tedious, I went over all that I had previously said in my letter, and she listened in blushing, quiet happiness. After a long, blissful hour together, my promised wife left me to dress for breakfast, and I, still almost unable to believe in my unhoped for happiness, sat on, listening in a sort of dream-like rapture to the pleasant sounds of morning.

A more prosaical turn was given to my thoughts after a time by seeing Captain Graham coming leisurely down the walk. He certainly did not look so miserable as I expected, but the latent fierceness with which he occasionally decapitated some harmless flower that grew within reach of his tiny cane proved his thoughts were not of a very pleasant character. Scarcely decided how to meet him, I silently waited his approach, but as soon as he saw me, he languidly said:

"Aw! Good morning, Saville. I'm deuced glad there's no necessity for that little affair between us coming off. 'Tis really as unpleasant to shoot at a fellow as to be shot at. Must say I was never in my life so taken aback, indeed, I may say stunned, as when Geraldine, hem! Miss Otway, I should say, informed me in one breath that I was an officious noodle, whom she hated as much as she liked yourself. You are a deuced sly fellow, Saville! Thought all along you were in love with that pretty little Merton girl."

"So I might have been at one time, only her affections were otherwise engaged," I answered, anxious to give my blue eyed friend a "lift."

"Really! To that big shouldered Chester, I suppose. Some women are so fond of giants. Yet no, she'd often cut him confoundedly short when he'd go up to talk to her. Perhaps it is that clever Canadian party who came from town last week, and wrote smart verses in French about her eyes and golden tresses. Wonder if he meant that Japanese switch, as the ladies call it, which she coils round her head?"

"The fact is, Captain Graham, Miss Merton never made me her confidant, but I have a considerable amount of sharpness, hem! where I am not concerned myself," I suddenly added, remembering my own late inveterate blindness in a case somewhat analogous, "and I have only to say that you are no coxcomb."

The significant emphasis, and significant look I favoured my companion with here must have been very eloquent indeed, for all at once opening his sleepy, hazel eyes very wide, his cheek slightly flushing at the same time, he said:

"You don't mean to say that I'm the favoured man?"

I smiled, but maintained a prudent silence.

"Well, I never dreamed of such a thing. I was so taken up with that shrewish, hem! with Miss Otway, I mean. But, say, hadn't you better try to look a little more like a man going to breakfast, and a little less like Speke, Livingston, or any of those other great travellers?"

Thanking him for the really serviceable hint, for my actual equipment was certainly not a proper, breakfast costume where ladies were expected to be present, my beard, owing to mental agitation, having remained unshorn, whilst my portmanteau lay prostrate on the ground a few paces from me, I left him, inwardly hoping that the saying about hearts being easily caught at a rebound, might hold good in his case and that of my fair ally.

Later it really did, and Fanny Merton, long since Mrs. Captain Graham, is still an intimate friend of Geraldine Saville, my well-loved wife.

In justice to the latter I must say before closing this short episode of my life, that Miss Otway showed me more temper and waywardness during the short period I knew her, than Mrs. Saville has done in the course of the sixteen years that have elasped since we joined our destinies together, a step, I may safely aver, neither of us have ever once regretted.

(1870)

John Hunter-Duvar
1830-1899

JOHN HUNTER-DUVAR was born in Scotland and emigrated as a young man to Halifax where he became a lieutenant-colonel in the colonial army. In 1875 he moved to Prince Edward Island where he was an inspector of fisheries from 1879 to 1889. During the last twenty years of his life, Hunter-Duvar published various works of fiction and poetry, and *De Roberval* (1888) a closet drama dealing with the leader of the first French colony in Canada. "D'Anville's Fleet" was published in *The Canadian Monthly and National Review* in 1876.

D'Anville's Fleet

Twas in the month October,
  On an Indian summer day,
That a fleet of foreign war-ships
  Sailed up Chebucto Bay, –
    On the waters of the Basin,
      Scarce heaving there they lay.

The ships seemed old and storm-beat,
  Their canvas was in strips,
The rust of smoke and ocean spray
  Hung on the cannons' lips,   10
    And in the lull, the *fleur-de-lys*
      Hung drooping o'er the ships.

There were but seventeen vessels,
  As our traditions tell,
Of seventy sail that three months since,
  Sailed out of gay Rochelle,
    Yet skilful were the captains,
      And they sailed their vessels well.

221

But fogs uprose, with never a noon,
  For clouds upclomb the heights,
And then would fall, as dark as pall,
  The long Atlantic nights,
      Save for the north wind's harbinger,
      The bright auroral lights.

    20

Whereby from out the nor'-west cloud
  Would storm come on to blow,
And in the wrack tall mast would crack,
  Till, shattered aloft and low,
      The gallant hulls like wearied things
      Lay rocking to and fro.

    30

Four enemies had that struggling fleet, –
  The tempest and the sea,
The English ships and the pestilence, –
  They might have withstood the three,
      But the angel of death sailed with the ships,
      And preyed there silently.

Every day the men grew fewer,
  And each day lost some ships,
For ever and anon came the boom
  From the alarum gun's lips,
      Telling that sail, and sail after sail
      Were hard in the British grips.

    40

They would get a glance of a straggling hull
  As the mist was drifting past,
When out of the fog dashed the English chase
  And had her hard and fast, –
      The Lily of France went down, and up
      Went George's flag on the mast!

Brave men! but yet stout hearts grew faint,
  For whispers dark and vague,
Of spectres such as legends tell
  Beleaguered the walls of Prague,
      Crept man to man, for men knew then
      On board them was *the plague!*

    50

At even-fire the bells were rung,
  To cast to the deep their dead;
At morning gun death's rites begun, –
  The sheet and the weight of lead,
    And all day long the dying groan
    Told another vacant bed.   60

The gunner who fired the sunrise gun,
  With a comrade by his side,
Ere eight bells told the hour of noon,
  Was drifting out on the tide;
    And his comrade ere the day was done
    Was ta'en with the plague and died.

And so from wearisome day to day
  The pestilence walked the decks,
Till hands were so few that scarce a crew
  Could man those floating specks,   70
    And at length, when they lay in Chebucto Bay,
    They were little but death and wrecks.

Of seventy sail of armèd ships
  That were fitted out in June,
But seventeen sail made up the tale, –
  With their Admiral sick, – that noon;
    And there, the shattered hulks, they lay
    In form of a half-moon.

Arrived at last, men glances cast
  At the coast of rock and tree,   80
While thoughts of home came winging fast
  From over the sorrowful sea,
    And the little sailor-boy up on the mast,
    Up on the mast sang he:

"My cousin spinning at her wheel,
  My sister Nanette's tread,
As watches she so kind and leal
  By my sick mother's bed, –
Ah! do they in their evening prayer
  Pray God and Mary for me?   90
    Oh never again! Oh never again!
    My home in Picardie."

Kneeling, the Admiral sadly prayed,
   And sadly himself he crossed:
"My soul to God and my sword to the King,
   And tell him that all is lost.
      Oh weary my life! Oh weary my death!
      Oh weary and tempest-tost!"

Next morn the Admiral's barge of state
   Was rowed adown the Bay,   100
And in it, wrapped in the flag of France,
   The Admiral d'Anville lay,
      And sad the boom of his funeral guns
      Made the heart of the fleet that day.

Then cried the Seigneur d'Estournelle: –
   "Shall I command this host?
Shall *I* go back to gallant France
   And say that all is lost?
      No! weary *my* life, Oh weary my death,
      Oh weary and tempest-tost!"   110

Again the Admiral's barge of state
   Was rowed adown the Bay,
And in it, wrapped in the flag of France,
   Sieur d'Estournelle he lay,
      And sad the sound of his funeral guns
      Made the heart of the fleet that day.

Then spoke the crews among themselves:
   "Is this without remede?
Ho! Scotsman, Sieur de Ramsay,
   St. André be thy speed!   120
      Now that the Admiral's dead and gone,
      You help us in our need!"

Up spake the Sieur de Ramsay:
   "Make ready to advance!
This is the hand of God, my men,
   And not the work of chance;
      And by God's help and St. Denis,
      I'll take this fleet to France!

"Ho! mates, there! beat to quarters, –
  Tell off each man and gun –   130
Fire wrecks! the rest make sailing-trim
  Ere rising of the sun, –
      Who is there fears to follow me?
        Who? Men of France? Not one!"

All night the forges' sparkles flew,
  All night rang hammers' clank,
All night the boat and swift canoe
  Plied to and from the bank, –
      When morning broke the shattered fleet
        Was rearranged in rank.   140

With swelling hearts, yet steady front,
  They turned them to the west;
The pine grove lay in its shadow grey
  Above their comrades' rest,
      And the wrecks, a fleet of fire they lay
        Reddening the water's breast.

(1876)

From
De Roberval

[Niagara]

.... How august are thy works, O God of Might.
...... This masterpiece of Thine Almighty hand
Transcends the range of words..... O, soul of man,
What can'st thou do but wonder and adore.
An ocean poured into a giant chasm
With one majestic sweep of quiet force,
Embodiment of power ineffable,
Resistless beyond utmost stretch of thought,
Too grand to have its features analysed,
Too vast to pick and speculate on parts,   10
But in its whole so dread it numbs the mind,

And merges all sensations into awe,
Visible image of immensity.
This wall of falling waters to the eye
Itself a miracle, but when conjoined
With that incessant slumberous monotone
That causes heart and ear alike to throb,
Addressing ear and eye alike, it reads
The occult riddle, how, in former times,
The very God came down and talked with men.   20
What can the hearer do but reverent say
This is the voice of God. The resonant rocks
And caverns echo it. Above the flume
And all along the stately rocking shore
The agëd forests that, like sentinels
With their gaunt shadows dim and tenebrous
Shut in the world's wonder, echo it,
While leagues away, through all the sylvan shades,
Outborne by the vibrating earth and air,
The cause unseen, the deep-toned murmur sounds   30
Like rolling of the Almighty's chariot wheels.
Nature's grand pæan to that Nature's God,
Throughout the ages an unresting hymn.
No fitful leaping, no impetuous rush,
But stern and slow in solemn majesty,
With the dread calm of the inevitable
And cold serenity of shunless fate;
That ever-falling wall could, effortless,
Submerge a capital, sweep nations' fleets
In splinters to unfathomable depths,   40
Or whirl whole armies of the empires, light
Upon its face as floating thistle-down.
The beauty and the terror of it! The sprays,
In spiral smoke-wreaths, rise in shifting forms,
More than the incense of a thousand fanes,
Until they mingle viewless with the clouds,
While, as reminder of the promise made –
Water should not again destroy the world,
Rainbow tiaras span the dreadful fall,
And through them flash the flung-up water-drops,   50
Making a rain of rainbows. Mystery
That the Creator should this marvel make,

And shut it in with dreadest solitude.
How few the eyes that ere have looked on this,
How far transcendant beyond painter's dream,
Or the most vivid fancy ever poet,
Wrapt in the world of faërie, ever had;
More wondrous even than the visions seen
By the Beloved in the apocalypse,
This wonder of the world – Niagara.   60

(1888)   (1888)

James De Mille
1833-1880

————◆————

BORN IN SAINT John, New Brunswick, James De Mille attended Acadia
College and, following a tour of Europe, enrolled at Brown University,
Rhode Island, where he received his M.A. in 1854. Soon after his
graduation, De Mille opened a bookshop in Saint John; later he taught
classics at Acadia College. From 1864 until his death he was professor
of English at Dalhousie University. One of the most prolific Canadian
writers of his time, De Mille wrote thirty books in fewer than twenty
years. Among his most interesting novels are *The Lady of the Ice* (1870)
and *A Strange Manuscript Found in a Copper Cylinder* (1888).

From
The Lady of the Ice

[Crossing the St. Lawrence]

ON THE FOLLOWING day I found myself compelled to go on some
routine duty cross the river to Point Levy. The weather was the most
abominable of that abominable season. It was winter, and yet not
Winter's self. The old gentleman had lost all that bright and hilarious
nature; all that sparkling and exciting stimulus which he owns and
holds here so joyously in January, February, and even March. He was
decrepit, yet spiteful; a hoary, old, tottering, palsied villain, hurling
curses at all who ventured into his evil presence. One look outside
showed me the full nature of all that was before me, and revealed the
old tyrant in the full power of his malignancy. The air was raw and chill.
There blew a fierce, blighting wind, which brought with it showers of
stinging sleet. The wooden pavements were overspread with a thin
layer of ice, so glassy that walking could only be attempted at extreme
hazard; the houses were incrusted with the same cheerful coating;
and, of all the beastly weather that I had ever seen there had never been
any equal to this. However, there was no escape from it; and so,
wrapping myself up as well as I could, I took a stout stick with a sharp
iron ferrule, and plunged forth into the storm.

On reaching the river, the view was any thing but satisfactory. The wind here was tremendous, and the sleet blew down in long, horizontal lines, every separate particle giving its separate sting, while the accumulated stings amounted to perfect torment. I paused for a while to get a little shelter, and take breath before venturing across.

There were other reasons for pausing. The season was well advanced, and the ice was not considered particularly safe. Many things conspired to give indications of a break-up. The ice on the surface was soft, honey-combed, and crumbling. Near the shore was a channel of open water. Farther out, where the current ran strongest, the ice was heaped up in hillocks and mounds, while in different directions appeared crevices of greater or less width. Looking over that broad surface as well as I could through the driving storm, where not long before I had seen crowds passing and repassing, not a soul was now visible. This might have been owing to the insecurity of the ice; but it might also have been owing to the severity of the weather. Black enough, at any rate, the scene appeared; and I looked forth upon it from my temporary shelter with the certainty that this river before me was a particularly hard road to travel.

"Ye'll no be gangin' ower the day, sewer*ly*?" said a voice near me.

I turned and saw a brawny figure in a reefing-jacket and "sou'-wester." He might have been a sailor, or a scowman, or a hibernating raftsman.

"Why?" said I.

He said nothing, but shook his head with solemn emphasis.

I looked for a few moments longer, and hesitated. Yet there was no remedy for it, bad as it looked. After being ordered forward, I did not like to turn back with an excuse about the weather. Besides, the ice thus far had lasted well. Only the day before, sleds had crossed. There was no reason why I should not cross now. Why should I in particular be doomed to a catastrophe more than any other man? And, finally, was not McGoggin there? Was he not always ready with his warmest welcome? On a stormy day, did he not always keep his water up to the boiling-point, and did not the very best whiskey in Quebec diffuse about his chamber its aromatic odor?

I moved forward. The die was cast.

The channel near the shore was from six to twelve feet in width, filled with floating fragments. Over this I scrambled in safety. As I advanced, I could see that in one day a great change had taken place. The surface-ice was soft and disintegrated, crushing readily under the feet. All around me extended wide pools of water. From beneath these arose occasional groaning sounds – dull, heavy crunches, which seemed to indicate a speedy break-up. The progress of the season, with its thaws and rains, had been gradually weakening the ice; along the shore its hold had in some places at least been relaxed; and the gale of wind that was now blowing was precisely of that description which most frequently sweeps away resistlessly the icy fetters of the river, and sets all the imprisoned waters free. At every step new signs of this approaching break-up became visible. From time to time I encountered gaps in the ice, of a foot or two in width, which did not of themselves amount to much, but which nevertheless served to show plainly the state of things.

My progress was excessively difficult. The walking was laborious on account of the ice itself and the pools through which I had to wade. Then there were frequent gaps, which sometimes could only be traversed by a long detour. Above all, there was the furious sleet, which drove down the river, borne on by the tempest, with a fury and unrelaxing pertinacity that I never saw equalled. However, I managed to toil onward, and at length reached the centre of the river. Here I found a new and more serious obstacle. At this point the ice had divided; and in the channel thus formed there was a vast accumulation of ice-cakes, heaped up one above the other in a long ridge, which extended as far as the eye could reach. There were great gaps in it, however, and to cross it needed so much caution, and so much effort, that I paused for a while, and, setting my back to the wind, looked around to examine the situation.

Wild enough that scene appeared. On one side was my destination, but dimly visible through the storm; on the other rose the dark cliff of Cape Diamond, frowning gloomily over the river, crowned with the citadel where the flag of Old England was streaming straight out at the impulse of the blast, with a stiffness that made it seem as though it had been frozen in the air rigid in that situation. Up the river all was black and gloomy; and the storm which burst from that quarter obscured the view; down the river the prospect was as gloomy, but one thing was plainly visible – a wide, black surface, terminating the gray of the ice, and showing that there at least the break-up had begun, and the river had resumed its sway.

A brief survey showed me all this, and for a moment created a strong desire to go back. Another moment, however, showed that to go forward was quite as wise and as safe. I did not care to traverse again what I had gone over, and the natural reluctance to turn back from the half-way house, joined to the hope of better things for the rest of the way, decided me to go forward.

After some examination, I found a place on which to cross the central channel. It was a point where the heaps of ice seemed at once more easy to the foot, and more secure. At extreme risk, and by violent efforts, I succeeded in crossing, and, on reaching the other side,

I found the ice more promising. Then, hoping that the chief danger had been successfully encountered, I gathered up my energies, and stepped out briskly toward the opposite shore.

It was not without the greatest difficulty and the utmost discomfort that I had come thus far. My clothes were coated with frozen sleet; my hair was a mass of ice; and my boots were filled with water. Wretched as all this was, there was no remedy for it, so I footed it as best I could, trying to console myself by thinking over the peaceful pleasures which were awaiting me at the end of my journey in the chambers of the hospitable McGoggin.

Suddenly, as I walked along, peering with half-closed eyes through the stormy sleet before me, I saw at some distance a dark object approaching. After a time, the object drew nearer, and resolved itself into a sleigh. It came onward toward the centre of the river, which it reached at about a hundred yards below the point where I had crossed. There were two occupants in the sleigh, one crouching low and muffled in wraps; the other the driver, who looked like one of the common *habitans.* Knowing the nature of the river there, and wondering what might bring a sleigh out at such a time, I stopped, and watched them with a vague idea of shouting to them to go back. Their progress thus far from the opposite shore, so far at least as I could judge, made me conclude that the ice on this side must be comparatively good, while my own journey had proved that on the Quebec side it was utterly impossible for a horse to go.

As they reached the channel where the crumbled ice-blocks lay floating, heaped up as I have described, the sleigh stopped, and the driver looked anxiously around. At that very instant there came one of those low, dull, grinding sounds I have already mentioned, but very much louder than any that I had hitherto heard. Deep, angry thuds followed, and crunching sounds, while beneath all there arose a solemn murmur like the "voice of many waters." I felt the ice heave under my feet, and sway in long, slow undulations, and one thought, quick as lightning, flashed horribly into my mind. Instinctively I leaped forward toward my destination, while the ice rolled and heaved beneath me, and the dread sounds grew louder at every step.

Scarcely had I gone a dozen paces when a piercing scream arrested me. I stopped and looked back. For a few moments only had I turned away, yet in that short interval a fearful change had taken place. The long ridge of ice which had been heaped up in the mid-channel had increased to thrice its former height, and the crunching and grinding of the vast masses arose above the roaring of the storm. Far up the river there came a deeper and fuller sound of the same kind, which, brought down by the wind, burst with increasing terrors upon the ear. The ridge of ice was in constant motion, being pressed and heaped up in ever-increasing masses, and, as it heaped itself up, toppling over and falling with a noise like thunder. There could be but one cause for all this, and the fear which had already flashed through my brain was now confirmed to my sight. The ice on which I stood was breaking up!

As all this burst upon my sight, I saw the sleigh. The horse had stopped in front of the ridge of ice in the mid-channel, and was rearing and plunging violently. The driver was lashing furiously and trying to turn the animal, which, frenzied by terror, and maddened by the stinging sleet, refused to obey, and would only rear and kick. Suddenly the ice under the sleigh sank down, and a flood of water rolled over it, followed by an avalanche of ice-blocks which had tumbled from the ridge. With a wild snort of terror, the horse turned, whirling round the sleigh, and with the speed of the wind dashed back toward the shore. As the sleigh came near, I saw the driver upright and trying to regain his command of the horse, and at that instant the other passenger started erect. The cloak fell back. I saw a face pale, overhung with dishevelled hair, and filled with an anguish of fear. But the pallor and the fear could not conceal the exquisite loveliness of that woman-face, which was thus so suddenly revealed in the midst of the storm and in the presence of death; and which now, beautiful beyond all that I had ever dreamed of, arose before my astonished eyes. It was from her that the cry had come but a few moments before. As she passed she saw me, and another cry escaped her. In another moment she was far ahead.

And now I forgot all about the dangers around me, and the lessening chances of an interview with McGoggin. I hurried on, less to secure my own safety than to assist the lady. And thus as I rushed onward I became aware of a new danger which arose darkly between me and the shore. It was a long, black channel, gradually opening itself up, and showing in its gloomy surface a dividing line between me and life. To go back seemed now impossible – to go forward was to meet these black waters.

Toward this gulf the frightened horse ran at headlong speed. Soon he reached the margin of the ice. The water was before him and headed him off. Terrified again at this, he swerved aside, and bounded up the river. The driver pulled frantically at the reins. The lady, who had fallen back again in her seat, was motionless. On went the horse, and, at every successive leap in his mad career, the sleigh swung wildly first to one side and then to the other. At last there occurred a curve in the line of ice, and reaching this the horse turned once more to avoid it. In doing so, the sleigh was swung toward the water. The shafts broke. The harness was torn asunder. The off-runner of the sleigh slid from the ice – it tilted over; the driver jerked at the reins and made a wild leap. In vain. His feet were entangled in the fur robes which dragged him back. A shriek, louder, wilder, and far more fearful than before, rang out through the storm; and the next instant down went the sleigh with its occupants into the water, the driver falling out, while the horse, though free from the sleigh, was yet jerked aside by the reins, and before he could recover himself fell with the rest into the icy stream.

All this seemed to have taken place in an instant. I hurried on, with all my thoughts on this lady who was thus doomed to so sudden and so terrible a fate. I could see the sleigh floating for a time, and the head of the horse, that was swimming. I sprang to a place which seemed to give a chance of assisting them, and looked eagerly to see what had become of the lady. The sleigh drifted steadily along. It was one of that box-shaped kind called *pungs*, which are sometimes made so tight that they can resist the action of water, and float either in crossing a swollen stream, or in case of breaking through the ice. Such boat-like sleighs are not uncommon; and this one was quite buoyant. I could see nothing of the driver. He had probably sunk at once, or had been drawn under the ice. The horse, entangled in the shafts, had regained the ice, and had raised one foreleg to its surface, with which he was making furious struggles to emerge from the water, while snorts of terror escaped him. But where was the lady? I hurried farther up, and, as I approached, I could see something crouched in a heap at the bottom of the floating sleigh. Was it she – or was it only the heap of buffalo-robes? I could not tell.

The sleigh drifted on, and soon I came near enough to see that the bundle had life. I came close to where it floated. It was not more than six yards off, and was drifting steadily nearer. I walked on by the edge of the ice, and shouted. There was no answer. At length I saw a white hand clutching the side of the sleigh. A thrill of exultant hope passed through me. I shouted again and again, but my voice was lost in the roar of the crashing ice and the howling gale. Yet, though my voice had not been heard, I was free from suspense, for I saw that the lady thus far was safe, and I could wait a little longer for the chance of affording her assistance. I walked on, then, in silence, watching the sleigh which continued to float. We travelled thus a long distance – I, and the woman who had thus been so strangely wrecked in so strange a bark. Looking back, I could no longer see any signs of the horse. All this time the sleigh was gradually drifted nearer the edge of the ice on which I walked, until at last it came so near that I reached out my stick, and, catching it with the crooked handle, drew it toward me. The shock, as the sleigh struck against the ice, roused its occupant. She started up, stood upright, stared for a moment at me, and then at the scene around. Then she sprang out, and, clasping her hands, fell upon her knees, and

234 / James De Mille

seemed to mutter words of prayer. Then she rose to her feet, and looked around with a face of horror. There was such an anguish of fear in her face, that I tried to comfort her. But my efforts were useless.

"Oh! there is no hope! The river is breaking up!" she moaned. "They told me it would. How mad I was to try to cross!"

Finding that I could do nothing to quell her fears, I began to think what was best to be done. First of all, I determined to secure the sleigh. It might be the means of saving us, or, if not, it would at any rate do for a place of rest. It was better than the wet ice for the lady. So I proceeded to pull it on the ice. The lady tried to help me, and, after a desperate effort, the heavy pung was dragged from the water upon the frozen surface. I then made her sit in it, and wrapped the furs around her as well as I could.

She submitted without a word. Her white face was turned toward mine; and once or twice she threw upon me, from her dark, expressive eyes, a look of speechless gratitude. I tried to promise safety, and encouraged her as well as I could, and she seemed to make an effort to regain her self-control.

In spite of my efforts at consolation, her despair affected me. I looked all around to see what the chances of escape might be. As I took that survey, I perceived that those chances were indeed small. The first thing that struck me was, that Cape Diamond was far behind the point where I at present stood. While the sleigh had drifted, and I had walked beside it, our progress had been down the river; and since then the ice, which itself had all this time been drifting, had borne us on without ceasing. We were still drifting at the very moment that I looked around. We had also moved farther away from the shore which I wished to reach, and nearer to the Quebec side. When the sleigh had first gone over, there had not been more than twenty yards between the ice and the shore; but now that shore was full two hundred yards away. All this time the fury of the wind, and the torment of the blinding, stinging sleet, had not in the least abated; the grinding and roaring of the ice had increased; the long ridge had heaped itself up to a greater height, and opposite us it towered up in formidable masses.

I thought at one time of entrusting myself with my companion to the sleigh, in the hope of using it as a boat to gain the shore. But I could not believe that it would float with both of us, and, if it would, there were no means of moving or guiding it. Better to remain on the ice than to attempt that. Such a refuge would only do as a last resort. After giving up this idea, I watched to see if there was any chance of drifting back to the shore, but soon saw that there was none. Every moment drew us farther off. Then I thought of a score of desperate undertakings, but all of them were given up almost as soon as they suggested themselves.

All this time the lady had sat in silence – deathly pale, looking around with that same anguish of fear which I had noticed from the first, like one who awaits an inevitable doom. The storm beat about her pitilessly; occasional shudders passed through her; and the dread scene around affected me far less than those eyes of agony, that pallid face, and those tremulous white lips that seemed to murmur prayers. She saw, as well as I, the widening sheet of water between us and the shore on the one side, and on the other the ever-increasing masses of crumbling ice.

At last I suddenly offered to go to Quebec, and bring back help for her. So wild a proposal was in the highest degree impracticable; but I thought that it might lead her to suggest something. As soon as she heard it, she evinced fresh terror.

"Oh, sir!" she moaned, "if you have a human heart, do not leave me! For God's sake, stay a little longer."

"Leave you!" I cried; "never while I have breath. I will stay with you to the last."

But this, instead of reassuring her, merely had the effect of changing her feelings. She grew calmer.

"No," said she, "you must not. I was mad with fear. No – go. You at least can save yourself. Go – fly – leave me!"

"Never!" I repeated. "I only made that proposal – not thinking to save you, but merely supposing that you would feel better at the simple suggestion of something."

"I implore you," she reiterated. "Go – there is yet time. You only risk your life by delay. Don't waste your time on me."

"I could not go if I would," I said, "and I swear I would not go if I could," I cried, impetuously. "I hope you do not take me for any thing else than a gentleman."

"Oh, sir, pardon me. Can you think that? – But you have already risked your life once by waiting to save mine – and, oh, do not risk it by waiting again."

"Madame," said I, "you must not only not say such a thing, but you must not even think it. I am here with you, and, being a gentleman, I am here by your side either for life or death. But come – rouse yourself. Don't give up. I'll save you, or die with you. At the same time, let me assure you that I haven't the remotest idea of dying."

She threw at me, from her eloquent eyes, a look of unutterable gratitude, and said not a word.

I looked at my watch. It was three o'clock. There was no time to lose. The day was passing swiftly, and at this rate evening would come on before one might be aware. The thought of standing idle any longer, while the precious hours were passing, was intolerable. Once more I made a hasty survey, and now, pressed and stimulated by the dire exigencies of the hour, I determined to make an effort toward the Quebec side. On that side, it seemed as though the ice which drifted from the other shore was being packed in an unbroken mass. If so, a way over it might be found to a resolute spirit.

I hastily told my companion my plan. She listened with a faint smile.

"I will do all that I can," said she, and I saw with delight that the mere prospect of doing something had aroused her.

My first act was to push the sleigh with its occupant toward the ice-ridge in the centre of the river. The lady strongly objected, and insisted on getting out and helping me. This I positively forbade. I assured her that my strength was quite sufficient for the undertaking, but that hers was not; and if she would save herself, and me, too, she must husband all her resources and obey implicitly. She submitted under protest, and, as I pushed her along, she murmured the most touching expressions of sympathy and of gratitude. But pushing a sleigh over the smooth ice is no very difficult work, and the load that it contained did not increase the labor in my estimation. Thus we soon approached that long ice-ridge which I have so frequently mentioned. Here I stopped, and began to seek a place which might afford a chance for crossing to the ice-field on the opposite side.

The huge ice-blocks gathered here, where the fields on either side were forced against one another, grinding and breaking up. Each piece was forced up, and, as the grinding process continued, the heap rose higher. At times, the loftiest parts of the ridge toppled over with a tremendous crash, while many other piles seemed about to do the same. To attempt to pass that ridge would be to encounter the greatest peril. In the first place, it would be to invite an avalanche; and then, again, wherever the piles fell, the force of that fall broke the field-ice below, and the water rushed up, making a passage through it quite as hazardous as the former. For a long time I examined without seeing any place which was at all practicable. There was no time, however, to be discouraged; an effort had to be made, and that without delay; so I determined to try for myself, and test one or more places. One place appeared less dangerous than others – a place where a pile of uncommon size had recently fallen. The blocks were of unusual size, and were raised up but a little above the level of the ice on which I stood. These blocks, though swaying slowly up and down, seemed yet to be strong enough for my purpose. I sprang toward the place, and found it practicable. Then I returned to the lady. She was eager to go. Here we had to give up the sleigh, since to transport that also was not to be thought of.

"Now," said I, "is the time for you to exert all your strength."

"I am ready," said she.

"Hurry, then."

At that moment there burst a thundershock. A huge pile farther down had fallen, and bore down the surface-ice. The water rushed boiling and seething upward, and spread far over. There was not a moment to lose. It was now or never; so, snatching her hand, I rushed forward. The water was up to my knees, and sweeping past and whirling back with a furious impetuosity. Through that flood I dragged her, and she followed bravely and quickly. I pulled her up to the first block, then onward to another. Leaping over a third, I had to relinquish her hand for a moment, and then, extending mine once more, I caught hers, and she sprang after me. All these blocks were firm, and our weight did not move their massive forms. One huge piece formed the last stage in our hazardous path. It overlapped the ice on the opposite side. I sprang down, and the next instant the lady was by my side. Thank Heaven! we were over.

Onward then we hurried for our lives, seeking to get as far as possible from that dangerous channel of ice-avalanches and seething waters; and it was not till a safe distance intervened, that I dared to slacken my pace so as to allow my companion to take breath. All this time she had not spoken a word, and had shown a calmness and an energy which contrasted strongly with her previous lethargy and terror.

I saw that the ice in this place was rougher than it had been on the other side. Lumps were upheaved in many places. This was a good sign, for it indicated a close packing in this direction, and less danger of open water, which was the only thing now to be feared. The hope of reaching the shore was now strong within me. That shore, I could perceive, must be some distance below Quebec; but how far I could not tell. I could see the dark outline of the land, but Quebec was now no longer perceptible through the thick storm of sleet.

For a long time, my companion held out nobly, and sustained the rapid progress which I was trying to keep up; but, at length, she began to show evident signs of exhaustion. I saw this with pain, for I was fearful every moment of some new circumstance which might call for fresh exertion from both of us. I would have given any thing to have had the sleigh which we were forced to relinquish. I feared that her strength would fail at the trying moment. The distance before us was yet so great that we seemed to have traversed but little. I insisted on her taking my arm and leaning on me for support, and tried to cheer her by making her look back and see how far we had gone. She tried to smile; but the smile was a failure. In her weakness, she began to feel more sensibly the storm from which she had been sheltered to some extent before she left the sleigh. She cowered under the fierce pelt of the pitiless sleet, and clung to me, trembling and shivering with cold.

On and on we walked. The distance seemed interminable. The lady kept up well, considering her increasing exhaustion, saying nothing whatever; but her quick, short breathing was audible, as she panted with fatigue. I felt every shudder that ran through her delicate frame. And yet I did not dare to stop and give her rest; for, aside from the imminent danger of losing our hope of reaching land, a delay, even to take breath, would only expose her the more surely to the effect of the cold. At last, I stopped for a moment, and drew off my overcoat. This, in spite of her protestations, I forced her to put on. She threatened, at one time, to sit down on the ice and die, rather than do it.

"Very well, madame," said I. "Then, out of a punctilio, you will destroy, not only yourself, but me. Do I deserve this?"

At this, tears started to her eyes. She submitted.

"Oh, sir," she murmured, "what can I say? It's for your sake that I refuse. I will submit. God bless you — who sent you to my help! God forever bless you!"

I said nothing.

On and on!

Then her steps grew feebler — then her weight rested on me more heavily.

On and on!

She staggered, and low moans succeeded to her heavy panting. At last, with a cry of despair, she fell forward.

I caught her in my arms, and held her up.

"Leave me!" she said, in a faint voice. "I cannot walk any farther."

"No; I will wait for a while."

"Oh, leave me! Save yourself! Or go ashore, and bring help!"

"No; I will go ashore with you, or not at all."

She sighed, and clung to me.

After a time, she revived a little, and insisted on going onward. This time she walked for some distance. She did this with a stolid, heavy step, and mechanically, like an automaton moved by machinery. Then she stopped again.

"I am dizzy," said she, faintly.

I made her sit down on the ice, and put myself between her and the wind. That rest did much for her. But I was afraid to let her sit more than five minutes. Her feet were saturated, and, in spite of my overcoat, she was still shivering.

"Come," said I; "if we stay any longer, you will die."

She staggered up. She clung to me, and I dragged her on. Then, again, she stopped.

I now tried a last resort, and gave her some brandy from my flask. I had thought of it often, but did not wish to give this until other things were exhausted; for, though the stimulus is an immediate remedy for weakness, yet on the ice and in the snow the reaction is dangerous to the last degree. The draught revived her wonderfully.

Starting once more, with new life, she was able to traverse a very great distance; and at length, to my delight, the shore began to appear very near. But now the reaction from the stimulant appeared. She sank down without a word; and another draught, and yet another, was needed to infuse some false strength into her. At length, the shore seemed close by us. Here she gave out utterly.

"I can go no farther," she moaned, as she fell straight down heavily and suddenly on the ice.

"Only one more effort," I said, imploringly. "Take some more brandy."

"It is of no use. Leave me! Get help!"

"See – the shore is near. It is not more than a few rods away."

"I cannot."

I supported her in my arms, for she was leaning on her hand, and slowly sinking downward. Once more I pressed the brandy upon her lips, as her head lay on my shoulder. Her eyes were closed. Down on her marble face the wild storm beat savagely; her lips were bloodless, and her teeth were fixed convulsively. It was only by an effort that I could force the brandy into her mouth. Once more, and for the last time, the fiery liquid gave her a momentary strength. She roused herself from the stupor into which she was sinking, and springing to her feet with a wild, spasmodic effort, she ran with outstretched hands toward the shore. For about twenty or thirty paces she ran, and, before I could overtake her, she fell once more.

I raised her up, and again supported her. She could move no farther. I sat by her side for a little while, and looked toward the shore. It was close by us now; but, as I looked, I saw a sight which made any further delay impossible.

Directly in front, and only a few feet away, was a dark chasm lying between us and that shore for which we had been striving so earnestly. It was a fathom wide; and there flowed the dark waters of the river, gloomily, warningly, menacingly! To me, that chasm was nothing; but how could she cross it? Besides, there was no doubt that it was widening every moment.

I started up.

"Wait here for a moment," said I, hurriedly.

I left her half reclining on the ice, and ran hastily up and down the chasm. I could see that my fears were true, the whole body of ice was beginning to break away and drift from this shore also, as it had done from the other. I saw a place not more than five feet wide. Back I rushed to my companion. I seized her, and, lifting her in my arms, without a word, I carried her to that place where the channel was narrowest; and then, without stopping to consider, but impelled by the one fierce desire for safety, I leaped forward, and my feet touched the opposite side.

With a horrible crash, the ice broke beneath me, and I went down. That sound, and the awful sensation of sinking, I shall never forget. But the cake of ice which had given way beneath my feet, though it went down under me, still prevented my sinking rapidly. I flung myself forward, and held up my almost senseless burden as I best could with one arm, while with the other I dug my sharp-pointed stick into the ice and held on for a moment. Then, summoning up my strength, I passed my left arm under my companion, and raised her out of the water upon the ice. My feet seemed sucked by the water underneath the shelf of ice against which I rested; but the iron-pointed stick never slipped, and I succeeded. Then, with a spring, I raised myself up from the water, and clambered out.

My companion had struggled up to her knees, and grasped me feebly, as though to assist me. Then she started to her feet. The horror of sudden death had done this, and had given her a convulsive energy of recoil from a hideous fate. Thus she sprang forward, and ran for some distance. I hastened after her, and, seizing her arm, drew it in mine. But at that moment her short-lived strength failed her, and she sank once more. I looked all around – the shore was only a few yards off. A short distance away was a high, cone-shaped mass of ice, whose white sheen was distinct amid the gloom. I recognized it at once.

"Courage, courage!" I cried. "We are at Montmorency. There is a house not far away. Only one more effort."

She raised her head feebly.

"Do you see it? Montmorency! the ice-cone of the Falls!" I cried, eagerly.

Her head sank back again.

"Look! look! We are saved! we are near houses!"

The only answer was a moan. She sank down lower. I grasped her so as to sustain her, and she lay senseless in my arms.

There was now no more hope of any further exertion from her. Strength and sense had deserted her. There was only one thing to be done.

I took her in my arms, and carried her toward the shore. How I clambered up that steep bank, I do not remember. At any rate, I succeeded in reaching the top, and sank exhausted there, holding my burden under the dark, sighing evergreens.

Rising once more, I raised her up, and made my way to a house. The inmates were kind, and full of sympathy. I committed the lady to their care, and fell exhausted on a settee in front of the huge fireplace.

(1870)   (1870)

William Francis Butler
1838-1910

BORN IN TIPPERARY, Ireland, William Francis Butler first came to Canada as a member of a British army regiment assigned to resist Fenian raids in 1867. Three years later he returned to Canada as an intelligence officer with the expedition sent to put down the Red River Rebellion. After the flight of Louis Riel to the United States, Butler was sent to report on the Hudson's Bay Company's posts on the Saskatchewan River. His account of his experiences in the Red River Settlement and of his journey across northwestern Canada was published as *The Great Lone Land* (1872). A year later he published *The Wild North Land,* a description of his travels in the Lake Athabasca and Peace River districts in 1872.

From
The Great Lone Land

[An Ocean of Grass]

[1870]

EARLY IN THE second week of October I once more drew nigh the hallowed precincts of Fort Garry.

"I am so glad you have returned," said the governor, Mr. Archibald, when I met him on the evening of my arrival, "because I want to ask you if you will undertake a much longer journey than any thing you have yet done. I am going to ask you if you will accept a mission to the Saskatchewan Valley and through the Indian countries of the West. Take a couple of days to think over it, and let me know your decision."

"There is no necessity, sir," I replied, "to consider the matter, I have already made up my mind, and, if necessary, will start in half an hour."

This was on the 10th of October, and winter was already sending his breath over the yellow grass of the prairies.

And now let us turn our glance to this great North-west whither my wandering steps are about to lead me. Fully 900 miles as bird would fly, and 1200 as horse can travel, west of Red River an immense range of mountains, eternally capped with snow, rises in rugged masses from a vast stream-seared plain. They who first beheld these grand guardians of the central prairies named them the Montagnes des Rochers; a fitting title for such vast accumulation of rugged magnificence. From the glaciers and ice valleys of this great range of mountains innumerable streams descend into the plains. For a time they wander, as if heedless of direction, through groves and glades and green spreading declivities; then, assuming greater fixidity of purpose, they gather up many a wandering rill, and start eastward upon a long journey. At length the many detached streams resolve themselves into two great water systems; through hundreds of miles these two rivers pursue their parallel courses, now approaching, now opening out from each other. Suddenly, the southern river bends towards the north, and at a point some 600 miles from the mountains pours its volume of water into the northern channel. Then the united river rolls in vast majestic curves steadily towards the north-east, turns once more towards the south, opens out into a great reed-covered marsh, sweeps on into a large cedar-lined lake, and finally, rolling over a rocky ledge, casts its waters into the northern end of the great Lake Winnipeg, fully 1300 miles from the glacier cradle where it took its birth. This river, which has along it every diversity of hill and vale, meadow-land and forest, treeless plain and fertile hill-side, is called by the wild tribes who dwell along its glorious shores the Kissaskatchewan, or Rapid-flowing River. But this Kissaskatchewan is not the only river which unwaters the great central region lying between Red River and the Rocky Mountains. The Assineboine or Stony River drains the rolling prairie lands 500 miles west from Red River, and many a smaller stream and rushing, bubbling brook carries into its devious channel the waters of that vast country which lies between the American boundary-line and the pine woods of the lower Saskatchewan.

So much for the rivers; and now for the land through which they flow. How shall we picture it? How shall we tell the story of that great, boundless, solitary waste of verdure?

The old, old maps which the navigators of the sixteenth century framed from the discoveries of Cabot and Cartier, of Varrazanno and Hudson, played strange pranks with the geography of the New World. The coast-line, with the estuaries of large rivers, was tolerably accurate; but the centre of America was represented as a vast inland sea whose shores stretched far into the Polar North; a sea through which lay the much-coveted passage to the long-sought treasures of the old realms of Cathay. Well, the geographers of that period erred only in the description of ocean which they placed in the central continent, for an ocean there is, and an ocean through which men seek the treasures of Cathay, even in our own times. But the ocean is one of grass, and the shores are the crests of mountain ranges, and the dark pine forests of sub-Arctic regions. The great ocean itself does not present more infinite variety than does this prairie-ocean of which we speak. In winter, a dazzling surface of purest snow; in early summer, a vast expanse of grass and pale pink roses; in autumn too often a wild sea of raging fire. No ocean of water in the world can vie with its gorgeous sunsets; no solitude can equal the loneliness of a night-shadowed prairie: one feels the stillness, and hears the silence, the wail of the prowling wolf makes the voice of solitude audible, the stars look down through infinite silence upon a silence almost as intense. This ocean has no past — time has been nought to it; and men have come and gone, leaving behind them no track, no vestige, of their presence. Some French writer, speaking of these prairies, has said that the sense of this utter negation of life, this complete absence of history, has struck him with a loneliness oppressive and sometimes terrible in its intensity. Perhaps so; but, for my part, the prairies had nothing terrible in their aspect, nothing oppressive in their loneliness. One saw here the world as it had taken shape and form from the hands of the Creator. Nor did the scene look less beautiful because nature alone tilled the earth, and the unaided sun brought forth the flowers.

(1872)   (1872)

Charles Mair
1838-1927

———◆———

CHARLES MAIR WAS born in Lanark, Upper Canada, and studied at Queen's University. In 1868 he joined in the founding of the "Canada First" movement and in that same year he travelled to the Red River Settlement where he was captured by Louis Riel during the Rebellion of 1869. He later participated in the events of the North-West Rebellion of 1885. Mair published his first collection of lyrics *Dreamland and Other Poems* in 1868, and a blank verse drama, *Tecumseh,* in 1886. The declared purpose of this play was "to depict dramatically the time and scenes in which the great Indian so nobly played his part." The opening acts of the play portray Tecumseh as a victim of American oppression, while the final two acts present him as a hero of the British-Canadian cause in the War of 1812.

From
Tecumseh

Act II, Scene 2*

The portico of GENERAL HARRISON'S *house. An open grove at a little distance in front.*

Curtain rises and discovers GENERAL HARRISON, *army officers and citizens, of various quality, including* TWANG, SLAUGH, GERKIN *and* BLOAT, *seated in the portico. A sergeant and guard of soldiers near by.*
    Enter TECUMSEH *and his followers with* LEFROY *in Indian dress. They all stop at the grove.*

HARRISON. Why halts he there?
Go tell him he is welcome to our house.

An Orderly goes down with message.

---

*Mair's list of dramatis personae identifies General Harrison as the Governor of Indiana Territory, Tecumseh as Chief of the Shawanoes and Lefroy as a British poet-artist enamoured of Indian life.

1ST OFFICER. How grave and decorous they look — "the mien
Of pensive people born in ancient woods."
But look at him! Look at Tecumseh there —
How simple in attire! that eagle plume
Sole ornament, and emblem of his spirit.
And yet, far scanned, there's something in his face
That likes us not. Would we were out of this!

HARRISON. Yes; even at a distance I can see   10
His eyes distilling anger. 'Tis no sign
Of treachery, which ever drapes with smiles
The most perfidious purpose. Our poor strength
Would tail at once should he break out on us;
But let us hope 'tis yet a war of wits
Where firmness may enact the part of force.

                                    Orderly returns.

What answer do you bring?

ORDERLY.   Tecumseh says:
"Houses are built for whites — the red man's house,
Leaf-roofed, and walled with living oak, is there —   20

                         Pointing to the grove.

Let our white brother meet us in it!"

2ND OFFICER.   Oh!
White brother! So he levels to your height,
And strips your office of its dignity.

3RD OFFICER. 'Tis plain he cares not for your dignity,
And touchingly reminds us of our tenets.
Our nation spurns the outward shows of state,
And ceremony dies for lack of service.
Pomp is discrowned, and throned regality
Dissolved away in our new land and laws.   30
Man is the Presence here!

1ST OFFICER.   Well, for my part,
I like not that one in particular.

                    Pointing towards TECUMSEH.

3RD OFFICER. No more do I!   I wish I were a crab,
And had its courtly fashion of advancing.

HARRISON. Best yield to him, the rather that he now
Invites our confidence.   His heavy force
Scants good opinion somewhat, yet I know
There's honour, aye, and kindness in this Chief.

                                    Rising.

3RD OFFICER. Yes, faith, he loves us all, and means to keep   40
Locks of our hair for memory.   Here goes!

All rise.

Servants and soldiers carry chairs and benches to the grove, followed
by GENERAL HARRISON *and others, who seat themselves —* TECUMSEH
and his followers still standing in the lower part of the grove.

HARRISON. We have not met to bury our respect,
Or mar our plea with lack of courtesy.
The Great Chief knows it is his father's wish
That he should sit by him.
TECUMSEH.   My father's wish!
My father is the sun; the earth my mother,

Pointing to each in turn.

And on her mighty bosom I shall rest.

TECUMSEH *and his followers seat themselves on the grass.*

HARRISON. *(Rising.)* I asked Tecumseh to confer with me,
Not in war's hue, but for the ends of peace.   50
Our own intent — witness our presence here,
Unarmed save those few muskets and our swords.
How comes it, then, that he descends on us
With this o'erbearing and untimely strength?
Tecumseh's virtues are the theme of all;
Wisdom and courage, frankness and good faith —
To speak of these things is to think of him!
Yet, as one theft makes men suspect the thief —
Be all his life else spent in honesty —
So does one breach of faithfulness in man   60
Wound all his after deeds. There is a pause
In some men's goodness like the barren time
Of those sweet trees which yield each second year,
Wherein what seems a niggardness in nature
Is but good husbandry for future gifts.
But this tree bears, and bears most treacherous fruit!
Here is a gross infringement of all laws
That shelter men in council, where should sit
No disproportioned force save that of reason —
Our strong dependence still, and argument,   70
Of better consequence than that of arms,
If great Tecumseh should give ear to it.

TECUMSEH. *(Rising.)* You called upon Tecumseh and he came!
You sent your messenger, asked us to bring
Our wide complaint to you – and it is here!

Pointing to his followers.

Why is our brother angry at our force,
Since every man but represents a wrong?
Nay! rather should our force be multiplied!
Fill up your streets and overflow your fields,
And crowd upon the earth for standing room;   .   80
Still would our wrongs outweigh our witnesses,
And scant recital for the lack of tongues.
I know your reason, and its bitter heart,
Its form of justice, clad with promises –
The cloaks of death!   That reason was the snare
Which tripped our ancestors in days of yore –
Who knew not falsehood and so feared it not:
Men who mistook your fathers' vows for truth,
And took them, cold and hungry, to their hearts,
Filled them with food, and shared with them their homes,   90
With such return as might make baseness blush.
What tree e'er bore such treacherous fruit as this?
But let it pass! let wrongs die with the wronged!
The red man's memory is full of graves.
But wrongs live with the living, who are here –
Inheritors of all our fathers' sighs,
And tears, and garments wringing wet with blood.
The injuries which you have done to us
Cry out for remedy, or wide revenge.
Restore the forests you have robbed us of –   110
Our stolen homes and vales of plenteous corn!
Give back the boundaries, which are our lives,
Ere the axe rise! aught else is reasonless.

HARRISON. Tecumseh's passion is a dangerous flood
Which sweeps away his judgment.   Let him lift
His threatened axe to hit defenceless heads!
It cannot mar the body of our right,
Nor graze the even justice of our claim:
These still would live, uncancelled by our death.
Let reason rule us, in whose sober light   120
We read those treaties which offend him thus:

What nation was the first established here,
Settled for centuries, with title sound?
You know that people, the Miami, well.
Long ere the white man tripped his anchors cold,
To cast them by the glowing western isles,
They lived upon these lands in peace, and none
Dared cavil at their claim.   We bought from them,
For such equivalent to largess joined,
That every man was hampered with our goods,   130
And stumbled on profusion.   But give ear!
Jealous lest aught might fail of honesty –
Lest one lean interest or poor shade of right
Should point at us – we made the Kickapoo
And Delaware the sharer of our gifts,
And stretched the arms of bounty over heads
Which held but by Miami sufferance.
But, you! whence came you? and what rights have you?
The Shawanoes are interlopers here –
Witness their name! mere wanderers from the South!   140
Spurned thence by angry Creek and Yamasee –
Now here to stir up strife, and tempt the tribes
To break the seals of faith.   I am surprised
That they should be so led, and more than grieved
Tecumseh has such ingrates at his back.

TECUMSEH. Call you those ingrates who but claim their own,
And owe you nothing but revenge?   Those men
Are here to answer and confront your lies.

                           Turning to his followers.

Miami, Delaware and Kickapoo!
Ye are alleged as signers of those deeds –   150
Those dark and treble treacheries of Fort Wayne.
Ye chiefs, whose cheeks are tanned with battle-smoke,
Stand forward, then, and answer if you did it!

KICKAPOO CHIEF. *(Rising.)* Not I!   I disavow them!
   They were made
By village chiefs whose vanity o'ercame
Their judgment, and their duty to our race.

DELAWARE CHIEF. *(Rising.)* And I reject the treaties in the name
Of all our noted braves and warriors.
They have no weight save with the palsied heads   160
Which dote on friendly compacts in the past.

MIAMI CHIEF. *(Rising.)* And I renounce them also.
    They were signed
By sottish braves – the Long-Knife's tavern chiefs –
Who sell their honour like a pack of fur,
Make favour with the pale-face for his fee,
And caper with the hatchet for his sport.
I am a chief by right of blood, and fling
Your false and flimsy treaties in your face.
I am my nation's head, and own but one   170
As greater than myself, and he is here!

                          Pointing to TECUMSEH.

TECUMSEH. You have your answer, and from those whose
  rights
Stand in your own admission. But from me –
The Shawanoe – the interloper here –
Take the full draught of meaning, and wash down
Their dry and bitter truths. Yes! from the South
My people came – fall'n from their wide estate
Where Altamaha's uncongealing springs
Kept a perpetual summer in their sight,
Sweet with magnolia blooms, and dropping balm,   180
And scented breath of orange and of pine.
And from the East the hunted Delawares came,
Flushed from their coverts and their native streams;
Your old allies, men ever true to you,
Who, resting after long and weary flight,
Are by your bands shot sitting on the ground.

HARRISON. Those men got ample payment for their land,
Full recompense, and just equivalent.

TECUMSEH. They flew from death to light upon it here!
And many a tribe comes pouring from the East,   190
Smitten with fire – their outraged women, maimed,
Screaming in horror o'er their murdered babes,
Whose sinless souls, slashed out by white men's swords,
Whimper in Heaven for revenge.   O God!
'Tis thus the pale-face prays, then cries "Amen"; –
He clamours, and his Maker answers him,
Whilst our Great Spirit sleeps!   Oh, no, no, no –
He does not sleep!   He will avenge our wrongs!
That Christ the white men murdered, and thought dead –
Who, if He died for mankind, died for us –   200
He is alive, and looks from heaven on this!

Oh, we have seen your baseness and your guile;
Our eyes are opened and we know your ways!
No longer shall you hoax us with your pleas,
Or with the serpent's cunning wake distrust,
Range tribe 'gainst tribe – then shoot the remnant down,
And in the red man's empty cabin grin,
And shake with laughter o'er his desolate hearth.
No, we are one! the red men all are one
In colour as in love, in lands and fate!   210

HARRISON. Still, with the voice of wrath Tecumseh speaks,
And not with reason's tongue.

TECUMSEH.   Oh, keep your reason!
It is a thief which steals away our lands.
Your reason is our deadly foe, and writes
The jeering epitaphs for our poor graves.
It is the lying maker of your books,
Wherein our people's vengeance is set down,
But not a word of crimes which led to it.
These are hushed up and hid, whilst all our deeds,   220
Even in self-defence, are marked as wrongs
Heaped on your blameless heads.
                              But to the point!
Just as our brother's Seventeen Council Fires
Unite for self-protection, so do we.
How can you blame us, since your own example
Is but our model and fair precedent?
The Long-Knife's craft has kept our tribes apart,
Nourished dissensions, raised distinctions up,
Forced us to injuries which, soon as done,   230
Are made your vile pretexts for bloody war.
But this is past. Our nations now are one –
Ready to rise in their imbanded strength.
You promised to restore our ravaged lands
On proof that they are ours – that proof is here,
And by the tongues of truth has answered you.
Redeem your sacred pledges, and no more
Our "leaden birds" will sing amongst your corn;
But love will shine on you, and startled peace
Will come again, and build by every hearth.   240
Refuse – and we shall strike you to the ground!
Pour flame and slaughter on your confines wide,

Till the charred earth, up to the cope of Heaven,
Reeks with the smoke of smouldering villages,
And steam of awful fires half quenched with blood.

TWANG. Did you ever hear the like?   If I hed my
shootin'-iron, darn me if I wouldn't draw a bead on that
barkin' savage.   The hungry devil gits under-holts on our
Guvner every time.

SLAUGH. You bet!   I reckon he'd better put a lump o'   250
bacon in his mouth to keep his bilin' sap o' passion down.

BLOAT. That's mor'n I'd do.   This is jest what we git
for allowin' the skulkin' devils to live.   I'd vittle 'em on
lead pills if I was Guvner.

TWANG. That's so!   Our civilizashun is jest this – we
know what's what.   If I hed *my* way –

HARRISON. Silence, you fools!   If you provoke him
here your blood be on your heads.

GERKIN. Right you air, Guvner!   We'll close our
dampers.   260

TECUMSEH. My brother's ears have heard.   Where is
   his tongue?

HARRISON. My honest ears ache in default of reason.
Tecumseh is reputed wise, yet now
His fuming passions from his judgment fly,
Like roving steeds which gallop from the catch,
And kick the air, wasting in wantonness
More strength than in submission.   His threats fall
On fearless ears.   Knows he not of our force,
Which in the East swarms like mosquitoes here?
Our great Kentucky and Virginia fires?   270
Our mounted men and soldier-citizens?
These all have stings – let him beware of them!

TECUMSEH. Who does not know your vaunting citizens!
Well drilled in fraud and disciplined in crime;
But in aught else – as honour, justice, truth –
A rabble, and a base disordered herd.
We know them; and our nations, knit in one,
Will challenge them, should this, our last appeal,
Fall on unheeding ears.   My brother, hearken!
East of Ohio you possess our lands,   280
Thrice greater than your needs, but west of it

We claim them all; then, let us make its flood
A common frontier, and a sacred stream
Of which our nations both may drink in peace.

HARRISON. Absurd!   The treaties of Fort Wayne must stand.
Your village chiefs are heads of civil rule,
Whose powers you seek to centre in yourself,
Or vest in warriors whose trade is blood.
We bought from those, and from your peaceful men –
Your wiser brothers – who had faith in us.   290

TECUMSEH. Poor, ruined brothers, weaned from honest lives!

HARRISON. They knew our wisdom, and preferred to sell
Their cabins, fields, and wilds of unused lands
For rich reserves and ripe annuities.
As for your nations being one like ours –
'Tis false – else would they speak one common tongue.
Nay, more! your own traditions trace you here –
Widespread in lapse of ages through the land –
From o'er the mighty ocean of the West.
What better title have you than ourselves,   300
Who came from o'er the ocean of the East,
And meet with you on free and common ground?
Be reasonable, and let wisdom's words
Displace your passion, and give judgment vent.
Think more of bounty, and talk less of rights –
Our hands are full of gifts, our hearts of love.

TECUMSEH. My brother's love is like the trader's warmth –
O'er with the purchase.   Oh, unhappy lives –
Our gifts which go for yours!   Once we were strong.
Once all this mighty continent was ours,   310
And the Great Spirit made it for our use.
He knew no boundaries, so had we peace
In the vast shelter of His handiwork,
And, happy here, we cared not whence we came.
We brought no evils thence – no treasured hate,
No greed of gold, no quarrels over God;
And so our broils, to narrow issues joined,
Were soon composed, and touched the ground of peace.
Our very ailments, rising from the earth,
And not from any foul abuse in us,   320
Drew back, and let age ripen to death's hand.
Thus flowed our lives until your people came,

Till from the East our matchless misery came!
Since then our tale is crowded with your crimes,
With broken faith, with plunder of reserves —
The sacred remnants of our wide domain —
With tamp'rings, and delirious feasts of fire,
The fruit of your thrice-cursèd stills of death,
Which make our good men bad, our bad men worse,
Ay! blind them till they grope in open day,   330
And stumble into miserable graves.
Oh, it is piteous, for none will hear!
There is no hand to help, no heart to feel,
No tongue to plead for us in all your land.
But every hand aims death, and every heart,
Ulcered with hate, resents our presence here;
And every tongue cries for our children's land
To expiate their crime of being born.
Oh, we have ever yielded in the past,
But we shall yield no more! Those plains are ours!   340
Those forests are our birth-right and our home!
Let not the Long-Knife build one cabin there —
Or fire from it will spread to every roof,
To compass you, and light your souls to death!

HARRISON. Dreams he of closing up our empty plains?
Our mighty forests waiting for the axe?
Our mountain steeps engrailed with iron and gold?
There's no asylumed madness like to this!
Mankind shall have its wide possession here;
And these rough assets of a virgin world   350
Stand for its coming, and await its hand.
The poor of every land shall come to this,
Heart-full of sorrows, and shall lay them down.

LEFROY. *(Springing to his feet.)* The poor!   What care your
   rich thieves for the poor?
Those graspers hate the poor, from whom they spring,
More deeply than they hate this injured race.
Much have they taken from it — let them now
Take this prediction, with the red man's curse!
The time will come when that dread power — the Poor —
Whom, in their greed and pride of wealth, they spurn —   360
Will rise on them, and tear them from their seats;
Drag all their vulgar splendours down, and pluck

Their shallow women from their lawless beds,
Yea, seize their puling and unhealthy babes,
And fling them as foul pavement to the streets.
In all the dreaming of the Universe
There is no darker vision of despairs!

1ST OFFICER. What man is this? 'Tis not an Indian.

HARRISON. Madman, you rave! – you know not what you say.

TECUMSEH. Master of guile, this axe should speak for him!

> *Drawing his hatchet as if to hurl it at* HARRISON.

2ND OFFICER. This man means mischief! Quick! Bring
up the guard!

> GENERAL HARRISON *and officers draw their swords. The warriors
> spring to their feet and cluster about* TECUMSEH, *their eyes fixed
> intently upon* HARRISON, *who stands unmoved.* TWANG *and his
> friends disappear. The soldiers rush forward and take aim, but are
> ordered not to fire.*

(1886)   (1901)

Louis Fréchette
1839-1908

—◆—

BORN AT LEVIS, Lower Canada, Louis Fréchette studied law at Laval University and was admitted to the bar of Lower Canada in 1864. His first volume of poetry, *Mes loisirs*, was published in 1863 and two years later he emigrated to Chicago. After returning to Canada in 1871, Fréchette practised law in Lévis, sat as a Member of Parliament from 1874 to 1878, and published more than a dozen volumes of poetry, stories, essays and plays.

The Discovery of the Mississippi

I

The mighty river slept in the savannahs;
In the dim distance passed the caravan
Of the wild herds of elk and buffalo.
Clothed in the radiance of the morning sun,
The wilderness its virgin splendour spread
      Far as the endless skies.

June glittered! O'er the waters and the grass,
O'er the high places and the secret depths,
Fertile Summer intoned her savage love;
From North to South, from sunset's place to dawn's,   10
All the immense expanse seemed still to hold
      Grandeur of primal days.

Mysterious workings! Rocks with hairless brows,
Pampas and bayous, woods and caverns wild,
All seemed to quiver under a passionate breath;
A stirring in this sad wilderness was felt,
As on the day when hymns of the new-born world
      Throbbed in unending space.

The Nameless, throned in primal might, was there:
Splendid, and freaked with shadow and with light,
Like a huge reptile torpid in the sun,
Old Meschacébé, still untouched by man,
Dispread his shining rings, from bank to bank,
      Down to the southern gulfs.

20

Like a Titan's bandolier slung on the globe,
The mighty river took his limpid way
From where the Bear to where Orion shines,
Bathing both arid plains and orange groves,
And joining in one marvellous nuptial bond
      The Equator and the North.

30

Exulting in the freedom of his waves
And in the mysterious woods which gave him shade,
The King of Waters had not yet laid down
(Wherever he had ta'en his wandering way)
The tribute of his mighty current save
      Before the sun and God!

II

Jolliet! Jolliet! What magic must have struck
Upon thine eyes when thy historic bark
Danced on the gold waves of the unknown stream!
What lordly smile have flowered upon thy lips,
What light of triumph, in that fiery moment,
      Glowed on thy naked brow!

40

Ah, see him there, prophetic and erect,
His face bright with Ambition realized,
His hand outstretched towards the embrownèd west,
Claiming this vast dominion in the name
Of the living God, and of the King of France,
      And of the civilized world!

Then, rocked by the swell and cradled by his dreams,
His ear attuned to the harmonious strand,
Breathing the sharp scent of the fragrant woods,
Skimming green isles and banks of opal sand,
He followed the winding thread of the pale wave,
      The wandering current's course!

50

Seeing him, from a core of floating boughs
Rose, like a concert, songs and murmurings;
Flights of water-birds started from the reeds
And, pointing the way to his fragile canoe,
Fled all before him, etching slender shadows
      In the water's luminous folds;   60

And while he drove along with full-blown sails,
It was as if the distant river-trees
In perfumed arches leaning o'er his path,
Bowed to the hero whose bold energy
Had just inscribed once more our race's name
      In the annals of the soul!

          III
O mighty Meschacébé, silent pilgrim,
Many a time, by starlight, have I come
To sit beside thy sleeping banks, and there,
Alone and dreaming under the mighty elms,   70
Have mused upon the curious forms that rise
      In the mists of evening.

Sometimes I saw, beneath the green arcades,
The cavalcade of fierce De Soto pass,
Offering its solemn challenge to the wastes;
Or 'twas Marquette, far-wandering o'er the plains,
Burning to offer a world to his own native land
      And souls to Almighty God;

Or, in the brushwood, my deceiving eye
Imaged the sparkle of La Salle's own sword;   80
Or a formless group of savage warriors,
Going I know not where, sombre and tragic-eyed,
Before a humble cross – O magic power! –
Passed, bending the knee!

And then, steeping my soul in poet's dreams,
I caught a glimpse, too, of white silhouettes,
Sweet phantoms floating on the waves of night:
Atala, Gabriel, Chactas, Evangeline,
And the shade of René, upright on a hill,
      Weeping immortal woes.   90

And so I put to sleep such memories…
But, amid those bright gleams of poesy,
The one that oftenest came to charm my eye
Was he who passed in a far-off gleam of glory,
That hardy pioneer whom our young history
      Denominates with pride.

IV

Jolliet! Jolliet! Two centuries of conquest,
Two matchless centuries have now gone by
Since the exalted hour when thy strong hand
Inscribed in one stroke on the mappemonde   100
These regions vast, this huge and fertile zone,
      This future granary of mankind!

Two centuries have passed since thy great spirit
Showed us the highway to the blessed land
Which God created with such lavishness:
May it still keep, in the foldings of its gown,
For the outcasts of all nations of the earth
      Both bread and liberty!

Two centuries gone! The virgin solitude
Is now no more! The rising tide of progress   110
Drowns the last signs of an extinguished past.
The city rises where the desert slept;
And the shackled river curves his mighty shoulder
      Beneath granitic spans!

No more the boundless forests: steam is there!
The sun of modern times shines everywhere;
The child of nature has been evangelized;
The peasant's ploughshare cultivates the plain
And the gold surplus of his teeming harvest
      Feeds the effete Old World!   120

v

From the purest sacrifice, the marvellous seed!
Who of us could have dreamed this mighty work,
O Jolliet, and you ingenuous apostles,
God's valiant soldiers without pride or fear,
Who bore the flaming torch of holy truth
      To latitudes unknown?

O humble instruments of Heaven's will,
You were the guide-posts that make easier
The rugged paths humanity must tread...
Glory unto you all! Leaping the gulfs of Time,   130
Your names, ringed by exalted aureoles,
     Shall win immortal fame!

And thou, o'erflowing country of these heroes,
Dear Canada, thou whom I idolize,
I see the share which Heaven has granted thee
In the fulfilment of these mighty works:
O fated land, I view the future and I trust
     In thy new destiny!

(1879)   (1970)

JOHN GLASSCO (TR.)

January

The storm has ceased. The keen and limpid air
Has spread a silver carpet on the stream
Where, on intrepid leg, the skater glides
With shimmering flame upon his iron shoe.

Far from her warm boudoir, a lady braves
Beneath her bearskin robes the biting air;
With a sound of golden bells her rapid sleigh
Flashes like lightning past our dazzled eyes.

And later, through the nights' ideal cold
While thousands of auroras in the sky   10
Flutter their plumage like fantastic birds,

In ambered salons – deity's new shrines –
T'orchestral strains, 'neath sparkling chandeliers,
The gay quadrille unreels its sinuous web!

(1879)   (1970)

JOHN GLASSCO (TR.)

Cap Eternité

It is one block, a crushing weight, whose edge
Looms over the black waves, whose brow
Fixed above the fog can break or cow
The storm's wing, the gulf's hurled sledge.

Great slab, colossal rock, whose menacing
Ribbed side shrugs off bomb and cannon ball,
Rising in one sweep into the skies, to fall
Sheer to its dark, unfathomed mortising!

What caprice has raised this wall of braille?
Caprice! Who knows? Rash would he be to rail   10
At the blind workings of fecundity!

The mass sustains a million flowers and bracts;
Whole flocks of swallows nest within the cracks;
And own, yes, this brute has his paternity!

(1879)   (1977)

D.G. JONES (TR.)

Edward William Thomson
1849-1924

———◆———

BORN IN PEEL County, Canada West, Edward William Thomson enlisted in the Union Army during the American Civil War and served in
the Queen's Own Rifles during the Fenian Raids of 1866. From 1879 to
1891 he was an editorial writer for the Toronto *Globe* and in 1891 he
became the editor of *The Youth's Companion* of Boston. He returned to
Canada in 1902 and settled in Ottawa. Although Thomson published
three volumes of poetry, his literary reputation is based on collections
of short stories such as *Old Man Savarin and Other Stories* (1895).

Privilege of the Limits

"YES, INDEED, MY grandfather wass once in jail," said old Mrs.
McTavish, of the county of Glengarry, in Ontario, Canada; "but that
wass for debt, and he wass a ferry honest man whateffer, and he would
not broke his promise – no, not for all the money in Canada. If you will
listen to me, I will tell chust exactly the true story about the debt, to
show you what an honest man my grandfather wass.

"One time Tougal Stewart, him that wass the poy's grandfather that
keeps the same store in Cornwall to this day, sold a plough to my
grandfather, and my grandfather said he would pay half the plough in
October, and the other half whateffer time he felt able to pay the
money. Yes, indeed, that was the very promise my grandfather gave.

"So he was at Tougal Stewart's store on the first of October early in
the morning pefore the shutters wass taken off, and he paid half chust
exactly to keep his word. Then the crop wass ferry pad next year, and
the year after that one of his horses wass killed py lightning, and the
next year his brother, that wass not rich and had a big family, died, and
do you think wass my grandfather to let the family be disgraced
without a good funeral? No, indeed. So my grandfather paid for the
funeral, and there was at it plenty of meat and drink for eferypody, as
wass the right Hielan' custom those days; and after the funeral my
grandfather did not feel chust exactly able to pay the other half for the
plough that year either.

"So, then, Tougal Stewart met my grandfather in Cornwall next day after the funeral, and asked him if he had some money to spare.

" 'Wass you in need of help, Mr. Stewart?' says my grandfather, kindly. 'For if it's in any want you are, Tougal,' says my grandfather, 'I will sell the coat off my back, if there is no other way to lend you a loan'; for that wass always the way of my grandfather with all his friends, and a bigger-hearted man there never wass in all Glengarry, or in Stormont, or in Dundas, moreofer.

" 'In want!' says Tougal – 'in want, Mr. McTavish!' says he, very high. 'Would you wish to insult a gentleman, and him of the name of Stewart, that's the name of princes of the world?' he said, so he did.

"Seeing Tougal had his temper up, my grandfather spoke softly, being a quiet, peaceable man, and in wonder what he had said to offend Tougal.

" 'Mr. Stewart,' says my grandfather, 'it wass not in my mind to anger you whatefer. Only I thought, from your asking me if I had some money, that you might be looking for a wee bit of a loan, as many a gentleman has to do at times, and no shame to him at all,' said my grandfather.

" 'A loan?' says Tougal, sneering. 'A loan, is it? Where's your memory, Mr. McTavish? Are you not owing me half the price of the plough you've had these three years?'

" 'And wass you asking me for money for the other half of the plough?' says my grandfather, very astonished.

" 'Just that,' says Tougal.

" 'Have you no shame or honor in you?' says my grandfather, firing up. 'How could I feel able to pay that now, and me chust yesterday been giving my poor brother a funeral fit for the McTavishes' own grand-nephew, that wass as good chentleman's plood as any Stewart in Glengarry. You saw the expense I wass at, for there you wass, and I thank you for the politeness of coming, Mr. Stewart,' says my grandfather, ending mild, for the anger would never stay in him more than a minute, so kind was the nature he had.

" 'If you can spend money on a funeral like that, you can pay me for my plough,' says Stewart; for with buying and selling he wass become a poor creature, and the heart of a Hielan'man wass half gone out of him, for all he wass so proud of his name of monarchs and kings.

"My grandfather had a mind to strike him down on the spot, so he often said; but he thought of the time when he hit Hamish Cochrane in anger, and he minded the penances the priest put on him for breaking the silly man's jaw with that blow, so he smothered the heat that wass in him, and turned away in scorn. With that Tougal Stewart went to court, and sued my grandfather, puir mean creature.

"You might think that Judge Jones – him that wass judge in Cornwall before Judge Jarvis that's dead – would do justice. But no, he made it the law that my grandfather must pay at once, though Tougal Stewart could not deny what the bargain wass.

" 'Your Honor,' says my grandfather, 'I said I'd pay when I felt able. And do I feel able now? No, I do not,' says he. 'It's a disgrace to Tougal Stewart to ask me, and himself telling you what the bargain wass,' said my grandfather. But Judge Jones said that he must pay, for all that he did not feel able.

" 'I will nefer pay one copper till I feel able,' says my grandfather; 'but I'll keep my Hielan' promise to my dying day, as I always done,' says he.

"And with that the old judge laughed, and said he would have to give judgment. And so he did; and after that Tougal Stewart got out an execution. But not the worth of a handful of oatmeal could the bailiff lay hands on, because my grandfather had chust exactly taken the precaution to give a bill of sale on his gear to his neighbor, Alexander Frazer, that could be trusted to do what was right after the law play was over.

"The whole settlement had great contempt for Tougal Stewart's conduct; but he wass a headstrong body, and once he begun to do wrong against my grandfather, he held on, for all that his trade fell away; and finally he had my grandfather arrested for debt, though you'll understand, sir, that he was owing Stewart nothing that he ought to pay when he didn't feel able.

"In those times prisoners for debt wass taken to jail in Cornwall, and if they had friends to give bail that they would not go beyond the posts that wass around the sixteen acres nearest the jail walls, the prisoners could go where they liked on that ground. This was called 'the privilege of the limits.' The limits, you'll understand, wass marked by cedar posts painted white about the size of hitching-posts.

"The whole settlement wass ready to go bail for my grandfather if he wanted it, and for the health of him he needed to be in the open air, and so he gave Tuncan Macdonnell of the Greenfields, and Æneas Macdonald of the Sandfields, for his bail, and he promised, on his Hielan' word of honor, not to go beyond the posts. With that he went where he pleased, only taking care that he never put even the toe of his foot beyond a post, for all that some prisoners of the limits would chump ofer them and back again, or maybe swing round them, holding by their hands.

"Efery day the neighbors would go into Cornwall to give my grandfather the good word, and they would offer to pay Tougal Stewart for the other half of the plough, only that vexed my grandfather, for he wass too proud to borrow, and, of course, efery day he felt less and less able to pay on account of him having to hire a man to be doing the spring ploughing and seeding and making the kale-yard.

"All this time, you'll mind, Tougall Stewart had to pay five shillings a week for my grandfather's keep, the law being so that if the debtor swore he had not five pounds' worth of property to his name, then the creditor had to pay the five shillings, and, of course, my grandfather had nothing to his name after he gave the bill of sale to Alexander Frazer. A great diversion it was to my grandfather to be reckoning up that if he lived as long as his father, that was hale and strong at ninety-six, Tougal would need to pay five or six hundred pounds for him, and there was only two pound five shillings to be paid on the plough.

"So it was like that all summer, my grandfather keeping heartsome, with the neighbors coming in so steady to bring him the news of the settlement. There he would sit, just inside one of the posts, for to pass his jokes, and tell what he wished the family to be doing next. This way it might have kept going on for forty years, only it came about that my grandfather's youngest child – him that was my father – fell sick, and seemed like to die.

"Well, when my grandfather heard that bad news, he wass in a terrible way, to be sure, for he would be longing to hold the child in his arms, so that his heart was sore and like to break. Eat he could not, sleep he could not: all night he would be groaning, and all day he would be walking around by the posts, wishing that he had not passed his Hielan' word of honor not to go beyond a post; for he thought how he could have broken out like a chentleman, and gone to see his sick child, if he had stayed inside the jail wall. So it went on three days and three nights pefore the wise thought came into my grandfather's head to show him how he need not go beyond the posts to see his little sick poy. With that he went straight to one of the white cedar posts, and pulled it up out of the hole, and started for home, taking great care to carry it in his hands pefore him, so he would not be beyond it one bit.

"My grandfather wass not half a mile out of Cornwall, which was only a little place in those days, when two of the turnkeys came after him.

" 'Stop, Mr. McTavish,' says the turnkeys.

" 'What for would I stop?' says my grandfather.

" 'You have broke your bail,' says they.

" 'It's a lie for you,' says my grandfather, for his temper flared up for anybody to say he would broke his bail. 'Am I beyond the post?' says my grandfather.

"With that they run in on him, only that he knocked the two of them over with the post, and went on rejoicing, like an honest man should, at keeping his word and overcoming them that would slander his good name. The only thing pesides thoughts of the child that troubled him was questioning whether he had been strictly right in turning round for to use the post to defend himself in such a way that it was nearer the jail than what he wass. But when he remembered how the jailer never complained of prisoners of the limits chumping ofer the posts, if so they chumped back again in a moment, the trouble went out of his mind.

"Pretty soon after that he met Tuncan Macdonnell of Greenfields, coming into Cornwall with the wagon.

" 'And how is this, Glengatchie?' says Tuncan. 'For you were never the man to broke your bail.'

"Glengatchie, you'll understand, sir, is the name of my grandfather's farm.

" 'Never fear, Greenfields,' says my grandfather, 'for I'm not beyond the post,'

"So Greenfields looked at the post, and he looked at my grandfather, and he scratched his head a wee, and he seen it was so; and then he fell into a great admiration entirely.

" 'Get in with me, Glengatchie – it's proud I'll be to carry you home'; and he turned his team around. My grandfather did so, taking great care to keep the post in front of him all the time; and that way he reached home. Out comes my grandmother running to embrace him; but she had to throw her arms around the post and my grandfather's neck at the same time, he was that strict to be within his promise. Pefore going ben the house, he went to the back end of the kale-yard which was farthest from the jail, and there he stuck the post; and then he went back to see his sick child, while all the neighbors that came round was glad to see what a wise thought the saints had put into his mind to save his bail and his promise.

"So there he stayed a week till my father got well. Of course the constables came after my grandfather, but the settlement would not let the creatures come within a mile of Glengatchie. You might think, sir, that my grandfather would have stayed with his wife and weans, seeing the post was all the time in the kale-yard, and him careful not to go beyond it; but he was putting the settlement to a great deal of trouble day and night to keep the constables off, and he was fearful that they might take the post away, if ever they got to Glengatchie, and give him the name of false, that no McTavish ever had. So Tuncan Greenfields and Æneas Sandfield drove my grandfather back to the jail, him with the post behind him in the wagon, so as he would be between it and the jail. Of course Tougal Stewart tried his best to have the bail declared forfeited; but old Judge Jones only laughed, and said my grandfather was a Hielan' gentleman, with a very nice sense of honor, and that was chust exactly the truth.

"How did my grandfather get free in the end? Oh, then, that was because of Tougal Stewart being careless – him that thought he knew so much of the law. The law was, you will mind, that Tougal had to pay five shillings a week for keeping my grandfather in the limits. The money wass to be paid efery Monday, and it wass to be paid in lawful money of Canada, too. Well, would you belief that Tougal paid in four shillings in silver one Monday, and one shilling in coppers, for he took up the collection in church the day pefore, and it wass not till Tougal had gone away that the jailer saw that one of the coppers was a Brock copper, – a medal, you will understand, made at General Brock's death, and not lawful money of Canada at all. With that the jailer came out to my grandfather.

" 'Mr. McTavish,' says he, taking off his hat, 'you are a free man, and I'm glad of it.' Then he told him what Tougal had done.

" 'I hope you will not have any hard feelings toward me, Mr. McTavish,' said the jailer; and a decent man he wass, for all that there wass not a drop of Hielan' blood in him. 'I hope you will not think hard of me for not being hospitable to you, sir,' says he; 'but it's against the rules and regulations for the jailer to be offering the best he can command to the prisoners. Now that you are free, Mr. McTavish,' says the jailer, 'I would be a proud man if Mr. McTavish of Glengatchie would do me the honor of taking supper with me this night. I will be asking your leave to invite some of the gentlemen of the place, if you will say the word, Mr. McTavish,' says he.

"Well, my grandfather could never bear malice, the kind man he was, and he seen how bad the jailer felt, so he consented, and a great company came in, to be sure, to celebrate the occasion.

"Did my grandfather pay the balance on the plough? What for should you suspicion, sir, that my grandfather would refuse his honest debt? Of course he paid for the plough, for the crop was good that fall.

" 'I would be paying you the other half of the plough now, Mr. Stewart,' says my grandfather, coming in when the store was full.

" 'Hoich, but YOU are the honest McTavish!' says Tougal, sneering.

"But my grandfather made no answer to the creature, for he thought it would be unkind to mention how Tougal had paid out six pounds four shillings and eleven pence to keep him in on account of a debt of two pound five that never was due till it was paid."

(1895)   (1895)

Isabella Valancy Crawford
1850-1887

———◆———

BORN IN DUBLIN, Ireland, Isabella Valancy Crawford emigrated with
her family to Paisley, Canada West, in 1858. After practising medicine
there for several years, her father moved his family to Lakefield and
then to Peterborough. When he died in 1875, Crawford settled in
Toronto and attempted to earn a living from the sale of her poems,
short stories and novels. Her single book of verse, *Old Spookses' Pass,
Malcolm's Katie, and Other Poems* (1884), was printed in Toronto at her
own expense. Crawford's *Collected Poems* was published posthumously
in 1905.

Malcolm's Katie: A Love Story

PART I.

Max placed a ring on little Katie's hand,
A silver ring that he had beaten out
From that same sacred coin — first well prized wage
For boyish labour, kept thro' many years.
"See, Kate," he said, "I had no skill to shape
Two hearts fast bound together, so I graved
Just 'K' and 'M,' for Katie and for Max."

"But look! you've run the lines in such a way
That 'M' is part of 'K,' and 'K' of 'M,'"
Said Katie, smiling. "Did you mean it thus?   10
I like it better than the double hearts."

"Well, well," he said, "but womankind is wise!
Yet tell me, dear, will such a prophecy
Not hurt you sometimes when I am away?
Will you not seek, keen-eyed, for some small break

In those deep lines to part the 'K' and 'M'
For you? Nay, Kate, look down amid the globes
Of those large lilies that our light canoe
Divides, and see within the polished pool
That small rose face of yours, so dear, so fair, —   20
A seed of love to cleave into a rock
And bourgeon thence until the granite splits
Before its subtle strength. I being gone –
Poor soldier of the axe – to bloodless fields
(Inglorious battles, whether lost or won),
That sixteen-summered heart of yours may say:
'I but was budding, and I did not know
My core was crimson and my perfume sweet;
I had not seen the sun, and blind I swayed
To a strong wind, and thought because I swayed   30
'Twas to the wooer of the perfect rose –
That strong, wild wind has swept beyond my ken,
The breeze I love sighs thro' my ruddy leaves.'"

"O words!" said Katie, blushing, "only words!
You build them up that I may push them down.
If hearts are flowers, I know that flowers can root,
Bud, blossom, die – all in the same loved soil.
They do so in my garden. I have made
Your heart my garden. If I am a bud
And only feel unfoldment feebly stir   40
Within my leaves, wait patiently; some June
I'll blush a full-blown rose, and queen it, dear,
In your loved garden. Tho' I be a bud,
My roots strike deep, and torn from that dear soil
Would shriek like mandrakes – those witch things I read
Of in your quaint old books. Are you content?"

"Yes, crescent-wise, but not to round, full moon.
Look at yon hill that rounds so gently up
From the wide lake; a lover king it looks,
In cloth of gold, gone from his bride and queen,   50
And yet delayed because her silver locks
Catch in his gilded fringe. His shoulders sweep
Into blue distance, and his gracious crest,
Not held too high is plumed with maple groves –
One of your father's farms: a mighty man,
Self-hewn from rock, remaining rock through all."

"He loves me, Max," said Katie.

         "Yes, I know –
A rock is cup to many a crystal spring.
Well, he is rich; those misty, peak-roofed barns –
Leviathans rising from red seas of grain –   60
Are full of ingots shaped like grains of wheat.
His flocks have golden fleeces, and his herds
Have monarchs worshipful as was the calf
Aaron called from the furnace; and his ploughs,
Like Genii chained, snort o'er his mighty fields.
He has a voice in Council and in Church – "

"He worked for all," said Katie, somewhat pained.

"Ay, so, dear love, he did. I heard him tell
How the first field upon his farm was ploughed.
He and his brother Reuben, stalwart lads,   70
Yoked themselves, side by side, to the new plough;
Their weaker father, in the grey of life –
But rather the wan age of poverty
Than many winters – in large, gnarlèd hands
The plunging handles held; with mighty strains
They drew the ripping beak through knotted sod,
Thro' tortuous lanes of blackened, smoking stumps,
And past great flaming brush-heaps, sending out
Fierce summers, beating on their swollen brows.
O such a battle! had we heard of serfs   80
Driven to like hot conflict with the soil,
Armies had marched and navies swiftly sailed
To burst their gyves. But here's the little point –
The polished-diamond pivot on which spins
The wheel of difference – they OWNED the soil,
And fought for love – dear love of wealth and power –
And honest ease and fair esteem of men.
One's blood heats at it!"

         "Yet you said such fields
Were all inglorious," Katie, wondering, said.   90

"Inglorious? Yes! They make no promises
Of Star or Garter, or the thundering guns
That tell the earth her warriors are dead.

Inglorious? Ay, the battle done and won
Means not a throne propped up with bleaching bones,
A country saved with smoking seas of blood,
A flag torn from the foe with wounds and death,
Or Commerce, with her housewife foot upon
Colossal bridge of slaughtered savages,
The Cross laid on her brawny shoulder, and   100
In one sly, mighty hand her reeking sword,
And in the other all the woven cheats
From her dishonest looms. Nay, none of these.
It means — four walls, perhaps a lowly roof;
Kine in a peaceful posture; modest fields;
A man and woman standing hand in hand
In hale old age, who, looking o'er the land,
Say, 'Thank the Lord, it all is mine and thine!'
It means, to such thewed warriors of the Axe
As your own father — well, it means, sweet Kate,   110
Outspreading circles of increasing gold,
A name of weight, one little daughter heir
Who must not wed the owner of an axe,
Who owns naught else but some dim, dusky woods
In a far land, two arms indifferent strong, — "

"And Katie's heart," said Katie, with a smile; —
For yet she stood on that smooth violet plain
Where nothing shades the sun; nor quite believed
Those blue peaks closing in were aught but mist
Which the gay sun could scatter with a glance.   120
For Max, he late had touched their stones, but yet
He saw them seamed with gold and precious ores,
Rich with hill flowers and musical with rills, —
"Or that same bud that will be Katie's heart
Against the time your deep, dim woods are cleared,
And I have wrought my father to relent."

"How will you move him, sweet? Why, he will rage
And fume and anger, striding o'er his fields,
Until the last bought king of herds lets down
His lordly front and, rumbling thunder from   130
His polished chest, returns his chiding tones.
How will you move him, Katie, tell me how?"

"I'll kiss him and keep still; that way is sure,"
Said Katie, smiling; "I have often tried."

"God speed the kiss," said Max, and Katie sighed,
  With prayerful palms close sealed, "God speed the axe!"

> O light canoe, where dost thou glide?
> Below thee gleams no silvered tide,
> But concave heaven's chiefest pride.

> Above thee burns Eve's rosy bar;   140
> Below thee throbs her darling star;
> Deep 'neath thy keel her round worlds are.

> Above, below – O sweet surprise
> To gladden happy lover's eyes!
> No earth, no wave – all jewelled skies.

PART II.

The South Wind laid his moccasins aside,
Broke his gay calumet of flowers, and cast
His useless wampum, beaded with cool dews,
Far from him northward; his long, ruddy spear
Flung sunward, whence it came, and his soft locks
Of warm, fine haze grew silvery as the birch.
His wigwam of green leaves began to shake;
The crackling rice-beds scolded harsh like squaws;
The small ponds pouted up their silver lips;
The great lakes eyed the mountains, whispered "Ugh!   10
Are ye so tall, O chiefs? Not taller than
Our plumes can reach," and rose a little way,
As panthers stretch to try their velvet limbs
And then retreat to purr and bide their time.

At morn the sharp breath of the night arose
From the wide prairies, in deep-struggling seas,
In rolling breakers, bursting to the sky;
In tumbling surfs, all yellowed faintly thro'
With the low sun; in mad, conflicting crests,
Voiced with low thunder from the hairy throats   20
Of the mist-buried herds. And for a man
To stand amid the cloudy roll and moil,
The phantom waters breaking overhead,
Shades of vexed billows bursting on his breast,
Torn caves of mist walled with a sudden gold –
Resealed as swift as seen – broad, shaggy fronts,

Fire-eyed, and tossing on impatient horns
The wave impalpable – was but to think
A dream of phantoms held him as he stood.
The late, last thunders of the summer crashed   30
Where shrieked great eagles, lords of naked cliffs.

The pulseless forest, locked and interlocked
So closely bough with bough and leaf with leaf,
So serfed by its own wealth, that while from high
The moons of summer kissed its green-glossed locks,
And round its knees the merry West Wind danced,
And round its ring, compacted emerald,
The South Wind crept on moccasins of flame,
And the red fingers of th' impatient Sun
Plucked at its outmost fringes, its dim veins   40
Beat with no life, its deep and dusky heart
In a deep trance of shadow felt no throb
To such soft wooing answer. Thro' its dream
Brown rivers of deep waters sunless stole;
Small creeks sprang from its mosses, and, amazed,
Like children in a wigwam curtained close
Above the great, dead heart of some red chief,
Slipped on soft feet, swift stealing through the gloom,
Eager for light and for the frolic winds.

In this shrill moon the scouts of Winter ran   50
From the ice-belted north, and whistling shafts
Struck maple and struck sumach and a blaze
Ran swift from leaf to leaf, from bough to bough,
Till round the forest flashed a belt of flame,
And inward licked its tongues of red and gold
To the deep-crannied inmost heart of all.
Roused the still heart – but all too late, too late!
Too late the branches, welded fast with leaves,
Tossed, loosened, to the winds; too late the Sun
Poured his last vigour to the deep, dark cells   60
Of the dim wood. The keen two-bladed Moon
Of Falling Leaves rolled up on crested mists,
And where the lush, rank boughs had foiled the Sun
In his red prime, her pale, sharp fingers crept
After the wind and felt about the moss,
And seemed to pluck from shrinking twig and stem
The burning leaves, while groaned the shuddering wood.

Who journeyed where the prairies made a pause
Saw burnished ramparts flaming in the sun
With beacon fires, tall on their rustling walls.   70
And when the vast horned herds at sunset drew
Their sullen masses into one black cloud,
Rolling thundrous o'er the quick pulsating plain,
They seemed to sweep between two fierce, red suns
Which, hunter-wise, shot at their glaring balls
Keen shafts with scarlet feathers and gold barbs.

By round, small lakes with thinner forests fringed —
More jocund woods that sung about the feet
And crept along the shoulders of great cliffs —
The warrior stags, with does and tripping fawns,   80
Like shadows black upon the throbbing mist
Of evening's rose, flashed thro' the singing woods,
Nor tim'rous sniffed the spicy cone-breathed air;
For never had the patriarch of the herd
Seen, limned against the farthest rim of light
Of the low-dipping sky, the plume or bow
Of the red hunter; nor, when stooped to drink,
Had from the rustling rice-bed heard the shaft
Of the still hunter hidden in its spears —
His bark canoe close knotted in its bronze,   90
His form as stirless as the brooding air,
His dusky eyes two fixed, unwinking fires,
His bow-string tightened, till it subtly sang
To the long throbs and leaping pulse that rolled
And beat within his knotted, naked breast.

There came a morn the Moon of Falling Leaves
With her twin silver blades had only hung
Above the low set cedars of the swamp
For one brief quarter, when the Sun arose
Lusty with light and full of summer heat,   100
And, pointing with his arrows at the blue
Closed wigwam curtains of the sleeping Moon,
Laughed with the noise of arching cataracts,
And with the dove-like cooing of the woods,
And with the shrill cry of the diving loon,
And with the wash of saltless rounded seas,
And mocked the white Moon of the Falling Leaves:

"Esa! esa! shame upon you, Pale Face!
Shame upon you, Moon of Evil Witches!
Have you killed the happy, laughing Summer?   110
Have you slain the mother of the flowers
With your icy spells of might and magic?
Have you laid her dead within my arms?
Wrapped her, mocking, in a rainbow blanket?
Drowned her in the frost-mist of your anger?
She is gone a little way before me;
Gone an arrow's flight beyond my vision.
She will turn again and come to meet me
With the ghosts of all the stricken flowers,
In a blue mist round her shining tresses,   120
In a blue smoke in her naked forests.
She will linger, kissing all the branches;
She will linger, touching all the places,
Bare and naked, with her golden fingers,
Saying, 'Sleep and dream of me, my children;
Dream of me, the mystic Indian Summer, –
I who, slain by the cold Moon of Terror,
Can return across the path of Spirits,
Bearing still my heart of love and fire,
Looking with my eyes of warmth and splendour,   130
Whisp'ring lowly thro' your sleep of sunshine.
I, the laughing Summer, am not turnèd
Into dry dust, whirling on the prairies,
Into red clay, crushed beneath the snowdrifts.
I am still the mother of sweet flowers
Growing but an arrow's flight beyond you
In the Happy Hunting-Ground – the quiver
Of great Manitou, where all the arrows
He has shot from His great bow of Power,
With its clear, bright singing cord of Wisdom,   140
Are re-gathered, plumed again and brightened,
And shot out, re-barbed with Love and Wisdom;
Always shot, and evermore returning.
Sleep, my children, smiling in your heart-seeds
At the spirit words of Indian Summer.'
Thus, O Moon of Falling Leaves, I mock you!
Have you slain my gold-eyed squaw, the Summer?"

The mighty Morn strode laughing up the land,
And Max, the lab'rer and the lover, stood
Within the forest's edge beside a tree –   150

The mossy king of all the woody tribes —
Whose clatt'ring branches rattled, shuddering,
As the bright axe cleaved moon-like thro' the air,
Waking strange thunders, rousing echoes linked,
From the full lion-throated roar to sighs
Stealing on dove-wings thro' the distant aisles.
Swift fell the axe, swift followed roar on roar,
Till the bare woodland bellowed in its rage
As the first-slain slow toppled to his fall.
"O King of Desolation, art thou dead?"   160
Cried Max, and laughing, heart and lips, leaped on
The vast prone trunk. "And have I slain a king?
Above his ashes will I build my house;
No slave beneath its pillars, but — a king!"

Max wrought alone but for a half-breed lad
With tough, lithe sinews, and deep Indian eyes
Lit with a Gallic sparkle. Max the lover found
The lab'rer's arms grow mightier day by day,
More iron-welded, as he slew the trees;
And with the constant yearning of his heart   170
Toward little Kate, part of a world away,
His young soul grew and shewed a virile front,
Full-muscled and large-statured like his flesh.

Soon the great heaps of brush were builded high,
And, like a victor, Max made pause to clear
His battle-field high strewn with tangled dead.
Then roared the crackling mountains, and their fires
Met in high heaven, clasping flame with flame;
The thin winds swept a cosmos of red sparks
Across the bleak midnight sky; and the sun   180
Walked pale behind the resinous black smoke.

And Max cared little for the blotted sun,
And nothing for the startled, outshone stars;
For love, once set within a lover's breast,
Has its own sun, its own peculiar sky,
All one great daffodil, on which do lie
The sun, the moon, the stars, all seen at once
And never setting, but all shining straight
Into the faces of the trinity —
The one beloved, the lover, and sweet love.   190

It was not all his own, the axe-stirred waste.
In these new days men spread about the earth
With wings at heel, and now the settler hears,
While yet his axe rings on the primal woods,
The shrieks of engines rushing o'er the wastes;
Nor parts his kind to hew his fortunes out.
And as one drop glides down the unknown rock
And the bright-threaded stream leaps after it
With welded billions, so the settler finds
His solitary footsteps beaten out   200
With the quick rush of panting human waves
Upheaved by throbs of angry poverty,
And driven by keen blasts of hunger from
Their native strands, so stern, so dark, so drear!
O then to see the troubled, groaning waves
Throb down to peace in kindly valley beds,
Their turbid bosoms clearing in the calm
Of sun-eyed Plenty, till the stars and moon,
The blessed sun himself, have leave to shine
And laugh in their dark hearts!   210

                  So shanties grew
Other than his amid the blackened stumps;
And children ran with little twigs and leaves
And flung them, shouting, on the forest pyres
Where burned the forest kings; and in the glow
Paused men and women when the day was done.
There the lean weaver ground anew his axe,
Nor backward looked upon the vanished loom,
But forward to the ploughing of his fields,
And to the rose of plenty in the cheeks   220
Of wife and children; nor heeded much the pangs
Of the roused muscles tuning to new work.
The pallid clerk looked on his blistered palms
And sighed and smiled, but girded up his loins
And found new vigour as he felt new hope.
The lab'rer with trained muscles, grim and grave,
Looked at the ground, and wondered in his soul
What joyous anguish stirred his darkened heart
At the mere look of the familiar soil,
And found his answer in the words, *"Mine own!"*   230

Then came smooth-coated men with eager eyes
And talked of steamers on the cliff-bound lakes,
And iron tracks across the prairie lands,
And mills to crush the quartz of wealthy hills,
And mills to saw the great wide-armèd trees,
And mills to grind the singing stream of grain.
And with such busy clamour mingled still
The throbbing music of the bold, bright Axe –
The steel tongue of the present; and the wail
Of falling forests – voices of the past.   240

Max, social-souled, and with his practised thews,
Was happy, boy-like, thinking much of Kate,
And speaking of her to the women-folk,
Who, mostly happy in new honeymoons
Of hope themselves, were ready still to hear
The thrice-told tale of Katie's sunny eyes
And Katie's yellow hair and household ways;
And heard so often, "There shall stand our home
On yonder slope, with vines about the door,"
That the good wives were almost made to see   250
The snowy walls, deep porches, and the gleam
Of Katie's garments flitting through the rooms;
And the black slope all bristling with burnt stumps
Was known amongst them all as "Max's house."

     O Love builds on the azure sea,
          And Love builds on the golden sand,
     And Love builds on the rose-winged cloud,
          And sometimes Love builds on the land!

     O if Love build on sparkling sea,
          And if Love build on golden strand,   260
     And if Love build on rosy cloud,
          To Love these are the solid land!

     O Love will build his lily walls,
          And Love his pearly roof will rear
     On cloud, or land, or mist, or sea –
          Love's solid land is everywhere!

PART III.

The great farmhouse of Malcolm Graem stood,
Square-shouldered and peak-roofed, upon a hill,
With many windows looking everywhere,
So that no distant meadow might lie hid,
Nor corn-field hide its gold, nor lowing herd
Browse in far pastures, out of Malcolm's ken.
He loved to sit, grim, grey, and somewhat stern,
And thro' the smoke-clouds from his short clay pipe
Look out upon his riches, while his thoughts
Swung back and forth between the bleak, stern past   10
And the near future; for his life had come
To that close balance when, a pendulum,
The memory swings between the "then" and "now."
His seldom speech ran thus two different ways:
"When I was but a laddie, thus I did";
Or, "Katie, in the fall I'll see to build
Such fences or such sheds about the place;
And next year, please the Lord, another barn."
Katie's gay garden foamed about the walls,
Assailed the prim-cut modern sills, and rushed   20
Up the stone walls to break on the peaked roof.
And Katie's lawn was like a poet's sward,
Velvet and sheer and diamonded with dew;
For such as win their wealth most aptly take
Smooth urban ways and blend them with their own.
And Katie's dainty raiment was as fine
As the smooth, silken petals of the rose,
And her light feet, her nimble mind and voice,
In city schools had learned the city's ways,
And, grafts upon the healthy, lovely vine,   30
They shone, eternal blossoms 'mid the fruit;
For Katie had her sceptre in her hand
And wielded it right queenly there and here,
In dairy, store-room, kitchen – every spot
Where woman's ways were needed on the place.

And Malcolm took her through his mighty fields
And taught her lore about the change of crops,
And how to see a handome furrow ploughed,
And how to choose the cattle for the mart,
And how to know a fair day's work when done,   40
And where to plant young orchards; for he said,
"God sent a lassie, but I need a son –

"Bethankit for His mercies all the same."
And Katie, when he said it, thought of Max,
Who had been gone two winters and two springs,
And sighed and thought, "Would he not be your son?"
But all in silence, for she had too much
Of the firm will of Malcolm in her soul
To think of shaking that deep-rooted rock;
But hoped the crystal current of his love   50
For his one child, increasing day by day,
Might fret with silver lip until it wore
Such channels thro' the rock that some slight stroke
Of circumstance might crumble down the stone.

The wooer, too, Max prophesied, had come;
Reputed wealthy; with the azure eyes
And Saxon-gilded locks, the fair, clear face
And stalwart form that most of women love;
And with the jewels of some virtues set
On his broad brow; with fires within his soul   60
He had the wizard skill to fetter down
To that mere pink, poetic, nameless glow
That need not fright a flake of snow away,
But, if unloosed, could melt an adverse rock,
Marrowed with iron, frowning in his way.

And Malcolm balanced him by day and night,
And with his grey-eyed shrewdness partly saw
He was not one for Kate, but let him come
And in chance moments thought, "Well, let it be;
They make a bonnie pair; he knows the ways   70
Of men and things; can hold the gear I give,
And, if the lassie wills it, let it be;"
And then, upstarting from his midnight sleep,
With hair erect and sweat upon his brow
Such as no labour e'er had beaded there,
Would cry aloud, wide staring thro' the dark,
"Nay, nay! She shall not wed him! Rest in peace!"
Then, fully waking, grimly laugh and say,
"Why did I speak and answer when none spake?"
But still lie staring, wakeful, through the shades,   80
List'ning to the silence, and beating still
The ball of Alfred's merits to and fro,
Saying, between the silent arguments,
"But would the mother like it, could she know?
I would there were a way to ring a lad

Like silver coin, and so find out the true.
But Kate shall say him 'Nay' or say him 'Yea'
At her own will."

      And Katie said him "Nay"
In all the maiden, speechless, gentle ways
A woman has. But Alfred only laughed   90
To his own soul, and said in his walled mind,
"O Kate, were I a lover I might feel
Despair flap o'er my hopes with raven wings,
Because thy love is given to other love.
And did I love, unless I gained thy love
I would disdain the golden hair, sweet lips,
True violet eyes and gentle air-blown form,
Nor crave the beauteous lamp without the flame,
Which in itself would light a charnel house.
Unloved and loving, I would find the cure   100
Of Love's despair in nursing Love's disdain –
Disdain of lesser treasure than the whole.
One cares not much to place against the wheel
A diamond lacking flame, nor loves to pluck
A rose with all its perfume cast abroad
To the bosom of the gale. Not I, in truth!
If all man's day's are three-score years and ten,
He needs must waste them not, but nimbly seize
The bright, consummate blossom that his will
Calls for most loudly. Gone, long gone the days   110
When Love within my soul forever stretched
Fierce hands of flame, and here and there I found
A blossom fitted for him, all up-filled
With love as with clear dew: – they had their hour
And burned to ashes with him as he drooped
In his own ruby fires. No phœnix he
To rise again, because of Katie's eyes,
On dewy wings from ashes such as his!
But now another passion bids me forth
To crown him with the fairest I can find,   120
And makes me lover, not of Katie's face,
But of her father's riches. O high fool,
Who feels the faintest pulsing of a wish
And fails to feed it into lordly life,
So that, when stumbling back to Mother Earth,
His freezing lip may curl in cold disdain
Of those poor, blighted fools who starward stare

For that fruition, nipped and scanted here!
And while the clay o'ermasters all his blood,
And he can feel the dust knit with his flesh,   130
He yet can say to them, 'Be ye content;
I tasted perfect fruitage thro' my life,
Lighted all lamps of passion till the oil
Failed from their wicks; and now, O now I know
There is no Immortality could give
Such boon as this – to simply cease to be!
There lies your Heaven, O ye dreaming slaves,
If ye would only live to make it so,
Nor paint upon the blue skies lying shades
Of – *what is not.* Wise, wise and strong the man   140
Who poisons that fond haunter of the mind,
Craving for a hereafter with deep draughts
Of wild delights so fiery, fierce, and strong,
That when their dregs are deeply, deeply drained,
What once was blindly craved of purblind Chance –
Life, life eternal, throbbing thro' all space –
Is strongly loathed; and, with his face in dust,
Man loves his only heaven – six feet of earth.
So, Katie, tho' your blue eyes say me 'Nay,'
My pangs of love for gold must needs be fed,   150
And shall be, Katie, if I know my mind."

Events were winds close nestling in the sails
Of Alfred's bark, all blowing him direct
To his wished harbour. On a certain day
All set about with roses and with fire –
One of three days of heat which frequent slip,
Like triple rubies, in between the sweet,
Mild, emerald days of summer – Katie went,
Drawn by a yearning for the ice-pale blooms,
Natant and shining, firing all the bay   160
With angel fires built up of snow and gold.
She found the bay close packed with groaning logs
Prisoned between great arms of close-hinged wood,
All cut from Malcolm's forests in the west
And floated thither to his noisy mills,
And all stamped with the potent "M" and "G"
Which much he loved to see upon his goods –
The silent courtiers owning him their king.
Out clear beyond, the rustling rice-beds sang,
And the cool lilies starred the shadowed wave.   170

"This is a day for lily-love," said Kate,
While she made bare the lilies of her feet
And sang a lily-song that Max had made
That spoke of lilies — always meaning Kate:

"While, Lady of the silvered lakes —
Chaste goddess of the sweet, still shrine
    The jocund river fitful makes
    By sudden, deep gloomed brakes —
Close sheltered by close warp and woof of vine,
Spilling a shadow gloomy-rich as wine   180
Into the silver throne where thou dost sit,
Thy silken leaves all dusky round thee knit!

"Mild Soul of the unsalted wave,
    White bosom holding golden fire,
Deep as some ocean-hidden cave
    Are fixed the roots of thy desire,
Thro' limpid currents stealing up,
And rounding to the pearly cup.
    Thou dost desire,
With all thy trembling heart of sinless fire,   190
    But to be filled
    With dew distilled
From clear, fond skies that in their gloom
    Hold, floating high, thy sister moon.
    Pale chalice of a sweet perfume,
    Whiter-breasted than a dove,
    To thee the dew is — love!"

Kate bared her little feet and poised herself
On the first log close grating on the shore;
And with bright eyes of laughter and wild hair —   200
A flying wind of gold — from log to log
Sped, laughing as they wallowed in her track
Like brown-scaled monsters, rolling as her foot
Spurned deftly each in turn with rose-white sole.
A little island, out in middle wave,
With its green shoulder held the great drive braced
Between it and the mainland, — here it was
The silver lilies drew her with white smiles —
And as she touched the last great log of all
It reeled, upstarting, like a column braced   210
A second on the wave, and when it plunged

Rolling upon the froth and sudden foam,
Katie had vanished, and with angry grind
The vast logs rolled together; nor a lock
Of drifting, yellow hair, an upflung hand,
Told where the rich man's chiefest treasure sank
Under his wooden wealth.

        But Alfred, prone
With pipe and book upon the shady marge
Of the cool isle, saw all, and seeing hurled   220
Himself, and hardly knew it, on the logs.
By happy chance a shallow lapped the isle
On this green bank; and when his iron arms
Dashed the barked monsters, as frail stems of rice,
A little space apart, the soft, slow tide
But reached his chest, and in a flash he saw
Kate's yellow hair, and by it drew her up,
And lifting her aloft, cried out, "O Kate!"
And once again cried, "Katie! is she dead?"
For like the lilies broken by the rough   230
And sudden riot of the armoured logs,
Kate lay upon his hands; and now the logs
Closed in upon him, nipping his great chest,
Nor could he move to push them off again
For Katie in his arms. "And now," he said,
"If none should come, and any wind arise
To weld these woody monsters 'gainst the isle,
I shall be cracked like any broken twig;
And as it is, I know not if I die,
For I am hurt – ay, sorely, sorely hurt!"   240
Then looked on Katie's lily face, and said,
"Dead, dead or living? Why, an even chance.
O lovely bubble on a troubled sea,
I would not thou shouldst lose thyself again
In the black ocean whence thy life emerged,
But skyward steal on gales as soft as love,
And hang in some bright rainbow overhead,
If only such bright rainbow spanned the earth."
Then shouted loudly, till the silent air
Roused like a frightened bird, and on its wings   250
Caught up his cry and bore it to the farm.
There Malcolm, leaping from his noontide sleep,
Upstarted as at midnight, crying out,
"She shall not wed him! Rest you, wife, in peace!"

They found him, Alfred, haggard-eyed and faint,
But holding Katie ever toward the sun,
Unhurt, and waking in the fervent heat,
And now it came that Alfred, being sick
Of his sharp hurts and tended by them both
With what was like to love – being born of thanks –   260
Had choice of hours most politic to woo,
And used his deed, as one might use the sun
To ripe unmellowed fruit; and from the core
Of Katie's gratitude hoped yet to nurse
A flower all to his liking – Katie's love.

But Katie's mind was like the plain, broad shield
Of a table diamond, nor had a score of sides;
And in its shield, so precious and so plain,
Was cut thro' all its clear depths Max's name.
And so she said him "Nay" at last, in words   270
Of such true-sounding silver that he knew
He might not win her at the present hour,
But smiled and thought, "I go, and come again;
Then shall we see. Our three-score years and ten
Are mines of treasure, if we hew them deep,
Nor stop too long in choosing out our tools."

PART IV.

From his far wigwam sprang the strong North Wind
And rushed with war-cry down the steep ravines,
And wrestled with the giants of the woods;
And with his ice-club beat the swelling crests
Of the deep watercourses into death;
And with his chill foot froze the whirling leaves
Of dun and gold and fire in icy banks;
And smote the tall reeds to the hardened earth,
And sent his whistling arrows o'er the plains,
Scattering the lingering herds; and sudden paused,   10
When he had frozen all the running streams,
And hunted with his war-cry all the things
That breathed about the woods, or roamed the bleak,
Bare prairies swelling to the mournful sky.

"White squaw!" he shouted, troubled in his soul,
 "I slew the dead, unplumed before; wrestled
 With naked chiefs scalped of their leafy plumes;
 I bound sick rivers in cold thongs of death,
 And shot my arrows over swooning plains,
 Bright with the paint of death, and lean and bare.   20
 And all the braves of my loud tribe will mock
 And point at me when our great chief, the Sun,
 Relights his council fire in the Moon
 Of Budding Leaves: 'Ugh, ugh! he is a brave!
 He fights with squaws and takes the scalps of babes!"
 And the least wind will blow his calumet,
 Filled with the breath of smallest flowers, across
 The war-paint on my face, and pointing with
 His small, bright pipe, that never moved a spear
 Of bearded rice, cry, 'Ugh! he slays the dead!"   30
 O my white squaw, come from thy wigwam grey,
 Spread thy white blanket on the twice-slain dead,
 And hide them ere the waking of the Sun!"

High grew the snow beneath the low-hung sky,
 And all was silent in the wilderness;
 In trance of stillness Nature heard her God
 Rebuilding her spent fires, and veiled her face
 While the Great Worker brooded o'er His work.

"Bite deep and wide, O Axe, the tree!
 What doth thy bold voice promise me?"   40

"I promise thee all joyous things
 That furnish forth the lives of kings;

"For every silver ringing blow
 Cities and palaces shall grow."

"Bite deep and wide, O Axe, the tree!
 Tell wider prophecies to me."

"When rust hath gnawed me deep and red
 A nation strong shall lift his head.

"His crown the very heavens shall smite,
 Æons shall build him in his might."   50

"Bite deep and wide, O Axe, the tree!
Bright Seer, help on thy prophecy!"

Max smote the snow-weighed tree and lightly laughed.
"See, friend," he cried to one that looked and smiled,
"My axe and I, we do immortal tasks;
We build up nations – this my axe and I."

"Oh!" said the other with a cold, short smile,
"Nations are not immortal. Is there now
One nation throned upon the sphere of earth
That walked with the first gods and with them saw   60
The budding world unfold its slow-leaved flower?
Nay, it is hardly theirs to leave behind
Ruins so eloquent that the hoary sage
Can lay his hand upon their stones and say:
'These once were thrones!'"

       "The lean lank lion peals
His midnight thunders over lone, red plains,
Long-ridged and crested on their dusty waves
With fires from moons red-hearted as the sun,
And deep re-thunders all the earth to him;   70
For, far beneath the flame-flecked, shifting sands,
Below the roots of palms, and under stones
Of younger ruins, thrones, towers and cities
Honeycomb the earth. The high, solemn walls
Of hoary ruins – their foundings all unknown
But to the round-eyed worlds that walk
In the blank paths of Space and blanker Chance –
At whose stones young mountains wonder, and the seas'
New-silvering, deep-set valleys pause and gaze –
Are reared upon old shrines whose very gods   80
Were dreams to the shrine-builders of a time
They caught in far-off flashes – as the child
Half thinks he can remember how one came
And took him in her hand and showed him that,
He thinks, she called the sun.

       "Proud ships rear high
On ancient billows that have torn the roots
Of cliffs, and bitten at the golden lips
Of firm, sleek beaches, till they conquered all

And sowed the reeling earth with salted waves;   90
Wrecks plunge, prow foremost, down still, solemn slopes,
And bring their dead crews to as dead a quay –
Some city built, before that ocean grew,
By silver drops from many a floating cloud,
By icebergs bellowing in their throes of death,
By lesser seas tossed from their rocking cups,
And leaping each to each; by dewdrops flung
From painted sprays, whose weird leaves and flowers
Are moulded for new dwellers on the earth,
Printed in hearts of mountains and of mines.   100

"Nations immortal? Where the well-trimmed lamps
Of long-past ages? When Time seemed to pause
On smooth, dust-blotted graves that, like the tombs
Of monarchs, held dead bones and sparkling gems,
She saw no glimmer on the hideous ring
Of the black clouds; no stream of sharp, clear light
From those great torches passed into the black
Of deep oblivion. She seemed to watch, but she
Forgot her long-dead nations. When she stirred
Her vast limbs in the dawn that forced its fire   110
Up the black East, and saw the imperious red
Burst over virgin dews and budding flowers,
She still forgot her mouldered thrones and kings,
Her sages and their torches and their gods,
And said, 'This is my birth – my primal day!'
She dreamed new gods, and reared them other shrines,
Planted young nations, smote a feeble flame
From sunless flint, re-lit the torch of mind.
Again she hung her cities on the hills,
Built her rich towers, crowned her kings again;   120
And with the sunlight on her awful wings
Swept round the flowery cestus of the earth,
And said, 'I build for Immortality!'
Her vast hand reared her towers, her shrines, her thrones;
The ceaseless sweep of her tremendous wings
Still beat them down and swept their dust abroad.
Her iron finger wrote on mountain sides
Her deeds and prowess, and her own soft plume
Wore down the hills. Again drew darkly on
A night of deep forgetfulness; once more   130
Time seemed to pause upon forgotten graves;

Once more a young dawn stole into her eyes;
Again her broad wings stirred, and fresh, clear airs
Blew the great clouds apart; again she said,
'This is my birth — my deeds and handiwork
Shall be immortal!' Thus and so dream on
Fooled nations, and thus dream their dullard sons.
Naught is immortal save immortal — Death!"

Max paused and smiled: "O preach such gospel, friend,
To all but lovers who most truly love;   140
For *them*, their gold-wrought scripture glibly reads,
All else is mortal but immortal — Love!"

"Fools! fools!" his friend said, "most immortal fools!
But pardon, pardon, for perchance you love?"

"Yes," said Max, proudly smiling, "thus do I
Possess the world and feel eternity."

Dark laughter blackened in the other's eyes:
"Eternity! why did such Iris arch
Enter our worm-bored planet? Never lived
One woman true enough such tryst to keep."   150

"I'd swear by Kate," said Max; "and then I had
A mother, and my father swore by her."

"By Kate? Ah, that were lusty oath, indeed!
Some other man will look into her eyes
And swear me roundly, 'By true Catherine!'
As Troilus swore by Cressèd — so they say."

"You never knew my Kate," said Max, and poised
His axe again on high; "but let it pass.
You are too subtle for me; argument
Have I none to oppose yours with but this: 160
Get you a Kate, and let her sunny eyes
Dispel the doubting darkness in your soul."

"And have not I a Kate? Pause, friend, and see.
She gave me this faint shadow of herself
The day I slipped the watch-star of our loves –
A ring – upon her hand; she loves me, too.
Yet tho' her eyes be suns, no gods are they
To give me worlds, or make me feel a tide
Of strong eternity set toward my soul;
And tho' she loves me, yet am I content   170
To know she loves me by the hour, the year,
Perchance the second – as all women love."

The bright axe faltered in the air and ripped
Down the rough bark and bit the drifted snow,
For Max's arm fell, withered in its strength,
'Long by his side. "Your Kate," he said, "your Kate?"

"Yes, mine – while holds her mind that way, my Kate;
I saved her life, and had her love for thanks.
Her father is Malcolm Graem – Max, my friend,
You pale! What sickness seizes on your soul?"   180

Max laughed, and swung his bright axe high again:
"Stand back a pace; a too far-reaching blow
Might level your false head with yon prone trunk!
Stand back and listen while I say, 'You lie!'
That is my Katie's face upon your breast,
But 'tis my Katie's love lives in my breast!
Stand back, I say! my axe is heavy, and
Might chance to cleave a liar's brittle skull!
Your Kate! your Kate! your Kate! – hark, how the woods
Mock at your lie with all their woody tongues!   190
O silence, ye false echoes! Not his Kate
But mine – I'm certain! I will have your life!"
All the blue heaven was dead in Max's eyes;
Doubt-wounded lay Kate's image in his heart,
And could not rise to pluck the sharp spear out.

" Well, strike, mad fool," said Alfred, somewhat pale;
"I have no weapon but these naked hands!"

"Ay, but," said Max, "you smote my naked heart!
O shall I slay him? Satan, answer me;
I cannot call on God for answer here!   200
O Kate – !"

A voice from God came thro' the silent woods
And answered him; for suddenly a wind
Caught the great tree-tops, coned with high-piled snow,
And smote them to and fro, while all the air
Was sudden filled with busy drifts; and high
White pillars whirled amid the naked trunks,
And harsh, loud groans, and smiting, sapless boughs
Made hellish clamour in the quiet place.
With a shrill shriek of tearing fibres, rocked   210
The half-hewn tree above his fated head,
And, tott'ring, asked the sudden blast, "Which way?"
And, answering, its windy arms down crashed
Thro' other lacing boughs with one loud roar
Of woody thunder. All its pointed boughs
Pierced the deep snow; its round and mighty corpse,
Bark-flayed and shudd'ring, quivered into death.
And Max, as some frail, withered reed, the sharp
And piercing branches caught at him, as hands
In a death-throe, and beat him to the earth;   220
And the dead tree upon its slayer lay.

"Yet hear we much of gods! If such there be,
They play at games of chance with thunderbolts,"
Said Alfred, "else on me this doom had come.
This seals my faith in deep and dark unfaith.
Now, Katie, are you mine, for Max is dead –
Or will be soon, imprisoned by those boughs,
Wounded and torn, soothed by the deadly palms
Of the white, traitorous frost; and buried then
Under the snows that fill those vast, grey clouds,   230
Low sweeping on the fretted forest roof.
And Katie shall believe you false – not dead.
False, false! – And I? O she shall find me true –
True as a fabled devil to the soul
He longs for with the heat of all Hell's fires.
These myths serve well for simile, I see,
And yet – down, Pity! knock not at my breast,
Nor grope about for that dull stone, my heart.

I'll stone thee with it, Pity! Get thee hence!
Pity, I'll strangle thee with naked hands;   240
For thou dost bear upon thy downy breast
Remorse, shaped like a serpent, and her fangs
Might dart at me and pierce my marrow thro'!
Hence, beggar, hence – and keep with fools, I say!
He bleeds and groans! Well, Max, thy God or mine,
Blind Chance, here played the butcher – 'twas not I.
Down, hands! ye shall not lift his fallen head!
What cords tug at ye? What? Ye'd pluck him up
And staunch his wounds? There rises in my breast
A strange, strong giant, throwing wide his arms   250
And bursting all the granite of my heart.
How like to quivering flesh a stone may feel!
Why, it has pangs! I'll none of them! I know
Life is too short for anguish and for hearts!
So I wrestle with thee, giant, and my will
Turns the thumb, and thou shalt take the knife!
Well done! I'll turn thee on the arena dust
And look on thee – What? thou wert Pity's self,
Stolen in my breast; and I have slaughtered thee!
But hist! where hast thou hidden they fell snake,   260
Fire-fanged Remorse? Not in my breast, I know,
For all again is chill and empty there,
And hard and cold – the granite knitted up!

"So lie there, Max – poor fond and simple Max!
'Tis well thou diest! Earth's children should not call
Such as thee father – let them ever be
Fathered by rogues and villains fit to cope
With the black dragon Chance and the black knaves
Who swarm in loathsome masses in the dust!
True Max, lie there, and slumber into death!"   270

PART V.

Said the high hill, in the morning, "Look on me!
Behold, sweet earth, sweet sister sky, behold
The red flames on my peaks, and how my pines
Are cressets of pure gold, my quarried scars

Of black crevasse and shadow-filled canyon
Are traced in silver mist. Now on my breast
Hang the soft purple fringes of the night;
Close to my shoulder droops the weary moon,
Dove-pale, into the crimson surf the sun
Drives up before his prow; and blackly stands   10
On my slim, softiest peak an eagle with
His angry eyes set sunward, while his cry
Falls fiercely back from all my ruddy heights,
And his bald eaglets, in their bare, broad nest,
Shrill pipe their angry echoes: 'Sun, arise,
And show me that pale dove beside her nest,
Which I shall strike with piercing beak and tear
With iron talons for my hungry young!'

"And that mild dove, secure for yet a space,
Half wakened, turns her ringed and glossy neck   20
To watch dawn's ruby pulsing on my breast,
And see the first bright golden motes slip down
The gnarlèd trunks about her leaf-deep nest,
Nor sees nor fears the eagle on the peak."

"Ay, lassie, sing! I'll smoke my pipe the while;
And let it be a simple, bonnie song,
Such as an old, plain man can gather in
His dulling ear, and feel it slipping thro'
The cold, dark, stony places of his heart."

"Yes, sing, sweet Kate," said Alfred in her ear;   30
"I often heard you singing in my dreams
When I was far away the winter past."
So Katie on the moonlit window leaned,
And in the airy silver of her voice
Sang of the tender blue Forget-me-not:

> Could every blossom find a voice
> And sing a strain to me,
> I know where I would place my choice,
> Which my delight should be.
> I would not choose the lily tall,   40
> The rose from musky grot,
> But I would still my minstrel call
> The blue Forget-me-not.

And I on mossy bank would lie,
   Of brooklet, rippling clear;
And she of the sweet azure eye,
   Close at my listening ear,
Should sing into my soul a strain
   Might never be forgot –
So rich with joy, so rich with pain,   50
   The blue Forget-me-not.

Ah, every blossom hath a tale,
   With silent grace to tell,
From rose that reddens to the gale
   To modest heather-bell;
But O the flower in every heart
   That finds a sacred spot
To bloom, with azure leaves apart,
   Is the Forget-me-not.

Love plucks it from the mosses green   60
   When parting hours are nigh,
And places it Love's palms between
   With many an ardent sigh;
And bluely up from grassy graves
   In some loved churchyard spot,
It glances tenderly and waves –
   The dear Forget-me-not.

And with the faint, last cadence stole a glance
At Malcolm's softened face – a bird-soft touch
Let flutter on the rugged, silver snarls   70
Of his thick locks – and laid her tender lips
A second on the iron of his hand.

"And did you ever meet," he sudden asked
Of Alfred, sitting pallid in the shade,
"Out by yon unco place, a lad, – a lad
Named Maxwell Gordon; tall and straight and strong;
About my size, I take it, when a lad?"

And Katie at the sound of Max's name,
First spoken for such space by Malcolm's lips,
Trembled and started, and let down her brow,   80
Hiding its sudden rose on Malcolm's arm.

"Max Gordon? Yes. Was he a friend of yours?"

"No friend of mine, but of the lassie's here.
How comes he on? I wager he's a drone,
And never will put honey in the hive."

"No drone," said Alfred, laughing; "when I left,
He and his axe were quarreling with the woods
And making forests reel. Love steels a lover's arm."

O blush that stole from Katie's swelling heart,
And with its hot rose brought the happy dew   90
Into her hidden eyes!

                "Ay, ay! is that the way?"
Said Malcolm, smiling. "Who may be his love?"

"In that he is a somewhat simple soul;
Why, I suppose he loves – " he paused, and Kate
Looked up with two forget-me-nots for eyes,
With eager jewels in their centres set
Of happy, happy tears, and Alfred's heart
Became a closer marble than before –
"Why, I suppose he loves – his lawful wife."   100

"His wife! his wife!" said Malcolm, in amaze,
And laid his heavy hand on Katie's head;
"Did you two play me false, my little lass?
Speak and I'll pardon. Katie, lassie, what?"

"He has a wife," said Alfred, "lithe and bronzed,
An Indian woman, comelier than her kind,
And on her knee a child with yellow locks,
And lake-like eyes of mystic Indian brown."
And so you knew him? he is doing well."

"False, false!" cried Katie, lifting up her head;   110
"Oh, you know not the Max my father means!"
"He came from yonder farm-house on the slope."
"Some other Max – we speak not of the same."
"He has a red mark on his temple set."
"It matters not – 'tis not the Max we know."

"He wears a turquoise ring slung round his neck."
"And many wear them; they are common stones."
"His mother's ring – her name was Helen Wynde."
"And there be many Helens who have sons."
"O Katie, credit me – it is the man!"   120
"O not the man! Why, you have never told
  Us of the true soul that the true Max has;
  The Max we know has such a soul, I know."

"How know you that, my foolish little lass?"
  Her father said, a storm of anger bound
  Within his heart like Samson with green withes;
  "Belike it is the false young cur we know."

"No, no," said Katie, simply, and low-voiced,
  "If he be traitor I must needs be false,
  For long ago love melted our two hearts,   130
  And time has moulded those two hearts in one,
  And he is true since I am faithful still."
  She rose and parted, trembling as she went,
  Feeling the following steel of Alfred's eyes,
  And with the icy hand of scorned mistrust
  Searching about the pulses of her heart,
  Feeling for Max's image in her breast.

"Tonight she conquers Doubt; tomorrow's noon
  His following soldiers sap the golden wall,
  And I shall enter and possess the fort,"   140
  Said Alfred, in his mind. "O Katie, child,
  Wilt thou be Nemesis with yellow hair
  To rend my breast? for I do feel a pulse
  Stir when I look into thy pure-barbed eyes.
  Oh, am I breeding that false thing, a heart,
  Making my breast all tender for the fangs
  Of sharp Remorse to plunge their hot fire in?
  I am a certain dullard. Let me feel
  But one faint goad, fine as a needle's point,
  And it shall be the spur in my soul's side   150
  To urge the maddening thing across the jags
  And cliffs of life into the soft embrace
  Of that cold mistress, who is constant, too,
  And never flings her lovers from her arms, –
  Not Death, for she is still a fruitful wife,

Her spouse the Dead; and their cold marriage yields
A million children, born of mouldering flesh.
So Death and Flesh live on; immortal they!
I mean the blank-eyed queen whose wassail bowl
Is brimmed from Lethe, and whose porch is red   160
With poppies, as it waits the panting soul.
She, she alone is great! No sceptred slave
Bowing to blind, creative giants, she!
No forces seize her in their strong, mad hands,
Nor say, 'Do this – be that!' Were there a God,
His only mocker, she, great Nothingness;
And to her, close of kin, yet lover, too,
Flies this large nothing that we call the soul."

Doth true Love lonely grow?
                    Ah, no! ah, no!   170
Ah, were it only so,
That it alone might show
   Its ruddy rose upon its sapful tree,
      Then, then in dewy morn
      Joy might his brow adorn
   With Love's young rose as fair and glad as he.

But with Love's rose doth blow,
                    Ah, woe! ah, woe!
Truth, with its leaves of snow,
And Pain and Pity grow   180
   With Love's sweet roses on its sapful tree!
      Love's rose buds not alone,
      But still, but still doth own
   A thousand blossoms cypress-hued to see!

PART VI.

Who curseth Sorrow knows her not at all.
Dark matrix she, from which the human soul
Has its last birth; whence it, with misty thews
Close knitted in her blackness, issues out
Strong for immortal toil up such great heights
As crown o'er crown rise through Eternity.
Without the loud, deep clamour of her wail,
The iron of her hands, the biting brine

Of her black tears, the soul, but lightly built
Of indeterminate spirit, like a mist   10
Would lapse to chaos in soft, gilded dreams,
As mists fade in the gazing of the sun.
Sorrow, dark mother of the soul, arise!
Be crowned with spheres where thy blest children dwell,
Who, but for thee, were not. No lesser seat
Be thine, thou Helper of the Universe,
Than planet on planet piled – thou instrument
Close clasped within the great Creative Hand!

The Land had put his ruddy gauntlet on,
Of harvest gold, to dash in Famine's face;   20
And like a vintage wain deep dyed with juice
The great moon faltered up the ripe, blue sky,
Drawn by silver stars – like oxen white
And horned with rays of light. Down the rich land
Malcolm's small valleys, filled with grain lip high,
Lay round a lonely hill that faced the moon
And caught the wine kiss of its ruddy light.
A cusped, dark wood caught in its black embrace
The valleys and the hill, and from its wilds,
Spiced with dark cedars, cried the whippoorwill.   30
A crane, belated, sailed across the moon.
On the bright, small, close linked lakes green islets lay –
Dusk knots of tangled vines, or maple boughs,
Or tufted cedars, bossed upon the waves.
The gay, enamelled children of the swamp
Rolled a low bass to treble, tinkling notes
Of little streamlets leaping from the woods.
Close to old Malcolm's mills two wooden jaws
Bit up the water on a sloping floor;
And here, in season, rushed the great logs down   40
To seek the river winding on its way.
In a green sheen, smooth as a naiad's locks,
The water rolled between the shuddering jaws,
Then on the river level roared and reeled
In ivory-armèd conflict with itself.

"Look down," said Alfred, "Katie, look and see
How that but pictures my mad heart to you.
It tears itself in fighting that mad love
You swear is hopeless. Hopeless – is it so?"
"Ah, yes," said Katie, "ask me not again!"   50

"But Katie, Max is false; no word has come,
Nor any sign from him for many months,
And – he is happy with his Indian wife."

She lifted eyes fair as the fresh, grey dawn
With all its dews and promises of sun.
"O Alfred, saver of my little life,
Look in my eyes and read them honestly!"
He laughed till all the isles and forests laughed.
"O simple child! what may the forest flames
See in the woodland ponds but their own fires?   60
And have you, Katie, neither fears nor doubts?"
She with the flower-soft pinkness of her palm
Covered her sudden tears, then quickly said,
"Fears – never doubts, for true love never doubts."

Then Alfred paused a space, as one who holds
A white doe by the throat and searches for
The blade to slay her. "This your answer still?
You doubt not – doubt not this far love of yours,
Tho' sworn a false young recreant, Kate, by me?"
"He is as true as I am," Katie said,   70
"And did I seek for stronger simile
I could not find such in the universe."
"And were he dead? what, Katie, were he dead –
A handful of brown dust, a flame blown out –
What then? would love be strongly true to – naught?"
"Still true to love my love would be," she said,
And, faintly smiling, pointed to the stars.

"O fool!" said Alfred, stirred as craters rock
To their own throes, while over his pale lips
Rolled flaming stone – his molten heart. "Then, fool,   80
Be true to what thou wilt, for he is dead,
And there have grown this gilded summer past
Grasses and buds from his unburied flesh!
I saw him dead. I heard his last, loud cry,
'O Kate!' ring thro' the woods; in truth I did!"
She half raised up a piteous, pleading hand,
Then fell along the mosses at his feet.

"Now will I show I love you, Kate," he said,
"And give you gift of love; you shall not wake
To feel the arrow feather-deep within   90
Your constant heart. For me, I never meant
To crawl an hour beyond what time I felt
The strange fanged monster that they call Remorse
Fold round my wakened heart. The hour has come;
And as Love grew the welded folds of steel
Slipped round in horrid zones. In Love's flaming eyes
Stared its fell eyeballs, and with hydra head
It sank hot fangs in breast and brow and thigh.
Come, Kate! O Anguish is a simple knave
Whom hucksters could outwit with small trade lies,   100
When thus so easily his smarting thralls
May flee his knout! Come, come, my little Kate;
The black porch with its fringe of poppies waits, –
A propylaeum hospitably wide, –
No lictors with their fasces at its jaws,
Its floor as kindly to my fire-veined feet
As to thy silver-lilied, sinless ones!
O you shall slumber soundly, tho' the white,
Wild waters pluck the crocus of your hair,
And scaly spies stare with round, lightless eyes   110
At your small face laid on my stony breast!
Come, Kate; I must not have you wake, dear heart,
To hear you cry, perchance, on your dead Max!"

He turned her still face close upon his breast,
And with his lips upon her soft-ringed hair
Leaped from the bank, low shelving o'er the knot
Of frantic waters at the long slide's foot.
And as the severed waters crashed and smote
Together once again, within the wave-
Stunned chamber of his ear there pealed a cry,   120
"O Kate! Stay, madman, traitor, stay! O Kate!"

Max, gaunt as prairie wolves in famine time
With long-drawn sickness, reeled upon the bank,
Katie, new rescued, waking in his arms.
On the white riot of the waters gleamed
The face of Alfred, calm, with close sealed eyes,
And blood red on his temple where it smote
The mossy timbers of the groaning slide.

"O God!" cried Max, as Katie's opening eyes
Looked up to his, slow budding to a smile   130
Of wonder and of bliss, "my Kate, my Kate!"
She saw within his eyes a larger soul
Than that light spirit that before she knew,
And read the meaning of his glance and words.
"Do as you will, my Max; I would not keep
You back with one light falling finger-tip!"
And cast herself from his large arms upon
The mosses at his feet, and hid her face
That she might not behold what he would do;
Or lest the terror in her shining eyes   140
Might bind him to her, and prevent his soul
Work out its greatness; and her long, wet hair
Drew massed about her ears, to shut the sound
Of the vexed waters from her anguished brain.

Max looked upon her, turning as he looked.
A moment came a voice in Katie's soul:
"Arise, be not dismayed, arise and look;
If he shall perish, 'twill be as a god,
For he will die to save his enemy."
But answered her torn heart: "I cannot look –   150
I cannot look and see him sob and die
In those pale, angry arms. O let me rest
Blind, blind and deaf until the swift-paced end.
My Max! O God! was that his Katie's name?"
Like a pale dove, hawk-hunted, Katie ran,
Her fear's beak in her shoulder; and below,
Where the coiled waters straightened to a stream,
Found Max all bruised and bleeding on the bank,
But smiling with man's truimph in his eyes
When he has on fierce Danger's lion neck   160
Placed his right hand and plucked the prey away.
And at his feet lay Alfred, still and white,
A willow's shadow trembling on his face.
"There lies the false, fair devil, O my Kate,
Who would have parted us, but could not, Kate!"
"But could not, Max," said Katie. "Is he dead?"
But, swift perusing Max's strange, dear face,
Close clasped against his breast, forgot him straight
And every other evil thing upon
The broad green earth.   170

PART VII.

Again rang out the music of the axe,
And on the slope, as in his happy dreams,
The home of Max with wealth of drooping vines
On the rude walls, and in the trellised porch
Sat Katie, smiling o'er the rich, fresh fields.
And by her side sat Malcolm, hale and strong,
Upon his knee a little smiling child
Named – Alfred, as the seal of pardon set
Upon the heart of one who sinned and woke
To sorrow for his sins; and whom they loved   10
With gracious joyousness, nor kept the dusk
Of his past deeds between their hearts and his.
Malcolm had followed with his flocks and herds
When Max and Katie, hand in hand, went out
From his old home; and now, with slow, grave smile,
He said to Max, who twisted Katie's hair
About his naked arm, bare from his toil:
"It minds me of old times, this house of yours;
It stirs my heart to hearken to the axe,
And hear the windy crash of falling trees.   20
Ay, these fresh forests make an old man young."

"Oh, yes!" said Max, with laughter in his eyes;
"And I do truly think that Eden bloomed
Deep in the heart of tall, green maple groves,
With sudden scents of pine from mountain sides,
And prairies with their breasts against the skies.
And Eve was only little Katie's height."

"Hoot, lad! you speak as every Adam speaks
About his bonnie Eve; but what says Kate?"

"Oh, Adam had not Max's soul," she said;   30
"And these wild woods and plains are fairer far
Than Eden's self. O bounteous mothers they,
Beckoning pale starvelings with their fresh, green hands,
And with their ashes mellowing the earth,
That she may yield her increase willingly!
I would not change these wild and rocking woods,
Dotted by little homes of unbarked trees,
Where dwell the fleers from the waves of want,
For the smooth sward of selfish Eden bowers,
Nor – Max for Adam, if I knew my mind!"   40

(1884)   (1905)

Said the Canoe

My masters twain made me a bed
Of pine-boughs resinous, and cedar;
Of moss, a soft and gentle breeder
Of dreams of rest; and me they spread
With furry skins and, laughing, said:
"Now she shall lay her polished sides
As queens do rest, or dainty brides,
Our slender lady of the tides!"

My masters twain their camp-soul lit:
Streamed incense from the hissing cones;   10
Large crimson flashes grew and whirled;
Thin golden nerves of sly light curled
Round the dun camp; and rose faint zones,
Half way about each grim bole knit,
Like a shy child that would bedeck
With its soft clasp a Brave's red neck,
Yet sees the rough shield on his breast,
The awful plumes shake on his crest,
And, fearful, drops his timid face,
Nor dares complete the sweet embrace.   20

Into the hollow hearts of brakes —
Yet warm from sides of does and stags
Passed to the crisp, dark river-flags —
Sinuous, red as copper-snakes,
Sharp-headed serpents, made of light,
Glided and hid themselves in night.

My masters twain the slaughtered deer
Hung on forked boughs with thongs of leather:
Bound were his stiff, slim feet together,
His eyes like dead stars cold and drear.   30
The wandering firelight drew near
And laid its wide palm, red and anxious,
On the sharp splendour of his branches,
On the white foam grown hard and sere
      On flank and shoulder.
Death — hard as breast of granite boulder —
      Under his lashes
Peered thro' his eyes at his life's grey ashes.

My masters twain sang songs that wove –
As they burnished hunting-blade and rifle –   40
A golden thread with a cobweb trifle,
Loud of the chase and low of love:

"O Love! art thou a silver fish,
   Shy of the line and shy of gaffing,
   Which we do follow, fierce, yet laughing,
   Casting at thee the light-winged wish?
   And at the last shall we bring thee up
   From the crystal darkness, under the cup
         Of lily folden
         On broad leaves golden?   50

"O Love! art thou a silver deer
   With feet as swift as wing of swallow,
   While we with rushing arrows follow?
   And at the last shall we draw near
   And o'er thy velvet neck cast thongs
   Woven of roses, stars and songs –
         New chains all moulden
         Of rare gems olden?"

They hung the slaughtered fish like swords
   On saplings slender; like scimitars,   60
   Bright, and ruddied from new-dead wars,
Blazed in the light the scaly hordes.

They piled up boughs beneath the trees,
   Of cedar web and green fir tassel.
   Low did the pointed pine tops rustle,
The camp-fire blushed to the tender breeze.

The hounds laid dewlaps on the ground
   With needles of pine, sweet, soft and rusty,
   Dreamed of the dead stag stout and lusty;
A bat by the red flames wove its round.   70

The darkness built its wigwam walls
   Close round the camp, and at its curtain
   Pressed shapes, thin, woven and uncertain
As white locks of tall waterfalls.

(1884)   (1905)

The City Tree

I STAND within the stony, arid town,
   I gaze forever on the narrow street,
I hear forever passing up and down
   The ceaseless tramp of feet.

I know no brotherhood with far-locked woods,
   Where branches bourgeon from a kindred sap,
Where o'er mossed roots, in cool, green solitudes,
   Small silver brooklets lap.

No emerald vines creep wistfully to me
   And lay their tender fingers on my bark;   10
High may I toss my boughs, yet never see
   Dawn's first most glorious spark.

When to and fro my branches wave and sway,
   Answ'ring the feeble wind that faintly calls,
They kiss no kindred boughs, but touch alway
   The stones of climbing walls.

My heart is never pierced with song of bird;
   My leaves know nothing of that glad unrest
Which makes a flutter in the still woods heard
   When wild birds build a nest.   20

There never glance the eyes of violets up,
   Blue, into the deep splendour of my green;
Nor falls the sunlight to the primrose cup
   My quivering leaves between.

Not mine, not mine to turn from soft delight
   Of woodbine breathings, honey sweet and warm;
With kin embattled rear my glorious height
   To greet the coming storm!

Not mine to watch across the free, broad plains
   The whirl of stormy cohorts sweeping fast,   30
The level silver lances of great rains
   Blown onward by the blast!

Not mine the clamouring tempest to defy,
  Tossing the proud crest of my dusky leaves —
Defender of small flowers that trembling lie
  Against my barky greaves!

Not mine to watch the wild swan drift above,
  Balanced on wings that could not choose between
The wooing sky, blue as the eye of love,
  And my own tender green!   40

And yet my branches spread, a kingly sight.
  In the close prison of the drooping air:
When sun-vexed noons are at their fiery height
  My shade is broad, and there

Come city toilers, who their hour of ease
  Weave out to precious seconds as they lie
Pillowed on horny hands, to hear the breeze
  Through my great branches die.

I see no flowers, but as the children race
  With noise and clamour through the dusty street,   50
I see the bud of many an angel face,
  I hear their merry feet.

No violets look up, but, shy and grave,
  The children pause and lift their crystal eyes
To where my emerald branches call and wave
  As to the mystic skies.

(1884)   (1905)

The Camp of Souls

My white canoe, like the silvery air
  O'er the River of Death that darkly rolls
When the moons of the world are round and fair,
  I paddle back from the "Camp of Souls."
When the wishton-wish in the low swamp grieves
Come the dark plumes of red "Singing Leaves."

Two hundred times have the moons of spring
    Rolled over the bright bay's azure breath
Since they decked me with plumes of an eagle's wing,
    And painted my face with the "paint of death,"   10
And from their pipes o'er my corpse there broke
The solemn rings of the blue "last smoke."

Two hundred times have the wintry moons
    Wrapped the dead earth in a blanket white;
Two hundred times have the wild sky loons
    Shrieked in the flush of the golden light
Of the first sweet dawn, when the summer weaves
Her dusky wigwam of perfect leaves.

Two hundred moons of the falling leaf
    Since they laid my bow in my dead right hand   20
And chanted above me the "song of grief"
    As I took my way to the spirit land;
Yet when the swallow the blue air cleaves
Come the dark plumes of red "Singing Leaves."

White are the wigwams in that far camp,
    And the star-eyed deer on the plains are found;
No bitter marshes or tangled swamp
    In the Manitou's happy hunting-ground!
And the moon of summer forever rolls
Above the red men in their "Camp of Souls."   30

Blue are its lakes as the wild dove's breast,
    And their murmurs soft as her gentle note;
As the calm, large stars in the deep sky rest,
    The yellow lilies upon them float;
And canoes, like flakes of the silvery snow,
Thro' the tall, rustling rice-beds come and go.

Green are its forests; no warrior wind
    Rushes on war trail the dusk grove through,
With leaf-scalps of tall trees mourning behind;
    But South Wind, heart friend of Great Manitou,   40
When ferns and leaves with cool dews are wet,
Blows flowery breaths from his red calumet.

Never upon them the white frosts lie,
    Nor glow their green boughs with the "paint of death";
Manitou smiles in the crystal sky,
    Close breathing above them His life-strong breath;
And He speaks no more in fierce thunder sound,
So near is His happy hunting-ground.

Yet often I love, in my white canoe,
    To come to the forests and camps of earth: 50
'Twas there death's black arrow pierced me through;
    'Twas there my red-browed mother gave me birth;
There I, in the light of a young man's dawn,
Won the lily heart of dusk "Springing Fawn."

And love is a cord woven out of life,
    And dyed in the red of the living heart;
And time is the hunter's rusty knife,
    That cannot cut the red strands apart:
And I sail from the spirit shore to scan
Where the weaving of that strong cord began.   60

But I may not come with a giftless hand,
    So richly I pile, in my white canoe,
Flowers that bloom in the spirit land,
    Immortal smiles of Great Manitou.
When I paddle back to the shores of earth
I scatter them over the white man's hearth.

For love is the breath of the soul set free;
    So I cross the river that darkly rolls,
That my spirit may whisper soft to thee
    Of *thine* who wait in the "Camp of Souls."   70
When the bright day laughs, or the wan night grieves,
Come the dusky plumes of red "Singing Leaves."

(1905)   (1905)

The Dark Stag

A startled stag, the blue-grey Night,
  Leaps down beyond black pines.
Behind – a length of yellow light –
  The hunter's arrow shines:
His moccasins are stained with red,
  He bends upon his knee,
From covering peaks his shafts are sped,
The blue mists plume his mighty head, –
  Well may the swift Night flee!

The pale, pale Moon, a snow-white doe,   10
  Bounds by his dappled flank:
They beat the stars down as they go,
  Like wood-bells growing rank.
The winds lift dewlaps from the ground,
  Leap from the quaking reeds;
Their hoarse bays shake the forests round,
With keen cries on the track they bound, –
  Swift, swift the dark stag speeds!

Away! his white doe, far behind,
  Lies wounded on the plain;   20
Yells at his flank the nimblest wind,
  His large tears fall in rain;
Like lily-pads, small clouds grow white
  About his darkling way;
From his bald nest upon the height
The red-eyed eagle sees his flight;
He falters, turns, the antlered Night, –
  The dark stag stands at bay!

His feet are in the waves of space;
  His antlers broad and dun   30
He lowers; he turns his velvet face
  To front the hunter, Sun;
He stamps the lilied clouds, and high
  His branches fill the west.
The lean stork sails across the sky,
The shy loon shrieks to see him die,
  The winds leap at his breast.

Roar the rent lakes as thro' the wave
    Their silver warriors plunge,
As vaults from core of crystal cave   40
    The strong, fierce muskallunge;
Red torches of the sumach glare,
    Fall's council-fires are lit;
The bittern, squaw-like, scolds the air;
The wild duck splashes loudly where
    The rustling rice-spears knit.

Shaft after shaft the red Sun speeds:
    Rent the stag's dappled side.
His breast, fanged by the shrill winds, bleeds,
    He staggers on the tide;   50
He feels the hungry waves of space
    Rush at him high and blue;
Their white spray smites his dusky face,
Swifter the Sun's fierce arrows race
    And pierce his stout heart thro'.

His antlers fall; once more he spurns
    The hoarse hounds of the day;
His blood upon the crisp blue burns,
    Reddens the mounting spray;
His branches smite the wave – with cries   60
    The loud winds pause and flag –
He sinks in space – red glow the skies,
The brown earth crimsons as he dies,
    The strong and dusky stag.

(1905)   (1905)

Wilfred Campbell
1858-1918

———◆———

WILFRED CAMPBELL WAS born in Berlin (Kitchener), Canada West, and educated at the University of Toronto, Wycliffe College and the Episcopal Theological School of Cambridge, Massachusetts. He was ordained as a minister in the Episcopal Church in 1885. Six years later he resigned from the ministry and took a position with the civil service in Ottawa. Before moving to Ottawa, Campbell published two volumes of verse including his best-known collection, *Lake Lyrics and Other Poems* (1889). He subsequently published several other volumes of poetry, travel books on Canada, fiction and verse dramas.

The Winter Lakes

Out in a world of death far to the northward lying,
    Under the sun and the moon, under the dusk and the day;
Under the glimmer of stars and the purple of sunsets dying,
    Wan and waste and white, stretch the great lakes away.

Never a bud of spring, never a laugh of summer,
    Never a dream of love, never a song of bird;
But only the silence and white, the shores that grow chiller
        and dumber,
    Wherever the ice winds sob, and the griefs of winter are
        heard.

Crags that are black and wet out of the gray lake looming,
    Under the sunset's flush and the pallid, faint glimmer of
        dawn;
Shadowy, ghost-like shores, where midnight surfs are
        booming
    Thunders of wintry woe over the spaces wan.

10

Lands that loom like specters, whited regions of winter,
   Wastes of desolate woods, deserts of water and shore;
A world of winter and death, within these regions who enter,
   Lost to summer and life, go to return no more.

Moons that glimmer above, waters that lie white under,
   Miles and miles of lake far out under the night;
Foaming crests of waves, surfs that shoreward thunder,
   Shadowy shapes that flee, haunting the spaces white.   20

Lonely hidden bays, moon-lit, ice-rimmed, winding,
   Fringed by forests and crags, haunted by shadowy shores;
Hushed from the outward strife, where the mighty surf is
      grinding
   Death and hate on the rocks, as sandward and landward it
      roars.

(1889)   (1889)

Indian Summer

Along the line of smoky hills
   The crimson forest stands,
And all the day the blue-jay calls
   Throughout the autumn lands.

Now by the brook the maple leans
   With all his glory spread,
And all the sumachs on the hills
   Have turned their green to red.

Now by great marshes wrapt in mist,
   Or past some river's mouth,   10
Throughout the long, still autumn day
   Wild birds are flying south.

(1889)   (1889)

How One Winter Came in the Lake Region

For weeks and weeks the autumn world stood still,
  Clothed in the shadow of a smoky haze;
The fields were dead, the wind had lost its will,
And all the lands were hushed by wood and hill,
  In those grey, withered days.

Behind a mist the blear sun rose and set,
  At night the moon would nestle in a cloud;
The fisherman, a ghost, did cast his net;
The lake its shores forgot to chafe and fret,
  And hushed its caverns loud.   10

Far in the smoky woods the birds were mute,
  Save that from blackened tree a jay would scream,
Or far in swamps the lizard's lonesome lute
Would pipe in thirst, or by some gnarlèd root
  The tree-toad trilled his dream.

From day to day still hushed the season's mood,
  The streams stayed in their runnels shrunk and dry;
Suns rose aghast by wave and shore and wood,
And all the world, with ominous silence, stood
  In weird expectancy: 20

When one strange night the sun like blood went down,
  Flooding the heavens in a ruddy hue;
Red grew the lake, the sere fields parched and brown,
Red grew the marshes where the creeks stole down,
  But never a wind-breath blew.

That night I felt the winter in my veins,
  A joyous tremor of the icy glow;
And woke to hear the north's wild vibrant strains,
While far and wide, by withered woods and plains,
  Fast fell the driving snow.   30

(1893)   (1893)

September in the Laurentian Hills

Already Winter in his sombre round,
    Before his time hath touched these hills austere
With lonely flame. Last night, without a sound,
    The ghostly frost walked out by wood and mere.
And now the sumach curls his frond of fire,
    The aspen-tree reluctant drops his gold,
And down the gullies the North's wild vibrant lyre
    Rouses the bitter armies of the cold.

O'er this short afternoon the night draws down,
    With ominous chill, across these regions bleak;   10
Wind-beaten gold, the sunset fades around
    The purple loneliness of crag and peak,
Leaving the world an iron house wherein
Nor love nor life nor hope hath ever been.

(1899)   (1900)

The Higher Kinship

Life is too grim with anxious, eating care
    To cherish what is best. Our souls are scarred
    By daily agonies, and our conscience marred
By petty tyrannies that waste and wear.
Why is this human fate so hard to bear?
    Could we but live with hill-lakes silver-starred,
    Or where the eternal silence leaneth toward
The awful front of nature, waste and bare,

Then might we, brothers to the lofty thought
    And inward self-communion of her dream,   10
Into that closer kin with love be brought,
Where mighty hills and woods and waters, wan,
Moon-paved at midnight, or godlike at dawn,
    Hold all earth's aspirations in their gleam.

(1905)   (1923)

The Politician

Carven in leathern mask or brazen face,
　　Were I time's sculptor, I would set this man.
　　Retreating from the truth, his hawk-eyes scan
The platforms of all public thought for place.
There wriggling with insinuating grace,
　　He takes poor hope and effort by the hand,
　　And flatters with half-truths and accents bland,
Till even zeal and earnest love grow base.

Knowing no right, save power's grim right-of-way;
　　No nobleness, save life's ignoble praise;　　　　　　　　10
No future, save this sordid day to day;
　　He is the curse of these material days:
Juggling with mighty wrongs and mightier lies,
This worshipper of Dagon and his flies!

(1905)　　　　　　　　　　　　　　　　　　　　　　(1923)

Nature

Nature, the dream that wraps us round,
　　One comforting and saving whole;
And as the clothes to the body of man,
　　The mantle of the soul.

Nature, the door that opens wide
　　From this close, fetid house of ill;
That lifts from curse of street to vast
　　Receding hill on hill.

Nature, the mood, now sweet of night,
　　Now grand and splendid, large of day;　　　　　　　10
From vast skyline and cloudy towers,
　　To stars in heaven that stray.

Nature, the hope, the truth, the gleam,
　　Beyond this bitter cark and dole;
Whose walls the infinite weft of dream,
　　Whose gift is to console.

(1905)　　　　　　　　　　　　　　　　　　　　　　(1923)

Charles Gordon
1860 – 1937

THE SON OF a Presbyterian clergyman, Charles Gordon spent his early years in Glengarry County, Canada West. After studying at the University of Toronto and at the University of Edinburgh, he became a minister of the Presbyterian Church in 1890. Gordon's first novel, *Black Rock*, appeared in serial form in 1898 under the pseudonym Ralph Connor. With its blend of type characters, Christian didacticism and sentimental plots, this novel exemplifies the characteristic qualities of the more than twenty novels which followed it. In his autobiography, *Postscript to Adventure* (1938), Gordon reveals many of the same interests and commitments which are given fictional treatment in his novels.

From
Postscript to Adventure

Highland Religion

FROM THE TIME of Constantine, Christianity has been a polemic religion. Its early conquests were won by its spiritual powers only. By the end of the fourth century, however, after the church had made alliance with the state, it lost much of primitive power. The Reformation in Britain was largely political and both in England and in Scotland was closely identified with political movements.

The Presbyterian Church in England, and especially in Scotland, assumed powers of state control. In Scotland the Presbyterian Church became the state church and exercised large influence and control in the temporal affairs of the people. This union of temporal and spiritual power had its natural reaction in the claim of the state to authority over the church. As a protest against this claim of state control, some six hundred ministers in what is known in Scottish ecclesiastical history as the Disruption, in 1843, walked out from their manses, and with their congregations left their churches and formed the Free Church of Scotland, which soon grew to be a vigorous and missionary church.

In the early days of Canadian history Presbyterian settlers from Scotland, Ireland, Holland and from the United States, retaining their ecclesiastical affiliations with their home churches, settled in large numbers in Eastern and Central Canada, so that at one time in the Canadian provinces, Maritime and Central, there were no fewer than ten types of Presbyterians with their separate churches.

In Glengarry the first Presbyterians were for the most part associated with the Church of Scotland – the Auld Kirk, as it was known. The Disruption in Scotland was a very real protest against the encroachment by the state upon the independence of the church, but in Canada there was no such invasion by the state and therefore no cause for division. But the Free Church in the homeland, feeling that the great principles of religious freedom were threatened wherever the Established, or Auld, Kirk was in existence, dispatched delegates to Canada under whose influence the Free Presbyterian Church was set up.

At the time of the Disruption in Scotland my father was a student in theology in Aberdeen. For conscience' sake he left the Auld Kirk College, surrendering a bursary, and became an ardent Free Churchman. He carried the memory of this experience with him to Canada, and naturally joined the Free Presbyterian Church.

In his Glengarry congregation there was at first no distinction between the Auld Kirk and the Free. But the division soon appeared and trouble ensued. The congregation was overwhelmingly Free Church. But the church building and about two hundred acres of land belonged to the Auld Kirk of whom there were half a dozen or so members in the congregation. These Auld Kirkers claimed the church building, although it had been erected almost entirely with Free Church money. The minister protested. The church ought to belong to those who had paid for it.

On a certain Sabbath morning the minister, my father, a fiery Highlander, found the church door locked with a new padlock and his congregation outside waiting admission. They had not long to wait.

"Donald McEwen, open this door," ordered the minister.

"There is a new lock on the door, sir," said the beadle.

"Give me the key!" said the minister. Donald handed him the key.

"Is this the key of this church?"

"Yes, sir, but they have put on a new lock, sir."

"I ask you, is this the key which you have always used to open this church?"

"Yes, sir, but this lock – "

"Answer my question! Is this the key of this church? Yes or no."

"Yes, sir, it is the key, but –"

"This is the key which ordinarily opens this door? Yes or no."

"It is the key."

The minister with slow and painstaking care, but with no result, tries the key.

"Donald, and you Mr. McNaughton, and all of you will notice that there is something wrong with this lock. The key will not open it. Stand clear!"

With a quick step the minister drives his foot against the door. The padlock is snapped, the door stands open. The people pass in for the public worship of God.

The minister is summoned to court in Cornwall to answer the charge of housebreaking and unlawful entry. On his black stallion, for the roads were muddy, and followed by a great cavalcade of mounted Free Kirkers, the minister rides twenty-five miles to the courts. The scene, as described in the book, *Torches Through the Bush,* is enacted.

The minister escapes jail but the Free Kirkers lose the church.

Religion in Glengarry in those days was a solemn and serious matter, a thing of life and death. An arrangement was made by the court for the use of the building by the Free Church folk, those of the Auld Kirk being too few to support a minister of their own. In a short time the Free Church people with great enthusiasm proceeded to erect a new brick church for themselves, which thereupon became the only Presbyterian church for the community, and Auld Kirkers remaining aloof from these housebreakers and seceders were without church privileges.

They tell a story, how true it is I cannot say, of how the chief champion of the Auld Kirk was won back to membership in the new church. One cold winter day the minister on his pastoral rounds, with his wife in the cutter beside him, came to the house of the leading Auld Kirker, Duncan Cameron.

"Mary," he said to his wife, "are you not cold?"

"Oh, just a little," she replied.

"Mary, you are very cold indeed," asserted the minister. "We will drive in and get warm at Duncan Cameron's."

"But, papa, Duncan Cameron –"

"Whisht, woman! Will he refuse shelter to a woman starving with the cold?" asked the minister with a twinkle in his eye.

He drove up to the door. Old Duncan himself appeared at the door, stern and forbidding.

"My wife is feeling the cold, Mr. Cameron," said the minister. "Perhaps you will not be keeping us out."

"God bless my soul, minister!" said the old man. "Is it a heathen you will be thinking that I am?"

In a few minutes they were cozily sitting in the large and comfortable kitchen before a blazing fire, with a cup of tea in their hands and Mrs. Cameron pressing oatcakes and scones upon them.

After half an hour of kindly inquiry about the family and especially about Christy's new baby, a lusty grandson, the minister in a voice of solemn authority said:

"Duncan, you will pass me the Book."

What could a man do? The Bible was brought. Family worship ended, the minister and his wife, with the eager aid of Duncan and his wife, wrapped themselves up warmly and proceeded to thank their hosts for their hospitality.

"If thine enemy hunger feed him, eh, Duncan?" said the minister with a little twinkle in his eye.

"My God! minister, don't be saying them words," said Duncan in a husky voice.

"Well, I will say no more than this, Duncan," said the minister in a voice kind but solemn. "The Church is there. It is not my church nor is it your church. It is the house of God. And He Himself will give you a welcome on the Sabbath Day."

The following Sabbath the congregation was astonished beyond measure to see Duncan Cameron and his wife, followed by their daughter, Christy, with her new baby in her arms, and her husband walk down the aisle to their seats in the church. A little later Duncan Cameron explained the phenomenon to his friend Kenneth McRae.

"God pity me, could I turn them freezing from my door? And when he 'took the books' you know yourself how it was."

There was little denominational rivalry, however, in the community for the sufficient reason that there were no rival churches. There were Baptists, few in number, but very stanch. They had no settled minister, but occasionally a minister would visit the district and hold a series of meetings in the homes of his people. One I remember well, a Mr. R. Rainboth, a handsome man and very courteous in his manners. Riding by the school one day he lifted his stovepipe hat in salutation of the pupils out at recess, which act of courtesy we considered a clear indication of pride. This opinion was strengthened by the revelation that his hair was "split in the middle," an unforgivable display of pride in the opinion of the boys. Mr. Rainboth was an eloquent and ardent exponent of the Baptist faith and had the hardihood, moreover, to challenge the Presbyterian minister to public debate.

The stage was set in the Presbyterian church. The church was packed. Glengarry folks, being mostly of Highland stock, love a fight. That the fight was of a spiritual nature relieved it of all carnal elements. Even churchmen and churchwomen could enjoy it with a clear conscience.

The Presbyterian minister was to open the debate, which he did by a dissertation on the origin and nature, worship and sacraments of the Old Testament church, together with its limitations and imperfections. At the end of the second day he was still in the Old Testament and going strong. But such was the overwhelming passion of his eloquence, so furious were his denunciations of the Baptist heresies, so truly terrible was his aspect as he marched up and down the platform that his opponent failed to appear on the third day, and the debate was over. The Presbyterians were jubilant, the Baptists scornfully disgusted.

"Debate?" exclaimed a Baptist brother, "Would you call that a debate?"

"What else?" inquired a Presbyterian.

"Well, all I will say is, it was God's mercy he did not have a claymore in his fist."

No, there was little denominational rivalry within the confines of the Presbyterian area. Methodists there were none. Never as a boy did I behold a Methodist in the flesh. At Moose Creek, ten miles or so away, there were said to be Methodists. But what sort of creatures they were I knew not. To my mind they were of such a nature that I would hate to meet them in the dark.

There were, however, Congregationalists, with whom the Presbyterians were on the most friendly terms. This was doubtless due to the fact that the minister's wife had been a Congregationalist. The younger generation, however, bore towards the Congregationalists a feeling of rivalry that amounted almost to contempt. The Congregational church was a small wooden structure, unpainted and without a steeple. Its windows had little square panes like those of the school. It was altogether contemptible. Its very name was contemptible: it was known as the Little Church. And there it stood right across the road from the new Presbyterian church, grand with steeple and proper church windows and everything.

My brother and I, passing by the Little Church one day, paused to look at it. Its mere existence was an affront to our church. Unprotected the square panes of the Little Church glowed in the sunlight. Denominational zeal suddenly flamed up in my heart. By an evil chance a number of perfectly smooth stones lay in the dust at my feet. The temptation proved irresistible. I picked up a stone and flung it at a window. The stone crashed through one of the square panes. My brother with shocked but delighted admiration rocked with laughter. Excited with the success of my own daring achievement and stimulated by his glee, I sent a second stone smashing through the window. Not to be outdone, my brother tried a shot, with perfect success. The thing became a contest of skill and daring. When most of the panes were shattered a sudden conviction of the enormity of our offense dawned upon us. We dashed off homeward filled with a feeling of mingled pride and terror, but also with a dread of doom. We were undoubtedly possessed of the devil. Nothing that I can think of could be a finer testimony both to the high esteem and affection in which our parents were held by the Congregational community and to the spirit of Christian forbearance shown by the members of the Little Church than the fact that the windows were quietly repaired without a word of complaint to the parents of the offenders.

(1938)   (1938)

Charles G.D. Roberts
1860 – 1943

THE SON OF an Anglican minister, Charles George Douglas Roberts was born at Douglas, New Brunswick, and raised in a country parish near the Tantramar marshes. Following his graduation from the University of New Brunswick, Roberts published his first collection of verse, *Orion, and Other Poems*, in 1880. During his career, Roberts was an editor, critic, historian, translator, poet, novelist and short story writer. Among his best-known works are his realistic animal stories and the lyrics and sonnets which appeared in two early collections, *In Divers Tones* (1886) and *Songs of the Common Day* (1893). "The Poetry of Nature" first appeared in *Forum* in 1897.

Dedication

[To *Orion and Other Poems*]

These first-fruits, gathered by distant ways,
In brief, sweet moments of toilsome days,
    When the weary brain was a thought less weary,
And the heart found strength for delight and praise, –

I bring them and proffer them to thee,
All blown and beaten by winds of the sea,
    Ripened beside the tide-vext river, –
The broad, ship-laden Miramichi.

Even though on my lips no Theban bees
Alighted, – though harsh and ill-formed these,   10
    Of alien matters in distant regions
Wrought in the youth of the centuries, –

Yet of some worth in thine eyes be they,
For bare mine innermost heart they lay;
    And the old, firm love that I bring thee with them
Distance shall quench not, or time bewray.

(1880)   (1949)

The Tantramar Revisited

Summers and summers have come, and gone with the flight of
     the swallow;
Sunshine and thunder have been, storm, and winter, and
     frost;
Many and many a sorrow has all but died from remembrance,
Many a dream of joy fall'n in the shadow of pain.
Hands of chance and change have marred, or moulded, or
     broken,
Busy with spirit or flesh, all I most have adored;
Even the bosom of Earth is strewn with heavier shadows, —
Only in these green hills, aslant to the sea, no change!
Here where the road that has climbed from the inland valleys
     and woodlands,
Dips from the hill-tops down, straight to the base of the hills, —   10
Here, from my vantage-ground, I can see the scattering
     houses,
Stained with time, set warm in orchards, and meadows, and
     wheat,
Dotting the broad bright slopes outspread to southward and
     eastward,
Wind-swept all day long, blown by the south-east wind.
Skirting the sunbright uplands stretches a riband of meadow,
Shorn of the labouring grass, bulwarked well from the sea,
Fenced on its seaward border with long clay dikes from the
     turbid
Surge and flow of the tides vexing the Westmoreland shores.
Yonder, toward the left, lie broad the Westmoreland
     marshes, —
Miles on miles they extend, level, and grassy, and dim,   20
Clear from the long red sweep of flats to the sky in the
     distance,
Save for the outlying heights, green-rampired Cumberland
     Point;
Miles on miles outrolled, and the river-channels divide them, —
Miles on miles of green, barred by the hurtling gusts.

Miles on miles beyond the tawny bay is Minudie.
There are low blue hills; villages gleam at their feet.
Nearer a white sail shines across the water, and nearer
Still are the slim, grey masts of fishing boats dry on the flats.
Ah, how well I remember those wide red flats, above tide-mark

Pale with scurf of the salt, seamed and baked in the sun! 30
Well I remember the piles of blocks and ropes, and the net-reels
Wound with the beaded nets, dripping and dark from the sea!
Now at this season the nets are unwound: they hang from the rafters
Over the fresh-stowed hay in upland barns, and the wind
Blows all day through the chinks, with the streaks of sunlight and
        sways them
Softly at will; or they lie heaped in the gloom of a loft.

Now at this season the reels are empty and idle; I see them
Over the lines of the dikes, over the gossiping grass.
Now at this season they swing in the long strong wind, thro' the
        lonesome
Golden afternoon, shunned by the foraging gulls. 40
Near about sunset the crane will journey homeward above them;
Round them, under the moon, all the calm night long,
Winnowing soft grey wings of marsh-owls wander and wander,
Now to the broad, lit marsh, now to the dusk of the dike.
Soon, thro' their dew-wet frames, in the live keen freshness of
        morning,
Out of the teeth of the dawn blows back the awakening wind.
Then, as the blue day mounts, and the low-shot shafts of the sunlight
Glance from the tide to the shore, gossamers jewelled with dew
Sparkle and wave, where late sea-spoiling fathoms of drift-net
Myriad-meshed, uploomed sombrely over the land. 50

Well I remember it all. The salt raw scent of the margin;
While, with men at the windlass, groaned each reel, and the net,
Surging in ponderous lengths, uprose and coiled in its station;
Then each man to his home, — well I remember it all!

Yet, as I sit and watch, this present peace of the landscape, —
Stranded boats, these reels empty and idle, the hush,
One grey hawk slow-wheeling above yon cluster of haystacks, —
More than the old-time stir this stillness welcomes me home.
Ah, the old-time stir, how once it stung me with rapture, —
Old-time sweetness, the winds freighted with honey and salt! 60
Yet will I stay my steps and not go down to the marsh-land, —
Muse and recall far off, rather remember than see, —
Lest on too close sight I miss the darling illusion,
Spy at their task even here the hands of chance and change.

(1886) (1974)

An Ode for the Canadian Confederacy

Awake, my country, the hour is great with change!
　　Under this gloom which yet obscures the land,
From ice-blue strait and stern Laurentian range
　　　　To where giant peaks our western bounds command,
A deep voice stirs, vibrating in men's ears
　　As if their own hearts throbbed that thunder forth,
A sound wherein who hearkens wisely hears
　　The voice of the desire of this strong North,
　　　　This North whose heart of fire
　　　　Yet knows not its desire   10
　　Clearly, but dreams, and murmurs in the dream.
The hour of dreams is done. Lo, in the hills the gleam!

Awake, my country, the hour of dreams is done!
　　Doubt not, nor dread the greatness of thy fate.
Tho' faint souls fear the keen confronting sun,
　　And fain would bid the morn of splendour wait;
Tho' dreamers, rapt in starry visions, cry
　　　　'Lo, yon thy future, yon thy faith, thy fame!'
And stretch vain hands to stars, thy fame is nigh,
　　Here in Canadian hearth, and home, and name; –   20
　　　　　This name which yet shall grow
　　　　　Till all the nations know
Us for a patriot people, heart and hand
Loyal to our native earth, our own Canadian land!

O strong hearts, guarding the birthright of our glory,
　　Worth your best blood this heritage that ye guard!
These mighty streams resplendent with our story,
　　These iron coasts by rage of seas unjarred, –
What fields of peace these bulwarks well secure!
　　What vales of plenty those calm floods supply!   30
Shall not our love this rough, sweet land make sure,
　　Her bounds preserve inviolate, though we die?
　　　　O strong hearts of the North,
　　　　　Let flame your loyalty forth,
　　And put the craven and base to an open shame,
Till earth shall know the Child of Nations by her name!

(1886)   (1974)

In September

This windy, bright September afternoon
    My heart is wide awake, yet full of dreams.
    The air, alive with hushed confusion, teems
With scent of grain-fields, and a mystic rune,
Foreboding of the fall of Summer soon,
    Keeps swelling and subsiding; till there seems
    O'er all the world of valleys, hills, and streams,
Only the wind's inexplicable tune.

My heart is full of dreams, yet wide awake.
    I lie and watch the topmost tossing boughs   10
    Of tall elms, pale against the vaulted blue;
But even now some yellowing branches shake,
    Some hue of death the living green endows: –
    If beauty flies, fain would I vanish too.

(1886)   (1974)

In the Wide Awe
and Wisdom of the Night

In the wide awe and wisdom of the night
    I saw the round world rolling on its way,
Beyond significance of depth or height,
    Beyond the interchange of dark and day.
I marked the march to which is set no pause,
    And that stupendous orbit, round whose rim
The great sphere sweeps, obedient unto laws
    That utter the eternal thought of Him.
I compassed time, outstripped the starry speed,
    And in my still soul apprehended space,   10
Till, weighing laws which these but blindly heed,
    At last I came before Him face to face, –
And knew the Universe of no such span
As the august infinitude of Man.

(1893)   (1974)

The Herring Weir

Back to the green deeps of the outer bay
    The red and amber currents glide and cringe,
    Diminishing behind a luminous fringe
Of cream-white surf and wandering wraiths of spray.
Stealthily, in the old reluctant way,
    The red flats are uncovered, mile on mile,
    To glitter in the sun a golden while.
Far down the flats, a phantom sharply grey,
The herring weir emerges, quick with spoil.
    Slowly the tide forsakes it. Then draws near,   10
    Descending from the farm-house on the height,
A cart, with gaping tubs. The oxen toil
    Sombrely o'er the level to the weir,
    And drag a long black trail across the light.

(1893)   (1974)

The Salt Flats

Here clove the keels of centuries ago
    Where now unvisited the flats lie bare.
    Here seethed the sweep of journeying waters, where
No more the tumbling flats of Fundy flow,
And only in the samphire pipes creep slow
    The salty currents of the sap. The air
Hums desolately with wings that seaward fare,
Over the lonely reaches beating low.

The wastes of hard and meagre weeds are thronged
With murmurs of a past that time has wronged;   10
    And ghosts of many an ancient memory
Dwell by the brackish pools and ditches blind,
In these low-lying pastures of the wind,
    These marshes pale and meadows by the sea.

(1893)   (1974)

The Pea-Fields

These are the fields of light, and laughing air,
   And yellow butterflies, and foraging bees,
   And whitish, wayward blossoms winged as these,
And pale green tangles like a seamaid's hair.
Pale, pale the blue, but pure beyond compare,
   And pale the sparkle of the far-off seas,
   A-shimmer like these fluttering slopes of peas,
And pale the open landscape everywhere.

From fence to fence a perfumed breath exhales
   O'er the bright pallor of the well-love fields, –   10
My fields of Tantramar in summer-time;
   And, scorning the poor feed their pasture yields,
Up from the busy lots the cattle climb,
   To gaze with longing through the grey, mossed rails.

(1893)   (1974)

The Mowing

This is the voice of high midsummer's heat.
   The rasping vibrant clamour soars and shrills
   O'er all the meadowy range of shadeless hills,
As if a host of giant cicadae beat
The cymbals of their wings with tireless feet,
   Or brazen grasshoppers with triumphing note
   From the long swath proclaimed the fate that smote
The clover and timothy-tops and meadowsweet.

The crying knives glide on; the green swath lies.
   And all noon long the sun, with chemic ray,   10
   Seals up each cordial essence in its cell,
That in the dusky stalls, some winter's day,
   The spirit of June, here prisoned by his spell,
   May cheer the herds with pasture memories.

(1893)   (1974)

Marsyas

A little grey hill-glade, close-turfed, withdrawn
Beyond resort or heed of trafficking feet,
Ringed round with slim trunks of the mountain ash.
Through the slim trunks and scarlet bunches flash —
Beneath the clear chill glitterings of the dawn —
Far off, the crests, where down the rosy shore
The Pontic surges beat.
The plains lie dim below. The thin airs wash
The circuit of the autumn-coloured hills,
And this high glade, whereon   10
The satyr pipes, who soon shall pipe no more.
He sits against the beech-tree's mighty bole, —
He leans, and with persuasive breathing fills
The happy shadows of the slant-set lawn.
The goat-feet fold beneath a gnarlèd root;
And sweet, and sweet the note that steals and thrills
From slender stops of that shy flute.
Then to the goat-feet comes the wide-eyed fawn
Hearkening; the rabbits fringe the glade, and lay
Their long ears to the sound;   20
In the pale boughs the partridge gather round,
And quaint hern from the sea-green river reeds;
The wild ram halts upon a rocky horn
O'erhanging; and, unmindful of his prey,
The leopard steals with narrowed lids to lay
His spotted length along the ground.
The thin airs wash, the thin clouds wander by,
And those hushed listeners move not. All the morn
He pipes, soft-swaying, and with half-shut eye,
In rapt content of utterance, —   30
               nor heeds
The young God standing in his branchy place,
The languor on his lips, and in his face,
Divinely inaccessible, the scorn.

(1893)   (1974)

The Skater

My glad feet shod with the glittering steel
I was the god of the winged heel.

The hills in the far white sky were lost;
The world lay still in the wide white frost;

And the woods hung hushed in their long white dream
By the ghostly, glimmering, ice-blue stream.

Here was a pathway, smooth like glass,
Where I and the wandering wind might pass

To the far-off palaces, drifted deep,
Where Winter's retinue rests in sleep.   10

I followed the lure, I fled like a bird,
Till the startled hollows awoke and heard

A spinning whisper, a sibilant twang,
As the stroke of the steel on the tense ice rang;

And the wandering wind was left behind
As faster, faster I followed my mind;

Till the blood sang high in my eager brain,
And the joy of my flight was almost pain.

Then I stayed the rush of my eager speed
And silently went as a drifting seed, –   20

Slowly, furtively, till my eyes
Grew big with the awe of a dim surmise,

And the hair of my neck began to creep
At hearing the wilderness talk in sleep.

Shapes in the fir-gloom drifted near.
In the deep of my heart I heard my fear.

And I turned and fled, like a soul pursued,
From the white, inviolate solitude.

(1901)   (1974)

The Prisoners of the Pitcher-Plant

AT THE EDGE of a rough piece of open, where the scrubby bushes which clothed the plain gave space a little to the weeds and harsh grasses, stood the clustering pitchers of a fine young sarracenia. These pitchers, which were its leaves, were of a light, cool green, vividly veined with crimson and shading into a bronzy red about the lip and throat. They were of all sizes, being at all stages of growth; and the largest, which had now, on the edge of summer, but barely attained maturity, were about six inches in length and an inch and a quarter in extreme diameter. Down in the very heart of the cluster, hardly to be discerned, was a tiny red-tipped bud, destined to shoot up, later in the season, into a sturdy flower-stalk.

Against the fresh, warm green of the sunlit world surrounding it, the sarracenia's peculiar colouring stood out conspicuously, its streaks and splashes of red having the effect of blossoms. This effect, at a season when bright-hued blooms were scarce, made the plant very attractive to any insects that chanced within view of it. There was nearly always some flutterer or hummer poising above it, or touching it eagerly to dart away again in disappointment. But every once in a while some little wasp, or fly, or shining-winged beetle, or gauzy ichneumon, would alight on the alluring lip, pause, and peer down into the pitcher. As a rule the small investigator would venture farther and farther, till it disappeared. Then it never came out again.

On a leaf of a huckleberry bush, overhanging the pitcher-plant, a little black ant was running about with the nimble curiosity of her kind. An orange and black butterfly, fluttering lazily in the sun, came close beside the leaf. At this moment a passing shrike swooped down and caught the butterfly in his beak. One of his long wings, chancing to strike the leaf, sent it whirling from its stem; and the ant fell directly upon one of the pitchers below.

It was far down upon the red, shining lip of the pitcher that she fell; and there she clung resolutely, her feet sinking into a sort of fur of smooth, whitish hairs. When she had quite recovered her equanimity she started to explore her new surroundings; and, because that was the easiest way to go, she went in the direction toward which the hairs all pointed. In a moment, therefore, she found herself just on the edge of the precipitous slope from the lip to the throat of the pitcher. Here, finding the slope strangely slippery, she thought it best to stop and retrace her steps. But when she attempted this she found it impossible.

The little, innocent-looking hairs all pressed against her, thrusting her downward. The more she struggled, the more energetically and elastically they pushed back at her; till all at once she was forced over the round, smooth edge, and fell.

To her terrified amazement, it was water she fell into. The pitcher was about half full of the chilly fluid. In her kickings and twistings she brought herself to the walls of her green prison, and tried to clamber out, – but here, again, were those cruel hairs on guard to foil her. She tried to evade them, to break them down, to bite them off with her strong, sharp mandibles. At last, by a supreme effort, she managed to drag herself almost clear, – but only to be at once hurled back, and far out into the water, by the sharp recoil of her tormentors.

Though pretty well exhausted by now, she would not give up the struggle; and presently her convulsive efforts brought her alongside of a refuge. It was only the floating body of a dead moth, but to the ant it was a safe and ample raft. Eagerly she crept out upon it, and lay very still for awhile, recovering her strength. More fortunate than most shipwrecked voyagers, she had an edible raft and was therefore in no imminent peril of starvation.

The light that came through the veined, translucent walls of this watery prison was of an exquisite cool beryl, very different from the warm daylight overhead. The ant had never been in any such surroundings before, and was bewildered by the strangeness of them. After a brief rest she investigated minutely every corner of her queer retreat, and then, finding that there was nothing she could do to better the situation, she resumed her attitude of repose, with only the slight waving of her antennae to show that she was awake.

For a long time nothing happened. No winds were astir that day, and no sounds came down into the pitcher save the shrill, happy chirping of birds in the surrounding bushes. But suddenly the pitcher began to tip and rock slightly, and the water to wash within its coloured walls. Something had alighted on the pitcher's lip.

It was something comparatively heavy, that was evident. A moment or two later it came sliding down those treacherous hairs, and fell into the water with a great splash which nearly swept the ant from her refuge.

The new arrival was a bee. And now began a tremendous turmoil within the narrow prison. The bee struggled, whirled around on the surface with thrashing wings, and sent the water swashing in every direction, till the ant was nearly drowned. She hung to her raft, however, and waited philosophically for the hubbub to subside. At length the bee too, after half a dozen vain and exhausting struggles to climb out against the opposing array of hairs, encountered the body of the dead moth. Instantly she tried to raise herself upon it, so as to escape the chill of the water and dry her wings for flight. But she was too heavy. The moth sank, and rolled over, at the same time being thrust against the wall of the pitcher. The ant, in high indignation clutched a bundle of the hostile hairs in her mandibles, and held herself at anchor against the wall.

Thoroughly used up, and stupid with panic and chill, the bee kept on futilely grappling with the moth's body, which, in its turn, kept on sinking and rolling beneath her. A very few minutes of such disastrous folly sufficed to end the struggle, and soon the bee was floating, drowned and motionless, beside the moth. Then the ant, with satisfaction, returned to her refuge.

When things get started happening, they are quite apt to keep it up for awhile, as if events invited events. A large hunting spider, creeping among the grass and weeds, discovered the handsome cluster of the sarracenia. She was one of the few creatures who had learned the secret of the pitcher-plant and knew how to turn it to account. More than once had she found easy prey in some trapped insect struggling near the top of a well-filled pitcher.

Selecting the largest pitcher as the one most likely to yield results, the spider climbed its stem. Then she mounted the bright swell of the pitcher itself, whose smooth outer surface offered no obstacle to such visitors. The pitcher swayed and bowed. The water within washed heavily. And the ant, with new alarm, marked the big, black shadow of the spider creeping up the outside of her prison.

Having reached the lip of the leaf and cautiously crawled over upon it, the spider took no risks with those traitor hairs. She threw two or three stout cables of web across the lip; and then, with this secure anchorage by which to pull herself back, she ventured fearlessly down the steep of that perilous throat. One hooked claw, outstretched behind her, held aloft the cable which exuded from her spinnerets as she moved.

On the extreme of the slope she stopped, and her red, jewelled cluster of eyes glared fiercely down upon the little black ant. The latter shrank and crouched, and tried to hide herself under the side of the dead moth to escape the light of those baleful eyes. This new peril was one which appalled her far more than all the others she had encountered.

At this most critical of all crises in the destiny of the little black ant, the fickle Fortune of the Wild was seized with another whim. An overwhelming cataclysm descended suddenly upon the tiny world of the pitcher-plant. The soft, furry feet of some bounding monster – rabbit, fox, or wildcat – came down amongst the clustered pitchers, crushing several to bits and scattering wide the contents of all the rest. Among these latter was that which contained the little black ant.

Drenched, astonished, but unhurt, she found herself lying in a tuft of splashed grass, once more free. Above her, on a grass-top, clung the bewildered spider. As it hung there, conspicious to all the foraging world, a great black-and-yellow wasp pounced upon it, stung it into helplessness, and carried it off on heavily humming wing.

(1907)   (1907)

The Poetry of Nature

"THE POETRY OF earth is never dead," wrote Keats; and, though the statement sounds, at first thought, a dangerously sweeping one, there is no doubt that if he had been called upon to argue the point he would have successfully maintained his thesis. Regarded subjectively, the poetry of earth, or, in other words, the quality which makes for poetry in external nature, is that power in nature which moves us by suggestion, which excites in us emotion, imagination, or poignant association, which plays upon the tense-strings of our sympathies with the fingers of memory or desire. This power may reside not less in a bleak pasture-lot than in a paradisal close of bloom and verdure, not less in a roadside thistle-patch than in a peak that soars into the sunset. It works through sheer beauty or sheer sublimity; but it may work with equal effect through austerity or reticence or limitation or change. It may use the most common scenes, the most familiar facts and forms, as the vehicle of its most penetrating and most illuminating message. It is apt to make the drop of dew on a grass-blade as significant as the starred sphere of the sky.

The poetry of nature, by which I mean this "poetry of earth" expressed in words, may be roughly divided into two main classes: that which deals with pure description, and that which treats of nature in some one of its many relations with humanity. The latter class is that which alone was contemplated in Keats's line. It has many subdivisions; it includes much of the greatest poetry that the world has known; and there is little verse of acknowledged mastery that does not depend upon it for some portion of its appeal.

The former class has but a slender claim to recognition as poetry, under any definition of poetry that does not make metrical form the prime essential. The failures of the wisest to enunciate a satisfactory definition of poetry make it almost presumptuous for a critic now to attempt the task; but from an analysis of these failures one may educe something roughly to serve the purpose. To say that *poetry is the metrical expression in words of thought fused in emotion,* is of course incomplete; but it has the advantage of defining. No one can think that anything other than poetry is intended by such a definition; and nothing is excluded that can show a clear claim to admittance. But the poetry of pure description might perhaps not pass without challenge, so faint is the flame of its emotion, so imperfect the fusion of its thought.

It is verse of this sort that is meant by undiscriminating critics when they inveigh against "nature-poetry," and declare that the only poetry worth man's attention is that which has to do with the heart of man.

Merely descriptive poetry is not very far removed from the work of the reporter and the photographer. Lacking the selective quality of creative art, it is in reality little more than a presentation of some of the raw materials of poetry. It leaves the reader unmoved, because little emotion has gone to its making. Poetry of this sort, at its best, is to be found abundantly in Thomson's "Seasons." At less than its best it concerns no one.

Nature becomes significant to man when she is passed through the alembic of his heart. Irrelevant and confusing details having been purged away, what remains is single and vital. It acts either by interpreting, recalling, suggesting, or symbolizing some phase of human feeling. Out of the fusing heat born of this contact comes the perfect line, luminous, unforgettable, with something of mystery in its beauty that eludes analysis. Whatever it be that is brought to the alembic, — naked hill, or barren sand-reach, sea or meadow, weed or star, — it comes out charged with a new force, imperishable and active wherever it finds sympathies to vibrate under its currents.

In the imperishable verse of ancient Greece and Rome, nature-poetry of the higher class is generally supposed to play but a small part. In reality, it is nearly always present, nearly always active in that verse; but it appears in such a disguise that its origin is apt to be overlooked.

The Greeks — and the Romans, of course, following their pattern — personified the phenomena of nature till these, for all purposes of art, became human. The Greeks made their anthropomorphic gods of the forces of nature which compelled their adoration. Of these personifications they sang, as of men of like passions with themselves; but in truth it was of external nature that they made their songs. Bion's wailing "Lament for Adonis," human as it is throughout, is in its final analysis a poem of nature. By an intense, but perhaps unconscious, subjective process, the ancients supplied external nature with their own moods, impulses, and passions.

The transitions from the ancient to the modern fashion of looking at nature are to be found principally in the work of the Celtic bards, who, rather than the cloistered students of that time, kept alive the true fire of poetry through the long darkness of the Middle Ages.

The modern attitude toward nature, as distinguished from that of the Greeks, begins to show itself clearly in English song very soon after the great revivifying movement which we call the Renaissance. At first, it is a very simple matter indeed. Men sing of nature because nature is impressing them directly. A joyous season calls forth a joyous song: —

> "Summer is icumen in,
>   Lhude sing, cuccu.
> Groweth sed and bloweth med
>   And springth the wude nu."

This is the poet's answering hail, when the spring-time calls to his blood. With the fall of the leaf, his singing has a sombre and foreboding note; and winter in the world makes winter in his song.

This is nature-poetry in its simplest form, — the form which it chiefly took with the spontaneous Elizabethans. But it soon became more complex, as life and society became entangled in more complex conditions. The artificialities of the Queen Anne period delayed this evolution; but with Gray and Collins we see it fairly in process. Man, looking upon external nature, projects himself into her workings. His own wrath he apprehends in the violence of the storm; his own joy in the loveliness of opening blossoms; his own mirth in the light waves running in the sun; his own gloom in the heaviness of the rain and wind. In all nature he finds but phenomena of himself. She becomes but an expression of his hopes, his fears, his cravings, his despair. This intense subjectivity is peculiarly characteristic of the nature-poetry produced by Byron and his school. When this Titan of modern song apostrophizes the storm thundering over Jura, he speaks to the tumult in the deeps of his own soul. When he addresses the stainless tranquillities of "clear, placid Leman," what moves him to utterance is the contemplation of such a calm as his vexed spirit often craved.

When man's heart and the heart of nature had become thus closely involved, the relationship between them and, consequently, the manner of its expression in song became complex almost beyond the possibilities of analysis. Wordsworth's best poetry is to be found in the utterances of the high-priest in nature's temple, interpreting the mysteries. The "Lines Composed a Few Miles Above Tintern Abbey" are, at first glance, chiefly descriptive; but their actual function is to convey to a restless age, troubled with small cares seen in too close perspective, the large, contemplative wisdom which seemed to Wordsworth the message of the scene which moved him

Keats, his soul aflame with the worship of beauty, was impassioned toward the manifestations of beauty in the world about him, and, at the same time, he used these freely as symbols to express other aspects of the same compelling spirit. Shelley, the most complex of the group, sometimes combined all these methods, as in the "Ode to the West Wind." But he added a new note, – which was yet an echo of the oldest, – the note of nature-worship. He saw continually in nature the godhead which he sought and adored, youthful protestations and affectations of atheism to the contrary notwithstanding. Most of Shelley's nature-poetry carries a rich vein of pantheism, allied to that which colors the oldest verse of time and particularly characterizes ancient Celtic song. With this significant and stimulating revival, goes a revival of that strong sense of kinship, of the oneness of earth and man, which the Greeks and Latins felt so keenly at times, which Omar knew and uttered, and which underlies so much of the verse of these later days.

That other unity – the unity of man and God, which forms so inevitable a corollary to the pantheistic proposition – comes to be dwelt upon more and more insistently throughout the nature-poetry of the last fifty years.

The main purpose of these brief suggestions is to call attention to the fact that nature-poetry is not mere description of landscape in metrical form, but the expression of one or another of many vital relationships between external nature and "the deep heart of man." It may touch the subtlest chords of human emotion and human imagination not less masterfully than the verse which sets out to be a direct transcript from life. The most inaccessible truths are apt to be reached by indirection. The divinest mysteries of beauty are not possessed exclusively by the eye that loves, or by the lips of a child, but are also manifested in some bird-song's unforgotten cadence, some flower whose perfection pierces the heart, some ineffable hue of sunset or sunrise that makes the spirit cry out for it knows not what. And whosoever follows the inexplicable lure of beauty, in color, form, sound, perfume, or any other manifestation, – reaching out to it as perhaps a message from some unfathomable past, or a premonition of the future, – knows that the mystic signal beckons nowhere more imperiously than from the heights of nature-poetry.

(1974)   (1897)

Bliss Carman
1861-1929

———◆———

BLISS CARMAN, A cousin of Charles G. D. Roberts, was born in Fredericton and received his B.A. from the University of New Brunswick in
1881. After several months of study at Oxford and the University of
Edinburgh, he returned to Fredericton in 1883. Three years later he
began graduate courses at Harvard where he came under the influence
of the philosopher, Josiah Royce, and a young American poet, Richard
Hovey. Carman's first authorized collection of verse, *Low Tide on Grand
Pré*, appeared in 1893 and with the numerous volumes that followed he
achieved international recognition.

Low Tide on Grand Pré

The sun goes down, and over all
   These barren reaches by the tide
Such unelusive glories fall,
   I almost dream they yet will bide
   Until the coming of the tide.

And yet I know that not for us,
   By any ecstasy of dream,
He lingers to keep luminous
   A little while the grievous stream,
   Which frets, uncomforted of dream —   10

A grievous stream, that to and fro
   Athrough the fields of Acadie
Goes wandering, as if to know
   Why one beloved face should be
   So long from home and Acadie.

Was it a year or lives ago
  We took the grasses in our hands,
And caught the summer flying low
  Over the waving meadow lands,
  And held it there between our hands?   20

The while the river at our feet –
  A drowsy inland meadow stream –
At set of sun the after-heat
  Made running gold, and in the gleam
  We freed our birch upon the stream.

There down along the elms at dusk
  We lifted dripping blade to drift,
Through twilight scented fine like musk,
  Where night and gloom awhile uplift,
  Nor sunder soul and soul adrift.   30

And that we took into our hands
  Spirit of life or subtler thing –
Breathed on us there, and loosed the bands
  Of death, and taught us, whispering,
  The secret of some wonder-thing.

Then all your face grew light, and seemed
  To hold the shadow of the sun;
The evening faltered, and I deemed
  That time was ripe, and years had done
  Their wheeling underneath the sun.   40

So all desire and all regret,
  And fear and memory, were naught;
One to remember or forget
  The keen delight our hands had caught;
  Morrow and yesterday were naught.

The night has fallen, and the tide...
  Now and again comes drifting home,
Across these aching barrens wide,
  A sigh like driven wind or foam;
  In grief the flood is bursting home.   50

(1893)   (1893)

A Northern Vigil

Here by the gray north sea,
    In the wintry heart of the wild,
Comes the old dream of thee,
    Guendolen, mistress and child.

The heart of the forest grieves
    In the drift against my door;
A voice is under the eaves,
    A footfall on the floor.

Threshold, mirror and hall,
10   Vacant and strangely aware,
Wait for their soul's recall
    With the dumb expectant air.

Here when the smouldering west
    Burns down into the sea,
I take no heed of rest
    And keep the watch for thee.

I sit by the fire and hear
    The restless wind go by,
On the long dirge and drear,
20   Under the low bleak sky.

When day puts out to sea
    And night makes in for land,
There is no lock for thee,
    Each door awaits thy hand!

When night goes over the hill
    And dawn comes down the dale,
It's O for the wild sweet will
    That shall no more prevail!

When the zenith moon is round,
30   And snow-wraiths gather and
            run,
And there is set no bound
    To love beneath the sun,

O wayward will, come near
    The old mad willful way,
The soft mouth at my ear
    With words too sweet to say!

Come, for the night is cold,
    The ghostly moonlight fills
Hollow and rift and fold
    Of the eerie Ardise hills!   40

The windows of my room
    Are dark with bitter frost,
The stillness aches with doom
    Of something loved and lost.

Outside, the great blue star
    Burns in the ghostland pale,
Where giant Algebar
    Holds on the endless trail.

Come, for the years are long,
    And silence keeps the door,   50
Where shapes with the
            shadows throng
    The firelit chamber floor.

Come, for thy kiss was warm,
    With the red embers' glare
Across thy folding arm
    And dark tumultuous hair!

And though thy coming rouse
    The sleep-cry of no bird,
The keepers of the house
    Shall tremble at thy word.   60

Come, for the soul is free!
    In all the vast dreamland
There is no lock for thee,
    Each door awaits thy hand.

Ah, not in dreams at all,
   Fleering, perishing, dim,
But thy old self, supple and tall,
   Mistress and child of whim!

The proud imperious guise,
70   Impetuous and serene,
The sad mysterious eyes,
   And dignity of mien!

Yea, wilt thou not return,
   When the late hill-winds veer,
And the bright hill-flowers burn
   With the reviving year?

(1893)

When April comes, and the sea
   Sparkles as if it smiled,
Will they restore to me
   My dark Love, empress and   80
     child?

The curtains seem to part;
   A sound is on the stair,
As if at the last ... I start;
   Only the wind is there.

Lo, now far on the hills
   The crimson fumes uncurled,
Where the caldron mantles and
    spills
   Another dawn on the world!

(1893)

A Windflower

Between the roadside and the wood,
   Between the dawning and the dew,
A tiny flower before the sun,
   Ephemeral in time, I grew.

And there upon the trail of spring,
   Not death nor love nor any name
Known among men in all their lands
   Could blur the wild desire with shame.

But down my dayspan of the year
   The feet of straying winds came by;   10
And all my trembling soul was thrilled
   To follow one lost mountain cry.

And then my heart beat once and broke
   To hear the sweeping rain forebode
Some ruin in the April world,
   Between the woodside and the road.

To-night can bring no healing now;
The calm of yesternight is gone;
Surely the wind is but the wind,
And I a broken waif thereon.   20

(1893)   (1893)

The Ships of St. John

Smile, you inland hills and rivers!
Flush, you mountains in the dawn!
But my roving heart is seaward
With the ships of gray St. John.

Fair the land lies, full of August,
Meadow island, shingly bar,
Open barns and breezy twilight,
Peace and the mild evening star.

Gently now this gentlest country
10   The old habitude takes on,
But my wintry heart is outbound
With the great ships of St. John.

Once in your wide arms you held
        me,
Till the man-child was a man,
Canada, great nurse and mother
Of the young sea-roving clan.

Always your bright face above me
Through the dreams of boyhood
        shone;
Now far alien countries call me
20   With the ships of gray St. John.

Swing, you tides, up out of Fundy!
Blow, you white fogs, in from sea!
I was born to be your fellow;
You were bred to pilot me.

At the touch of your strong
        fingers,
Doubt, the derelict, is gone;
Sane and glad I clear the
        headland
With the white ships of St. John.

Loyalists, my fathers, builded
This gray port of the gray sea,   30
When the duty to ideals
Could not let well-being be.

When the breadth of scarlet
        bunting
Puts the wreath of maple on,
I must cheer too, – slip my
        moorings
With the ships of gray St. John.

Peerless-hearted port of heroes,
Be a word to lift the world,
Till the many see the signal
Of the few once more unfurled.   40

Past the lighthouse, past the
        nunbuoy,
Past the crimson rising sun,
There are dreams go down the
        harbor
With the tall ships of St. John.

In the morning I am with them
As they clear the island bar, –
Fade, till speck by speck the midday
Has forgotten where they are.

(1897)

But I sight a vaster sea-line,
Wider lee-way, longer run,   50
Whose discoverers return not
With the ships of gray St. John.

(1897)

Overlord

Lord of the grass and hill,
Lord of the rain,
White Overlord of will,
Master of pain,

I who am dust and air
Blown through the halls of death,
Like a pale ghost of prayer, –
I am thy breath.

Lord of the blade and leaf,
10   Lord of the bloom,
Sheer Overlord of grief,
Master of doom,

Lonely as wind or snow,
Through the vague world and
      dim,
Vagrant and glad I go;
I am thy whim.

Lord of the storm and lull,
Lord of the sea,
I am thy broken gull,
20   Blown far alee.

(1902)

Lord of the harvest dew,
Lord of the dawn,
Star of the paling blue
Darkling and gone,

Lost on the mountain height
Where the first winds are stirred,
Out of the wells of night
I am thy word.

Lord of the haunted hush,
Where raptures throng,   30
I am thy hermit thrush,
Ending no song.

Lord of the frost and cold,
Lord of the North,
When the red sun grows old
And day goes forth,

I shall put off this girth, –
Go glad and free,
Earth to my mother earth,
Spirit to thee.   40

(1902)

At the Yellow of the Leaf

The falling leaf is at the door;
The autumn wind is on the hill;
Footsteps I have heard before
Loiter at my cabin sill.

Full of crimson and of gold
Is the morning in the leaves;
And a stillness pure and cold
Hangs about the frosty eaves.

The mysterious autumn haze
10   Steals across the blue ravine,
Like an Indian ghost that strays
Through his olden lost demesne.

Now the goldenrod invades
Every clearing in the hills;
The dry glow of August fades,
And the lonely cricket shrills.

Yes, by every trace and sign
The good roving days are here.
Mountain peak and river line
20   Float the scarlet of the year.

Lovelier than ever now
Is the world I love so well.
Running water, waving bough,
And the bright wind's magic spell

Rouse the taint of migrant blood
With the fever of the road, —
Impulse older than the flood
Lurking in its last abode.

Did I once pursue your way,
30   Little brothers of the air,
Following the vernal ray?
Did I learn my roving there?

Was it on your long spring rides,
Little brothers of the sea,
In the dim and peopled tides,
That I learned this vagrancy?

Now the yellow of the leaf
Bids away by hill and plain,
I shall say good-bye to grief,
Wayfellow with joy again.   40

The glamour of the open door
Is on me, and I would be gone, —
Speak with truth or speak no more,
House with beauty or with none.

Great and splendid, near and far,
Lies the province of desire;
Love the only silver star
Its discoverers require.

I shall lack nor tent nor food,
Nor companion in the way,   50
For the kindly solitude
Will provide for me to-day.

Few enough have been my needs;
Fewer now they are to be;
Where the faintest follow leads,
There is heart's content for me.

Leave the bread upon the board;
Leave the book beside the chair;
With the murmur of the ford,
Light of spirit I shall fare.   60

Leave the latch-string in the door,
And the pile of logs to burn;
Others may be here before
I have leisure to return.

(1903)   (1903)

Lord of My Heart's Elation

Lord of my heart's elation,
Spirit of things unseen,
Be thou my aspiration
Consuming and serene!

Bear up, bear out, bear onward
This mortal soul alone,
To selfhood or oblivion,
Incredibly thine own, –

As the foamheads are loosened
10 And blown along the sea,
Or sink and merge forever
In that which bids them be.

(1903)

I, too, must climb in wonder,
Uplift at thy command, –
Be one with my frail fellows
Beneath wind's strong hand,

A fleet and shadowy column
Of dust or mountain rain,
To walk the earth a moment
And be dissolved again.   20

Be thou my exaltation
Or fortitude of mien,
Lord of the world's elation
Thou breath of things unseen!

(1903)

The Great Return

O Mother, I have loved thee without fear
And looked upon the mystery of change,
Since first, a child, upon the closing year
I saw the snowflakes fall and whispered, "Strange!"

Because in these pale border lands of fate
Grief hath companioned me, I have not quailed;
And when love passed into the outer strait,
I have not faltered and thou hast not failed.

When I have lifted up my heart to thee,
Then hast thou ever hearkened and drawn near,   10
And bowed thy shining face close over me,
Till I could hear thee as hill-flowers hear.

When I have cried to thee in lonely need,
Being but a child of thine bereft and wrung,
Then all the rivers in the hills gave heed;
And the great hill-winds in thy holy tongue –

That ancient incommunicable speech
The April stars and autumn sunsets know —
Soothed me and calmed with solace beyond reach
Of human ken, mysterious and low.   20

Then in that day, when the last snow shall come
And chill the fair round world within its fold,
Leave me not friendless in the gathering gloom,
But gird thine arms about me as of old.

When that great storm out of the dark shall drive,
And blur the sun, and bugle my release,
Let not thy weary earthling faint nor strive,
Faring beyond the tumult to thy peace.

(1904)   (1954)

Softer than the Hill-Fog to the Forest

Softer than the hill-fog to the forest
Are the loving hands of my dear lover,
When she sleeps beside me in the starlight
And her beauty drenches me with rest.

As the quiet mist enfolds the beech-trees,
Even as she dreams her arms enfold me,
Half awaking with a hundred kisses
On the scarlet lily of her mouth.

(1905)   (1954)

Easter Eve

If I should tell you I saw Pan lately down by the shallows of
    Silvermine,
Blowing an air on his pipe of willow, just as the moon began to
    shine;
Or say that, coming from town on Wednesday, I met Christ
    walking in Ponus Street;
You might remark, "Our friend is flighty! Visions, for want of
    enough red meat!"

Then let me ask you: Last December, when there was skating
    on Wampanaw,
Among the weeds and sticks and grasses under the hard black
    ice I saw
An old mud-turtle poking about, as if he were putting his
    house to rights,
Stiff with the cold perhaps, yet knowing enough to prepare
    for the winter nights.

And here he is on a log this morning, sunning himself as calm
    as you please.
But I want to know, when the lock of winter was sprung of a
    sudden, who kept the keys?   10
Who told old nibbler to go to sleep safe and sound with the lily
    roots,
And then in the first warm days of April – out to the sun with
    the greening shoots?

By night a flock of geese went over, honking north on the
    trails of air,
The spring express – but who despatched it, equipped with
    speed and cunning care?
Hark to our bluebird down in the orchard trolling his chant of
    the happy heart,
As full of light as a theme of Mozart's – but where did he learn
    that more than art?

Where the river winds through grassy meadows, as sure as the
      south wind brings the rain,
Sounding his reedy note in the alders, the redwing comes
      back to his nest again.
Are these not miracles? Prompt you answer: "Merely the
      prose of natural fact;
Nothing but instinct plain and patent, born in the creatures,   20
      that bids them act."

Well, I have an instinct as fine and valid, surely, as that of the
      beasts and birds,
Concerning death and the life immortal, too deep for logic,
      too vague for words.
No trace of beauty can pass nor perish, but other beauty is
      somewhere born;
No seed of truth or good be planted, but the yield must grow
      as the growing corn.

Therefore this ardent mind and spirit I give to the glowing
      days of earth,
To be wrought by the Lord of life to something of lasting
      import and lovely worth.
If the toil I give be without self-seeking, bestowed to the limit
      of will and power,
To fashion after some form ideal the instant task and the
      waiting hour,

It matters not though defeat undo me, though faults betray
      me and sorrows scar,
Already I share the life eternal with the April buds and the   30
      evening star,
The slim new moon is my sister now; the rain, my brother; the
      wind, my friend.
Is it not well with these forever? Can the soul of man fare ill in
      the end?

(1909)   (1976)

Morning in the Hills.

How quiet is the morning in the hills!
The stealthy shadows of the summer clouds
Trail through the cañon, and the mountain stream
Sounds his sonorous music far below
In the deep-wooded wind-enchanted clove.

Hemlock and aspen, chestnut, beech, and fir
Go tiering down from storm-worn crest and ledge,
While in the hollows of the dark ravine
See the red road emerge, then disappear
Towards the wide plain and fertile valley lands.   10

My forest cabin half-way up the glen
Is solitary, save for one wise thrush,
The sound of falling water, and the wind
Mysteriously conversing with the leaves.

Here I abide unvisited by doubt,
Dreaming of far-off turmoil and despair,
The race of men and love and fleeting time,
What life may be, or beauty, caught and held
For a brief moment at eternal poise.

What impulse now shall quicken and make live   20
This outward semblance and this inward self?
One breath of being fills the bubble world,
Colored and frail, with fleeting change on change.

Surely some God contrived so fair a thing
In the vast leisure of uncounted days,
And touched it with the breath of living joy,
Wondrous and fair and wise! It must be so.

(1912)   (1912)

Sara Jeannette Duncan
1861-1922

———◆———

BORN IN BRANTFORD, Canada West, Sara Jeannette Duncan began a career as a novelist in 1890 with the publication of *A Social Departure*. In the following year she married Everard Charles Cotes, the curator of the Indian Museum of Calcutta, and spent most of her later life in India and England. Although Duncan published eighteen novels, only two directly reflect her Canadian experience: *The Imperialist* (1904) and *Cousin Cinderella* (1908). Before beginning her career as a novelist, Duncan was a successful journalist and worked for newspapers such as the Toronto *Globe*, the *Washington Post* and the *Montreal Star*. Some of her most interesting work appears in "Saunterings," a column which she wrote during the late 1880s for the Toronto journal, *The Week*.

From
Saunterings

November 25, 1886

THAT IT WAS quite possible to enjoy life, Anastasia, the Youth, and I discovered last summer, and to do it in the orthodox and approved fashion set by those who leave town for the purpose, without either going a prodigious distance or paying a prodigious price. These negative advantages were supplemented by a positive opportunity of gaining some knowledge of local life and character as it is in the Province of Ontario. Local life and character being sought for by Canadians usually anywhere but in Canada, we were fired by a sense of originality in our plan to discover it in the wilds of Prince Edward County.

There may be a few among the great untravelled that do not live in the vicinity of the place who will follow us geographically to the "Sand Banks," on the shores of Lake Ontario. A dotted line vaguely indicates them on the map, which gives no sign, however, of their being inhabited. The most speculative architect of castles in the air would never dream of constructing upon the basis of that wavering and watery indication the magnificence of a pine palace for the accommodation of the transient public, flanked by a grocery and surrounded by every sylvan and sandy attraction: yet such there is. The sand banks are phenomenal, and where there is a phenomenon there is sure to be a hotel.

To get to Picton from almost anywhere in the summer, one sails up the long, narrow, picturesquely irregular Bay of Quinté. Thrice happy is he who takes the trip in that magical time between the day and the darkness of the glowing July weather, when the little steamer almost noiselessly furrows her way through the still, shining water, with its dark tree-shadows and sunset tints of rose and amber, carrying her voyagers, one fancies, to some sure haven where the purple and the gold and the violet and the opal do not slip away. The solid old farm-houses that send their straggling boundaries down to the steep, rocky, moss-grown water's edge, have a look of having been built for comfort and endurance. The fences are all of stones piled on top of one another. Here and there the blossoming water betrays the idyl of a love-tryst at the water-foot of one of these primitive divisions, where Corydon and Phyllis are discussing the advisability of taking it down. And now and then our little craft makes a convulsive hiatus in her peaceful puffing toward an ideal port, and rubs up along a weather-beaten old wharf to receive a solitary passenger, or some half-dozen bags of an agricultural product, the lumpy and uninteresting nature of which will never be made public through the medium of this pen. One feels disposed to speculate upon the forgotten past of these discouraged-looking little settlements, each with its demoralised landing or dilapidated pier, its dusty road curving down to the water out of the woods and pastures, and its church spire rising from a parti-coloured sprinkling of village houses, and softly throwing its doctrinal significance against the evening sky – a chapter folded back in a book that few turn the leaves of; and yet what open page of Canadian history is more bravely illuminated than that which burns with the steadfast loyalty of the strong-hearted ten thousand who preferred allegiance as subjects to disaffection as citizens, even at the expense of all that exile meant in 1783!

It is ten o'clock when we puff into Picton, and at eleven we are driving through the soft radiance of a July moon, that shows us on one side of the road symmetrical maples, set out by the beauty-loving Prince Edward County farmers; on the other, glimmering whitely through the dark cedars and wild undergrowth, the sand banks that have given the narrow peninsula its local fame. Here and there the sand has gradually forced its way through and over the trees to the road, which curves in as the sure yearly encroach is made. Silhouetted against the sky, the dead cedars stretch pathetic arms above us, and every now and then a plash from Lake Ontario, quiet to-night, sounds from behind them. Two hours of this and a sudden bend in the road discloses the hotel, all alight, apparently for the accommodation of a large and fraternal number of circus companies, who have pitched the colossal tents which shine like snow in the moonlight, in most friendly proximity.

We are welcomed by a special benefaction in the shape of a young married person, who finds that her olive branches thrive in the doubtful fertility of the Sand Banks, and who shows us the way to the dining room.

There is nobody else to do it – not a hint of a clerk with an old-gold necktie, not a suggestion of a porter without any necktie at all. In fact, there is not a human being visible except a tall, loose-jointed man without a coat, who slouches into the room after us, appropriates a chair at the head of our table, and addresses us familiarly upon the subject of cold apple-pie. Our relative seems to take his presence there quite as a matter of course, so we feel that it behooves us not to be premature with our indignation. We are too hungry to be dignified, anyway, so we content ourselves with bestowing our undivided attention upon such fragments of the feast as remain after forty boarders, ravenous with the fresh lake air, have partaken of their evening meal. We merely observe that he is guilelessly innocent of conventionality and cuffs; that he tips his chair with accustomed grace, and leans forward on his elbows with the air of a part of the establishment. Later, in the seclusion of an apartment which we share with the young married person aforesaid and all the olive branches, we learn that the gentleman who had honoured us with his society was a sort of Pooh-Bah compendium of all the officials whose services we had missed, that he habitually distinguished himself by the non-performance of any of them, that his name was Byers, and that he was had in reputation and respect upon various accounts throughout the whole length and breadth of the county.

We are drawn in from our early stroll among the pines and the rocks and the blossoming elder-bushes next morning by a clamorous bell, which seemed to speak griddle-cakes to our waiting souls. Approaching the veranda, we see that Byers is ringing it, and, having seated ourselves in the plank-walled dining-room, with the lake breeze blowing straight through it, Byers brings us the griddle-cakes of our anticipation. Daylight discloses him the possessor of a long, bristling, yellow moustache, overshadowing a mouth turned down at the corners, with a chronic expression of disgust at things in general. His nose hooks over it, and his gray eyes have a speculative expression. His movements are so mechanical that the Youth whispers, in an awe-struck voice, his conviction that a disrobing would find him wooden, with joints. We feel sure that he superintends the dish-washing; but we are mistaken, for he waylays us in the hall to "register." This we proceed to do, with the forty boarders in a curious line behind us. Only when a guest comes to stay for at least a week is that precious record produced. On being interrogated as to its seclusion from the public eye, Byers had responded to the effect that, while there was nothing mean about him, paper cost something; and "them darned picnickers 'ud fill it up in a week." In fact, nothing happens to exercise this functionary that is not laid directly at the door of the irresponsible, unprofitable, but smilingly guileless rustic visitors, who come for the day with their baskets, disport themselves on the two capacious swings, make love publicly and unrestrainedly on the veranda, but in no wise add to the revenue of the big pine hotel. So in his heart Byers hateth them.

Next day is Sunday – a gala day at the Sand Banks. From nine o'clock in the morning until nine at night, trim top-buggies, weather-beaten "democrats," and comfortable family carriages deposit their loads of bashful youths and blushing maidens, farmers' families, shopmen, bank clerks, and all sorts and conditions of townspeople, chiefly come to keep cool, wander about, amuse themselves, and see their friends, for the place is purely local, and everybody is "acquainted." Quoits or croquet, being untaxable, Mr. Byers strictly forbids as violations of the Sabbath; but any and all of the visitors may indulge in rifle-shooting, back of the stables, at a dozen shots for a quarter, without incurring anybody's censure. Of course, ill-natured people make remarks about it; but Byers scorns to justify himself, and goes about persecuted for righteousness' sake. The boarders lie in hammocks under the trees, sing, smoke, and read novels; occasionally making an incursion upon the dining-room, where the tables are always set. They do not dance or play cards. One is almost inclined to record it to their credit.

"Mr. Byers, why don't you have church here, in the dance-hall? You often have a minister over Sunday," asks a lady with a troubled conscience this afternoon.

"Well, ma'am ther' was a church here onct. Right down there." An expressive finger is pointed toward the great white banks. "The sand buried it. Discovered it myself, three weeks ago. Ther's a Presbyterian minister in it, just pernouncin' the benediction. But the congregation had gone hum to dinner! Honest though, no foolin', folks don't want no church here. They come here to have a good time, an' darn it all, they're goin' to *have* it – while I'm boss!"

But we discover that Mr. Byers' views are subject to fluctuation – the weather, or the surroundings, or the social atmosphere affect them equally. He brings a chair down to the lake shore one bright evening, where we sit staring at the shimmering water and the fleecy clouds, and the dark island-outlines, and proceeds to give us various doctrinal views. He begins by inquiring what church we "patronise." We respond, with kindling recollection of our covenanting forefathers, that we are Presbyterians.

"Thought so," giving his chair a hitch to avoid a ledge at the back of his head. Byers never utilises all the legs of his chair. "Ther's somethin' about Presbyterians that gives 'em away every time. Fine people though, the Presbyterians – finer 'n the Methodists by a long sight. I tell *you* I've come across some pretty darn mean Methodists, considerin' the way they whoop 'er up! You never heard tell of 'Bijah Crooks, I 'spose. Well, 'Bijah Crooks is my wife's own second cousin, but I'm bound to say he's the biggest Methodist an' the smallest man in the hull country!"

He pauses for an expression of interest in 'Bijah, which comes with promptitude.

"You see he's the feller that keeps the pound. He got an old white horse in there one day last spring. Jake Smith he owned the beast, an' had turned him out on the road to die. When 'Bijah found after keepin' him nigh onto a fortnight ther' wasn't nothin' to be made out o' Jake, what 'd he do but up an' tell old Doctor Burdock, the best-naturedest man ever was, that *his brother's* white mare was goin' to be sold fer poundage ef he didn't pay two dollars an' git her out. Jim Burdock never owned a white mare in his life far's I know, but the Doctor, knowin' no better, up an' paid the two dollars like a man. He's ben lookin' fer 'Bijah ever since."

"And the poor old white horse –" breathlessly from the Youth.

"Oh, it died in the Doctor's back yard over to Ameliasburg. But that wasn't just square ef 'Bijah, was it now? I'm always thankful I don't worship 'long with *his* sex, if they do make more noise."

If I am a blue Presbyterian, Anastasia is a pink and white Methodist, but she doesn't champion her cause. Perhaps 'Bijah's derelictions strike her as too overwhelming to be lightly dealt with, and Anastasia never deals with things seriously – in the hot weather. So in a somnolent spirit of peace and good will, she inquires our entertainer's denominational tendencies.

"Me? Oh, I'm a Brethern. In other words, my wife is. Deacon, too, I am; but she does it fer both of us in the season. Sunday's no day fer me to leave. Lots o' Brethern round here. An' there's no church like 'em – not fer good works. I ain't undoctrinatin' any other denomination, either; dare say there's good in all of 'em. But fer liberal views and proper methods of interpolatin' Scripter I'll back the Brethern. Ef a man thinks a thing's right, why it *is* right – that's all ther' is about it; en' ef he thinks it's wrong, it's wrong." Here he becomes ornate and gesticulative. "An' we don't believe in goin' mournin' all our days, an' callin' this a world of woe. Ef mirthfulness ain't enj'ined in Scripter, I want to know what is. I don't hang my harp on no willow, an' ther's a good deal o' dance in me yet, ef I am married an' settled. 'Nother thing, we believe in immersion as the only symptom o' baptism in the hull Bible. Ef ther's one *re*diculous doctern in your church, it's that sprinklin' the kids!"

The moon shines down upon us, and the waves curl over the big stones and slip back again, leaving them covered with the filmy lacework of the foam. The blue-bells growing in the rock crevices sway with the wind; there is a sound of laughter from the pine-hid veranda; and still Byers continues to discourse with intent to prove that this world is a very tolerable place to live in, if one only possesses a rightly-constituted conscience. And by and by we leave him to his comfortable theory.

It is the day to press flowers, to pack mementoes, to take parting looks at things. The time of our departure is at hand. We are tenderly contemplating that fact and some very badly cooked beefsteak at breakfast when we become conscious of an unusual stir in the "office," that is, the place in which Byers keeps his beloved register. The door opens and a yachting party noisily takes possession of what is known as "the strangers' " table. Six gentlemen, all in becoming navy blue. Poor Anastasia! Her back is toward them, and nobody is interested in a back view.

"I'll have an egg – no, two."

"We haven't any eggs, sir, only for the boarders."

"A glass of milk – ice in it."

"Have to buy our milk, sir. Don't give it to nobody but the boarders' children, on special terms."

"Got any whitefish?"

"Not this morning, sir. Only enough cooked for the boarders. Like some beefsteak?"

"Yes, if the boarders don't mind. And if there's anything else they haven't disposed of, you can bring us that too. We're not particular."

We linger over our last griddle cakes, photograph the rough, bright room, with its shocking chromos, indelibly upon our minds and "settle." Nearly everybody is going to-day; two carriages are waiting now. It costs three cents to answer letters about rooms, and Byers never gratifies public curiosity at his own expense, on principle. Consequently the Sand Banks hostelry is overcrowded or empty always. He is everywhere this morning, coatless, hatless, as usual, with his slick, long, whitish hair pasted over his forehead, and his mouth turned down at the corners with its characteristic expression of disgusted forlornity. He shakes hands all round with genuine regret, and, just as we drive off, leans over toward me with a nod in Anastasia's direction. "Say," he whispers timorously, "what's her front name?"

(1886)

Pauline Johnson
1861-1913

THE DAUGHTER OF an Englishwoman and a Mohawk chief, Pauline Johnson was raised on the Six Nations Reserve near Brantford, Canada West, and adopted the Mohawk name Tekahionwake. She published her first poem in 1885 and in 1892 began the series of concert readings of her poems and stories which made her a popular and romantic figure to audiences in both Canada and England. Johnson's collected poems appeared in 1912 under the title *Flint and Feather*.

Shadow River

Muskoka

A stream of tender gladness,
Of filmy sun, and opal tinted skies;
Of warm midsummer air that lightly lies
In mystic rings,
Where softly swings
The music of a thousand wings
That almost tones to sadness.

Midway 'twixt earth and heaven,
A bubble in the pearly air, I seem
To float upon the sapphire floor, a dream   10
Of clouds of snow,
Above, below,
Drift with my drifting, dim and slow,
As twilight drifts to even.

The little fern-leaf, bending
Upon the brink, its green reflection greets,
And kisses soft the shadow that it meets

With touch so fine,
The border line
The keenest vision can't define;   20
So perfect is the blending.

The far, fir trees that cover
The brownish hills with needles green and gold,
The arching elms o'erhead, vinegrown and old,
Repictured are
Beneath me far,
Where not a ripple moves to mar
Shades underneath, or over.

Mine is the undertone;
The beauty, strength, and power of the land   30
Will never stir or bend at my command;
But all the shade
Is marred or made,
If I but dip my paddle blade;
And it is mine alone.

O! pathless world of seeming!
O! pathless life of mine whose deep ideal
Is more my own than ever was the real.
For others Fame
And Love's red flame,   40
And yellow gold: I only claim
The shadows and the dreaming.

(1895)   (1913)

Marshlands

A thin wet sky, that yellows at the rim,
And meets with sun-lost lip the marsh's brim.

The pools low lying, dank with moss and mould,
Glint through their mildews like large cups of gold.

Among the wild rice in the still lagoon,
In monotone the lizard shrills his tune.

The wild goose, homing, seeks a sheltering,
Where rushes grow, and oozing lichens cling.

Late cranes with heavy wing, and lazy flight,
Sail up the silence with the nearing night.   10

And like a spirit, swathed in some soft veil,
Steals twilight and its shadows o'er the swale.

Hushed lie the sedges, and the vapours creep,
Thick, grey and humid, while the marshes sleep.

(1895)   (1913)

Silhouette

The sky-line melts from russet into blue,
Unbroken the horizon, saving where
A wreath of smoke curls up the far, thin air,
And points the distant lodges of the Sioux.

Etched where the lands and cloudlands touch and die
A solitary Indian tepee stands,
The only habitation of these lands,
That roll their magnitude from sky to sky.

The tent poles lift and loom in thin relief,
The upward floating smoke ascends between,   10
And near the open doorway, gaunt and lean,
And shadow-like, there stands an Indian Chief.

With eyes that lost their lustre long ago,
With visage fixed and stern as fate's decree,
He looks towards the empty west, to see
The never-coming herd of buffalo.

Only the bones that bleach upon the plains,
Only the fleshless skeletons that lie
In ghastly nakedness and silence, cry
Out mutely that naught else to him remains.   20

(1903)   (1913)

The Corn Husker

Hard by the Indian lodges, where the bush
  Breaks in a clearing, through ill-fashioned fields,
She comes to labour, when the first still hush
  Of autumn follows large and recent yields.

Age in her fingers, hunger in her face,
  Her shoulders stooped with weight of work and years,
But rich in tawny colouring of her race,
  She comes a-field to strip the purple ears.

And all her thoughts are with the days gone by,
  Ere might's injustice banished from their lands   10
Her people, that to-day unheeded lie,
  Like the dead husks that rustle through her hands.

(1903)   (1913)

Archibald Lampman
1861-1899

THE SON OF an Anglican clergyman, Archibald Lampman was born in Morpeth, Canada West, and graduated from Trinity College, Toronto, in 1882. Following a brief period as a secondary school teacher, he joined the Post Office Department in Ottawa and worked there until his death. Generally regarded as one of the most important Canadian writers of the nineteenth century, Lampman published his first volume, *Among the Millet,* in 1888. Subsequent collections include *Lyrics of Earth* (1895), *Alcyone* (1899), *Poems* (1900) and *Lampman's Kate: Late Love Poems* (1975).

Heat

From plains that reel to southward, dim,
 The road runs by me white and bare;
Up the steep hill it seems to swim
 Beyond, and melt into the glare.
Upward half-way, or it may be
 Nearer the summit, slowly steals
A hay-cart, moving dustily
 With idly clacking wheels.

By his cart's side the wagoner
 Is slouching slowly at his ease,   10
Half-hidden in the windless blur
 Of white dust puffing to his knees.
This wagon on the height above,
 From sky to sky on either hand,
Is the sole thing that seems to move
 In all the heat-held land.

Beyond me in the fields the sun
  Soaks in the grass and hath his will;
I count the marguerites one by one;
  Even the buttercups are still. 20
On the brook yonder not a breath
  Disturbs the spider or the midge.
The water-bugs draw close beneath
  The cool gloom of the bridge.

Where the far elm-tree shadows flood
  Dark patches in the burning grass,
The cows, each with her peaceful cud,
  Lie waiting for the heat to pass.
From somewhere on the slope near by
  Into the pale depth of the noon 30
A wandering thrush slides leisurely
  His thin revolving tune.

In intervals of dreams I hear
  The cricket from the droughty ground;
The grasshoppers spin into mine ear
  A small innumerable sound.
I lift mine eyes sometimes to gaze:
  The burning sky-line blinds my sight:
The woods far off are blue with haze:
  The hills are drenched in light. 40

And yet to me not this or that
  Is always sharp or always sweet;
In the sloped shadow of my hat
  I lean at rest, and drain the heat;
Nay more, I think some blessèd power
  Hath brought me wandering idly here:
In the full furnace of this hour
  My thoughts grow keen and clear.

(1888)   (1900)

Among the Timothy

Long hours ago, while yet the morn was blithe,
   Nor sharp athirst had drunk the beaded dew,
A mower came, and swung his gleaning scythe
   Around this stump, and, shearing slowly, drew
   Far round among the clover, ripe for hay,
      A circle clean and gray;
And here among the scented swathes that gleam,
   Mixed with dead daisies, it is sweet to lie
And watch the grass and the few-clouded sky,
      Nor think but only dream.   10

For when the noon was turning, and the heat
   Fell down most heavily on field and wood,
I too came hither, borne on restless feet,
   Seeking some comfort for an aching mood.
   Ah! I was weary of the drifting hours,
      The echoing city towers,
The blind gray streets, the jingle of the throng,
   Weary of hope that like a shape of stone
   Sat near at hand without a smile or moan,
      And weary most of song.   20

And those high moods of mine that sometime made
   My heart a heaven, opening like a flower
A sweeter world where I in wonder strayed,
   Begirt with shapes of beauty and the power
   Of dreams that moved through that enchanted clime
      With changing breaths of rhyme,
Were all gone lifeless now, like those white leaves
   That hang all winter, shivering dead and blind
   Among the sinewy beeches in the wind,
      That vainly calls and grieves.   30

Ah! I will set no more mine overtaskèd brain
   To barren search and toil that beareth nought,
For ever following with sore-footed pain
   The crossing pathways of unbournèd thought;
   But let it go, as one that hath no skill,
      To take what shape it will,

An ant slow-burrowing in the earthy gloom,
 A spider bathing in the dew at morn,
 Or a brown bee in wayward fancy borne
  From hidden bloom to bloom.   40

Hither and thither o'er the rocking grass
 The little breezes, blithe as they are blind,
Teasing the slender blossoms pass and pass,
 Soft-footed children of the gipsy wind,
 To taste of every purple-fringèd head
  Before the bloom is dead;
And scarcely heed the daisies that, endowed
 With stems so short they cannot see, up-bear
 Their innocent sweet eyes distressed, and stare
  Like children in a crowd.   50

Not far to fieldward in the central heat,
 Shadowing the clover, a pale poplar stands
With glimmering leaves that, when the wind comes, beat
 Together like innumerable small hands,
 And with the calm, as in vague dreams astray,
  Hang wan and silver-gray;
Like sleepy maenads, who in pale surprise,
 Half-wakened by a prowling beast, have crept
 Out of the hidden covert, where they slept,
  At noon with languid eyes.   60

The crickets creak, and through the noonday glow,
 That crazy fiddler of the hot mid-year,
The dry cicada plies his wiry bow
 In long-spun cadence, thin and dusty sere;
 From the green grass the small grasshoppers' din
  Spreads soft and silvery thin;
And ever and anon a murmur steals
 Into mine ears of toil that moves alway,
 The crackling rustle of the pitch-forked hay
  And lazy jerk of wheels.   70

As so I lie and feel the soft hours wane,
 To wind and sun and peaceful sound laid bare,
That aching dim discomfort of the brain
 Fades off unseen, and shadowy-footed care
 Into some hidden corner creeps at last

To slumber deep and fast;
And gliding on, quite fashioned to forget,
   From dream to dream I bid my spirit pass
   Out into the pale green ever-swaying grass
      To brood, but no more fret.   80

And hour by hour among all shapes that grow
   Of purple mints and daisies gemmed with gold
In sweet unrest my visions come and go;
   I feel and hear and with quiet eyes behold;
   And hour by hour, the ever-journeying sun,
      In gold and shadow spun,
Into mine eyes and blood, and through the dim
   Green glimmering forest of the grass shines down,
   Till flower and blade, and every cranny brown,
      And I are soaked with him.   90

(1888)   (1900)

The Railway Station

The darkness brings no quiet here, the light
   No waking: ever on my blinded brain
   The flare of lights, the rush, and cry, and strain,
The engines' scream, the hiss and thunder smite:
I see the hurrying crowds, the clasp, the flight,
   Faces that touch, eyes that are dim with pain:
   I see the hoarse wheels turn, and the great train
Move labouring out into the bourneless night.
So many souls within its dim recesses,
   So many bright, so many mournful eyes: 10
Mine eyes that watch grow fixed with dreams and
         guesses;
   What threads of life, what hidden histories,
What sweet or passionate dreams and dark distresses,
   What unknown thoughts, what various agonies!

(1888)   (1900)

In November

The hills and leafless forests slowly yield
   To the thick-driving snow. A little while
   And night shall darken down. In shouting file
The woodmen's carts go by me homeward-wheeled,
Past the thin fading stubbles, half concealed,
   Now golden-gray, sowed softly through with snow,
   Where the last ploughman follows still his row,
Turning black furrows through the whitening field.
Far off the village lamps begin to gleam,
   Fast drives the snow, and no man comes this way;   10
     The hills grow wintry white, and bleak winds moan
     About the naked uplands. I alone
   Am neither sad, nor shelterless, nor gray,
Wrapped round with thought, content to watch and dream.

(1888)   (1900)

Snow

White are the far-off plains, and white
     The fading forests grow;
The wind dies out along the height,
     And denser still the snow,
A gathering weight on roof and tree,
     Falls down scarce audibly.

The road before me smoothes and fills
     Apace, and all about
The fences dwindle, and the hills
     Are blotted slowly out;   10
The naked trees loom spectrally
     Into the dim white sky.

The meadows and far-sheeted streams
     Lie still without a sound;
Like some soft minister of dreams

> The snow-fall hoods me round;
> In wood and water, earth and air,
>   A silence everywhere.
>
> Save when at lonely intervals
>   Some farmer's sleigh urged on,   20
> With rustling runners and sharp bells,
>   Swings by me and is gone;
> Or from the empty waste I hear
>   A sound remote and clear;
>
> The barking of a dog, or call
>   To cattle, sharply pealed,
> Borne echoing from some wayside stall
>   Or barnyard far afield;
> Then all is silent, and the snow
>   Falls, settling soft and slow.   30
>
> The evening deepens, and the gray
>   Folds closer earth and sky;
> The world seems shrouded far away;
>   Its noises sleep, and I,
> As secret as yon buried stream,
>   Plod dumbly on, and dream.

(1895)   (1900)

The City of the End of Things

> Beside the pounding cataracts
> Of midnight streams unknown to us
> 'Tis builded in the leafless tracts
> And valleys huge of Tartarus.
> Lurid and lofty and vast it seems;
> It hath no rounded name that rings,
> But I have heard it called in dreams
> The City of the End of Things.

Its roofs and iron towers have grown
None knoweth how high within the night,   10
But in its murky streets far down
A flaming terrible and bright
Shakes all the stalking shadows there,
Across the walls, across the floors,
And shifts upon the upper air
From out a thousand furnace doors;
And all the while an awful sound
Keeps roaring on continually,
And crashes in the ceaseless round
Of a gigantic harmony.   20
Through its grim depths re-echoing
And all its weary height of walls,
With measured roar and iron ring,
The inhuman music lifts and falls.
Where no thing rests and no man is,
And only fire and night hold sway;
The beat, the thunder and the hiss
Cease not, and change not, night nor day.

And moving at unheard commands,
The abysses and vast fires between,   30
Flit figures that with clanking hands
Obey a hideous routine;
They are not flesh, they are not bone,
They see not with the human eye,
And from their iron lips is blown
A dreadful and monotonous cry;
And whoso of our mortal race
Should find that city unaware,
Lean Death would smite him face to face,
And blanch him with its venomed air: 40
Or caught by the terrific spell,
Each thread of memory snapt and cut,
His soul would shrivel and its shell
Go rattling like an empty nut.

It was not always so, but once,
In days that no man thinks upon,
Fair voices echoed from its stones,
The light above it leaped and shone:

Once there were multitudes of men,
That built that city in their pride,   50
Until its might was made, and then
They withered age by age and died.
But now of that prodigious race,
Three only in an iron tower,
Set like carved idols face to face,
Remain the masters of its power;
And at the city gate a fourth,
Gigantic and with dreadful eyes,
Sits looking toward the lightless north,
Beyond the reach of memories;   60
Fast rooted to the lurid floor,
A bulk that never moves a jot,
In his pale body dwells no more,
Or mind, or soul, – an idiot!

But sometime in the end those three
Shall perish and their hands be still,
And with the master's touch shall flee
Their incommunicable skill.
A stillness absolute as death
Along the slacking wheels shall lie,   70
And, flagging at a single breath,
The fires shall moulder out and die.
The roar shall vanish at its height,
And over that tremendous town
The silence of eternal night
Shall gather close and settle down.
All its grim grandeur, tower and hall,
Shall be abandoned utterly,
And into rust and dust shall fall
From century to century;   80
Nor ever living thing shall grow,
Or trunk of tree, or blade of grass;
No drop shall fall, no wind shall blow,
Nor sound of any foot shall pass:
Alone of its accursèd state,
One thing the hand of Time shall spare,
For the grim Idiot at the gate
Is deathless and eternal there.

(1899)   (1972)

The Land of Pallas

Methought I journeyed along ways that led for ever
   Throughout a happy land where strife and care were dead,
And life went flowing by me like a placid river
   Past sandy eyots where the shifting shoals make head.

A land where beauty dwelt supreme, and right, the donor
   Of peaceful days; a land of equal gifts and deeds,
Of limitless fair fields and plenty had with honour;
   A land of kindly tillage and untroubled meads,

Of gardens, and great fields, and dreaming rose-wreathed alleys,
   Wherein at dawn and dusk the vesper sparrows sang;   10
Of cities set far off on hills down vista'd valleys,
   And floods so vast and old, men wist not whence they sprang,

Of groves, and forest depths, and fountains softly welling,
   And roads that ran soft-shadowed past the open doors,
Of mighty palaces and many a lofty dwelling,
   Where all men entered and no master trod their floors.

A land of lovely speech, where every tone was fashioned
   By generations of emotion high and sweet,
Of thought and deed and bearing lofty and impassioned;
   A land of golden calm, grave forms, and fretless feet.   20

And every mode and saying of that land gave token
   Of limits where no death or evil fortune fell,
And men lived out long lives in proud content unbroken,
   For there no man was rich, none poor, but all were well.

And all the earth was common, and no base contriving
   Of money of coined gold was needed there or known,
But all men wrought together without greed or striving,
   And all the store of all to each man was his own.

From all that busy land, gray town, and peaceful village,
   Where never jar was heard, nor wail nor cry of strife,   30
From every laden stream and all the fields of tillage,
   Arose the murmur and the kindly hum of life.

At morning to the fields came forth the men, each neighbour
  Hand-linked to other, crowned, with wreaths upon their hair,
And all day long with joy they gave their hands to labour,
  Moving at will, unhastened, each man to his share.

At noon the women came, the tall fair women, bearing
  Baskets of wicker in their ample hands for each,
And learned the day's brief tale, and how the fields were faring,
  And blessed them with their lofty beauty and blithe speech.   40

And when the great day's toil was over, and the shadows
  Grew with the flocking stars, the sound of festival
Rose in each city square, and all the country meadows,
  Palace, and paven court, and every rustic hall.

Beside smooth streams, where alleys and green gardens
          meeting
  Ran downward to the flood with marble steps, a throng
Came forth of all the folk, at even, gaily greeting,
  With echo of sweet converse, jest, and stately song.

In all their great fair cities there was neither seeking
  For power of gold, nor greed of lust, nor desperate pain   50
Of multitudes that starve, or in hoarse anger breaking,
  Beat at the doors of princes, break and fall in vain.

But all the children of that peaceful land, like brothers,
  Lofty of spirit, wise, and ever set to learn
The chart of neighbouring souls, the bent and need of others,
  Thought only of good deeds, sweet speech, and just return.

And there there was no prison, power of arms, nor palace,
  Where prince or judge held sway, for none was needed there;
Long ages since the very names of fraud and malice
  Had vanished from men's tongues, and died from all men's   60
          care.

And there there were no bonds of contract, deed or marriage,
  No oath, nor any form, to make the word more sure,
For no man dreamed of hurt, dishonour, or miscarriage,
  Where every thought was truth, and every heart was pure.

There were no castes of rich or poor, of slave or master,
  Where all were brothers, and the curse of gold was dead,
But all that wise fair race to kindlier ends and vaster
  Moved on together with the same majestic tread.

And all the men and women of that land were fairer
  Than even the mightiest of our meaner race can be;   70
The men like gentle children, great of limb, yet rarer
  For wisdom and high thought, like kings for majesty.

And all the women through great ages of bright living,
  Grown goodlier of stature, strong, and subtly wise,
Stood equal with the men, calm counsellors, ever giving
  The fire and succour of proud faith and dauntless eyes.

And as I journeyed in that land I reached a ruin,
  A gateway of a lonely and secluded waste,
A phantom of forgotten time and ancient doing,
  Eaten by age and violence, crumbled and defaced.   80

On its grim outer walls the ancient world's sad glories
  Were recorded in fire; upon its inner stone,
Drawn by dead hands, I saw, in tales and tragic stories,
  The woe and sickness of an age of fear made known.

And lo, in that gray storehouse, fallen to dust and rotten,
  Lay piled the traps and engines of forgotten greed,
The tomes of codes and canons, long disused, forgotten,
  The robes and sacred books of many a vanished creed.

An old grave man I found, white-haired and gently spoken,
  Who, as I questioned, answered with a smile benign,   90
'Long years have come and gone since these poor gauds
        were broken,
  Broken and banished from a life made more divine.

'But still we keep them stored as once our sires deemed fitting,
  The symbol of dark days and lives remote and strange,
Lest o'er the minds of any there should come unwitting
  The thought of some new order and the lust of change.

'If any grow disturbed, we bring them gently hither,
  To read the world's grim record and the sombre lore
Massed in these pitiless vaults, and they returning thither,
  Bear with them quieter thoughts, and make for change no   100
    no more.'

And thence I journeyed on by one broad way that bore me
  Out of that waste, and as I passed by tower and town
I saw amid the limitless plain far out before me
  A long low mountain, blue as beryl, and its crown

Was capped by marble roofs that shone like snow for
    whiteness,
  Its foot was deep in gardens, and that blossoming plain
Seemed in the radiant shower of its majestic brightness
  A land for gods to dwell in, free from care and pain.

And to and forth from that fair mountain like a river
  Ran many a dim gray road, and on them I could see   110
A multitude of stately forms that seemed for ever
  Going and coming in bright bands; and near to me

Was one that in his journey seemed to dream and linger,
  Walking at whiles with kingly step, then standing still,
And him I met and asked him, pointing with my finger,
  The meaning of the palace and the lofty hill.

Whereto the dreamer: 'Art thou of this land, my brother,
  And knowest not the mountain and its crest of walls,
Where dwells the priestless worship of the all-wise mother?
  That is the hill of Pallas; those her marble halls!   120

'There dwell the lords of knowledge and of thought
    increasing,
  And they whom insight and the gleams of song uplift;
And thence as by a hundred conduits flows unceasing
  The spring of power and beauty, an eternal gift.

Still I passed on until I reached at length, not knowing
  Whither the tangled and diverging paths might lead,
A land of baser men, whose coming and whose going
  Were urged by fear, and hunger, and the curse of greed.

I saw the proud and fortunate go by me, faring
   In fatness and fine robes, the poor oppressed and slow,   130
The faces of bowed men, and piteous women bearing
   The burden of perpetual sorrow and the stamp of woe.

And tides of deep solicitude and wondering pity
   Possessed me, and with eager and uplifted hands
I drew the crowd about me in a mighty city,
   And taught the message of those other kindlier lands.

I preached the rule of Faith and Brotherly Communion,
   The law of Peace and Beauty and the death of Strife,
And painted in great words the horror of disunion,
   The vainness of self-worship, and the waste of life.   140

I preached but fruitlessly; the powerful from their stations
   Rebuked me as an anarch, envious and bad,
And they that served them with lean hands and bitter patience
   Smiled only out of hollow orbs, and deemed me mad.

And still I preached, and wrought, and still I bore my
       message,
   For well I knew that on and upward without cease
The spirit works for ever, and by Faith and Presage
   That somehow yet the end of human life is Peace.

(1899)   (1900)

The Autumn Waste

There is no break in all the wide gray sky,
Nor light on any field, and the wind grieves
And talks of death. Where cold gray waters lie
Round grayer stones, and the new-fallen leaves
Heap the chill hollows of the naked woods,
A lisping moan, an inarticulate cry,
Creeps far among the charnel solitudes,
Numbing the waste with mindless misery.
In these bare paths, these melancholy lands,
What dream, or flesh, could ever have been young?   10
What lovers have gone forth with linkèd hands?
What flowers could ever have bloomed, what birds have sung?
Life, hopes, and human things seem wrapped away,
With shrouds and spectres, in one long decay.

(1899)   (1900)

On the Companionship with Nature

Let us be much with Nature; not as they
That labour without seeing, that employ
Her unloved forces, blindly without joy;
 Nor those whose hands and crude delights obey
The old brute passion to hunt down and slay;
But rather as children of one common birth,
Discerning in each natural fruit of earth
Kinship and bond with this diviner clay.
Let us be with her wholly at all hours,
With the fond lover's zest, who is content   10
If his ear hears, and if his eye but sees;
So shall we grow like her in mould and bent,
Our bodies stately as her blessèd trees,
Our thoughts as sweet and sumptuous as her flowers.

(1900)   (1900)

In the City

I wandered in a city great and old,
At morn, at noon, and when the evening fell,
And round my spirit gathered like a spell
Its splendour and its tumult and its gold,
The mysteries and the memories of its years,
Its victors and fair women, all the life,
The joy, the power, the passion, and the strife,
Its sighs of hand-locked lovers, and its tears.
And whereso in that mighty city, free
And with clear eyes and eager heart I trod,   10
My thought became a passion high and strong,
And all the spirit of humanity,
Soft as a child and potent as a god,
Drew near to me, and rapt me like a song.

(1900)   (1900)

A Sunset at Les Eboulements

Broad shadows fall.   On all the mountain side
The scythe-swept fields are silent.   Slowly home
By the long beach the high-piled hay-carts come,
Splashing the pale salt shallows.   Over wide
Fawn-coloured wastes of mud the slipping tide,
Round the dun rocks and wattled fisheries,
Creeps murmuring in.   And now by twos and threes,
O'er the slow spreading pools with clamorous chide,
Belated crows from strip to strip take flight.
Soon will the first star shine; yet ere the night   10
Reach onward to the pale-green distances,
The sun's last shaft beyond the gray sea-floor
Still dreams upon the Kamouraska shore,
And the long line of golden villages.

(1900)   (1900)

The Modern Politician

What manner of soul is his to whom high truth
Is but the plaything of a feverish hour,
A dangling ladder to the ghost of power!
Gone are the grandeurs of the world's iron youth,
When kings were mighty, being made by swords.
Now comes the transit age, the age of brass,
When clowns into the vacant empires pass,
Blinding the multitude with specious words.
To them faith, kinship, truth and verity,
Man's sacred rights and very holiest thing,   10
Are but the counters at a desperate play,
Flippant and reckless what the end may be,
So that they glitter, each his little day,
The little mimic of a vanished king.

(1900)   (1900)

A Forest Path in Winter

Along this secret and forgotten road
    All depths and forest forms, above, below,
    Are plumed and draped and hillocked with the snow.
A branch cracks now and then, and its soft load
Drifts by me in a thin prismatic shower;
    Else not a sound, but vistas bound and crossed
    With sheeted gleams and sharp blue shadows, frost,
And utter silence. In his glittering power
The master of mid-winter reveries
    Holds all things buried soft and strong and deep.   10
    The busy squirrel has his hidden lair;
And even the spirits of the stalwart trees
    Have crept into their utmost roots, and there,
Upcoiled in the close earth, lie fast asleep.

(1900)   (1900)

On Lake Temiscamingue

A single dreamy elm, that stands between
   The sombre forest and the wan-lit lake,
Halves with its slim gray stem and pendent green
   The shadowed point.   Beyond it without break
Bold brows of pine-topped granite bend away,
   Far to the southward, fading off in grand
Soft folds of looming purple.   Cool and gray,
   The point runs out, a blade of thinnest sand.
Two rivers meet beyond it: wild and clear,
   Their deepening thunder breaks upon the ear –   10
The one descending from its forest home
   By many an eddied pool and murmuring fall –
The other cloven through the mountain wall,
   A race of tumbled rocks, a roar of foam.

(1900)   (1900)

True Passion

I know I am not wise, my friend. Perchance
You think me very foolish and to blame.
But how could I keep measure, or how tame
The fiery grief by any ordinance?
Fate wills it so. By nature's own decree
I love you. With a rare and cunning hand,
In that dear soul and shape of yours, she planned
The fairest of all mortal things to me.

Nor did the choice so offer, would I part
From this true passion with its stress and sting;   10
Rather I praise and honour my own heart,
That holds so noble and so fair a thing.
True love is worth the having, though in vain,
And you worth loving, though the cost be pain!

(1975)   (1975)

Duncan Campbell Scott
1862-1947

THE SON OF a Methodist minister, Duncan Campbell Scott was born in Ottawa and educated at various schools in eastern Ontario and Quebec. At the age of seventeen he entered the Department of Indian Affairs where he eventually became deputy superintendent-general. After meeting Archibald Lampman in 1883, Scott began to write poetry and ten years later he published the first of nine volumes, *The Magic House and Other Poems* (1893). He also wrote two collections of short stories and collaborated with Lampman and Wilfred Campbell in "At the Mermaid Inn" (1892-1893), a column for the Toronto *Globe*.

Night and the Pines

Here in the pine shade is the nest of night,
   Lined deep with shadows, odorous and dim,
And here he stays his sweeping flight,
    Here where the strongest wind is lulled for him,
      He lingers brooding until dawn,
      While all the trembling stars move on and on.

Under the cliff there drops a lonely fall,
   Deep and half heard its thunder lifts and booms;
Afar the loons with eerie call
    Haunt all the bays, and breaking through the glooms   10
      Upfloats that cry of light despair,
      As if a demon laughed upon the air.

A raven croaks from out his ebon sleep,
   When a brown cone falls near him through the dark;
And when the radiant meteors sweep
    Afar within the larches wakes the lark;
      The wind moves on the cedar hill,
      Tossing the weird cry of the whip-poor-will.

Sometimes a titan wind, slumbrous and hushed,
  Takes the dark grove within his swinging power;   20
And like a cradle softly pushed,
    The shade sways slowly for a lulling hour;
      While through the cavern sweeps a cry,
      A Sibyl with her secret prophecy.

When morning lifts its fragile silver dome,
  And the first eagle takes the lonely air,
Up from his dense and sombre home
    The night sweeps out, a tireless wayfarer,
      Leaving within the shadows deep,
      The haunting mood and magic of his sleep.   30

And so we cannot come within this grove,
  But all the quiet dusk remembrance brings
Of ancient sorrow and of hapless love,
    Fate, and the dream of power, and piercing things
      Traces of mystery and might,
      The passion-sadness of the soul of night.

(1893)   (1893)

The Piper of Arll

There was in Arll a little cove
Where the salt wind came cool and free:
A foamy beach that one would love,
If he were longing for the sea.

A brook hung sparkling on the hill,
The hill swept far to ring the bay;
The bay was faithful, wild or still,
To the heart of the ocean far away.

There were three pines above the comb
That, when the sun flared and went down,   10
Grew like three warriors reaving home
The plunder of a burning town.

A piper lived within the grove,
Tending the pasture of his sheep;
His heart was swayed with faithful love,
From the springs of God's ocean clear and deep.

And there a ship one evening stood,
Where ship had never stood before;
A pennon bickered red as blood,
An angel glimmered at the prore.   20

About the coming on of dew,
The sails burned rosy, and the spars
Were gold, and all the tackle grew
Alive with ruby-hearted stars.

The piper heard an outland tongue,
With music in the cadenced fall;
And when the fairy lights were hung,
The sailors gathered one and all,

And leaning on the gunwales dark,
Crusted with shells and dashed with foam,   30
With all the dreaming hills to hark,
They sang their longing songs of home.

When the sweet airs had fled away,
The piper, with a gentle breath,
Moulded a tranquil melody
Of lonely love and longed-for death.

When the fair sound began to lull,
From out the fireflies and the dew,
A silence held the shadowy hull,
Until the eerie tune was through.   40

Then from the dark and dreamy deck
An alien song began to thrill;
It mingled with the drumming beck,
And stirred the braird upon the hill.

Beneath the stars each sent to each
A message tender, till at last
The piper slept upon the beach,
The sailors slumbered round the mast.

Still as a dream till nearly dawn,
The ship was bosomed on the tide;   50
The streamlet, murmuring on and on,
Bore the sweet water to her side.

Then shaking out her lawny sails,
Forth on the misty sea she crept;
She left the dawning of the dales,
Yet in his cloak the piper slept.

And when he woke he saw the ship,
Limned black against the crimson sun;
Then from the disc he saw her slip,
A wraith of shadow – she was gone.   60

He threw his mantle on the beach,
He went apart like one distraught,
His lips were moved – his desperate speech
Stormed his inviolable thought.

He broke his human-throated reed,
And threw it in the idle rill;
But when his passion had its mead,
He found it in the eddy still.

He mended well the patient flue,
Again he tried its varied stops;   70
The closures answered right and true,
And starting out in piercing drops,

A melody began to drip
That mingled with a ghostly thrill
The vision-spirit of the ship,
The secret of his broken will.

Beneath the pines he piped and swayed,
Master of passion and of power;
He was his soul and what he played,
Immortal for a happy hour.   80

He, singing into nature's heart,
Guiding his will by the world's will,
With deep, unconscious, childlike art
Had sung his soul out and was still.

And then at evening came the bark
That stirred his dreaming heart's desire;
It burned slow lights along the dark
That died in glooms of crimson fire.

The sailors launched a sombre boat,
And bent with music at the oars;   90
The rhythm throbbing every throat,
And lapsing round the liquid shores,

Was that true tune the piper sent,
Unto the wave-worn mariners,
When with the beck and ripple blent
He heard that outland song of theirs.

Silent they rowed him, dip and drip,
The oars beat out an exequy,
They laid him down within the ship,
They loosed a rocket to the sky.   100

It broke in many a crimson sphere
That grew to gold and floated far,
And left the sudden shore-line clear,
With one slow-changing, drifting star.

Then out they shook the magic sails,
That charmed the wind in other seas,
From where the west line pearls and pales,
They waited for a ruffling breeze.

But in the world there was no stir,
The cordage slacked with never a creak,   110
They heard the flame begin to purr
Within the lantern at the peak.

They could not cry, they could not move,
They felt the lure from the charmed sea;
They could not think of home or love
Or any pleasant land to be.

They felt the vessel dip and trim,
And settle down from list to list;
They saw the sea-plain heave and swim
As gently as a rising mist.   120

And down so slowly, down and down,
Rivet by rivet, plank by plank;
A little flood of ocean flown
Across the deck, she sank and sank.

From knee to breast the water wore,
It crept and crept; ere they were ware
Gone was the angel at the prore,
They felt the water float their hair.

They saw the salt plain spark and shine,
They threw their faces to the sky;   130
Beneath a deepening film of brine
They saw the star-flash blur and die.

She sank and sank by yard and mast,
Sank down the shimmering gradual dark;
A little drooping pennon last
Showed like the black fin of a shark.

And down she sank till, keeled in sand,
She rested safely balanced true,
With all her upward gazing band,
The piper and the dreaming crew.   140

And there, unmarked of any chart,
In unrecorded deeps they lie,
Empearled within the purple heart
Of the great sea for aye and aye.

Their eyes are ruby in the green
Long shaft of sun that spreads and rays,
And upward with a wizard sheen
A fan of sea-light leaps and plays.

Tendrils of or and azure creep,
And globes of amber light are rolled,   150
And in the gloaming of the deep
Their eyes are starry pits of gold.

And sometimes in the liquid night
The hull is changed, a solid gem,
That glows with a soft stony light,
The lost prince of a diadem.

And at the keel a vine is quick,
That spreads its bines and works and weaves
O'er all the timbers veining thick
A plenitude of silver leaves.   160

(1898)   (1898)

Watkwenies

Vengeance was once her nation's lore and law:
When the tired sentry stooped above the rill,
Her long knife flashed, and hissed, and drank its fill;
Dimly below her dripping wrist she saw,
One wild hand, pale as death and weak as straw,
Clutch at the ripple in the pool; while shrill
Sprang through the dreaming hamlet on the hill,
The war-cry of the triumphant Iroquois.

Now clothed with many an ancient flap and fold,
And wrinkled like an apple kept till May,   10
She weighs the interest-money in her palm,
And, when the Agent calls her valiant name,
Hears, like the war-whoops of her perished day,
The lads playing snow-snake in the stinging cold.

(1898)   (1898)

The Forsaken

I

Once in the winter
Out on a lake
In the heart of the north-land,
Far from the Fort
And far from the hunters,
A Chippewa woman
With her sick baby,
Crouched in the last hours
Of a great storm.
Frozen and hungry,   10
She fished through the ice
With a line of the twisted
Bark of the cedar,
And a rabbit-bone hook
Polished and barbed;
Fished with the bare hook
All through the wild day,
Fished and caught nothing;
While the young chieftain
Tugged at her breasts,   20
Or slept in the lacings
Of the warm *tikanagan.*
All the lake-surface
Streamed with the hissing
Of millions of iceflakes
Hurled by the wind;
Behind her the round
Of a lonely island
Roared like a fire
With the voice of the storm   30
In the deeps of the cedars.
Valiant, unshaken,
She took of her own flesh,
Baited the fish-hook,
Drew in a gray-trout,
Drew in his fellows,
Heaped them beside her,

Dead in the snow.
Valiant, unshaken,
She faced the long distance,   40
Wolf-haunted and lonely,
Sure of her goal
And the life of her dear one:
Tramped for two days,
On the third in the morning,
Saw the strong bulk
Of the Fort by the river,
Saw the wood-smoke
Hang soft in the spruces,
Heard the keen yelp   50
Of the ravenous huskies
Fighting for whitefish:
Then she had rest.

II

Years and years after,
When she was old and withered,
When her son was an old man
And his children filled with vigour,
They came in their northern tour on the verge of winter,
To an island in a lonely lake.
There one night they camped, and on the morrow   60
Gathered their kettles and birch-bark
Their rabbit-skin robes and their mink-traps,
Launched their canoes and slunk away through the islands,
Left her alone forever,
Without a word of farewell,
Because she was old and useless,
Like a paddle broken and warped,
Or a pole that was splintered.
Then, without a sigh,
Valiant, unshaken,   70
She smoothed her dark locks under her kerchief,
Composed her shawl in state,

Then folded her hands ridged with sinews and corded with
       veins,
Folded them across her breasts spent with the nourishing of
       children,
Gazed at the sky past the tops of the cedars,
Saw two spangled nights arise out of the twilight,
Saw two days go by filled with the tranquil sunshine,
Saw, without pain, or dread, or even a moment of longing: 80
Then on the third great night there came thronging and
       thronging
Millions of snowflakes out of a windless cloud;
They covered her close with a beautiful crystal shroud,
Covered her deep and silent.
But in the frost of the dawn,
Up from the life below,
Rose a column of breath
Through a tiny cleft in the snow,
Fragile, delicately drawn,
Wavering with its own weakness,   90
In the wilderness a sign of the spirit,
Persisting still in the sight of the sun
Till day was done.
Then all light was gathered up by the hand of God and hid in
       His breast,
Then there was born a silence deeper than silence,
Then she had rest.

(1905)   (1926)

On the Way to the Mission

They dogged him all one afternoon,
Through the bright snow,
Two whitemen servants of greed;
He knew that they were there,
But he turned not his head;
He was an Indian trapper;
He planted his snow-shoes firmly,
He dragged the long toboggan
Without rest.

The three figures drifted   10
Like shadows in the mind of a seer;
The snow-shoes were whisperers
On the threshold of awe;
The toboggan made the sound of wings,
A wood-pigeon sloping to her nest.

The Indian's face was calm.
He strode with the sorrow of fore-knowledge,
But his eyes were jewels of content
Set in circles of peace.

They would have shot him;   20
But momently in the deep forest,
They saw something flit by his side:
Their hearts stopped with fear.
Then the moon rose.
They would have left him to the spirit,

But they saw the long toboggan
Rounded well with furs,
With many a silver fox-skin,
With the pelts of mink and of otter.
They were the servants of greed;   30
When the moon grew brighter
And the spruces were dark with sleep,
They shot him.
When he fell on a shield of moonlight
One of his arms clung to his burden;

The snow was not melted:
The spirit passed away.

Then the servants of greed
Tore off the cover to count their gains;
They shuddered away into the shadows,   40
Hearing each the loud heart of the other.
Silence was born.

There in the tender moonlight,
    As sweet as they were in life,
Glimmered the ivory features,
    Of the Indian's wife.

In the manner of Montagnais women
    Her hair was rolled with braid;
Under her waxen fingers
    A crucifix was laid.   50

He was drawing her down to the Mission,
    To bury her there in spring,
When the bloodroot comes and the windflower
    To silver everything.

But as a gift of plunder
    Side by side were they laid,
The moon went on to her setting
    And covered them with shade.

(1905)   (1905)

The Sea by the Wood

I dwell in the sea that is wild and deep,
    But afar in a shadow still,
I can see the trees that gather and sleep
    In the wood upon the hill.

The deeps are green as an emerald's face,
    The caves are crystal calm,
But I wish the sea were a little trace
    Of moisture in God's palm.

The waves are weary of hiding pearls,
    Are aweary of smothering gold,   10
They would all be air that sweeps and swirls
    In the branches manifold.

They are weary of laving the seaman's eyes
    With their passion prayer unsaid,
They are weary of sobs and the sudden sighs
    And movements of the dead.

All the sea is haunted with human lips
    Ashen and sere and gray,
You can hear the sails of the sunken ships
    Stir and shiver and sway,   20

In the weary solitude;
    If mine were the will of God, the main
Should melt away in the rustling wood
    Like a mist that follows the rain.

But I dwell in the sea that is wild and deep
    And afar in the shadow still,
I can see the trees that gather and sleep
    In the wood upon the hill.

(1905)   (1926)

The Wood by the Sea

I dwell in the wood that is dark and kind
    But afar off tolls the main,
Afar, far off I hear the wind,
    And the roving of the rain.

The shade is dark as a palmer's hood,
    The air with balm is bland:
But I wish the trees that breathe in the wood
    Were ashes in God's hand.

The pines are weary of holding nests,
    Are aweary of casting shade;   10
Wearily smoulder the resin crests
    In the pungent gloom of the glade.

Weary are all the birds of sleep,
    The nests are weary of wings,
The whole wood yearns to the swaying deep,
    The mother of restful things.

The wood is very old and still,
    So still when the dead cones fall,
Near in the vale or away on the hill,
    You can hear them one and all,   20

And their falling wearies me;
    If mine were the will of God, – O, then
The wood should tramp to the sounding sea,
    Like a marching army of men!

But I dwell in the wood that is dark and kind,
    Afar off tolls the main;
Afar, far off I hear the wind
    And the roving of the rain.

(1905)   (1926)

The Height of Land

Here is the height of land:
   The watershed on either hand
Goes down to Hudson Bay
Or Lake Superior;
The stars are up, and far away
The wind sounds in the wood, wearier
Than the long Ojibway cadence
In which Potàn the Wise
Declares the ills of life
And Chees-que-ne-ne makes a mournful sound   10
Of acquiescence. The fires burn low
With just sufficient glow
To light the flakes of ash that play
At being moths, and flutter away
To fall in the dark and die as ashes:
Here there is peace in the lofty air,
And Something comes by flashes
Deeper than peace; –
The spruces have retired a little space
And left a field of sky in violet shadow   20
With stars like marigolds in a water-meadow.

Now the Indian guides are dead asleep;
   There is no sound unless the soul can hear
The gathering of the waters in their sources.

We have come up through the spreading lakes
   From level to level, –
Pitching our tents sometimes over a revel
Of roses that nodded all night,
Dreaming within our dreams,
To wake at dawn and find that they were captured   30
With no dew on their leaves;
Sometimes mid sheaves
Of bracken and dwarf-cornel, and again
On a wide blue-berry plain
Brushed with the shimmer of a bluebird's wing;

A rocky islet followed
With one lone poplar and a single nest
Of white-throat-sparrows that took no rest
But sang in dreams or woke to sing, –
To the last portage and the height of land – :   40
Upon one hand
The lonely north enlaced with lakes and streams,
And the enormous targe of Hudson Bay,
Glimmering all night
In the cold arctic light;
On the other hand
The crowded southern land
With all the welter of the lives of men.
But here is peace, and again
That Something comes by flashes   50
Deeper than peace, – a spell
Golden and inappellable
That gives the inarticulate part
Of our strange being one moment of release
That seems more native than the touch of time,
And we must answer in chime;
Though yet no man may tell
The secret of that spell
Golden and inappellable.

Now are there sounds walking in the wood,   60
    And all the spruces shiver and tremble,
And the stars move a little in their courses.
The ancient disturber of solitude
Breathes a pervasive sigh,
And the soul seems to hear
The gathering of the waters at their sources;
Then quiet ensues and pure starlight and dark;
The region-spirit murmurs in meditation,
The heart replies in exaltation
And echoes faintly like an inland shell   70
Ghost tremors of the spell;
Thought reawakens and is linked again
With all the welter of the lives of men.

Here on the uplands where the air is clear
    We think of life as of a stormy scene, –
Of tempest, of revolt and desperate shock;

And here, where we can think, on the bright uplands
Where the air is clear, we deeply brood on life
Until the tempest parts, and it appears
As simple as to the shepherd seems his flock: 80
A Something to be guided by ideals –
That in themselves are simple and serene –
Of noble deed to foster noble thought,
And noble thought to image noble deed,
Till deed and thought shall interpenetrate,
Making life lovelier, till we come to doubt
Whether the perfect beauty that escapes
Is beauty of deed or thought or some high thing
Mingled of both, a greater boon than either:
Thus we have seen in the retreating tempest   90
The victor-sunlight merge with the ruined rain,
And from the rain and sunlight spring the rainbow.

The ancient disturber of solitude
    Stirs his ancestral potion in the gloom,
And the dark wood
Is stifled with the pungent fume
Of charred earth burnt to the bone
That takes the place of air.
Then sudden I remember when and where, –
The last weird lakelet foul with weedy growths   100
And slimy viscid things the spirit loathes,
Skin of vile water over viler mud
Where the paddle stirred unutterable stenches,
And the canoes seemed heavy with fear,
Not to be urged toward the fatal shore
Where a bush fire, smouldering, with sudden roar
Leaped on a cedar and smothered it with light
And terror. It had left the portage-height
A tangle of slanted spruces burned to the roots,
Covered still with patches of bright fire   110
Smoking with incense of the fragrant resin
That even then began to thin and lessen
Into the gloom and glimmer of ruin.

'Tis overpast. How strange the stars have grown;
    The presage of extinction glows on their crests
And they are beautied with impermanence;
They shall be after the race of men

And mourn for them who snared their fiery pinions,
Entangled in the meshes of bright words.

A lemming stirs the fern and in the mosses   120
   Eft-minded things feel the air change, and dawn
Tolls out from the dark belfries of the spruces.
How often in the autumn of the world
Shall the crystal shrine of dawning be rebuilt
With deeper meaning! Shall the poet then,
Wrapped in his mantle on the height of land,
Brood on the welter of the lives of men
And dream of his ideal hope and promise
In the blush sunrise? Shall he base his flight
Upon a more compelling law than Love   130
As Life's atonement; shall the vision
Of noble deed and noble thought immingled
Seem as uncouth to him as the pictograph
Scratched on the cave side by the cave-dweller
To us of the Christ-time? Shall he stand
With deeper joy, with more complex emotion,
In closer commune with divinity,
With the deep fathomed, with the firmament charted,
With life as simple as a sheep-boy's song,
What lies beyond a romaunt that was read   140
Once on a morn of storm and laid aside
Memorious with strange immortal memories?
Or shall he see the sunrise as I see it
In shoals of misty fire the deluge-light
Dashes upon and whelms with purer radiance,
And feel the lulled earth, older in pulse and motion,
Turn the rich lands and the inundant oceans
To the flushed color, and hear as now I hear
The thrill of life beat up the planet's margin
And break in the clear susurrus of deep joy   150
That echoes and reëchoes in my being?
O Life is intuition the measure of knowledge
And do I stand with heart entranced and burning
At the zenith of our wisdom when I feel
The long light flow, the long wind pause, the deep
Influx of spirit, of which no man may tell
The Secret, golden and inappellable?

(1916)   (1916)

At Gull Lake: August, 1810

Gull Lake set in the rolling prairie –
Still there are reeds on the shore,
As of old the poplars shimmer
As summer passes;
Winter freezes the shallow lake to the core;
Storm passes,
Heat parches the sedges and grasses,
Night comes with moon-glimmer,
Dawn with the morning-star;
All proceeds in the flow of Time   10
As a hundred years ago.

Then two camps were pitched on the shore,
The clustered teepees
Of Tabashaw Chief of the Saulteaux.
And on a knoll tufted with poplars
Two gray tents of a trader –
Nairne of the Orkneys.
Before his tents under the shade of the poplars
Sat Keejigo, third of the wives
Of Tabashaw Chief of the Saulteaux;   20
Clad in the skins of antelopes
Broidered with porcupine quills
Coloured with vivid dyes,
Vermilion here and there
In the roots of her hair,
A half-moon of powder-blue
On her brow, her cheeks
Scored with light ochre streaks.
Keejigo daughter of Launay
The Normandy hunter   30
And Oshawan of the Saulteaux,
Troubled by fugitive visions
In the smoke of the camp-fires
In the close dark of the teepee,
Flutterings of colour
Along the flow of the prairies,
Spangles of flower tints
Caught in the wonder of dawn,
Dreams of sounds unheard –
The echoes of echo,   40

Star she was named for
Keejigo, star of the morning,
Voices of storm –
Wind-rush and lightning, –
The beauty of terror;
The twilight moon
Coloured like a prairie lily,
The round moon of pure snow,
The beauty of peace;
Premonitions of love and of beauty   50
Vague as shadows cast by a shadow.
Now she had found her hero,
And offered her body and spirit
With abject unreasoning passion,
As Earth abandons herself
To the sun and the thrust of the lightning.
Quiet were all the leaves of the poplars,
Breathless the air under their shadow,
As Keejigo spole of these things to her heart
In the beautiful speech of the Saulteaux.   60

> *The flower lives on the prairie,*
> *The wind in the sky,*
> *I am here my beloved;*
> *The wind and the flower.*
>
> *The crane hides in the sand-hills,*
> *Where does the wolverine hide?*
> *I am here my beloved,*
> *Heart's-blood on the feathers*
> *The foot caught in the trap.*
>
> *Take the flower in your hand,*   70
> *The wind in your nostrils;*
> *I am here my beloved;*
> *Release the captive*
> *Heal the wound under the feathers.*

A storm-cloud was marching
Vast on the prairie,
Scored with livid ropes of hail,
Quick with nervous vines of lightning –
Twice had Nairne turned her away
Afraid of the venom of Tabashaw,   80

Twice had the Chief fired at his tents
And now when two bullets
Whistled above the encampment
He yelled "Drive this bitch to her master."

Keejigo went down a path by the lake;
Thick at the tangled edges,
The reeds and the sedges
Were gray as ashes
Against the death-black water;
The lightning scored with double flashes   90
The dark lake-mirror and loud
Came the instant thunder.
Her lips still moved to the words of her music,
"Release the captive,
Heal the wound under the feathers."

At the top of the bank
The old wives caught her and cast her down
Where Tabashaw crouched by his camp-fire.
He snatched a live brand from the embers,
Seared her cheeks,   100
Blinded her eyes,
Destroyed her beauty with fire,
Screaming, "Take that face to your lover."
Keejigo held her face to the fury
And made no sound.
The old wives dragged her away
And threw her over the bank
Like a dead dog.

Then burst the storm —
The Indians' screams and the howls of the dogs   110
Lost in the crash of hail
That smashed the sedges and reeds,
Stripped the poplars of leaves,
Tore and blazed onwards,
Wasting itself with riot and tumult —
Supreme in the beauty of terror.

The setting sun struck the retreating cloud
With a rainbow, not an arc but a column
Built with the glory of seven metals;

Beyond in the purple deeps of the vortex   120
Fell the quivering vines of the lightning.
The wind withdrew the veil from the shrine of the moon,
She rose changing her dusky shade for the glow
Of the prairie lily, till free of all blemish of colour
She came to her zenith without a cloud or a star,
A lovely perfection, snow-pure in the heaven of midnight.
After the beauty of terror the beauty of peace.

But Keejigo came no more to the camps of her people;
Only the midnight moon knew where she felt her way,
Only the leaves of autumn, the snows of winter   130
Knew where she lay.

(1935)   (1935)

At Delos

An iris-flower with topaz leaves,
    With a dark heart of deeper gold,
Died over Delos when light failed
    And the night grew cold.

No wave fell mourning in the sea
    Where age on age beauty had died;
For that frail colour withering away
    No sea-bird cried.

There is no grieving in the world
    As beauty fades throughout the years: 10
The pilgrim with the weary heart
    Brings to the grave his tears.

(1947)   (1947)

Stephen Leacock
1869-1944

———————◆———————

BORN IN HAMPSHIRE, England, Stephen Leacock immigrated with his family to a farm near Lake Simcoe in 1875. He was educated at Upper Canada College, the University of Toronto and the University of Chicago. After earning his doctorate , he accepted an appointment to the Department of Economics and Political Science at McGill University in 1903. He remained at McGill until his retirement in 1936 and published books in areas as diverse as political science, literary criticism, history and autobiography. However, following the publication of *Literary Lapses* in 1910, his reputation as a teacher and scholar was overshadowed by his renown as a humorist. Leacock's *Sunshine Sketches of a Little Town*, a collection of linked sketches set in the mythical town of Mariposa, was published in 1912.

From
Sunshine Sketches of a Little Town

The Marine Excursions
of the Knights of Pythias

HALF-PAST SIX on a July morning! The Mariposa Belle is at the wharf, decked in flags, with steam up ready to start. Excursion day!

Half-past six on a July morning, and Lake Wissanotti lying in the sun as calm as glass. The opal colours of the morning light are shot from the surface of the water.

Out on the lake the last thin threads of the mist are clearing away like flecks of cotton wool.

The long call of the loon echoes over the lake. The air is cool and fresh. There is in it all the new life of the land of the silent pine and the moving waters. Lake Wissanotti in the morning sunlight! Don't talk to me of the Italian lakes, or the Tyrol or the Swiss Alps. Take them away. Move them somewhere else. I don't want them.

Excursion Day, at half-past six of a summer morning! With the boat all decked in flags and all the people in Mariposa on the wharf, and the band in peaked caps with big cornets tied to their bodies ready to play at any minute! I say! Don't tell me about the Carnival of Venice and the Delhi Durbar. Don't! I wouldn't look at them. I'd shut my eyes! For light and colour give me every time an excursion out of Mariposa down the lake to the Indian's Island out of sight in the morning mist. Talk of your Papal Zouaves and your Buckingham Palace Guard! I want to see the Mariposa band in uniform and the Mariposa Knights of Pythias with their aprons and their insignia and their picnic baskets and their five-cent cigars!

Half-past six in the morning, and all the crowd on the wharf and the boat due to leave in half an hour. Notice it! – in half an hour. Already she's whistled twice (at six, and at six fifteen), and at any minute now, Christie Johnson will step into the pilot house and pull the string for the warning whistle that the boat will leave in half an hour. So keep ready. Don't think of running back to Smith's Hotel for the sandwiches. Don't be fool enough to try to go up to the Greek Store, next to Netley's, and buy fruit. You'll be left behind for sure if you do. Never mind the sandwiches and the fruit! Anyway, here comes Mr. Smith himself with a huge basket of provender that would feed a factory. There must be sandwiches in that. I think I can hear them clinking. And behind Mr. Smith is the German waiter from the caff with another basket – indubitably lager beer; and behind him, the bar-tender of the hotel, carrying nothing, as far as one can see. But of course if you know Mariposa you will understand that why he looks so nonchalant and empty-handed is because he has two bottles of rye whiskey under his linen duster. You know, I think, the peculiar walk of a man with two bottles of whiskey in the inside pockets of a linen coat. In Mariposa, you see, to bring beer to an excursion is quite in keeping with public opinion. But, whiskey, – well, one has to be a little careful.

Do I say that Mr. Smith is here? Why, everybody's here. There's Hussell the editor of the Newspacket, wearing a blue ribbon on his coat, for the Mariposa Knights of Pythias are, by their constitution, dedicated to temperance; and there's Henry Mullins, the manager of the Exchange Bank, also a Knight of Pythias, with a small flask of Pogram's Special in his hip pocket as a sort of amendment to the constitution. And there's Dean Drone, the Chaplain of the Order, with a fishing-rod (you never saw such green bass as lie among the rocks at Indian's Island), and with a trolling line in case of maskinonge, and a landing net in case of pickerel, and with his eldest daughter, Lilian Drone, in case of young men. There never was such a fisherman as the Rev. Rupert Drone.

Perhaps I ought to explain that when I speak of the excursion as being of the Knights of Pythias, the thing must not be understood in any narrow sense. In Mariposa practically everybody belongs to the Knights of Pythias just as they do to everything else. That's the great thing about the town and that's what makes it so different from the city. Everybody is in everything.

You should see them on the seventeenth of March, for example, when everybody wears a green ribbon and they're all laughing and glad, – you know what the Celtic nature is, – and talking about Home Rule.

On St. Andrew's Day every man in town wears a thistle and shakes hands with everybody else and you see the fine old Scotch honesty beaming out of their eyes.

And on St. George's Day! – well, there's no heartiness like the good old English spirit after all; why shouldn't a man feel glad that he's an Englishman?

Then on the Fourth of July there are stars and stripes flying over half the stores in town, and suddenly all the men are seen to smoke cigars, and to know all about Roosevelt and Bryan and the Philippine Islands. Then you learn for the first time that Jeff Thorpe's people came from Massachusetts and that his uncle fought at Bunker Hill (it must have been Bunker Hill, – anyway Jefferson will swear it was in Dakota all right enough); and you find that George Duff has a married sister in Rochester and that her husband is all right; in fact, George was down there as recently as eight years ago. Oh, it's the most American town imaginable is Mariposa, – on the fourth of July.

But wait, just wait, if you feel anxious about the solidity of the British connection, till the twelfth of the month, when everybody is wearing an orange streamer in his coat and the Orangemen (every man in town) walk in the big procession. Allegiance! Well, perhaps you remember the address they gave to the Prince of Wales on the platform of the Mariposa station as he went through on his tour to the west. I think that pretty well settled that question.

So you will easily understand that of course everybody belongs to the Knights of Pythias and the Masons and Oddfellows, just as they all belong to the Snow Shoe Club and the Girls' Friendly Society.

And meanwhile the whistle of the steamer has blown again for a quarter to seven: – loud and long this time, for any one not here now is late for certain, unless he should happen to come down in the last fifteen minutes.

What a crowd upon the wharf and how they pile on to the steamer! It's a wonder that the boat can hold them all. But that's just the marvellous thing about the Mariposa Belle.

I don't know, – I have never known, – where the steamers like the Mariposa Belle come from. Whether they are built by Harland and

Wolff of Belfast or whether, on the other hand, they are not built by Harland and Wolff of Belfast, is more than one would like to say offhand.

The Mariposa Belle always seems to me to have some of those strange properties that distinguish Mariposa itself. I mean, her size seems to vary so. If you see her there in the winter, frozen in the ice beside the wharf with a snowdrift against the windows of the pilot house, she looks a pathetic little thing the size of a butternut. But in the summer time, especially after you've been in Mariposa for a month or two, and have paddled alongside of her in a canoe, she gets larger and taller, and with a great sweep of black sides, till you see no difference between the Mariposa Belle and the Lusitania. Each one is a big steamer and that's all you can say.

Nor do her measurements help you much. She draws about eighteen inches forward and more than that, – at least half an inch more, astern, and when she's loaded down with an excursion crowd, she draws a good two inches more. And above the water, – why, look at all the decks on her! There's the deck you walk on to, from the wharf, all shut in, with windows along it, and the after cabin with the long table, and above that the deck with all the chairs piled upon it, and the deck in front where the band stand round in a circle, and the pilot house is higher than that, and above the pilot house is the board with the gold name and the flag pole and the steel ropes and the flags; and fixed in somewhere on the different levels, is the lunch counter where they sell the sandwiches, and the engine room, and down below the deck level, beneath the water line, is the place where the crew sleep. What with steps and stairs and passages and piles of cordwood for the engine, – oh no, I guess Harland and Wolff didn't build her. They couldn't have.

Yet even with a huge boat like the Mariposa Belle, it would be impossible for her to carry all of the crowd that you see in the boat and on the wharf. In reality, the crowd is made up of two classes, – all of the people in Mariposa who are going on the excursion and all those who are not. Some come for the one reason and some for the other.

The two tellers of the Exchange Bank are both there standing side by side. But one of them, – the one with the cameo pin and the long face like a horse, – is going, and the other, – with the other cameo pin and the face like another horse, – is not. In the same way. Hussell of the Newspacket is going, but his brother, beside him, isn't. Lilian Drone is going, but her sister can't; and so on all through the crowd.

And to think that things should look like that on the morning of a steamboat accident.

How strange life is!

To think of all these people so eager and anxious to catch the steamer, and some of them running to catch it, and so fearful that they might miss it, – the morning of a steamboat accident. And the captain blowing his whistle, and warning them so severely that he would leave them behind, – leave them out of the accident! And everybody crowding so eagerly to be in the accident.

Perhaps life is like that all through.

Strangest of all to think, in a case like this, of the people who were left behind, or in some way or other prevented from going, and always afterwards told of how they had escaped being on board the Mariposa Belle that day!

Some of the instances were certainly extraordinary.

Nivens, the lawyer, escaped from being there merely by the fact that he was away in the city.

Towers, the tailor, only escaped owing to the fact that, not intending to go on the excursion he had stayed in bed till eight o'clock and so had not gone. He narrated afterwards that waking up that morning at half-past five, he had thought of the excursion and for some unaccountable reason had felt glad that he was not going.

The case of Yodel, the auctioneer, was even more inscrutable. He had been to the Oddfellows excursion on the train the week before and to the Conservative picnic the week before that, and had decided not to go on this trip. In fact, he had not the least intention of going. He narrated afterwards how the night before someone had stopped him on the corner of Nippewa and Tecumseh Streets (he indicated the very spot) and asked: "Are you going to take in the excursion to-morrow?"and he had said, just as simply as he was talking when narrating it: "No." And ten minutes after that, at the corner of Dalhousie and Brock Streets (he offered to lead a party of verification to the precise place) somebody else had stopped him and asked: "Well, are you going on the steamer trip to-morrow?" Again he had answered: "No," apparently almost in the same tone as before.

He said afterwards that when he heard the rumour of the accident it seemed like the finger of Providence, and he fell on his knees in thankfulness.

There was the similar case of Morison (I mean the one in Glover's hardware store that married one of the Thompsons). He said afterwards that he had read so much in the papers about accidents lately, – mining accidents, and aeroplanes and gasoline, – that he had grown nervous. The night before his wife had asked him at supper: "Are you going on the excursion?" He had answered: "No, I don't think I feel like it," and had added: "Perhaps your mother might like to go?" And the next evening just at dusk when the news ran through the town, he said the first thought that flashed through his head was: "Mrs. Thompson's on that boat."

He told this right as I say it – without the least doubt or confusion. He never for a moment imagined she was on the Lusitania or the Olympic or any other boat. He knew she was on this one. He said you could have knocked him down where he stood. But no one had. Not even when he got half-way down, – on his knees, and it would have been easier still to knock him down or kick him. People do miss a lot of chances.

Still, as I say, neither Yodel nor Morison nor anyone thought about there being an accident until just after sundown when they –

Well, have you ever heard the long booming whistle of a steamboat two miles out on the lake in the dusk, and while you listen and count and wonder, seen the crimson rockets going up against the sky and then heard the fire bell ringing right there beside you in the town, and seen the people running to the town wharf?

That's what the people of Mariposa saw and felt that summer evening as they watched the Mackinaw life-boat go plunging out into the lake with seven sweeps to a side and the foam clear to the gunwale with the lifting stroke of fourteen men!

But, dear me, I am afraid that this is no way to tell a story. I suppose the true art would have been to have said nothing about the accident till it happened. But when you write about Mariposa, or hear of it, if you know the place, it's all so vivid and real that a thing like the contrast between the excursion crowd in the morning and the scene at night leaps into your mind and you must think of it.

But never mind about the accident, – let us turn back again to the morning.

The boat was due to leave at seven. There was no doubt about the hour, – not only seven, but seven sharp. The notice in the Newspacket said: "The boat will leave sharp at seven;" and the advertising posters on the telegraph poles on Missinaba Street that began "Ho, for Indian's Island!" ended up with the words: "Boat leaves at seven sharp." There was a big notice on the wharf that said: "Boat leaves sharp on time."

So at seven, right on the hour, the whistle blew loud and long, and then at seven fifteen three short peremptory blasts and at seven thirty one quick angry call, – just one, – and very soon after that they cast off the last of the ropes and the Mariposa Belle sailed off in her cloud of flags, and the band of the Knights of Pythias, timing it to a nicety, broke into the "Maple Leaf for Ever!"

I suppose that all excursions when they start are much the same. Anyway, on the Mariposa Belle everybody went running up and down all over the boat with deck chairs and camp stools and baskets, and found places, splendid places to sit, and then got scared that there might be better ones and chased off again. People hunted for places out of the sun and when they got them swore that they weren't going to freeze to please anybody; and the people in the sun said that they hadn't paid fifty cents to be roasted. Others said that they hadn't paid fifty cents to get covered with cinders, and there were still others who hadn't paid fifty cents to get shaken to death with the propeller.

Still, it was all right presently. The people seemed to get sorted out into the places on the boat where they belonged. The women, the older ones, all gravitated into the cabin on the lower deck and by getting round the table with needlework, and with all the windows shut, they soon had it, as they said themselves, just like being at home.

All they young boys and the toughs and the men in the band got down on the lower deck forward, where the boat was dirtiest and where the anchor was and the coils of rope.

And upstairs on the after deck there were Lilian Drone and Miss Lawson, the high school teacher, with a book of German poetry, – Gothey I think it was, – and the bank teller and the younger men.

In the centre, standing beside the rail, were Dean Drone and Dr. Gallagher, looking through binocular glasses at the shore.

Up in front on the little deck forward of the pilot house was a group of the older men, Mullins and Duff and Mr. Smith in a deck chair, and beside him Mr. Golgotha Gingham, the undertaker of Mariposa, on a stool. It was part of Mr. Gingham's principles to take in an outing of this sort, a business matter, more or less, – for you never know what may happen at these water parties. At any rate, he was there in a neat suit of black, not, of course, his heavier or professional suit, but a soft clinging effect as of burnt paper that combined gaiety and decorum to a nicety.

"Yes," said Mr. Gingham, waving his black glove in a general way towards the shore, "I know the lake well, very well. I've been pretty much all over it in my time."

"Canoeing?" asked somebody.

"No," said Mr. Gingham, "not a canoe." There seemed a peculiar and quiet meaning in his tone.

"Sailing, I suppose," said somebody else.

"No," said Mr. Gingham. "I don't understand it."

"I never knowed that you went on to the water at all, Gol," said Mr. Smith, breaking in.

"Ah, not now," explained Mr. Gingham; "it was years ago, the first summer I came to Mariposa. I was on the water practically all day. Nothing like it to give a man an appetite and keep him in shape."

"Was you camping?" asked Mr. Smith.

"We camped at night," assented the undertaker, "but we put in practically the whole day on the water. You see we were after a party that had come up here from the city on his vacation and gone out in a sailing canoe. We were dragging. We were up every morning at sunrise, lit a fire on the beach and cooked breakfast, and then we'd light our pipes and be off with the net for a whole day. It's a great life," concluded Mr. Gingham wistfully.

"Did you get him?" asked two or three together.

There was a pause before Mr. Gingham answered.

"We did," he said, – "down in the reeds past Horseshoe Point. But it was no use. He turned blue on me right away."

After which Mr. Gingham fell into such a deep reverie that the boat had steamed another half mile down the lake before anybody broke the silence again.

Talk of this sort, – and after all what more suitable for a day on the water? – beguiled the way.

Down the lake, mile by mile over the calm water, steamed the Mariposa Belle. They passed Poplar Point where the high sand banks are with all the swallows' nests in them; and Dean Drone and Dr. Gallagher looked at them alternately through the binocular glasses, and it was wonderful how plainly one could see the swallows and the banks and the shrubs, – just as plainly as with the naked eye.

And a little further down they passed the Shingle Beach, and Dr. Gallagher, who knew Canadian history, said to Dean Drone that it was strange to think that Champlain had landed there with his French explorers three hundred years ago; and Dean Drone, who didn't know Canadian history, said it was stranger still to think that the hand of the Almighty had piled up the hills and rocks long before that; and Dr. Gallagher said it was wonderful how the French had found their way through such a pathless wilderness; and Dean Drone said that it was wonderful also to think that the Almighty had placed even the smallest shrub in its appointed place. Dr. Gallagher said it filled him with admiration. Dean Drone said it filled him with awe. Dr. Gallagher said he'd been full of it ever since he was a boy; and Dean Drone said so had he.

Then a little further, as the Mariposa Belle steamed on down the lake, they passed the Old Indian Portage where the great grey rocks are; and Dr. Gallagher drew Dean Drone's attention to the place where the narrow canoe track wound up from the shore to the woods, and Dean Drone said he could see it perfectly well without the glasses.

Dr. Gallagher said that is was just here that a party of five hundred French had made their way with all their baggage and accoutrements across the rocks of the divide and down to the Great Bay. And Dean

Drone said that it reminded him of Xenophon leading his ten thousand Greeks over the hill passes of Armenia down to the sea. Dr. Gallagher said that he had often wished he could have seen and spoken to Champlain, and Dean Drone said how much he regretted to have never known Xenophon.

And then after that they fell to talking of relics and traces of the past and Dr. Gallagher said that if Dean Drone would come round to his house some night he would show him some Indian arrow heads that he had dug up in his garden. And Dean Drone said that if Dr. Gallagher would come round to the rectory any afternoon he would show him a map of Xerxes' invasion of Greece. Only he must come some time between the Infant Class and the Mothers' Auxiliary.

So presently they both knew that they were blocked out of one another's houses for some time to come, and Dr. Gallagher walked forward and told Mr. Smith, who had never studied Greek, about Champlain crossing the rock divide.

Mr. Smith turned his head and looked at the divide for half a second and then said he had crossed a worse one up north back of the Wahnipitae and that the flies were Hades, – and then went on playing freezeout poker with the two juniors in Duff's bank.

So Dr. Gallagher realized that that's always the way when you try to tell people things, and that as far as gratitude and appreciation goes one might as well never read books or travel anywhere or do anything.

In fact, it was at this very moment that he made up his mind to give the arrows to the Mariposa Mechanics' Institute, – they afterwards became, as you know, the Gallagher Collection. But for the time being, the doctor was sick of them and wandered off round the boat and watched Henry Mullins showing George Duff how to make a John Collins without lemons, and finally went and sat down among the Mariposa band and wished that he hadn't come.

So the boat steamed on and the sun rose higher and higher, and the freshness of the morning changed into the full glare of noon, and they went on to where the lake began to narrow in at its foot, just where the Indian's Island is, – all grass and trees and with a log wharf running into the water. Below it the Lower Ossawippi runs out of the lake, and quite near are the rapids, and you can see down among the trees the red brick of the power house and hear the roar of the leaping water.

The Indian's Island itself is all covered with trees and tangled vines, and the water about it is so still that it's all reflected double and looks the same either way up. Then when the steamer's whistle blows as it comes into the wharf, you hear it echo among the trees of the island, and reverberate back from the shores of the lake.

The scene is all so quiet and still and unbroken, that Miss Cleghorn, –

the sallow girl in the telephone exchange, that I spoke of – said she'd like to be buried there. But all the people were so busy getting their baskets and gathering up their things that no one had time to attend to it.

I mustn't even try to describe the landing and the boat crunching against the wooden wharf and all the people running to the same side of the deck and Christie Johnson calling out to the crowd to keep to the starboard and nobody being able to find it. Everyone who has been on a Mariposa excursion knows all about that.

Nor can I describe the day itself and the picnic under the trees. There were speeches afterwards, and Judge Pepperleigh gave such offence by bringing in Conservative politics that a man called Patriotus Canadiensis wrote and asked for some of the invaluable space of the Mariposa Times-Herald and exposed it.

I should say that there were races too, on the grass on the open side of the island, graded mostly according to ages, – races for boys under thirteen and girls over nineteen and all that sort of thing. Sports are generally conducted on that plan in Mariposa. It is realized that a woman of sixty has an unfair advantage over a mere child.

Dean Drone managed the races and decided the ages and gave out the prizes; the Wesleyan minister helped, and he and the young student, who was relieving in the Presbyterian Church, held the string at the winning point.

They had to get mostly clergymen for the races because all the men had wandered off, somehow, to where they were drinking lager beer out of two kegs stuck on pine logs among the trees.

But if you've ever been on a Mariposa excursion you know all about these details anyway.

So the day wore on and presently the sun came through the trees on a slant and the steamer whistle blew with a great puff of white steam and all the people came straggling down to the wharf and pretty soon the Mariposa Belle had floated out on to the lake again and headed for the town, twenty miles away.

I suppose you have often noticed the contrast there is between an excursion on its way out in the morning and what it looks like on the way home.

In the morning everybody is so restless and animated and moves to and fro all over the boat and asks questions. But coming home, as the afternoon gets later and later and the sun sinks beyond the hills, all the people seem to get so still and quiet and drowsy.

So it was with the people on the Mariposa Belle. They sat there on the benches and deck chairs in little clusters, and listened to the regular beat of the propeller and almost dozed off asleep as they sat. Then when the sun set and the dusk drew on, it grew almost dark on the deck and so still that you could hardly tell there was anyone on board.

And if you had looked at the steamer from the shore or from one of the islands, you'd have seen the row of lights from the cabin windows shining on the water and the red glare of the burning hemlock from the funnel, and you'd have heard the soft thud of the propeller miles away over the lake.

Now and then, too, you could have heard them singing on the steamer, – the voices of the girls and the men blended into unison by the distance, rising and falling in long-drawn melody: *"O – Can-a-da – O – Can-a-da."*

You may talk as you will about the intoning choirs of your European cathedrals, but the sound of "O Can-a-da," borne across the waters of a silent lake at evening is good enough for those of us who know Mariposa.

I think that it was just as they were singing like this: *"O – Can-a-da,"* that word went round that the boat was sinking.

If you have ever been in any sudden emergency on the water, you will understand the strange psychology of it, – the way in which what is happening seems to become known all in a moment without a word being said. The news is transmitted from one to the other by some mysterious process.

At any rate, on the Mariposa Belle first one and then the other heard that the steamer was sinking. As far as I could ever learn the first of it was that George Duff, the bank manager, came very quietly to Dr. Gallagher and asked him if he thought that the boat was sinking. The doctor said no, that he had thought so earlier in the day but that he didn't now think that she was.

After that Duff, according to his own account, had said to Macartney, the lawyer, that the boat was sinking, and Macartney said that he doubted it very much.

Then somebody came to Judge Pepperleigh and woke him up and said that there was six inches of water in the steamer and that she was sinking. And Pepperleigh said it was perfect scandal and passed the news on to his wife and she said that they had no business to allow it and that if the steamer sank that was the last excursion she'd go on.

So the news went all round the boat and everywhere the people gathered in groups and talked about it in the angry and excited way that people have when a steamer is sinking on one of the lakes like Lake Wissanotti.

Dean Drone, of course, and some others were quieter about it, and said that one must make allowances and that naturally there were two sides to everything. But most of them wouldn't listen to reason at all. I think, perhaps, that some of them were frightened. You see the last time but one that the steamer had sunk, there had been a man drowned and it made them nervous.

What? Hadn't I explained about the depth of Lake Wissanotti? I had taken it for granted that you knew; and in any case parts of it are deep enough, though I don't suppose in this stretch of it from the big reed beds up to within a mile of the town wharf, you could find six feet of water in it if you tried. Oh, pshaw! I was not talking about a steamer sinking in the ocean and carrying down its screaming crowds of people into the hideous depths of green water. Oh, dear me, no! That kind of thing never happens on Lake Wissanotti.

But what does happen is that the Mariposa Belle sinks every now and then, and sticks there on the bottom till they get things straightened up.

On the lakes round Mariposa, if a person arrives late anywhere and explains that the steamer sank, everybody understands the situation.

You see when Harland and Wolff built the Mariposa Belle, they left some cracks in between the timbers that you fill up with cotton waste every Sunday. If this is not attended to, the boat sinks. In fact, it is part of the law of the province that all the steamers like the Mariposa Belle must be properly corked, – I think that is the word, – every season. There are inspectors who visit all hotels in the province to see that it is done.

So you can imagine now that I've explained it a little straighter, the indignation of the people when they knew that the boat had come uncorked and that they might be stuck out there on a shoal or a mud-bank half the night.

I don't say either that there wasn't any danger; anyway, it doesn't feel very safe when you realize that the boat is settling down with every hundred yards that she goes, and you look over the side and see only the black water in the gathering night.

Safe! I'm not sure now that I come to think of it that it isn't worse than sinking in the Atlantic. After all, in the Atlantic there is wireless tele-graphy, and a lot of trained sailors and stewards. But out on Lake Wissanotti, – far out, so that you can only just see the lights of the town away off to the south, – when the propeller comes to a stop, – and you can hear the hiss of steam as they start to rake out the engine fires to prevent an explosion, – and when you turn from the red glare that comes from the furnace doors as they open them, to the black dark that is gathering over the lake, – and there's a night wind beginning to run among the rushes, – and you see the men going forward to the roof of the pilot house to send up the rockets to rouse the town, – safe? Safe yourself, if you like; as for me, let me once get back into Mariposa again, under the night shadow of the maple trees, and this shall be the last, last time I'll go on Lake Wissanotti.

Safe! Oh, yes! Isn't it strange how safe other people's adventures seem after they happen. But you'd have been scared, too, if you'd been there just before the steamer sank, and seen them bringing up all the women on to the top deck.

I don't see how some of the people took it so calmly; how Mr. Smith, for instance, could have gone on smoking and telling how he'd had a steamer "sink on him" on Lake Nipissing and a still bigger one, a side-wheeler, sink on him in Lake Abbitibbi.

Then, quite suddenly, with a quiver, down she went. You could feel the boat sink, sink, – down, down, – would it never get to the bottom? The water came flush up to the lower deck, and then – thank heaven, – the sinking stopped and there was the Mariposa Belle safe and tight on a reed bank.

Really, it made one positively laugh! It seemed so queer and, anyway, if a man has a sort of natural courage, danger makes him laugh. Danger? pshaw! fiddlesticks! everybody scouted the idea. Why, it is just the little things like this that give zest to a day on the water.

Within half a minute they were all running round looking for sandwiches and cracking jokes and talking of making coffee over the remains of the engine fires.

I don't need to tell at length how it all happened after that.

I suppose the people on the Mariposa Belle would have had to settle down there all night or till help came from the town, but some of the men who had gone forward and were peering out into the dark said that it couldn't be more than a mile across the water to Miller's Point. You could almost see it over there to the left, – some of them, I think, said "off on the port bow," because you know when you get mixed up in these marine disasters, you soon catch the atmosphere of the thing.

So pretty soon they had the davits swung out over the side and were lowering the old lifeboat from the top deck into the water.

There were men leaning out over the rail of the Mariposa Belle with lanterns that threw the light as they let her down, and the glare fell on the water and the reeds. But when they got the boat lowered, it looked such a frail, clumsy thing as one saw it from the rail above, that the cry was raised: "Women and children first!" For what was the sense, if it should turn out that the boat wouldn't even hold women and children, of trying to jam a lot of heavy men into it?

So they put in mostly women and children and the boat pushed out into the darkness so freighted down it would hardly float.

In the bow of it was the Presbyterian student who was relieving the minister, and he called out that they were in the hands of Providence. But he was crouched and ready to spring out of them at the first moment.

So the boat went and was lost in the darkness except for the lantern in the bow that you could see bobbing on the water. Then presently it came back and they sent another load, till pretty soon the decks began to thin out and everybody got impatient to be gone.

It was about the time that the third boat-load put off that Mr. Smith took a bet with Mullins for twenty-five dollars, that he'd be home in Mariposa before the people in the boats had walked round the shore.

No one knew just what he meant, but pretty soon they saw Mr. Smith disappear down below into the lowest part of the steamer with a mallet in one hand and a big bundle of marline in the other.

They might have wondered more about it, but it was just at this time that they heard the shouts from the rescue boat – the big Mackinaw lifeboat – that had put out from the town with fourteen men at the sweeps when they saw the first rockets go up.

I suppose there is always something inspiring about a resue at sea, or on the water.

After all, the bravery of the lifeboat man is the true bravery, – expended to save life, not to destroy it.

Certainly they told for months after of how the rescue boat came out to the Mariposa Belle.

I suppose that when they put her in the water the lifeboat touched it, for the first time since the old Macdonald Government placed her on Lake Wissanotti.

Anyway, the water poured in at every seam. But not for a moment, – even with two miles of water between them and the steamer, – did the rowers pause for that.

By the time they were half-way there the water was almost up to the thwarts but they drove her on. Panting and exhausted (for mind you, if you haven't been in a fool boat like that for years, rowing takes it out of you), the rowers stuck to their task. They threw the ballast over and chucked into the water the heavy cork jackets and lifebelts that encumbered their movements. There was no thought of turning back. They were nearer to the steamer than the shore.

"Hang to it, boys," called the crowd from the steamer's deck, and hang they did.

They were almost exhausted when they got them; men leaning from the steamer threw them ropes and one by one every man was hauled aboard just as the lifeboat sank under their feet.

Saved! by Heaven, saved, by one of the smartest pieces of rescue work ever seen on the lake.

There's no use describing it; you need to see rescue work of this kind by lifeboats to understand it.

414 / Stephen Leacock

Nor were the lifeboat crew the only ones that distinguished themselves.

Boat after boat and canoe after canoe had put out from Mariposa to the help of the steamer. They got them all.

Pupkin, the other bank teller, with a face like a horse, who hadn't gone on the excursion, – as soon as he knew that the boat was signalling for help and that Miss Lawson was sending up rockets, – rushed for a row boat, grabbed an oar (two would have hampered him), and paddled madly out into the lake. He struck right out into the dark with the crazy skiff almost sinking beneath his feet. But they got him. They rescued him. They watched him almost dead with exhaustion, make his way to the steamer, where he was hauled up with ropes. Saved! Saved!!

They might have gone on that way half the night, picking up the rescuers, only, at the very moment when the tenth load of people left for the shore, – just as suddenly and saucily as you please, up came the Mariposa Belle from the mud bottom and floated.

FLOATED?

Why, of course she did. If you take a hundred and fifty people off a steamer that has sunk, and if you get a man as shrewd as Mr. Smith to plug the timber seams with mallet and marline, and if you turn ten bandsmen of the Mariposa band on to your hand pump on the bow of the lower decks – float? why, what else can she do?

Then, if you stuff in hemlock into the embers of the fire that you were raking out, till it hums and crackles under the boiler, it won't be long before you hear the propeller thud-thudding at the stern again, and before the long roar of the steam whistle echoes over to the town.

And so the Mariposa Belle, with all steam up again and with the long train of sparks careering from the funnel, is heading for the town.

But no Christie Johnson at the wheel in the pilot house this time.

"Smith! Get Smith!" is the cry.

Can he take her in? Well, now! Ask a man who has had steamers sink on him in half the lakes from Temiscaming to the Bay, if he can take her in? Ask a man who has run a York boat down the rapids of the Moose when the ice is moving, if he can grip the steering wheel of the Mariposa Belle. So there she steams safe and sound to the town wharf!

Look at the lights and the crowd! If only the federal census taker could count us now! Hear them calling and shouting back and forward from the deck to the shore! Listen! There is the rattle of the shore ropes as they get them ready, and there's the Mariposa band, – actually forming in a circle on the upper deck just as she docks, and the leader with his baton, – one – two – ready now, –

"O CAN-A-DA!"

(1912)   (1912)

Emily Carr
1871-1945

———◆———

EMILY CARR WAS born in Victoria, British Columbia, and studied art in
San Francisco, London and Paris. Following her graduation in 1902
from the Westminster School of Art in London, she returned to British
Columbia and began a series of visits to villages of the Indians of the
West Coast. These trips provided subjects for many of her most famous
paintings and much of her later literary work. Carr published several
autobiographical works including *Klee Wyck*, a collection of sketches
which won the Governor-General's Award for non-fiction in 1941, *The
Book of Small* (1942) and *The House of All Sorts* (1944).

D'Sonoqua

I WAS SKETCHING in a remote Indian village when I first saw her. The
village was one of those that the Indians use only for a few months in
each year; the rest of the time it stands empty and desolate. I went there
in one of its empty times, in a drizzling dusk.

When the Indian agent dumped me on the beach in front of the
village, he said "There is not a soul here. I will come back for you in two
days." Then he went away.

I had a small Griffon dog with me, and also a little Indian girl, who,
when she saw the boat go away, clung to my sleeve and wailed, "I'm
'fraid."

We went up to the old deserted Mission House. At the sound of the
key in the rusty lock, rats scuttled away. The stove was broken, the
wood wet. I had forgotten to bring candles. We spread our blankets on
the floor, and spent a poor night. Perhaps my lack of sleep played its
part in the shock that I got, when I saw her for the first time.

Water was in the air, half mist, half rain. The stinging nettles, higher
than my head, left their nervy smart on my ears and forehead, as I beat
my way through them, trying all the while to keep my feet on the plank
walk which they hid. Big yellow slugs crawled on the walk and slimed it.
My feet slipped, and I shot headlong to her very base, for she had no
feet. The nettles that were above my head reached only to her knee.

It was not the fall alone that jerked the "Oh's" out of me, for the great wooden image towering above me was indeed terrifying.

The nettle-bed ended a few yards beyond her, and then a rocky bluff jutted out, with waves battering it below. I scrambled up and went out on the bluff, so that I could see the creature above the nettles. The forest was behind her, the sea in front.

Her head and trunk were carved out of, or rather into, the bole of a great red cedar. She seemed to be part of the tree itself, as if she had grown there at its heart, and the carver had only chipped away the outer wood so that you could see her. Her arms were spliced and socketed to the trunk, and were flung wide in a circling, compelling movement. Her breasts were two eagle heads, fiercely carved. That much, and the column of her great neck, and her strong chin, I had seen when I slithered to the ground beneath her. Now I saw her face.

The eyes were two rounds of black, set in wider rounds of white, and placed in deep sockets under wide, black eyebrows. Their fixed stare bored into me as if the very life of the old cedar looked out, and it seemed that the voice of the tree itself might have burst from that great round cavity, with projecting lips, that was her mouth. Her ears were round, and stuck out to catch all sounds. The salt air had not dimmed the heavy red of her trunk and arms and thighs. Her hands were black, with blunt finger-tips painted a dazzling white. I stood looking at her for a long, long time.

The rain stopped, and white mist came up from the sea, gradually paling her back into the forest. It was as if she belonged there, and the mist were carrying her home. Presently the mist took the forest too, and, wrapping them both together, hid them away.

"Who is that image?" I asked the little Indian girl, when I got back to the house.

She knew which one I meant, but to gain time, she said, "What image?"

"The terrible one, out there on the bluff." The girl had been to Mission School, and fear of the old, fear of the new, struggled in her eyes. "I dunno," she lied.

I never went to that village again, but the fierce wooden image often came to me, both in my waking and in my sleeping.

Several years passed, and I was once more sketching in an Indian village. There were Indians in this village, and in a mild backward way it was "going modern". That is, the Indians had pushed the forest back a little to let the sun touch the new buildings that were replacing the old community houses. Small houses, primitive enough to a white man's thinking, pushed here and there between the old. Where some of the big community houses had been torn down, for the sake of the lumber, the great corner posts and massive roof-beams of the old structure were often left, standing naked against the sky, and the new little house was built inside, on the spot where the old one had been.

It was in one of these empty skeletons that I found her again. She had once been a supporting post for the great centre beam. Her pole-mate, representing the Raven, stood opposite her, but the beam that had rested on their heads was gone. The two poles faced in, and one judged the great size of the house by the distance between them. The corner posts were still in place, and the earth floor, once beaten to the hardness of rock by naked feet, was carpeted now with rich lush grass.

I knew her by the stuck-out ears, shouting mouth, and deep eye-sockets. These sockets had no eye-balls, but were empty holes, filled with stare. The stare, though not so fierce as that of the former image, was more intense. The whole figure expressed power, weight, domination, rather than ferocity. Her feet were planted heavily on the head of the squatting bear, carved beneath them. A man could have sat on either huge shoulder. She was unpainted, weather-worn, sun-cracked, and the arms and hands seemed to hang loosely. The fingers were thrust into the carven mouths of two human heads, held crowns down. From behind, the sun made unfathomable shadows in eye, cheek and mouth. Horror tumbled out of them.

I saw Indian Tom on the beach, and went to him.

"Who is she?"

The Indian's eyes, coming slowly from across the sea, followed my pointing finger. Resentment showed in his face, greeny-brown and wrinkled like a baked apple, – resentment that white folks should pry into matters wholly Indian.

"Who is that big carved woman?" I repeated.

"D'Sonoqua." No white tongue could have fondled the name as he did.

"Who is D'Sonoqua?"

"She is the wild woman of the woods."

"What does she do?"

"She steals children."

"To eat them?"

"No, she carries them to her caves; that," pointing to a purple scar on the mountain across the bay, "is one of her caves. When she cries 'OO-oo-oo-oeo', Indian mothers are too frightened to move. They stand like trees, and the children go with D'Sonoqua."

"Then she is bad?"

"Sometimes bad…sometimes good," Tom replied, glancing furtively at those stuck-out ears. Then he got up and walked away.

I went back, and, sitting in front of the image, gave stare for stare. But her stare so over-powered mine, that I could scarcely wrench my eyes away from the clutch of those empty sockets. The power that I felt was not in the thing itself, but in some tremendous force behind it, that the carver had believed in.

A shadow passed across her hands and their gruesome holdings. A little bird, with its beak full of nesting material, flew into the cavity of her mouth, right in the pathway of that terrible OO-oo-oo-oeo. Then my eye caught something that I had missed — a tabby cat asleep between her feet.

This was D'Sonoqua, and she was a supernatural being, who belonged to these Indians.

"Of course," I said to myself, "I do not believe in supernatural beings. Still – who understands the mysteries behind the forest? What would one do if one did meet a supernatural being?" Half of me wished that I could meet her, and half of me hoped I would not.

Chug – chug – the little boat had come into the bay to take me to another village, more lonely and deserted than this. Who knew what I should see there? But soon supernatural beings went clean out of my mind, because I was wholly absorbed in being naturally seasick.

When you have been tossed and wracked and chilled, any wharf looks good, even a rickety one, with its crooked legs stockinged in barnacles. Our boat nosed under its clammy darkness, and I crawled up the straight slimy ladder, wondering which was worse, natural seasickness, or supernatural "creeps". The trees crowded to the very edge of the water, and the outer ones, hanging over it, shadowed the shoreline into a velvet smudge. D'Sonoqua might walk in places like this. I sat for a long time on the damp, dusky beach, waiting for the stage. One by one dots of light popped from the scattered cabins, and made the dark seem darker. Finally the stage came.

We drove through the forest over a long straight road, with black pine trees marching on both sides. When we came to the wharf the little gas mail-boat was waiting for us. Smell and blurred light oozed thickly out of the engine room, and except for one lantern on the wharf everything else was dark. Clutching my little dog, I sat on the mail sacks which had been tossed on to the deck.

The ropes were loosed, and we slid out into the oily black water. The moon that had gone with us through the forest was away now. Black pine-covered mountains jagged up on both sides of the inlet like teeth. Every gasp of the engine shook us like a great sob. There was no rail round the deck, and the edge of the boat lay level with the black slithering horror below. It was like being swallowed again and again by some terrible monster, but never going down. As we slid through the water, hour after hour, I found myself listening for the OO-oo-oo-oeo.

Midnight brought us to a knob of land, lapped by the water on three sides, with the forest threatening to gobble it up on the fourth. There was a rude landing, a rooming-house, an eating-place, and a store, all for the convenience of fishermen and loggers. I was given a room, but after I had blown out my candle, the stillness and the darkness would not let me sleep.

In the brilliant sparkle of the morning when everything that was not superlatively blue was superlatively green, I dickered with a man who was taking a party up the inlet that he should drop me off at the village I was headed for.

"But," he protested, "there is nobody there."

To myself I said, "There is D'Sonoqua."

From the shore, as we rowed to it, came a thin feminine cry – the mewing of a cat. The keel of the boat had barely grated in the pebbles, when the cat sprang aboard, passed the man shipping his oars, and crouched for a spring into my lap. Leaning forward, the man seized the creature roughly, and with a cry of "Dirty Indian vermin!" flung her out into the sea.

I jumped ashore, refusing his help, and with a curt "Call for me at sun-down," strode up the beach; the cat followed me.

When we had crossed the beach and come to a steep bank, the cat ran ahead. Then I saw that she was no lean, ill-favoured Indian cat, but a sleek aristocratic Persian. My snobbish little Griffon dog, who usually refused to let an Indian cat come near me, surprised me by trudging beside her in comradely fashion.

The village was typical of the villages of these Indians. It had only one street, and that had only one side, because all the houses faced the beach. The two community houses were very old, dilapidated and bleached, and the handful of other shanties seemed never to have been young; they had grown so old before they were finished, that it was then not worth while finishing them.

Rusty padlocks carefully protected the gaping walls. There was the usual broad plank in front of the houses, the general sitting and sunning place for Indians. Little streams ran under it, and weeds poked up through every crack, half hiding the companies of tins, kettles, and rags, which patiently waited for the next gale and their next move.

In front of the Chief's house was a high, carved totem pole, sur-mounted by a large wooden eagle. Storms had robbed him of both wings, and his head had a resentful twist, as if he blamed somebody. The heavy wooden heads of two squatting bears peered over the nettle-tops. The windows were too high for peeping in or out. "But, save D'Sonoqua, who is there to peep?" I said aloud, just to break the silence. A fierce sun burned down as if it wanted to expose every ugliness and forlornness. It drew the noxious smell out of the skunk

420 / Emily Carr

cabbages, growing in the rich black ooze of the stream, scummed the water-barrels with green slime, and branded the desolation into my very soul.

The cat kept very close, rubbing and bumping itself and purring ecstatically; and although I had not seen them come, two more cats had joined us. When I sat down they curled into my lap, and then the strangeness of the place did not bite into me so deeply. I got up, determined to look behind the houses.

Nettles grew in the narrow spaces between the houses. I beat them down, and made my way over the bruised dank-smelling mass into a space of low jungle.

Long ago the trees had been felled and left lying. Young forest had burst through the slash, making an impregnable barrier, and sealing up the secrets which lay behind it. An eagle flew out of the forest, circled the village, and flew back again.

Once again I broke silence, calling after him, "Tell D'Sonoqua – " and turning, saw her close, towering above me in the jungle.

Like the D'Sonoqua of the other villages she was carved into the bole of a red cedar tree. Sun and storm had bleached the wood, moss here and there softened the crudeness of the modelling; sincerity underlay every stroke.

She appeared to be neither wooden nor stationary, but a singing spirit, young and fresh, passing through the jungle. No violence coarsened her; no power domineered to wither her. She was graciously feminine. Across her forehead her creator had fashioned the Sistheutl, or mythical two-headed sea-serpent. One of its heads fell to either shoulder, hiding the stuck-out ears, and framing her face from a central parting on her forehead which seemed to increase its womanliness.

She caught your breath, this D'Sonoqua, alive in the dead bole of the cedar. She summed up the depth and charm of the whole forest, driving away its menace.

I sat down to sketch. What was this noise of purring and rubbing going on about my feet? Cats. I rubbed my eyes to make sure I was seeing right, and counted a dozen of them. They jumped into my lap and sprang to my shoulders. They were real – and very feminine.

There we were – D'Sonoqua, the cats and I – the woman who only a few moments ago had forced herself to come behind the houses in trembling fear of the "wild woman of the woods" – wild in the sense that forest-creatures are wild – shy, untouchable.

(1941)   (1941)

Nellie McClung
1873-1951

———◆———

NELLIE (MOONEY) McCLUNG was born near Owen Sound, Ontario, and in 1880 moved with her family to Manitoba. In the early decades of the twentieth century she became an important leader of the Women's Christian Temperance Union and one of the early advocates of women's rights in Canada. In addition to her work as a social activist and politician, McClung wrote a number of novels, several collections of short stories and sketches and two volumes of autobiography, *Clearing in the West* (1935) and *The Stream Run Fast* (1945).

From
The Stream Runs Fast

[A Gentleman of the Old School]

THE BIG CITY gathered us in when the pleasant summer at the beach was over. Mark, our youngest child, was born on October of that year, and quickly became the idol of the family, with his blonde curls, blue eyes and quaint wisdom. The other children were all at school and Jack had started at Wesley College. Every day was full of interest. I enjoyed my association with the Canadian Women's Press Club, when we met once a week for tea in our own comfortable quarters. There great problems were discussed and the seed germ of the suffrage association was planted. It was not enough for us to meet and talk and eat chicken sandwiches and olives. We felt we should organize and create a public sentiment in favor of women's suffrage.

The visit of Mrs. Emmeline Pankhurst and of Miss Barbara Wiley, also one of the British Militant Suffragettes, created a profound impression. The immediate cause of our desire to organize was the plight of women workers in small factories. Some of our members had visited these and we were greatly stirred over the question of long hours, small wages and distressing working conditions.

Mrs. Claude Nash spoke one day on this subject at a Local Council meeting, and as a result of this meeting she and I were deputed to bring pressure to bear on the government for the appointment of a woman factory inspector. We decided to go to see Sir Rodmond Roblin, the Premier, and if possible, get him to come with us to see some of the factories. She knew him quite well and I had often listened to him in the Legislative Assembly from the visitors' gallery. He was a florid, rather good-looking man in his early sixties, somewhat pompous in manner but very popular with his party and firmly seated on the political throne by what was known as the "Machine". He believed in the patronage system and distributed governmental favors to the faithful in each riding. However, even in all the exposures which followed his defeat in 1914, there was no proof that he had ever enriched himself at the country's expense.

Mrs. Nash must have had some political standing, for I certainly had not, and we got an interview. We found Sir Rodmond in a very genial mood, and he expressed his delight at our coming. Mrs. Nash was a very handsome young woman, dressed that day in a grey lamb coat and crimson velvet hat. I wasn't looking so poorly myself for I, too, had youth on my side, and we could see that the old man was impressed favorably. I told him I had just come to live in the City from Manitou and I mentioned the name of W.H. Sharpe (afterwards Senator Sharpe) and I think that Sir Rodmond took it for granted that I, too, was a good Conservative, or, as he expressed it, was of the "household of faith". Sir Rodmond had once been a lay preacher in the Methodist Church, and scriptural references came natural to him. He balked a bit when we asked him if he would come with us to see some of the factories and tried to get us to be satisfied with one of his deputies, but Mrs. Nash and I held firm, and much to our surprise, he consented. He called his car and we set out. He looked very well in his beaver coat, and his car was the most pretentious I had ever ridden in. The cut glass vase filled with real carnations impressed my country eyes.

On the way to the first factory, the Premier, who sat between us, with his plump hands resting on a gold-headed cane, gave us his views on women working in factories. He believed in work, especially for young women. There was too much idleness now, with electricity and short cuts in labor. As a boy he had worked from sunrise, and before, until the shadows of evening fell, and enjoyed it. Happiest days of his life ... running barefoot under the apple trees. Perhaps we were over-sentimental about factory conditions.... Women's hearts were often too kind ... but he liked kind women – and hoped they would never change. And these young girls in the factories whom we thought were underpaid, no doubt they lived at home, and really worked because they wanted pin-money. Anyway, working wouldn't hurt them, it would keep them off the streets ...

Knowing what we did, we let the monologue go on. He advised us not to allow our kind hearts to run away with us. Most of the women in the factories, he understood, were from foreign countries, where life was strenuous (that word was in the first flush of its popularity then). They did not expect to be carried to the skies on a flowery bed of ease! It doesn't do women any harm to learn how money comes....Extravagant women are the curse of this age.

We conducted the Premier down dark, slippery stairs to an airless basement where light in mid-day came from gaunt light bulbs, hanging from smoky ceilings. The floor was littered with refuse of apple peelings and discarded clothing. There was no ventilation and no heat. The room was full of untidy women, operating sewing machines and equally unattractive men cutting out garments on long tables. We urged Sir Rodmond to speak to some of the workers, but he was willing to call it a day at the first glance. He was shocked at the filth of the place, and asked one of the women if anybody ever swept the floor? He had to shout to drown the sound of the machines. The woman shook her head and kept on working. Then we reminded him that all these people were on piece work.

We led the Premier through a side door into the foul passage where a queue had formed before a door marked "Toilet". We could see that Sir Rodmond was deeply shocked that we should know about such things but Mrs. Nash led the way, and I pushed him along from behind. We drew his attention to the fact that there was no separate accommodation for the women, and we did not need to mention that the plumbing had evidently gone wrong. We knew that he was soon going to bolt away from us, so we didn't spare him anything.

"For God's sake, let me out of here, " he cried at last. "I'm choking! I never knew such hell holes existed!"

"These people work from 8:30 to 6:00, Sir Rodmond. Six days a week," Mrs. Nash told him sweetly. "But no doubt they get used to it." I am afraid her sarcasm was lost on Sir Rodmond.

When we got him up on the street again, he remembered an important interview he had promised, but we coaxed him to come to one more factory where men's shirts were being made, and all the workers were young women, and by promising him that this would be the last one, he came with us. This workroom was in rather a better building and some daylight came in from the windows. We wanted him particularly to see these young girls who were being "kept off the streets". At one machine a girl worked with a bandaged hand, a badly hurt hand

and a very dirty bandage. At another one a girl coughed almost continuously. I asked her how long she had had her cold and she said she had no cold, it was just a bit of bronchitis she had every winter, but she daren't stop work for there were plenty more to take her place, and someone had to earn some money in their family, as their father was out of work. She said she had been lucky to get the job. The manager came over to speak to us, anxious to show us the fine product they were turning out. Mrs. Nash asked him how often the factory inspector came around, but he didn't seem to know anything about factory inspectors. "In fact," he said, "we hardly need one. All the girls are glad of the work. I have no trouble with them."

"How about the girl who coughs so much?" I asked. "Couldn't she be given a few days off with pay to get built up a bit?"

The manager regarded me sternly.

"The company is not a charitable institution," he said, "and makes no provision for anything like that. If the girl is sick, she can always quit!" He threw out his hands expressively in a fine gesture of freedom.

Sir Rodmond was moving towards the door, and we followed. When we got back into the car we could see that the fine old gentleman of the old school was really shocked at what he had seen.

"Now, Sir Rodmond," we said, "do you still think that these women are pleasurably employed in this rich land of wide spaces and great opportunites?"

Sir Rodmond let down one of the windows of the car and said:

"I still can't see why two women like you should ferret out such utterly disgusting things."

"Your factory inspector knows about these places," we told him. "We mailed him a list of them and described them, but he has done nothing. He takes your attitude: Why should women interfere with what does not concern them? But we are not discouraged and have no intention of allowing these conditions to continue. We would like you to appoint a woman factory inspector, a real, trained social worker."

Sir Rodmond grew impatient at that. "I tell you it's no job for a woman. I have too much respect for women to give any of them a job like this.... But I don't mind admitting that I'm greatly disturbed over all this, greatly disturbed," he repeated. "I'll admit I didn't know that such places existed and I promise you that I will speak to Fletcher about it."

With this understanding we parted, thanking Sir Rodmond for giving us so much of his time.

Our investigations went on. We were only amateurs but we did find out a few things about how the "other half" lived. We made some other discoveries too. We found out that the Local Council of Women could not be our medium. There were too many women in it who were afraid to be associated with any controversial subject. Their husbands would not let them "go active". It might imperil their jobs. The long tentacles of the political octopus reached far. So one night at Jane Hample's house on Wolsley Avenue we organized the Political Equality League, with a membership of about fifteen. We believed that fifteen good women who were not afraid to challenge public opinion could lay the foundations better than a thousand. Some good work had been already done by the Icelandic women of the city, who had organized the first suffrage society many years before, and the W.C.T.U. women could always be counted on and the same was true of the Labor women.

We wanted to get first-hand information on the status of women in Manitoba, and, of course, the whole Dominion. Then it was our purpose to train public speakers and proceed to arouse public sentiment. We would be ready for the next election and hoped to make our influence felt. We had all the courage of youth and inexperience with a fine underpinning of simplicity that bordered on ignorance, but anything we lacked in knowledge we made up in enthusiasm.

On a sudden impulse one day I phoned to the Premier's office when the House was in session and asked for an interview with Sir Rodmond Roblin, and to my surprise I found myself speaking to the gentleman himself, who in his most gracious manner assured me he would be pleased to see me and I could come at once, which I did. There in his private office with its red plush hangings and heavy leather furniture, I told the head of the government what we were doing and what we hoped to do. He listened with amused tolerance, but I was grateful to him for listening.

"Sir Rodmond," I said, "the women of Manitoba are going to be given the vote, either by you or someone else, and as you are the present Premier, it can be your proud privilege to have this piece of progressive legislation to your credit. I know what you're thinking; you're not impressed with the importance of this matter but that's because you never thought of it and you really should begin to think about it. You can no longer afford to take this attitude of indifference, and that's why I came to see you."

He looked up at me then and said:

"What in the world do women want to vote for? Why do women want to mix in the hurly-burly of politics? My mother was the best woman in the world, and she certainly never wanted to vote! I respect women," he went on, "I honor and reverence women, I lift my hat when I meet a woman."

"That's all very nice to hear," I said, "but unfortunately that's not enough. The women of Manitoba believe that the time has come to make an effort to obtain political equality. The laws are very unfair to women. I would like to tell you about some of them, for I don't believe you know, and what I would really like to do this afternoon is to have a chance to talk to you and your cabinet. It wouldn't take me long; I think fifteen minutes would be enough, and if you and the cabinet could be convinced that it is the right thing to do, it would certainly be easier, more dignified and less disturbing than if we are compelled to make a fight for it. But that is what we are prepared to do, if that is the way you want it. I wish you would call them in, Sir Rodmond, there's plenty of room here in your office."

Sir Rodmond removed the dead cigar from his mouth and his eyes hardened.

"The cabinet wouldn't listen to you," he said.

"You'd be surprised," I answered. "I'm really not hard to listen to, and I don't believe the cabinet would mind at all. In fact," I said brazenly, "I think they'd like it. It would be a welcome change in the middle of a dull day.

He could scarcely find words to express his astonishment and disapproval.

"You surprise me," he said slowly. "Now who do you think you are?"

"At this moment," I said, "I'm one of the best advisers you ever had in all your life. I'm not asking you for a favor, I'm really offering you help."

"What if I tell you that I don't need your help?" he said severely. "And that I think you're rather a conceited young woman, who has perhaps had some success at Friday afternoon entertainments at country school houses, and so are laboring under the delusion that you have the gift of oratory. What would you say to that?"

"I wouldn't mind," I answered. "I wouldn't even resent it. But I wish to tell you again, Sir Rodmond, as clearly as I can make it, that we are going to create public sentiment in this province, which will work against you at the next election. Did you ever hear that quotation about there being a tide in the affairs of men, which taken at the flood leads on to fortune?"

We looked at each other across the wide space of his mahogany desk and the silence was eloquent. Then Sir Rodmond's mood changed. His self confidence came back; for a moment a doubt had assailed him. But the absurdity of the situation gave him courage. After all, what had he to be afraid of? His party was firmly entrenched, having 29 of the 42 members. He grew jocular.

"It would never do to let you speak to the cabinet," he said in the tone that one uses to a naughty child. "Even if they listened to you, which I doubt, you would only upset them, and I don't want that to happen. They are good fellows – they do what they are told to do, now. Every government has to have a head, and I'm the head of this one; and I don't want dissension and arguments. I believe in leaving well enough alone. Take the Indians, for example, they were far happier eating muskrats and the bark of trees before the white man came with education and disturbing ideas. Now they've lost all their good old-fashioned ways. No, you can't come in here and make trouble with my boys, just when I have them trotting easy and eating out of my hand. Now you forget all this nonsense about women voting," he went on in his suavest tones. "You're a fine, smart young woman, I can see that. And take it from me, nice women don't want the vote."

His voice dripped fatness.

"By nice women," I said, "you probably mean selfish women who have no more thought for the underpaid, overworked women than a pussycat in a sunny window has for the starving kitten on the street. Now in that sense I am not a nice woman, for I do care. I care about those factory women, working in ill-smelling holes, and we intend to do something about it, and when I say 'we' I'm talking for a great many women, of whom you will hear more as the days go on."

I stood to go. Then he smiled good-humoredly at me and said:

"Now don't go away mad. You know you amuse me. Come any time, I'll always be glad to see you." My smile was just as good-natured as his when I said:

"I'll not be back, Sir Rodmond; not in your time. I hadn't much hope of doing any good by coming, but I thought it only fair to give you the chance. I'll not be back, but it's just possible that you will hear from me, not directly, but still you'll hear; and you may not like what you hear, either."

"Is this a threat?" he laughed.

"No," I said, "it's a prophecy."

(1945)   (1945)

Robert Service
1874-1958

———◆———

BORN IN LANCASHIRE, England, Robert Service attended high school in Glasgow and emigrated to Canada in 1894. After working as a bank clerk in British Columbia, he was transferred to the Yukon district in 1904 and remained there until 1912. In his first volume of poems, *Songs of a Sourdough* (1907), Service dealt with the Klondike goldrush of 1898. With this volume he won the fame and financial independence which enabled him to retire. In later years he lived in France, travelled widely and wrote novels of adventure and numerous volumes of popular verse.

The Shooting of Dan McGrew

A bunch of the boys were whooping it up in the Malamute
    saloon;
The kid that handles the music box was hitting a jag-time
    tune;
Back of the bar, in a solo game, sat Dangerous Dan McGrew,
And watching his luck was his light-o'-love, the lady that's
    known as Lou.

When out of the night, which was fifty below, and into the din
    and the glare,
There stumbled a miner fresh from the creeks, dog-dirty, and
    loaded for bear.
He looked like a man with a foot in the grave, and scarcely the
    strength of a louse,
Yet he tilted a poke of dust on the bar, and he called for drinks
    for the house.
There was none could place the stranger's face, though we
    searched ourselves for a clue;
But we drank his health, and the last to drink was Dangerous   10
    Dan McGrew.

There's men that somehow just grip your eyes, and hold them
      hard like a spell;
And such was he, and he looked to me like a man who had
      lived in hell;
With a face most hair, and the dreary stare of a dog whose day
      is done,
As he watered the green stuff in his glass, and the drops fell
      one by one.
Then I got to figgering who he was, and wondering what he'd
      do,
And I turned my head – and there watching him was the lady
      that's known as Lou.

His eyes went rubbering round the room, and he seemed in a
      kind of daze,
Till at last that old piano fell in the way of his wandering gaze.
The rag-time kid was having a drink; there was no one else on
      the stool,
So the stranger stumbles across the room, and flops down
      there like a fool.   20
In a buckskin shirt that was glazed with dirt he sat, and I saw
      him sway;
Then he clutched the keys with his talon hands – my God! but
      that man could play!

Were you ever out in the Great Alone, when the moon was
      awful clear,
And the icy mountains hemmed you in with a silence you most
      could *hear:*
With only the howl of a timber wolf, and you camped there in
      the cold,
A half-dead thing in a stark, dead world, clean mad for the
      muck called gold;
While high overhead, green, yellow and red, the North Lights
      swept in bars –
Then you've a haunch what the music meant...hunger and
      night and the stars.

And hunger not of the belly kind, that's banished with bacon
      and beans;
But the gnawing hunger of lonely men for a home and all that
      it means;   30
For a fireside far from the cares that are, four walls and a roof
      above;

But oh! so cramful of cosy joy, and crowned with a woman's
    love;
A woman dearer than all the world, and true as Heaven
    is true –
(God! how ghastly she looks through her rouge, – the lady
    that's known as Lou).

Then on a sudden the music changed, so soft that you scarce
    could hear;
But you felt that your life had been looted clean of all that it
    once held dear;
That someone had stolen the woman you loved; that her love
    was a devil's lie;
That your guts were gone, and the best for you was to crawl
    away and die.
'Twas the crowning cry of a heart's despair, and it thrilled you
    through and through –
"I guess I'll make it a spread misere," said Dangerous Dan   40
    McGrew.

The music almost died away…then it burst like a pent-up
    flood;
And it seemed to say, "Repay, repay," and my eyes were blind
    with blood.
The thought came back of an ancient wrong, and it stung like
    a frozen lash.
And the lust awoke to kill, to kill…then the music stopped
    with a crash.

And the stranger turned, and his eyes they burned in a most
    peculiar way;
In a buckskin shirt that was glazed with dirt he sat, and I saw
    him sway;
Then his lips went in in a kind of grin, and he spoke, and his
    voice was calm;
And, "Boys," says he, "you don't know me, and none of you
    care a damn;
But I want to state, and my words are straight, and I'll bet my
    poke they're true,
That one of you is a hound of hell…and that one is Dan   50
    McGrew."

Then I ducked my head, and the lights went out, and two
    guns blazed in the dark;
And a woman screamed, and the lights went up, and two men
    lay stiff and stark;
Pitched on his head, and pumped full of lead, was Dangerous
    Dan McGrew,
While the man from the creeks lay clutched to the breast of
    the lady that's known as Lou.

These are the simple facts of the case, and I guess I ought to
    know;
They say that the stranger was crazed with "hooch," and I'm
    not denying it's so.
I'm not so wise as the lawyer guys, but strictly between us two —
The woman that kissed him and – pinched his poke – was the
    lady that's known as Lou.

(1907)   (1907)

The Trail of Ninety-Eight

I

Gold! We leapt from our benches. Gold! We sprang from our
    stools.
Gold! We wheeled in the furrow, fired with the faith of fools.
Fearless, unfound, unfitted, far from the night and the cold,
Heard we the clarion summons, followed the master-lure –
    Gold!

Men from the sands of the Sunland; men from the woods of
    the West;
Men from the farms and the cities, into the Northland we
    pressed.
Greybeards and striplings and women, good men and bad
    men and bold,
Leaving our homes and our loved ones, crying exultantly –
    "Gold!"

Never was seen such an army, pitiful, futile, unfit;
Never was seen such a spirit, manifold courage and grit;   10
Never has been such a cohort under one banner enrolled,
As surged to the ragged-edged Arctic, urged by the
        arch-tempter – Gold.

"Farewell," we cried to our dearests; little we cared for their
        tears.
"Farewell," we cried to the humdrum and the yoke of the
        hireling years;
Just like a pack of school-boys, and the big crowd cheered us
        good-bye.
Never were hearts so uplifted, never were hopes so high.

The spectral shores flitted past us, and every whirl of the
        screw
Hurled us nearer to fortune, and ever we planned what we'd
        do –
Do with the gold when we got it – big, shiny nuggets like
        plums,
There in the sand of the river, gouging it out with our thumbs.   20

And one man wanted a castle, another a racing stud;
A third would cruise in a palace yacht like a red-necked prince
        of blood.
And so we dreamed and we vaunted, millionaires to a man,
Leaping to wealth in our visions long ere the trail began.

II

We landed in wind-swept Skagway. We joined the weltering
        mass,
Clamoring over their outfits, waiting to climb the Pass.
We tightened our girths and our pack-straps; we linked on the
        Human Chain,
Struggling up to the summit, where every step was a pain.

Gone was the joy of our faces; grim and haggard and pale;
The heedless mirth of the shipboard was changed to the care
        of the trail.
We flung ourselves in the struggle, packing our grub in relays,
Step by step to the summit in the bale of the winter days.

Floundering deep in the sump-holes, stumbling out again;
Crying with cold and weakness, crazy with fear and pain.　　　　10
Then from the depths of our travail, ere our spirits were
　　　　broke,
Grim, tenacious and savage, the lust of the trail awoke.

"Klondike or bust!" rang the slogan; every man for his own.
Oh, how we flogged the horses, staggering skin and bone!
Oh, how we cursed their weakness, anguish they could not
　　　　tell,
Breaking their hearts in our passion, lashing them on till they
　　　　fell!

For grub meant gold to our thinking, and all that could walk
　　　　must pack;
The sheep for the shambles stumbled, each with a load on its
　　　　back;
And even the swine were burdened, and grunted and
　　　　squealed and rolled,
And men went mad in the moment, huskily clamoring　　　　20
　　　　"Gold!"

Oh, we were brutes and devils, goaded by lust and fear!
Our eyes were strained to the Summit; the weaklings dropped
　　　　to the rear,
Falling in heaps by the trail-side, heart-broken, limp and wan;
But the gaps closed up in an instant, and heedless the chain
　　　　went on.

Never will I forget it, there on the mountain face,
Antlike, men with their burdens, clinging in icy space;
Dogged, determined and dauntless, cruel and callous and
　　　　cold,
Cursing, blaspheming, reviling, and ever that battle-cry –
　　　　"Gold!"

Thus toiled we, the army of fortune, in hunger and hope and
　　　　despair,
Till glacier, mountain and forest vanished, and radiantly fair　　　　30
There at our feet lay Lake Bennett, and down to its welcome
　　　　we ran:
The trail of the land was over, the trail of the water began.

III

We built our boats and we launched them. Never has been
        such a fleet;
A packing-case for a bottom, a mackinaw for a sheet.
Shapeless, grotesque, lopsided, flimsy, makeshift and crude,
Each man after his fashion builded as best he could.

Each man worked like a demon, as prow to rudder we raced;
The winds of the Wild cried "Hurry," the voice of the waters,
        "Haste."
We hated those driving before us; we dreaded those pressing
        behind;
We cursed the slow current that bore us; we prayed to the God
        of the wind.

Spring! and the hillsides flourished, vivid in jeweled green;
Spring! and our hearts' blood nourished envy and hatred and   10
        spleen.
Little cared we for the Spring-birth; much cared we to get on –
Stake in the Great White Channel, stake ere the best be gone.

The greed of the gold possessed us; pity and love were forgot;
Covetous visions obsessed us; brother with brother fought.
Partner with partner wrangled, each one claiming his due;
Wrangled and halved their outfits, sawing their boats in two.

Thuswise we voyaged Lake Bennett, Tagish, then Windy
        Arm,
Sinister, savage and baleful, boding us hate and harm.
Many a scow was shattered, there on that iron shore;
Many a heart was broken, straining at sweep and oar.   20

We roused Lake Marsh with a chorus, we drifted many a mile;
There was the canyon before us – cave-like its dark defile;
The shores swept faster and faster; the river narrowed to
        wrath;
Waters that hissed disaster reared upright in our path.

Beneath us the green tumult churning, above us the
        cavernous gloom;
Around us, swift twisting and turning, the black, sullen walls
        of a tomb.

We spun like a chip in a mill-race; our hearts hammered
        under the test;
Then – oh, the relief on each chill face! – we soared into
        sunlight and rest.

Hand sought for hand on the instant. Cried we: "our troubles
        are o'er."
Then, like a rumble of thunder, heard we a canorous roar.   30
Leaping and boiling and seething, saw we a cauldron afume;
There was the rage of the rapids, there was the menace of doom.

The river springs like a racer, sweeps through a gash in the rock;
Butts at the boulder-ribbed bottom, staggers and rears at the
        shock;
Leaps like a terrified monster, writhes in its fury and pain;
Then with the crash of a demon springs to the onset again.

Dared we that ravening terror; heard we its din in our ears;
Called on the God of our fathers, juggled forlorn with our
        fears;
Sank to our waists in its fury, tossed to the sky like a fleece;
Then, when our dread was the greatest, crashed into safety   40
        and peace.

But what of the others that followed, losing their boats by the
        score?
Well could we see them and hear them, strung down that
        desolate shore.
What of the poor souls that perished? Little of them shall be said –
On to the Golden Valley, pause not to bury the dead.

Then there were days of drifting, breezes soft as a sigh;
Night trailed her robe of jewels over the floor of the sky.
The moonlit stream was a python, silver, sinuous, vast,
That writhed on a shroud of velvet – well, it was done at last.

There were the tents of Dawson, there the scar of the slide;
Swiftly we poled o'er the shallows, swiftly leapt o'er the side.   50
Fires fringed the mouth of Bonanza; sunset gilded the dome;
The test of the trail was over – thank God, thank God, we were
        Home!

(1909)   (1909)

My Cross

I wrote a poem to the Moon
But no one noticed it;
Although I hoped that late or soon
Someone would praise a bit
Its purity and grace forlorn,
Its beauty tulip-cool...
But as my poem died still-born,
I felt a fool.

I wrote a verse of vulgar trend
Spiced with an oath or two;   10
I tacked a snapper at the end
And called it *Dan McGrew.*
I spouted it to bar-room boys,
Full fifty years away;
Yet still with rude and ribald noise
It lives today.

'Tis bitter truth, but there you are –
That's how a name is made;
Write of a rose, a lark, a star,
You'll never make the grade.   20
But write of gutter and of grime,
Of pimp and prostitute,
The multitude will read your rhyme,
And pay to boot.

So what's the use to burn and bleed
And strive for beauty's sake?
No one your poetry will read,
Your heart will only break.
But set your song in vulgar pitch,
If rhyme you will not rue,   30
And make your heroine a bitch...
Like *Lady Lou.*

(1951)   (1966)

Theodore Goodridge Roberts
1877-1953

THEODORE GOODRIDGE ROBERTS, a younger brother of Charles G. D. Roberts, was born and educated in Federicton, New Brunswick. He became a journalist and in 1898 worked as a correspondent for the New York *Independent* in the Spanish-American War. Later he lived in Newfoundland and edited *The Newfoundland Magazine*. Roberts' attachment to the Maritime region is apparent in his many adventure novels and historical romances, and in *The Leather Bottle* (1934), a selection of his poems.

River Morning

Mist along the river, creeping down
With spinning clots of drift and blinks of foam;
Terns screaming out along the sandbars;
A heron flapping from his reedy home.

Breath of pennyroyal on the gravel;
Breath of wet willows down the shore;
Start of life around the bushy islands,
And, at the East's gold gate, one blue day more.

(1934)   (1934)

The Blue Heron

In a green place lanced through
With amber and gold and blue;
A place of water and weeds
And roses pinker than dawn,

437

And ranks of lush young reeds,
And grasses straightly withdrawn
From graven ripples of sands,
The still blue heron stands.

Smoke-blue he is, and grey
As embers of yesterday.   10
Still he is, as death;
Like stone, or shadow of stone,
Without a pulse or breath,
Motionless and alone
There in the lily stems:
But his eyes are alive like gems.

Still as a shadow; still
Grey feather and yellow bill:
Still as an image made
Of mist and smoke half hid   20
By windless sunshine and shade,
Save when a yellow lid
Slides and is gone like a breath:
Death-still — and sudden as death!

(1934)   (1934)

The Desolate Cabin

Swings the door at the wind's will:
    Sun-dazed, the clearings swoon:
Over the stump-land washes
    The voiceless afternoon.

Creaks the roof at the wind's whim:
    Noiseless, the lean hares pass:
Snake-berries gleam in the shadows:
    Shadows glide in the grass.

No one crosses the threshold.
    The windows show no face.   10
The northern gable slouches
    Like the loser of a race.

Here are sunshine and silence,
   Shadow and empty air.
Did something gleam at the window,
   Like a thin hand waving there?

No bird calls from the spruces,
   No beast cries from the plain.
A spent wind runs on the roof,
   With the sound of forgotten rain: 20

And something stirs on the threshold
   Like the ghost of a drifting leaf,
And sobs in the yellow silence
   Like a lost soul of grief.

A mist at the edge of the wood
   The breath of the forest waits
Westward, the naked rampikes
   Stand at the crimson gates.

(1934)   (1934)

Fiddler's Green

> "At a place called Fiddler's Green, there do all honest Mariners take their pleasure after death; and there are Admirals with their dear Ladies, and Captains of lost voyages with the Sweethearts of their youth, and tarry-handed Sailormen singing in cottage gardens."

Never again shall we beat out to sea
In rain and mist and sleet like bitter tears,
And watch the harbour beacons fade a-lee,
And people all the sea-room with our fears.
Our toil is done. No more, no more do we
Square the slow yards and stagger on the sea.

No more for us the white and windless day
Undimmed, unshadowed, where the weed drifts by
And leaden fish pass, rolling, at their play,

And changeless suns glide up a changeless sky.   10
Our watch is done; and never more shall we
Whistle a wind across a fest'ring sea,

Cities we saw: white wall and glinting dome,
And palm-fringed islands gleaming on the blue.
To us more fair the kindly sights of home –
The climbing streets and windows shining true.
Our voyage is done, and never more shall we
Reef bucking topsails on a tossing sea.

Wonders we knew and beauty in far ports;
Laughter and peril round the swinging deep;   20
The wrath of God; the pomp of pagan courts ...
The rocks sprang black! ... *and we awoke from sleep!*
Our task is done; and never more shall we
Square the slow yards and stagger on the sea.

Here are the hearts we love, the lips we know,
The hands of seafarers who came before.
The eyes that wept for us, a night ago,
Are laughing now that we shall part no more.
All care is past; and never more shall we
Make sail at daybreak for the grievous sea.   30

(1934)   (1934)

The Wreckers' Prayer

In the old days before the building of the lighthouses, the poor "noddies" of many a Newfoundland outport prayed for wrecks – aye, and with easy conscience. Only the few hundreds of them who took to deep-sea voyaging ever learned anything of the world and its peoples. All the world excepting their own desolate bays and "down Nort'", was "up-along" to them. Montreal, Pernambuco, London, Oporto, Boston, Halifax – all were in-cluded in up-along to them; and up-along was a grand, rich place where all men were gentlemen wearing collars and coats, eating figgy-duff every day and smoking all they wanted to. The folk of up-along had the easy end of life; so why shouldn't they contribute something of their goods and gear to poor but honest noddies now and then, even if against their inclinations – aye, even if at the cost of their lives?

Give us a wrack or two, Good Lard,
For winter in Tops'il Tickle bes hard,
Wid grey frost creepin' like mortal sin
And perishin' lack of bread in the bin.

A grand, rich wrack, us do humbly pray,
Busted abroad at the break o' day
An' hove clear in 'crost Tops'il Reef,
Wid victuals an' gear to beguile our grief.

God of reefs an' tides an' sky,
Heed Ye our need an' hark to our cry!
Bread by the bag an' beef by the cask.
Ease for sore bellies bes all we ask.

One grand wrack – or maybe two? –
Wid gear an' victuals to see us through
'Til Spring starts up like the leap of day
An' the fish strike back into Tops'il Bay.

One rich wrack – for Thy hand bes strong!
A barque or a brig from up-along
Bemused by Thy twisty tides, O Lard!
For winter in Tops'il Tickle bes hard.

Loud an' long will us sing Yer praise,
Marciful Fadder, O Ancient of Days,
Master of fog an' tide an' reef!
Heave us a wrack to beguile our grief. Amen.

(1934)   (1934)

Emile Nelligan
1879-1941

———◆———

EMILE NELLIGAN WAS born in Montreal and became a leading poet of L'Ecole Littéraire de Montréal, an association founded in 1895 by poets interested in the work of the Parnassian and Symbolist poets of France. Most of his poems were written during the three years preceding his mental breakdown in 1899, and the first collection of his poetry, *Emile Nelligan et son oeuvre*, was edited by Louis Dantin in 1903. Nelligan's rejection of the patriotic and romantic traditions of earlier nineteenth-century poetry in French Canada marked a major development in the evolution of poetry in Quebec.

By the Fireside

In the old winters when we still were small,
In dresses, boisterous, pink, with chubby looks,
Our big and long-since vanished picture-books
Showed us the world; we seemed to own it all.

In groups around the fire at evening,
Picture by picture, ah! how happily
We turned the pages, starry-eyed to see
Squadrons of fine dragoons go galloping!

I once was happy, one of these; but now,
Feet on the fender, with dull, listless brow,   10
I with my always bitter heart descry

Flame-fashioned pictures where my youth goes by,
And, like a passing soldier, rides abroad
On life's black field, gripping a bloody sword.

(1903)   (1960)
P.F. WIDDOWS (TR.)

The Garden of the Past

Nothing is sweeter than the glad return,
  As after absent years abroad,
      Sweeter than the return
  By memory's flower-bestrewn
  Lily-innocent road
      To the garden of Childhood:

To the walled garden, private and entranced,
  Where rang our fresh cries of delight,
      Our walled garden entranced,
  Where once our sisters used to dance   10
  In the tree-dappled light,
      Our sisters dressed in white.

On April evenings, with cries of joy,
  Radiant, with refrains as well,
      They passed with songs of joy
  Under the leafy canopy
  The arbour's sudden chill,
      A living villanelle,

While somewhere from within the house came straying
  An old guitar's accompaniment   20
      From the old house came straying –
  Surely, you thought, a lady playing
  Behind cool shutters, bent
      Over an instrument.

But what more bitter than to think also
  Of all those ruined things of ours!
      Alas! to think also
  When back across our lives we go
  By paths of withered flowers
      Back to our youthful years,   30

And feel ourselves neurotic, growing old,
  Ill-treated, slighted and disarmed,
      Surly and growing old;
  And struggling free from the lost world
  Our weeping youth becomes
      Eternal with its charms.

(1903)   (1960)

P.F. WIDDOWS (TR.)

Christ on the Cross

This plaster Jesus always halted me,
Placed like a shrine at the old convent door,
A scaffold, stern and lowering, before
Which I would bend with meek idolatry.

Not long ago, in blue-eyed reverie
Roaming dim meadows at the cricket's hour
With wind-blown hair, declaiming "Eloa",
True to my rôle of art's young devotee,

I noticed near the ruins of that wall
Piled high, the ancient, massive cross with all   10
The plaster crumbled in the primroses.

And I stayed staring, sad, contemplative,
And heard in me convulsive hammers drive
Home the black nails of private Calvaries.

(1903)   (1960)
P.F. WIDDOWS (TR.)

A Woman Passing By

A woman in a veil. In the darkening park
Ghostlike she passed before me yesterday.
Mournful and singular she moved away
Hiding her pride beneath an opal mask.

One look from her was all I had to ask
To guess the grief that secret in her lay.
And then she vanished down a shadowy way
That seemed to match her mourning, dark to dark.

Compare my youth to that poor passer-by.
Many will meet it here, where joylessly   10
Life leads us down the pathway to the tomb;

All see it pass, like a leaf in the wind
That twists and falls and withers in the gloom:
But none will love it, none will understand.

(1903)   (1960)
P.F. WIDDOWS (TR.)

The Ship of Gold

There was a gallant vessel wrought of gold,
Whose tops'ls raked the skies in seas unknown;
Carved on the prow a naked Venus shone,
With wind-tossed locks, in the immoderate Sun.

But ah! one night she struck the famous reef
In teacherous Ocean where the Siren sings.
Ghastly, a slanting hulk, she twists and swings
Down the profound Abyss, her changeless shroud.

She was a golden ship whose glassy hull
Betrayed the treasure-trove for which the three   10
Foul Captains, *Hate, Disgust,* and *Frenzy* strove.

What rests at last after the hasty plunge?
What of my heart's lost fate, poor derelict?
— Foundered, alas! in the black gulf of Dream!

(1903)   (1970)
A.J.M. SMITH (TR.)

The Poet's Wine

Green gaiety, everything blended in a quick
Burst. O beautiful May evening, bird-choirs bringing
Their modulations to my wide window, singing
As my relinquished heart-hopes sing, changing music.

O beautiful May evening, joyful May evening!
A far-off organ chants its melancholy chant,
And the twilight rays, like purple rapiers, slant
Into the day's heart, perfumed in its dying.

How gay I am, how gay! Into the singing glass
With the wine! Keep pouring, never stop pouring!   10
Let me forget that the days are triste and boring,
The crowd contemptible and the world an ass.

Gay, I am gay! Exalted in wine and art! ...
How I dream of the lofty rhymes I shall make,
Rhymes trembling with the sighs of funeral music,
Winds of autumn passing through the haze, distant, apart.

Kingship of the bitter laughter, and the rage
Of knowing that one is a poet, pierced by scorn;
Of being a heart and not understood, forlorn
To all but the moon's night and thunder's equipage.   20

Ladies, I drink to you, smilers along the way
Where the Ideal beckons me to her pink embraces,
And to you, gentlemen, with your sombre faces,
You who disdain my hand, I drink especially.

When the blue pricks out its coming splendour of stars
And as it were a hymn praises the golden spring,
What tears have I to shed over the day's dying?
I, on a dark path, in the dark of my young years?

Gay, I am gay! Inexpressible May evening!
Ridiculously gay, can it be that I've —   30
Not drunk either — that I'm happy to be alive?
Has it at last been healed, my old wound of loving?

The bells cease, and the evening scents follow after
As the breeze takes them, and the wine rustles and throbs.
I am more than gay, hear my resonant laughter!
So gay, so gay, I am breaking into sobs.

(1903)   (1970)
GEORGE JOHNSTON (TR.)

Old Fantasist

At her window among her potted plants, from cold
and bluster sheltered, she pulls her Japanese
shawl around her, Miss Adèle, and reads one of these
Dumas novels, as she did as a twenty-year-old.

And all her boudoir is a distraction of bizarre
odds and ends, cloister of ancientnesses, herself
the type of her own cult, encrusted, like her shelf-
borne vases, onyx, portraits, books from everywhere.

On the random cushions a scar-faced Persian tom
purrs his contented thunder while his fading dame   10
coaxes her sad heart among the ochreing pages

unaware, in the pangs of her closeted sweet
dream, of a passing mocking face, an outrageous
organ-grinder's face, magnificent, out in the street.

(1903)   (1970)
GEORGE JOHNSTON (TR.)

Louis Hémon
1880-1913

———◆———

BORN IN BREST, France, Louis Hémon came to Canada in 1911. After spending his first winter in Montreal, Hémon moved to the Lake St. John area of the Saguenay district in 1912; he was killed in a railway accident at Chapleau, Ontario, the following year. In addition to his best-known work, *Maria Chapdelaine* (1916), Hémon left for posthumous publication the fragments of a travel book which appeared first in an English translation as *The Journal of Louis Hémon* (1924) and in French as "Au pays de Québec" in L.-J. Dalbis' *Le Bouclier Canadien-Français* (1928).

From
The Journal of Louis Hémon

[From Liverpool to Quebec]

AT THE OFFICE of the Allan Line, in Cockspur Street, a clerk presented the two horns of the dilemma in a concise and striking manner.

"To go to Montreal," he said, "you have the choice between two of our services: that from Liverpool, and that from London and Le Havre. By Liverpool, the crossing takes seven days. On the Le Havre line there is French cooking and wine with the meals. The crossing takes thirteen days."

For a professional investigator, notebook in hand, in search of easy generalizations, here was already a chance to establish a contrast between the essential haste of the Anglo-Saxons and the indolence of our compatriots who resign themselves very readily to crossing on an old boat, and devoting two weeks to it, provided they can eat in the French fashion and guzzle Medoc twice a day all the way to Montreal; but, after eight years of London, Anglo-French contrasts had lost their relief, and generalizations no longer seemed so easy or so sure. I thought only of weighing the pro and the con. Thirteen days at sea – it was tempting; but October was already advanced, and it would be good to have, on arriving, a few weeks to spare before the winter set in – that Canadian winter which one imagines so redoubtable at a distance. I therefore left from Liverpool, four days later.

Seven days at sea. A good sea, not rough enough to be bothersome, sufficiently so not to be insipid. Thus, few are sick, or at least few are frankly sick; but quite a number, upset by apprehension, keep, throughout this week, the curiously greenish complexion of those who are anxious, or else descend jauntily in the morning to the saloon, play with an egg or a bowl of gruel, and go back to the deck without waiting for the end of the meal. Oh! without precipitation, with dignity; but turning their quivering nostrils away from the victuals, and dropping some ingenious pretext to their table-companions.

All sorts of passengers: not a few Canadians who have spent the summer in England and are now returning; several young Englishmen who are crossing for the first time, sent by their business houses; and a handful of others who have left at a venture, and although it is the bad season. Among these last, a subtle bond seems to establish itself. They gauge each other furtively, and think: "Has that chap a better chance to succeed than I? How much money has he in his pocket?" That is to say, how long will he be able to wait, if he has to wait, before going hungry? And they note the shape of his shoulders and the expression of his face, half fraternally, half as rivals: "If that flat-chested clerk does not find the work he wants, will he measure up to the work he does find?"

For the optimism which, all told, is general among them, is of the most reasonable sort. Scarcely any are seen who imagine they are going to a magnificent Eldorado whence they will be able to return, after very few years, to live in ease at home. They hope, evidently, to succeed better there than in England, since they have left; but they are aware, also, that they will find a sterner struggle, a much harder climate, and, above all, that atmosphere of simple cruelty characteristic of a young country which is forging ahead and has hardly time to stop to pity and help those who fall by the way, having failed.

Thus one of them, who has been able to equip himself amply, pay his second-class passage and still keep a few pounds in his pocket, has, nevertheless, from time to time, several minutes of anxiety. Installed on the deck in his steamer-chair, he watches the long, monotonous roll of the Atlantic, and thinks:

"There are not more than three or four of us on this boat who have set out at a venture. It is the bad season...the bad season..." And he seeks to estimate, as nearly as possible, all the "x's" of the problem: the cold of the coming winter – the real, intense cold which he does not yet know – the conditions of life and of work in this new country, his chances of finding at once, or almost at once, a living wage.

Phrases from the official booklets on emigration come back to him..."Agricultural workers and artisans are those who should go to Canada, and the only ones sure to succeed...Men practising liberal professions, clerks, etc....etc....would be wrong to emigrate." There are artisans and peasants on this boat, but travelling third-class. They will find work as soon as they land, and have not the slightest reason for anxiety. The man belonging to one of those diverse classes "who would be wrong to emigrate," is, on the contrary, prey to a disquietude. He gets up and goes to join other passengers who are not making their first trip, to ask them for an indirect encouragement.

He questions negligently: "Had you something in view when you crossed the first time?"

One of them replies: "Yes." Another says: "No...but it was spring. Now it's the bad season, you see!"

The bad season....There is no more discouraging expression; and the silhouette of the continent we are approaching – a silhouette contemplated so often on the maps that it is automatically visualized when thought of – assumes a menacing, hostile aspect. All the young men who "would be wrong to emigrate," and who have, nevertheless, emigrated, strive to imagine some of the rigours awaiting them. They pass in review all the different trades they believe themselves capable of practising at a pinch; and they end by saying to themselves that they will "muddle through" all right, and by wrapping themselves comfortably in their rugs to enjoy fully what they are sure of: half a week longer of comfort, with four square meals a day, which appears important and precious at the approach of all this uncertainty.

Others have no sort of anxiety. They are those who are not going to Canada to succeed, but simply to travel and to see something they have not yet seen. They are not anxious, because what happens to them will necessarily be something new, and consequently welcome.

Five days out of Liverpool, a thick fog descends upon the sea, and it begins to be cold. One of the ship's officers explains that it is the wind from Labrador; and, for those of the passengers who are making their first trip, this name of "Labrador" in itself seems to make the temperature fall several degrees lower still.

We shall pass too far from Newfoundland to see the coast, nor shall we pass any icebergs; for at this season they have already passed, drifting majestically to the south, throughout the summer months, melting a little every day: a pilgrimage which is also a sort of slow suicide....

The first land sighted is, therefore, the island of Anticosti. As a good Frenchman, I have always made it a point of honour to know a little of the geography of those countries only where I have travelled. Accordingly, I was altogether ignorant of the existence of this island which has, however, several titles to glory. In the first place, it is just about the size of Corsica; and, as a matter of fact, where does it get this Italian-sounding name? But, above all, it belongs to M. Henri Menier.

The dynasty of the chocolate manufacturers has shown itself infinitely more modern and more prudent than that of the sugar-refiners in its territorial acquistions. M. Menier has not had to occupy Anticosti by main force. He has been satisfied to purchase it. I do not know the price; but, given the dimensions of this patch of ground, the square meter must have cost him very little. He comes here fairly regularly in his yacht, during the summer. Anticosti remains, naturally, a part of the Candian territory and is, therefore, indirectly a British dependency; but a landowner's powers are vast, and the legend runs that M. Menier has turned his island into a little Franco-Canadian colony from which English-speaking people are politely excluded. He has installed in it lumbering operations and several other industries, and comes like a czar, when it pleases him, to live several weeks among his good people, and to hunt the bear and the caribou.

Only – the eternal lesson of humility – the infinitely great, financially and territorially speaking, is prey to the persecutions of the infinitely small. The illustrious chocolate-maker carries on, year after year, an unsuccessful and hopeless struggle against the mosquitoes, which are the scourge of the damp, wooded regions during the warm season; and mosquito-nettings, gauze veils, divers lotions destined to inspire the mosquitoes with disgust for human flesh, scarcely succeed in rendering supportable the master of Anticosti's sojourn on his estates.

All we see of his island is an interminable coast, low, brown, distant, which the fog reveals and conceals, as if playing a game. Then when, towards evening, the fog lifts, we perceive that this coast has disappeared, and we seem to be at open sea. Only, the sight of this first trans-Atlantic land, and the memory of the often consulted maps, makes us almost feel the proximity of the two shores of the Gulf of Saint Lawrence – shores which are always out of sight, but which close in upon us hourly.

Next morning when, leaving stifling cabins, we go up on deck for a little breath before breakfast, one of these shores has become visible and, in a few hours, we come to skirt it quite close.

It is flat and bare at the water's level; but very soon hills appear in the interior, and their line draws nearer. The somewhat misty atmosphere lends them a factitious majesty, and shreds of clouds, hanging halfway up their sides, complacently exaggerate their height, which is only moderate; but it would not take so much to rivet the attention of the passengers, who are now all on deck and looking with a sort of candid interest. The least land takes on a striking relief, after a week on the water; but what marks this land with a moving grandeur in our eyes is, above all, the fact that it is the Canadian land, the outpost of the continent towards which we were bound. A coast with exactly the same silhouette, seen somewhere in Europe, in the Baltic or the Black Sea, would not have this magic; and I firmly believe it would be equally true of an Asiatic or African coast.

America remains essentially the country where one goes to seek one's fortune, the country for which one has left one's own country. A country which one visits in passing, or which one is going to inhabit a few years at most, has not this solemnity of a promised land, on the approach, or this aspect of a double enigma proper to countries where many men come to live forever, or for a long time: the enigma of what the continent hides behind its visible fringe, and the enigma of the life it will provide them. Even today, now that the colonization and the clearing have become prosaic industrial operations, devoid of all adventure, the first glimpse of the American coast in the distance awakes in many of us irrational, anachronistic, adventurous souls, and moves us curiously; but, without doubt, to feel this, one must travel otherwise than as a tourist – must have a little uncertainty in one's life, and find one's self among people for whom the passage from the old continent to the new is a poignantly important throw of the dice, on which they have staked almost everything!

One of the proud predictions heard and read most often on Canadian soil, is that the twentieth century will be "Canada's century," as the nineteenth was that of the United States. It is, doubtless, in drawing towards Quebec or Montreal that one recovers most easily and most exactly the state of mind of the *déracinés* who saw New York Bay open before them a hundred years ago. Those who, approaching that city today, watch the Statue of Liberty and the mass of the "sky-scrapers" loom up, can have very different impressions only, because the first aspect offered them by America is that of one city among others, and no longer the primitive, striking aspect of the empty country they are going to reclaim and to fill.

The ship ascending the Saint Lawrence, on the contrary, nears the shore on arriving at Rimouski, which is the first landing after Liverpool and the only one before Quebec. A little wooden tug, whose hull is extraordinarily massive and its prow singularly shaped to enable it to navigate in winter on the river filled with floating ice, comes, in midstream, to take the few passengers landing here. Of the city itself, which is hidden by an island, and of minor importance moreover, we see only a steeple and an indistinct mass of red, and brown-roofed houses; but this southern shore remains near and visible for a long time after our departure. A railroad line follows it, not far from the river. The strip of land bounded by this line and the river, is strewn with villages, collections of wooden houses in neutral tones, the browns predominating – houses always grouped about a pointed spire, but seeming, nevertheless, to stretch out deliberately, to attempt to bind the villages together, to make a good showing, and to fill up a little the empty spaces of the over-big country. For, behind this chaplet of fishing and farming villages, is the peninsula of New Brunswick and of Maine, the most easterly, the nearest to Europe, of all civilized America, where, however, there are still expanses of several thousand square kilometers without railroads and roads – almost without habitations – and deep forests which men penetrate at wide intervals only, in the autumn, to hunt the wolf and the elk.

It is the northern coast which, however, when we approach it, gives the strongest impression of a country scarcely tamed, still empty and wild. Perhaps the imagination counts for something in this – the recollection that, on this side, there is no longer any real civilization, any city deserving the name, nothing but here and there a few groups of houses timidly assembled, a few lost posts at the bends of the rivers and, farther still, nothing but the wigwams of the last Indians, scattered in the least inclement corners of Unguava and Labrador.

However, the part played by the imagination is not necessarily great, and its task is easy. Here and there this northern coast rises sheer up from the river in a series of rounded hills three-quarters covered with pines. The rock sometimes shows through the earth, but there are only a few precipices or escarpments: everywhere simple, severe lines, ample enough to keep the forest skirts which cover them from changing their profile; everywhere browns and sombre greens: the brown of the bare earth, the brown of the close-ranked tree-trunks, the sombre green of their foliage; and other neutral tones, too, of vegetation which has been sombre in colour and line, even in midsummer, and which is now fading or growing still darker.

From time to time, with a sort of surprise, are seen houses. Here is one halfway up a hillside, another on the water's edge, five or six are assembled in a fold of the ground; and, apparently, about their walls, stretch cleared spaces which must be fields. Yet between houses or groups of houses, there are several miles of steep slope, a deep valley, or a rounded summit – often a bit of forest that would have to be skirted – and one's eyes begin to seek – generally in vain – the rudimentary roads which should, nevertheless, unite them to each other or unite them to something, facilitate their approach for men from elsewhere. Then suddenly one fancies one sees the river lined with an icy crust, obstructed with heavy, serried blocks of ice floating down the current, the slopes covered with the deep winter snow; and the presence of these isolated houses, the existence of the people who live in them, become, for us men of the teeming countries, things almost inexplicable, pathetic.

All day long our ship ascends the river, approaching sometimes one shore, sometimes the other, to follow the line of deep water. This channel, by which all the Canadian traffic passes seven months in the year – the seven months during which the river is navigable – is marked with a care and a precision which constantly recall its importance. It is an uninterrupted chaplet of fires and of buoys; and yet, when the fog comes, in the afternoon, we must stop, drop anchor, and stay there an hour – a long hour of cold humidity, of impalpable opacity which the lugubrious appeal of the siren pierces every minute.

When a gust of wind disperses the fog and permits us to start again, the shores for a long time remain indistinct, drowned, in their turn, in this mist; and, soon after, night descends.

(1924)   (1924)

Marjorie Pickthall
1883-1922

———◆———

MARJORIE PICKTHALL WAS born near London, England, and accompanied her parents to Toronto in 1889. From 1912 to 1919 she lived in England and then returned to Canada and settled in British Columbia. In addition to novels, short stories and a poetic tragedy, Pickthall published several volumes of poetry beginning with *The Drift of Pinions* (1913). *The Complete Poems of Majorie Pickthall* was published in 1925.

Père Lalemant

I lift the Lord on high,
Under the murmuring hemlock boughs, and see
The small birds of the forest lingering by
And making melody.
These are mine acolytes and these my choir,
And this mine altar in the cool green shade,
Where the wild soft-eyed does draw nigh
Wondering, as in the byre
Of Bethlehem the oxen heard Thy cry
And saw Thee, unafraid.   10

My boatmen sit apart,
Wolf-eyed, wolf-sinewed, stiller than the trees.
Help me, O Lord, for very slow of heart
And hard of faith are these.
Cruel are they, yet Thy children. Foul are they,
Yet wert Thou born to save them utterly.
Then make me as I pray,
Just to their hates, kind to their sorrows, wise
After their speech, and strong before their free
Indomitable eyes.   20

Do the French lilies reign
Over Mont Royal and Stadacona still?
Up the St. Lawrence comes the spring again,
Crowning each southward hill
And blossoming pool with beauty, while I roam
Far from the perilous folds that are my home,
There where we built St. Ignace for our needs,
Shaped the rough roof tree, turned the first sweet sod,
St. Ignace and St. Louis, little beads
On the rosary of God.   30

Pines shall Thy pillars be,
Fairer than those Sidonian cedars brought
By Hiram out of Tyre, and each birch-tree
Shines like a holy thought.
But come no worshippers; shall I confess,
St. Francis-like, the birds of the wilderness?
O, with Thy love my lonely head uphold.
A wandering shepherd I, who hath no sheep;
A wandering soul, who hath no scrip, nor gold,
Nor anywhere to sleep.   40

My hour of rest is done;
On the smooth ripple lifts the long canoe;
The hemlocks murmur sadly as the sun
Slants his dim arrows through.
Whither I go I know not, nor the way,
Dark with strange passions, vexed with heathen charms,
Holding I know not what of life or death;
Only be Thou beside me day by day,
Thy rod my guide and comfort, underneath
Thy everlasting arms.   50

(1913)   (1913)

On Amaryllis

A TORTOYSE

My name was Amaryllis. I
From a harde Shell put forthe to fly;
No Bird, alas! with Beautie prim'd,
Hath Death th' inconstant Fowler lim'd.
No antick Moth on Blossoms set
Hath Judgement taken in a Net.
So dull, so slowe, so meeke I went
In my House-Roof that pay'd no Rent,
E'en my deare Mistresse guess'd no Spark
Could e'er enlight'n my dustie Dark.   10

    Judge not, ye Proud. Each lowlie Thing
    May lack the Voyce, not Heart, to sing.
    The Worme that from the Moulde suspires
    May be attun'd with heavenlie Quires,
    And I, a-crawling in my Straw,
    Was moved by Love, and made by Law.
    So all ye wise, who 'neath your Clod
    Go creeping onwards up to God,
    Take Heart of me, who by His Grace,
    Slough'd off my Pris'n and won my Race.   20

(1916)   (1916)

Two Souls

A LETTER FROM PERE JOGUES

Most reverend Father, I have borne all wrong,
Agonies, griefs, revengements. Yet not I,
But rather He Who knew and loved us long,
And came at last to die.
In my maimed hands ye see Him, in my face
His poor abiding place,

"Lo, they will hear My voice and understand;
Go, seek My wandering sheep," the Shepherd saith,
So o'er the world I sought them, hand in hand
With that dark brother of our Order, Death.   10
Under the shadow of his bitterest rod,
Behold, two souls for God!

Like the reed-feeding swans that cannot choose
But hear the voice of summer, in swift flight
Up from Three Rivers came the long canoes
Through calm of day and night,
I in the foremost, Coupil and Couture,
Whose fiery crowns are sure.

Sweet shines the summer over Normandy,
And bright on Arles among her blossoming vines,   20
But, O, more sweet than any land or sea
The northern summer shines.
Each night a silvered dream to cast away,
Each golden dream a day —

So we went on, and our dark Hurons smiled,
Singing the child-songs of the woodpecker,
Through clear green glooms and amber bars enisled
Of tamarack and fir.
Till one cried, "Lo, a shadow and a dread
Steals from the isles ahead!"   30

Death laid a sudden silence on his lips.
In tumult of torn waters at the side.
Crashing, he fell, and all our little ships
Shook on that reddening tide.
Then the blue noon was torn with steel and flame,
And the Five Nations came.

(1925)   (1927)

Stars

Now in the West the slender moon lies low,
And now Orion glimmers through the trees,

Clearing the earth with even pace and slow,
And now the stately-moving Pleiades,
In that soft infinite darkness overhead
Hang jewel-wise upon a silver thread.

And all the lonelier stars that have their place,
Calm lamps within the distant southern sky,
And planet-dust upon the edge of space,
Look down upon the fretful world, and I   10
Look up to outer vastness unafraid
And see the stars which sang when earth was made.

(1925)   (1927)

Snow in April

Over the boughs that the wind has shaken,
    Over the sands that are rippled with rain,
Over the banks where the buds awaken
    Cold cloud shadows are spreading again.
All the musical world is still,
    When sharp and sudden, a sparrow calls,
And down on the grass where the violets shiver,
Through the spruce on the height of the hill,
Down on the breadths of the shining river
    The faint snow falls.   10

Last weak word of a lord that passes –
    Why should the burgeoning woods be mute?
Spring is abroad in the spiring grasses,
    Life is awake in the robin's flute.
But high in the spruce a wind is wailing,
    And the birds in silence arise and go.
Is it that winter is still too near
For the heart of the world to cast out fear,
When over the sky the rack comes sailing
    And suddenly falls the snow?   20

(1925)   (1927)

Canada's Century

"Behold, a people shall come from the north, and a great nation."

I

Out of the north, O Lord,
Out of the north we have come at Thy word;
The forests have heard,
Yea, the tall cedars have heard, and they bow;
The plains have rejoiced at the wound of the plow,
They have laughed, they have laughed at the kiss of the rain
In the bountiful beauty of grain;
The waters have sung of the ships to be.
We are come, a people new-risen, and free
As our wide deep rivers that run from the snows to the sea.   10

II

Into our hands they are given, the unknown opening years,
That, like a seed close-furled,
Hide all their growth and sovereignty and fears
And glories from the world.
Ours is the coming time, and ours the stress
To hold from Thee Thy gifts in worthiness, –
Honour and labour, law to right the wrong,
Courage and peace divine,
Life, clean as prairie of the north, and strong
As the rock-rooted pine, –   20
These shall be ours, and ours, of all, in all, is Thine.

III

Speak yet again,
Thou Who of old to wandering Israel came
In cloud and flame;
But not in wrath
Of human words, nor show an unveiled sword.
Lead us in mercy, Lord.
Behold, the long sweet year Thy word fulfills.
We see Thy prophets' visions on the plain,
Thy signs and wonders writ upon the hills, –   30
The free hills of the North.

(1927)   (1927)

Bibliography

In compiling this bibliography we have listed principal reference works for the study of Canadian literature and a selection of works by each author represented in this volume. Entries in Parts I, II, and III are presented in alphabetical order; in Part IV the books of each author are arranged in chronological order. We would like to acknowledge our indebtedness to the bibliographical studies of Michael Gnarowski, R.G. Moyles, Gérard Tougas, and especially to R.E. Watters for *A Checklist of Canadian Literature and Background Materials 1628-1960*.

I BIBLIOGRAPHIES AND GENERAL REFERENCES

BARBEAU, VICTOR and ANDRE FORTIER, *Dictionnaire bibliographique du Canada français* (Montreal, Académie canadienne-française,1974) 246p.

The Brock Bibliography of Published Canadian Stage Plays in English 1900-1972 (St. Catharines, Brock University, 1972) vi + 35p. [*First Supplement* (St. Catharines, Brock University, 1973) 47p.]

"Canadian Literature; An Annotated Bibliography." [Published annually in *Journal of Canadian Fiction* from 1973.]

"Canadian Literature; a Checklist." [Published annually in *Canadian Literature* from 1960 to 1971.]

Canadian Periodical Index [A continuing serial.]

COLOMBO, JOHN ROBERT, *Colombo's Canadian Quotations* (Edmonton, Hurtig, 1974) x + 735p.

———, *Colombo's Canadian References* (Toronto, Oxford University Press, 1976) viii + 576p.

FEE, MARGERY and RUTH CAWKER, *Canadian Fiction. An Annotated Bibliography* (Toronto, Peter Martin Associates, 1976) xiii + 170p.

GNAROWSKI, MICHAEL, *A Concise Bibliography of English-Canadian Literature* (Toronto, McClelland and Stewart, 1973) 125p.

HAYNE, DAVID M. and MARCEL TIROL, *Bibliographie critique du roman canadien-française 1837-1900* (Toronto, University of Toronto Press, 1968) viii + 144p.

"Letters in Canada." [Published annually in *University of Toronto Quarterly* from 1935.]

Livres et auteurs canadiens (Montreal, Editions Jumonville, 1962.) [Published annually from 1962 to 1969.]

Livres et auteurs québécois (Montreal, Editions Jumonville, 1970.) [Published annually from 1970.]

LOCHHEAD, DOUGLAS, *Bibliography of Canadian Bibliographies/Bibliographie des bibliographies canadiennes* (Toronto, University of Toronto Press, 1972) xiv + 312p.

MOYLES, R.G., *English-Canadian Literature to 1900. A Guide to Information Sources* (Detroit, Gale Research Company, 1976) xi + 346p.

MOYLES, R.G. and CATHERINE SIEMENS, *English-Canadian Literature: A Student Guide and Annotated Bibliography* (Edmonton, Athabascan Publishing Company, 1972) 44p.

NEW, WILLIAM, *Critical Writing on Commonwealth Literature* (University Park, Pennsylvania, Pennsylvania State University Press, 1975) 333p.

NEWMAN, MAUREEN and PHILIP STRATFORD, *Bibliography of Canadian Books in Translation: French to English and English to French/Bibliographie de livres canadiens traduits de l'anglais au français et du français à l'anglais* (Ottawa, Humanities Research Council of Canada, 1975) vi + 57p.

TOUGAS, GERARD, *A Checklist of Printed Materials Relating to French-Canadian Literature 1763-1968. /Liste de référence 1763-1968.* [Revised edition (Vancouver, University of British Columbia Press, 1973) xvi + 174p.]

TREMBLAY, JEAN PIERRE, *Bibliographie québécoise (Quebec, Educo Media,* 1973) 252p.

WATTERS, REGINALD, *A Checklist of Canadian Literature and Background Materials,* 1628-1960. [Revised edition (Toronto, University of Toronto Press, 1972) xxiv + 1085p.]

—— and Inglis Bell, *On Canadian Literature 1806-1960* (Toronto, University of Toronto Press, 1966) ix + 165p.

WOODCOCK, GEORGE, *Canadian Poets, 1960-1973* (Ottawa, Golden Dog Press, 1976) x + 69p.

II LITERARY HISTORY AND BIOGRAPHY

BAILLARGEON, SAMUEL, *Littérature canadienne-français.* Revised edition (Montreal, Fides, 1965) 525p.

BAKER, RAY P., *A History of English-Canadian Literature to the Confederation* (Cambridge, Massachusetts, Harvard University Press, 1920) xi + 200p.

BEAULIEU, VICTOR-LEVY, *Manuel de la petite littérature du Québec* (Montreal, L'Aurore, 1974) 268p.

BESSETTE, GERARD et al, *Histoire de la littérature canadienne-française par les textes* (Montreal, Centre Educatif et Culturel, 1968) 704p.

Dictionary of Canadian Biography (Toronto, University of Toronto Press, 1966)

DUHAMEL, ROGER, *Manuel de littérature canadienne-française* (Ottawa, Editions de Renouveau Pédagogique, 1967) 161p.

EDWARDS, MURRAY, *A Stage in Our Past: English-Language Theatre in Eastern Canada from the 1790's to 1914* (Toronto, University of Toronto Press, 1968) xii + 211p.

GAY, PAUL, *Notre Littérature. Guide littéraire du Canada Français* (Montreal, Editions H.M.H., 1969) xvi + 214p.

GRANDPRE, PIERRE DE et al, *Histoire de la littérature française du Québec* (Montreal, Beauchemin, 1967-1969) 4 vols.

KLINCK, CARL F. (ed.), *Literary History of Canada: Canadian Literature in English* [Revised edition (Toronto, University of Toronto Press, 1976) 3 vols.]

PACEY, DESMOND, *Creative Writing in Canada: A Short History of English-Canadian Literature.* [Revised edition (Toronto, Ryerson, 1961) ix + 314p.]

——, *Ten Canadian Poets* (Toronto, Ryerson, 1958) ix + 350p.

STORY, NORAH, *Oxford Companion to Canadian History and Literature* (Toronto, Oxford University Press, 1967) xi + 935p. [*Supplement* edited by William Toye (Toronto, Oxford University Press, 1973) v + 318p.]

SYLVESTRE, GUY et al, *Canadian Writers/Ecrivains Canadiens* (Toronto, University of Toronto Press, 1966) xviii + 186p.

THOMAS, CLARA, *Our Nature, Our Voices* (Toronto, New Press, 1973) 175p.

TOUGAS, GERARD, *Histoire de la littérature canadienne-française.* Second edition (Paris, Presses universitaires de France, 1964) xii + 312p. Also published as *La littérature canadienne-française* (Paris, Presses Universitaires de France, 1974) 270p. [Second editon translated into English by A.L. Cook (Toronto, Ryerson, 1966) ix + 301p.]

WALLACE, W. STEWART, *The Macmillan Dictionary of Canadian Biography* (Toronto, Macmillan, 1963) 822p.

III CRITICAL STUDIES

ATWOOD, MARGARET, *Survival* (Toronto, Anansi, 1972) 287p.

BALLSTADT, CARL, *The Search for English-Canadian Literature* (Toronto, University of Toronto Press, 1975) L + 214p.

BESSETTE, GERARD, *Une littérature en ébullition* (Montreal, Editions du Jour, 1968) 315p.

BRAZEAU, J. RAYMOND, *An Outline of Contemporary French-Canadian Literature* (Toronto, Forum House, 1972) xii + 126p.

BROWN, E. K., *On Canadian Poetry* [Revised edition (Toronto, Ryerson, 1944) xi +312p.]

————, *Responses and Evaluations. Essays on Canada.* Edited with an Introduction by David Staines (Toronto, McClelland and Stewart, 1977) xviii +314p.

CAMERON, DONALD, *Conversations with Canadian Novelists* (Toronto, Macmillan, 1973) 2 vols.

COLLIN, W. E., *The White Savannahs* (Toronto, Macmillan, 1936) 288p.

DAVEY, FRANK, *From There to Here* (Erin, Ontario, Press Porcépic, 1974) 288p.

DORSONVILLE, MAX, *Caliban Without Prospero: Essay on Quebec and Black Literature* (Erin, Ontario, Press Porcépic, 1974) 227p.

DUDEK, LOUIS and MICHAEL GNAROWSKI, *The Making of Modern Poetry in Canada* (Toronto, Ryerson, 1967) 303p.

EGGLESTON, WILFRED, *The Frontier and Canadian Letters* (Toronto, Ryerson, 1957) ix + 164p.

EGOFF, SHIELA, *The Republic of Childhood* [Revised edition (Toronto, Oxford University Press, 1975) vii +335p.]

FARLEY, T. E., *Exiles and Pioneers* (Ottawa, Borealis Press, 1976) xvii +302p.

FRYE, NORTHROP, *The Bush Garden: Essays on the Canadian Imagination* (Toronto, Anansi, 1971) x +256p.

GARNET, ELDON, *Where? The Other Canadian Poetry* (Erin, Press Porcépic, 1974) ii + 188p.

GIBSON, GRAEME, *Eleven Canadian Novelists* (Toronto, Anansi, 1973) 324p.

JONES, DOUGLAS, *Butterfly on Rock. A Study of Themes and Images in Canadian Literature* (Toronto, University of Toronto Press, 1970) + 197p.

LE MOYNE, JEAN, *Convergences* (Montreal, Editions H.M.H., 1961) 324p. [Translated by Philip Stratford (Toronto, Ryerson, 1966) xii + 256p.]

MCCOURT, EDWARD, *The Canadian West in Fiction* [Revised edition (Toronto, Ryerson, 1970) 128p.]

MCMULLEN, LORRAINE (ed.), *Twentieth Century Essays on Confederation Literature* (Ottawa, The Tecumseh Press, 1976) 151p.

MANDEL, ELI (ed.), *Contexts of Canadian Criticism* (Chicago, University Of Chicago Press, 1971) vii + 304p.

MARCOTTE, GILLES, *Une littérature qui se fait* [Revised edition (Montreal, Editions H.M.H., 1968) 307p.]

MATTHEWS, JOHN, *Tradition in Exile* (Toronto, University of Toronto Press, 1962) viii + 197p.

NEW, WILLIAM, *Among Worlds* (Erin, Ontario, Press Porcépic, 1975) 287p.

————, *Articulating West* (Toronto, New Press, 1972) xxvi + 282p.

NORTHEY, MARGOT, *The Haunted Wilderness* (Toronto, University of Toronto Press, 1976) 131p.

PACEY, DESMOND, *Essays in Canadian Criticism, 1938-1968* (Toronto, Ryerson, 1969) 294p.

RASHLEY, R. E., *Poetry in Canada. The First Three Steps* (Toronto, Ryerson, 1958) xvii + 166p.

SHEK, BEN-ZION, *Social Realism in the French-Canadian Novel* (Montreal, Harvest House, 1977) 326p.

SMITH, A.J.M. *Masks of Fiction* (Toronto, McClelland and Stewart, 1961) 176p.

————, *Masks of Poetry* (Toronto, McClelland and Stewart, 1962) 144p.

————, *Towards a View of Canadian Letters* (Vancouver, University of British Columbia Press, 1973) xi + 230p.

————, *On Poetry and Poets* (Toronto, McClelland and Stewart, 1977) viii + 122p.

SUTHERLAND, RONALD, *Second Image* (Toronto, New Press, 1971) 189p.

URBAS, JEANETTE, *From Thirty Acres to Modern Times* (Toronto, McGraw-Hill Ryerson, 1976) xiv + 158p.

WARWICK, JACK, *The Long Journey* (Toronto, University of Toronto Press, 1968) x + 172p.

WATERSTON, ELIZABETH, *Survey* (Toronto, Methuen, 1973) 215p.

WILSON, EDMUND, *O Canada: An American's Notes on Canadian Culture* (New York, Farrar Strauss, 1964) 245p.

WOODCOCK, GEORGE (ed.), *The Canadian Novel in the Twentieth Century* (Toronto, McClelland and Stewart, 1975) xi + 337p.
——, (ed.), *A Choice of Critics* (Toronto, Oxford, 1966) xxi + 247p.
——, (ed.), *Colony and Confederation* (Vancouver, University of British Columbia Press, 1974) vii +218p.
——, *Odysseus Ever Returning* (Toronto, McClelland and Stewart, 1970) xv + 158p.
——, (ed.), *Poets and Critics* (Toronto, Oxford, 1974) x + 246p.

IV INDIVIDUAL AUTHORS

ADAM ALLAN (1757-1823)
The New Gentle Shepherd. A Pastoral Comedy Originally Written in the Scotch Dialect, by Allan Ramsay. Reduced to English by Lieutenant Adam Allan. To which is annexed a Description of the Great Falls of the River Saint John (London, Richardson, 1798) 75p.

HENRY ALLINE (1748-1784)
Two Mites on Some of the Most Important and Much Disputed Points of Divinity (Halifax, 1781) Also published as *Two Mites, Cast into the Offering of God, for the Benefit of Mankind* (Dover, New Hampshire, 1804).
A court for the Trial of Anti-Traditionist. [Halifax], [1783].
Sermon Preached to, and at the Request, of a Religious Society of Young Men United and Engaged for the Maintaining and Enjoying of Religious Worship in Liverpool, on the 19th November, 1782 (Halifax, [1783]).
A Sermon on a Day of Thanksgiving Preached at Liverpool, By Henry Alline. On the 21st of November 1782 (Halifax, [1783]).
A Sermon Preached on the 19th of February 1783 at Fort-Midway (Halifax, [1783].) [Also published as *A Gospel Call to Sinners* (Newburyport, Massachusetts, Blunt & March, 1795).]
Hymns and Spiritual Songs (Stonington-Port, Connecticut, Turnbull, 1802) 281p. [First published Boston, 1786.]
The Life and Journey of the Rev. Mr. Henry Alline (Boston, Gilbert & Dean, 1806) 180p.

PHILIPPE AUBERT DE GASPE (1786-1871)
Les Anciens Canadiens (Quebec, Desbarats, 1863) 413p. [Translated as *The Canadians of Old* by Georgiana M. Penée (Quebec, Desbarats, 1864) 333p. This translation reprinted with changes as *Seigneur d'Haberville* (Toronto, Musson, 1929) 333p. Translated as *The Canadians of Old* by Charles G.D. Roberts (New York, Appleton, 1890) 287p. This translation reprinted as *Cameron of Lochiel* (Toronto, Copp Clark, 1905) xvii + 287p.]
Mémoires (Ottawa, Desbarats, 1866) 563p.
Divers (Montreal, Beauchemin, 1893) 145p.

JACOB BAILEY (1731-1808)
The Frontier Missionary. A Memoir of the Life of the Rev. Jacob Bailey, Missionary of Pownalborough, Maine, Cornwallis and Annapolis, N.S. Edited by William S. Bartlett (Boston, Ide & Dutton, 1853) 365p.

FRANCES BROOKE (1724-1789)
Virginia, a Tragedy, with Odes, Pastorals, and Translations (London, Author, 1756) 159p.
The History of Lady Julia Mandeville (London, Dodsley, 1782) 2 vols. [First published 1763, 218p.]
The Old Maid, By Mary Singleton, Spinster [pseud.] (London, Millar, 1764) 304p.
The History of Emily Montague (London, Dodsley, 1769) 4 vols.
The Excursion (London, Cadell, 1777) 2 vols.
The Siege of Sinope. A Tragedy (London, Cadell, 1781) 71p.
Rosina. A Comic Opera in Two Acts (London, Cadell, 1783) 46p.
The History of Charles Mandeville (London, Lane, 1790) 2 vols.
Marian. A Comic Opera in Two Acts (London, Longmans, 1800) 31p.

WILLIAM FRANCIS BUTLER (1838-1910)
A Narrative of the Historical Events Connected With the Sixty-ninth Regiment (London, Mitchell, 1870) 130p.
The Great Lone Land. A Narrative of Travel and Adventure in the North-West (London, Sampson Low, 1872) 388p.
The Wild North Land. Being the Story of a Winter Journey, with Dogs, Across Northern North America (London, Sampson Low, 1873) 358p.

Akim-foo: The History of a Failure (London, Sampson Low, 1875) 300p.

Far Out: Roving Re-told (London, Isbister, 1880) xxiv + 386p.

Red Cloud, the Solitary Sioux. A Tale of the Great Prairie (London, Low & Marston, 1882) 327p. [Also published as *The Hero of Pine Ridge* (Boston, C.E. Brown, [188?]) 327p.]

The Campaign of the Cataracts; being a personal narrative of the Great Nile Expedition of 1884-5. With illustrations from drawings by Lady Butler (London, Sampson Low, 1887) vii + 389p.

Charles George Gordon (London, Macmillan, 1889) vi + 255p.

Sir Charles Napier (London, Macmillan, 1890) 216p.

The Life of Sir George Pomeroy Colley, 1835-1881 (London, Murray, 1899) 430p.

The Light of the West, With Some Other Wayside Thoughts, 1865-1908 (Dublin, Gill, 1909) 246p.

Sir William Butler. An Autobiography (London, Constable, 1911) 476p.

WILFRED CAMPBELL (1858-1918)

Snowflakes and Sunbeams (St. Stephen, New Brunswick, St. Croix Courier, 1888) 36p.

Lake Lyrics and Other Poems (St. John, New Brunswick, McMillan, 1889) 160p.

The Dread Voyage and Other Poems (Toronto, Briggs, 1893) 190p.

Mordred and Hildebrand. A Book of Tragedies (Ottawa, Durie, 1895) 168p.

Beyond the Hills of Dream (Boston, Houghton, 1899) 137p.

The Poems of Wilfred Campbell (Toronto, Briggs, 1905) 354p.

Ian of the Orcades; or, The Armourer of Girnigoe (London, Oliphant, 1906) 320p.

Canada. Painted By T. Mower Martin. Described by Wilfred Campbell (London, Black, 1907) 272p.

Poetical Tragedies (Toronto, Briggs, 1908) 316p.

A Beautiful Rebel. A Romance of Upper Canada in 1812 (Toronto, Westminster, 1909) 318p.

The Beauty, History, Romance and Mystery of the Canadian Lake Region (Toronto, Musson, 1910) 191p. [Enlarged and revised edition (1914) 215p.]

The Scotsman in Canada. Vol. 1: Eastern Canada (Toronto, Musson, [1911]) 423p.

Sagas of Vaster Britain. Poems of the Race, the Empire, and the Divinity of Man (Toronto, Musson, 1914) 163p.

The Poetical Works of Wilfred Campbell. Edited with a Memoir by W.J. Sykes (London, Hodder, 1923) 363p.

At the Mermaid Inn, Conducted by Archibald Lampman, W. W. Campbell, Duncan C. Scott. Being selections from Essays...which appeared in the Toronto *Globe,* 1892-1893. Edited by Arthur S. Bourinot (Ottawa, Bourinot, 1958) 96p.

Selected Poems. Edited by C. F. Klinck (Ottawa, The Tecumseh Press, 1976) 59p.

BLISS CARMAN (1861-1929)

Low Tide on Grand Pré. A Book of Lyrics (New York, Webster, 1893) 120p. [Also an unauthorized publication in the Canadian Series of Pamphlets (Toronto, Copp Clark, [1889]) 26p.]

Songs From Vagabondia. By Bliss Carman and Richard Hovey (Boston, Copeland 1894) 54p.

Behind the Arras. A Book of the Unseen (Boston, Lamson Wolffe, 1895) 102p.

More Songs from Vagabondia. By Bliss Carman and Richard Hovey (Boston, Copeland, 1896) 72p.

Ballads of Lost Haven. A Book of the Sea (Boston, Lamson Wolffe, 1897) 117p.

By the Aurelian Wall, and Other Elegies (Boston, Lamson Wolffe, 1898) 132p.

The Green Book of the Bards (Cambridge, Massachusetts, University Press, 1898) 12p.

The Vengeance of Noel Brassard. A Tale of the Acadian Expulsion (Cambridge, Massachusetts, Bradley, 1899) 23p.

A Winter Holiday (Boston, Small Maynard, 1899) 43p.

Last Songs from Vagabondia. By Bliss Carman and Richard Hovey (Boston, Small Maynard, 1901) 79p.

Ballads and Lyrics (London, Bullen, 1902) 79p.

...From the Book of Myths (Boston, Page, 1902) 88p.

Ode on the Coronation of King Edward (Boston, Page, 1902) 34p.

Sappho. Lyrics. With Excerpts from a Literal Rendering by H. T. Wharton (n.p., Author, 1902) 8p.

...From the Green Book of the Bards (Boston, Page, 1903) 137p.

The Friendship of Art (Boston, Page, 1904) 303p.

The Kinship of Nature (Boston, Page, 1904) 298p. [Published 1903]

...*Poems* (London, Murray, 1904) 2 vols.

Sappho: One Hundred Lyrics. With an Introduction by Charles G. D. Roberts (Boston, Page, 1904) 130p.

...*Songs from a Northern Garden* (Boston, Page, 1904) 121p.

...*Songs of the Sea Children* (Boston, Page, 1904) 182p.

...*From the Book of Valentines* (Boston, Page, 1905) 103p.

Pipes of Pan. Containing "From the Book of Myths," "From the Green Book of the Bards," "Songs of the Sea Children," "Songs from a Northern Garden," "From the Book of Valentines" (Boston, Page, 1903-1905) 5 vols in 1. [First Canadian Edition (Toronto, Ryerson, 1942).]

The Poetry of Life (Boston, Page, 1905). 258p.

The Making of Personality. [With Mary Perry King] (Boston, Page, 1908) 375p.

The Rough Rider, and Other Poems (New York, Kennerley, 1909) 78p.

A Painter's Holiday, and Other Poems (New York, F. F. Sherman, 1911) 43p.

Songs from Vagabondia, More Songs from Vagabondia, Last Songs from Vagabondia. By Bliss Carman and Richard Hovey (Boston, Small Maynard, [1911]) 3 vols. in 1.

Echoes from Vagabondia. (Boston, Small Maynard, 1912) 65p.

Daughters of Dawn. A Lyrical Pageant... by Bliss Carman and Mary Perry King (New York, Kennerley, 1913) 118p.

Earth Deities, and Other Rhythmic Masques. By Bliss Carman and Mary Perry King (New York, Kennerley, 1914) 85p.

April Airs. A Book of New England Lyrics (Boston, Small Maynard, 1916) 77p.

Later Poems. With an Appreciation by R. H. Hathaway (Toronto, McClelland and Stewart, [1921]) 203p.

Ballads and Lyrics (Toronto, McClelland and Stewart, 1923) 293p.

Far Horizons (Boston, Small Maynard, [1925]) 85p.

Our Canadian Literature. Representative Verse, English. Chosen by Bliss Carman and Lorne Pierce (Toronto, Ryerson, 1925) 361p.

Talks on Poetry and Life. Five Lectures Delivered before the University of Toronto, December, 1925. (Toronto, Ryerson, 1926) 58p.

Sanctuary. Sunshine House Sonnets (New York, Dodd Mead, 1929) 55p.

Wild Garden (New York, Dodd Mead, [1929]) 76p.

Bliss Carman's Poems (Toronto, McClelland and Stewart, 1931) 546p.

Bliss Carman's Scrap Book. A Table of Contents. Edited with a Postscript by Lorne Pierce (Toronto, Ryerson, [1931]) 18p.

The Music of Earth. Foreword and Notes by Lorne Pierce (Toronto, Ryerson, 1931) 45p.

The Selected Poems of Bliss Carman. Edited with an Introduction by Lorne Pierce (Toronto, McClelland and Stewart, 1954) 122p.

The Poems of Bliss Carman. Edited with an Introduction by Robert Sorfleet (Toronto, McClelland and Stewart, 1976) 169p.

EMILY CARR (1871-1945)

Klee Wyck (Toronto, Oxford University Press, 1941) 155p.

The Book of Small (Toronto, Oxford University Press, 1942) 245p.

The House of All Sorts (Toronto, Oxford University Press, 1944) 222p.

Emily Carr: Her Paintings and Sketches (Toronto, Oxford University Press, 1945) 64p.

Growing Pains. The Autobiography of Emily Carr (Toronto, Oxford University Press, 1946) 381p.

The Heart of a Peacock. Edited by Ira Dilworth (Toronto, Oxford University Press, 1953) 234p.

Pause. A Sketch Book (Toronto, Clarke Irwin, 1953) 148p.

An Address by Emily Carr. With an Introduction by Ira Dilworth (Toronto, Oxford University Press, 1955) ix + 13p.

Hundreds and Thousands. The Journals of Emily Carr (Toronto, Clarke Irwin, 1966) 332)p.

Fresh Seeing. Two Addresses (Toronto, Clarke Irwin, 1973) 38p.

JACQUES CARTIER (1491-1557)

Brief récit de la navigation. Faicte es ysles de Canada (Paris, P. Roffet & A. LeClerc, 1545).

Discours du voyage fait par le Capitaine Iaques Cartier au Terresneufes de Canadas, Norembergue, Hochelage, Labrador, & pays adiacens, dite nouvelle France avec particulieres moeurs, langage, & ceremonies des habitans d'icelle

(Rouen, l'Imprimerie de R. du Petit Val, 1598) 64p. [This account of Cartier's first voyage was first published in Italian in 1556; this text was then translated into English in 1580 and into this French edition in 1598.]
The Voyages of Jacques Cartier. Published from the Originals with Translations, Notes and Appendices by H.P. Biggar (Ottawa, Publications of the Public Archives of Canada, 1924) xiv + 330p.

ISABELLA VALANCY CRAWFORD
(1850-1887)
Old Spookses' Pass, Malcolm's Katie, and Other Poems (Toronto, James Bain, 1884) 224p.
The Collected Poems of Isabella Valancy Crawford. Edited by J.W. Garvin with an Introduction by Ethelwyn Wetherald (Toronto, Briggs, 1905) 309p.
Selected Stories of Isabella Valancy Crawford. Edited with an Introduction by Penny Petrone (Ottawa, University of Ottawa Press, 1975) 90p.

OCTAVE CREMAZIE (1827-1879)
Oeuvres complètes (Montreal, Beauchemin, 1882) 543p.
Lettres et fragments de lettres (Montreal, Beauchemin, 1886) 316p.
Poésies (Montreal, Beauchemin, 1886) 230p.
Poésies (Montreal, Beauchemin, 1912) 236p.
Poésies (Montreal, Beauchemin, 1925) 202p.
Crémazie. Texte établi et annoté par Michel Dassonville (Montreal, Fides, [1956].) 95p.
Oeuvres I. Poésies. Texte établi annoté et presenté par Odette Condemine (Ottawa, Editions de L'Université d'Ottawa, 1972) 613p.
Oeuvres II. Prose. Texte établi, annoté et presenté par Odette Condemine (Ottawa, Editions de L'Université d'Ottawa, 1976) 438p.

JAMES DE MILLE (1833-1880)
John Wheeler's Two Uncles; or, Launching into Life. [Anon] (New York, Carlton & Porter, [1860]).
Andy O'Hara: or, The Child of Promise. [Anon] (New York, Carlton & Porter, 1861).
The Martyr of the Catacombs. A Tale of Ancient Rome. [Anon] (New York, Carlton & Porter, 1865) 202p.

Helena's Household. A Tale of Rome in the First Century. [Anon] (New York, Carter, 1868) 422p. [Also published as *Helena's Household.* An Ideal of Roman Life in the Time of Paul and Nero (New York, Ward & Drummond, 1890).]
The "B.O.W.C.". A Book for Boys. By the author of *The Dodge Club,* etc. [pseud] (Boston, Lee & Shepard, 1869) 322p.
Cord and Creese. A Novel (New York, Harper, 1869) 305p.
The Dodge Club; or, Italy in 1859 (New York, Harper, 1869) 133p.
The Boys of Grand Pré School (Boston, Lee & Shepard, 1870) 348p.
The Lady of the Ice. A Novel (New York, Appleton, 1870) 146p.
Lost in the Fog (Boston, Lee & Shepard, [1870]) 316p.
Among the Brigands (Boston, Lee & Shepard, 1871) 328p.
The Cryptogram. A Novel (New York, Harper, 1871) 261p.
The American Baron (New York, Harper, 1872) 132p.
A Comedy of Terrors (Boston, Osgood, 1872) 152p.
Fire in the Woods (Boston, Lee & Shepard, 1872) 323p.
Picked Up Adrift (Boston, Lee & Shepard, 1872) 335p.
An Open Question. A Novel (New York, Appleton, 1872) 233p.
The Seven Hills (Boston, Lee & Shepard, 1872) p.
The Treasure of the Seas (Boston, Lee & Shepard, 1873) 336p.
The Lily and the Cross. A Tale of Acadia (Boston, Lee & Shepard, 1874) 264p.
The Living Link. A Novel (New York, Harper, 1874) 171p.
The Babes in the Wood. A Tragic Comedy. A Tale of the Italian Revolution of 1848 (Boston, Gill, 1875) 142p.
The Winged Lion; or, Stories of Venice (New York, Dillingham, 1877) 323p.
The Elements of Rhetoric (New York, Harper, 1878) 564p.
A Castle in Spain. A Novel (New York, Harper, 1883) 183p.
Old Garth. A Story of Sicily (New York, Munro, 1883) 52p.
A Strange Manuscript Found in a Copper Cylinder. [Anon] (New York, Harper, 1888) 291p.
Behind the Veil. A Poem (Halifax, Allen, 1893) 30p.

SARA JEANNETTE DUNCAN (1861-1922)
A Social Departure. How Orthodocia and I Went Round the World by Ourselves (London, Chatto and Windus, 1890) 417p.
An American Girl in London (London, Chatto and Windus, 1891) 321p.
The Simple Adventures of a Memsahib (New York, Appleton, 1893) 311p.
A Daughter of To-Day (New York, Appleton, 1894) 392p.
The Story of Sonny Sahib (London, Macmillan, 1894) 114p.
Vernon's Aunt. Being the Oriental Experience of Miss Lavinia Moffat (London, Chatto and Windus, 1894) 200p.
His Honour and a Lady (Toronto, Rose, 1896) 321p.
Hilda. A Story of Calcutta (New York, Stokes, 1898) 317p.
A Voyage of Consolation. Being…a Sequel to… *An American Girl in London* (London, Methuen, 1898) 318p.
The Path of a Star (London, Methuen, 1899) 311p.
On the Other Side of the Latch (London, Methuen, 1901) 266p. [Also published as *The Crow's Nest* (New York, Dodd Mead, 1901) 248p.]
Those Delightful Americans (New York, Appleton, 1902) 352p.
The Pool in the Desert (New York, Appleton, 1903) 318p.
The Imperialist (Toronto, Copp Clark, 1904) 472p.
Set in Authority (London, Constable, 1906) 344p.
Cousin Cinderella. A Canadian Girl in London (Toronto, Macmillan, 1908) 365p.
The Burnt Offering (London, Methuen, 1909) 324p.
The Consort (London, Stanley Paul, 1912) 344p.
His Royal Happiness (New York, Appleton, 1914) 377p.
Title Clear. A Novel (London, Hutchinson, 1922) 288p.
The Gold Cure. A Novel (London, Hutchinson, 1924) 286p.

LOUIS FRECHETTE (1839-1908)
Mes loisirs (Quebec, Brousseau, 1863) 200p.
La Voix d'un exilé (Chicago, Imprimerie de l'Amerique, 1869) 26p.
Félix Poutré (Montreal, n.p., 1871) 59p.
Pêle-mêle. Fantaisies et souvenirs poétiques (Montreal, Lovell, 1877) 274p.

Les Fleurs boréales. Les Oiseaux de neige: Poésies Canadiennes (Quebec, Darveau, 1879) 268p.
Poésies choisies (Quebec, Darveau, 1879) 182p.
Papineau. Drame historique canadien en quatre actes et neuf tableaux (Montreal, Chapleau et Lavigne, 1880) 100p.
Le Retour de l'exilé. Drame en cinq actes et huit tableaux (Montreal, Chapleau et Lavigne, 1880) 72p.
La Legende d'un peuple. Avec une préface de Jules Claretie. (Paris, Librairie Illustrée, 1888) vii + 347p.
Feuilles volantes: Poésies canadiennes (Quebec, Darveau, 1890) 228p.
Originaux et détraqués. Douze types québécquois (Montreal, Patenaude, 1892) 360p.
Christmas in French Canada. With illustrations by Frederic Simpson Coburn (Toronto, Morang, 1899) xv + 262p.[Published as *La Noël au Canada: Contes et récits* (Toronto, Morang, 1900) xix + 288p.]
Poésies choisies (Montreal, Beauchemin, 1908) 3 vols.
Cent morceaux choisis. Recueillis par sa fille, Pauline Fréchette ([Beauceville], [L'Eclaireur], 1924) 240p.
Fréchette. Textes choisis et présentés par Michel Dassonville (Montreal, Fides, 1959) 95p.
Mémoires intimes. Texte établi et annoté par George A. Klinck (Montreal, Fides, [1961]) 200p.
Contes. Préface de Maurice Lemire et Jacques Roy (Montreal, Fides, 1974) 189p.
Contes, Tome II. Masques et fantômes et les autres contes. Texte présenté par Aurélien Boivin et Maurice Lemire (Montreal, Fides, 1977) 379p.

OLIVER GOLDSMITH (1794-1861)
The Rising Village. A Poem (London, Sharpe, 1825) 48p.
The Rising Village, with Other Poems (Saint John, New Brunswick, McMillan, 1834) 144p.
The Autobiography of Oliver Goldsmith. Published for the First Time from the Original Manuscript of the Author of "The Rising Village." Introduction and Notes by Rev. Wilfrid E. Myatt (Toronto, Ryerson, 1943) 76p.
The Manuscript Book of Oliver Goldsmith, Author of "The Rising Village." With Descrip-

tion and Comment by E. Cockburn Kyte. (Toronto, Bibliographical Society of Canada, 1950) 13p.

The Rising Village. Edited by Michael Gnarowski (Montreal, Delta, 1968) 47p.

CHARLES GORDON (1860-1937)

Beyond the Marshes. By Ralph Connor [pseud] (Toronto, Westminster, 1898) 36p.

Black Rock. A Tale of the Selkirks. By Ralph Connor [pseud] (Toronto, · Westminster, 1898) 327p.

The Sky Pilot. A Tale of the Foothills. By Ralph Connor [pseud] (Chicago, Revell, 1899) 300p.

The Man From Glengarry. A Tale of the Ottawa. By Ralph Connor [pseud] (Toronto, Westminster, 1901) 473p.

Glengarry School Days. A Story of Early Days in Glengarry. By Ralph Connor [pseud] (Chicago, Revell, 1902) 340p. [Also published as *Glengarry Days* (London, Hodder, 1902) 252p.]

Gwen. An Idyll of the Canyon. By Ralph Connor [pseud] (New York, Revell, 1904) 94p.

The Prospector. A Tale of the Crow's Nest Pass. By Ralph Connor [pseud] (New York, Revell, 1904) 401p.

The Pilot at Swan Creek (London, Hodder, 1905) 184p.

The Doctor. A Tale of the Rockies. By Ralph Connor [pseud] (Toronto, Westminster, 1906) 399p. [Also published as *The Doctor of Crow's Nest* (London, Hodder, 1906) 399p.]

The Life of James Robertson, Missionary Superintendent in the Northwest Territories (Toronto, Westminster, 1908) 403p.

The Foreigner. A Tale of Saskatchewan, By Ralph Connor [pseud] (Toronto, Westminster, 1909) 384p. [Also published as *The Settler.* A Tale of Saskatchewan (London, Hodder, 1909) 307p.]

Corporal Cameron of the North West Mounted Police. A Tale of the Macleod Trail. By Ralph Connor [pseud] (New York, Hodder, 1912) 454p.

The Patrol of the Sun Dance Trail. By Ralph Connor [pseud] (New York, Doran, 1914) 363p.

The Major. By Ralph Connor [pseud] (Toronto, McClelland and Stewart, 1917) 383p.

The Sky Pilot in No Man's Land. By Ralph Connor [pseud] (Toronto, McClelland and Stewart, 1919) 349p.

To Him That Hath. A Novel of the West of Today. By Ralph Connor [pseud] (New York, Doran, 1921) 291p.

The Gaspards of Pine Croft. A Romance of the Windermere. By Ralph Connor [pseud] (Toronto, McClelland and Stewart, 1923) 318p.

Treading the Winepress. By Ralph Connor [pseud] (Toronto, McClelland and Stewart, 1925) 394p.

The Friendly Four, and Other Stories. By Ralph Connor [pseud] (New York, Doran, 1926) 275p.

The Runner. A Romance of the Niagaras. By Ralph Connor [pseud] (Garden City, Doubleday, 1929) 481p.

The Rock and the River. A Romance of Quebec. By Ralph Connor [pseud] (New York, Dodd Mead, 1931) 377p.

The Arm of Gold, By Ralph Connor [pseud]. (New York, Dodd Mead, 1932) 314p.

The Girl from Glengarry. By Ralph Connor [pseud] (New York, Dodd Mead, 1933) 312p. [Also published as *The Glengarry Girl* (London, Lane, 1934) 314p.]

Torches Through the Bush. A Tale of Glengarry. By Ralph Connor [pseud] (New York, Dodd Mead, 1934) 300p.

The Rebel Loyalist. By Ralph Connor [pseud] (Toronto, McClelland and Stewart 1935) 328p.

The Gay Crusader. A Romance of Quebec. By Ralph Connor [pseud] (New York, Dodd Mead, 1936) 376p.

He Dwelt Among Us. By Ralph Connor [pseud] (New York, Revell, 1936) 174p.

Postscript to Adventure. The Autobiography of Ralph Connor (New York, Farrar, 1938) 430p.

JOHN GYLES (1680-1755)

Memoirs of odd adventures, strange deliverances, etc. in the captivity of John Gyles, esq., commander of the garrison on Saint George River, in the district of Maine (Boston, S. Kneeland and T. Green, 1736) 48p. [Also published in *Tragedies of the Wilderness.* Edited by Samuel G. Drake (Boston, Antiquarian Bookstore and Institute, 1841) 360p.]

THOMAS CHANDLER HALIBURTON (1796-1865)

A General Description of Nova Scotia (Halifax, Royal Canadian School, 1823) 200p.

An Historical and Statistical Account of Nova Scotia (Halifax, Joseph Howe, 1829) 2 vols.

The Clockmaker; or, The Sayings and Doings of Samuel Slick, of Slickville [Anon] [First Series] (Halifax, Joseph Howe, 1836) 221p.; [Second Series] (London, Bentley, 1838); [Third Series] (London, Bentley, 1840).

The Bubbles of Canada (London, Bentley, 1839) 332p.

A Reply to the Report of The Earl of Durham. By a colonist [pseud] (London, Bentley, 1839) 91p.

The Letter-Bag of the Great Western; or, Life in a Steamer (London, Bentley, 1840) 323p.

The Attaché; or, Sam Slick in England [First Series] (London, Bentley, 1843) 2 vols.; [Second Series] (London, Bentley, 1844) 2 vols.

The Old Judge; or, Life in a Colony (London, Colburn, 1849) 2 vols.

Rule and Misrule of the English in America (London, Colburn, 1851) 2 vols.

Traits of American Humor, By Native Authors. Edited and Adapted by the Author of "Sam Slick" (London, Colburn, 1852) 3 vols.

Sam Slick's Wise Saws and Modern Instances; or, What He Said, Did or Invented (London, Hurst & Blackett, 1853) 2 vols.

The Americans at Home; or, Byeways, Backwoods, and Prairies. Edited by the Author of "Sam Slick" (London, Hurst & Blackett, 1854) 3 vols.

Nature and Human Nature (London, Hurst & Blackett, 1855) 2 vols.

An Address on the Present Condition, Resources, and Prospects of British North America (London, Hurst & Blackett, 1857) 44p.

The Season Ticket (London, Bentley, 1860) 376p.

Fragments from Sam Slick. Selected and Arranged by Lawrence J. Burpee (Toronto, Musson, 1909) 91p.

Sam Slick. Edited with a Critical Estimate and a Bibliography by Ray Palmer Baker (Toronto, McClelland and Stewart, 1923) 420p.

Selections from Sam Slick. Edited by Paul A. W. Wallace (Toronto, Ryerson, 1923) 150p.

The Old Judge, or Life in a Colony. A Selection of Sketches. Edited and Introduced by R. E. Watters (Toronto, Clarke Irwin, 1968) 247p.

The Sam Slick Anthology. Selected and Introduced by R. E. Watters. Edited for Modern Readers by W. S. Avis (Toronto, Clarke Irwin, 1969) 263p.

ROBERT HAYMAN (1575-1629)

Quodlibets Lately Come Over From New Britaniola, Old Newfound-Land. Epigrams and Other Small Parcels, Both Morall and Divine. By R.H., Sometimes Governour of the Plantation (London, Mitchell, 1628) 64p.

SAMUEL HEARNE (1745-1792)

A Journey From Prince of Wales's Fort in Hudson's Bay, to the Northern Ocean ... in the Years 1769, 1770, 1771 & 1772 (London, Strahan & Cadell, 1775) xliv + 458p.

Journals of Samuel Hearne and Philip Turnor. Edited with an Introduction by J. B. Tyrrell (Toronto, Champlain Society, 1934) xviii + 611 + xiip.

CHARLES HEAVYSEGE (1816-1876)

The Revolt of Tartarus. A Poem (London, Simpkin, Marshall & Company [1852]) 155p.

Sonnets. By the Author of *The Revolt of Tartarus.* [pseud] (Montreal, Rose, 1855) 61p.

Saul. A Drama, in Three Parts. [Anon] (Montreal, Rose, 1857) 315p.

Count Filippo; or, The Unequal Marriage. A Drama in Five Acts by the Author of *Saul* [pseud] (Montreal, Author, 1860) 153p.

The Dark Huntsman. [Anon] (Montreal, 'Witness' Steam Printing House, 1864) 8p.

The Owl. [Anon] (n.p., 1864)

The Advocate. A Novel (Montreal, Worthington, 1865) 125p.

Jephthah's Daughter (Montreal, Dawson, 1865) 94p.

Jezebel. A Poem in Three Cantos (Montreal, The Golden Dog Press, 1972) 31p.

The Dark Huntsman (1864 and 1876 texts). Edited by Michael Gnarowski (Ottawa, The Golden Dog Press, 1973)

LOUIS HEMON (1880-1913)

Maria Chapdelaine. Récit du Canada français. Précédé de deux préfaces par M. Emile Boutroux de l'Académie française et par M. Louvigny de Montigny de la Société Royale du Canada. Illustrations originales du Suzor-Coté (Montreal, LeFebvre, 1916) 243p. [Many translations including W. H. Blake, (Toronto, Macmillan, 1921) 263p.]

La Belle que voila (Paris, Grasset, 1923) 239p. [Translated by W. A. Bradley as *My Fair Lady* (New York, Macmillan, 1923) 226p.]

Colin-Maillard (Paris, Grasset, 1924) 278p. [Translated by Arthur Richmond as *Blind Man's Buff* (New York, Macmillan, 1924) 244p.]

The Journal of Louis Hémon. Translated by W. A. Bradley (New York, Macmillan, 1924) [French text appears as "Au pays de Québec" in L.-J. Dalbis. *Le Bouclier canadien-français* (Montreal, Deom, 1925) 246p.]

Battling Malone, Pugiliste. Préface de Daniel Halévy (Paris, Grasset, 1925) 268p. [Translated by W.A. Bradley as *Battling Malone and Other Stories* (London, T. Butterworth, 1925).]

Monsieur Ripois and Nemesis. Translated by W.A. Bradley (New York, Macmillan, 1925) 359p. [French text appears as *Monsieur Ripois et la Némésis* (Paris, Grasset, 1950) 315p.]

Louis Hémon: Lettres à sa famille. Edité par Nicole Deschamps (Montreal, Presses de l'Université de Montréal, 1968) 219p.

ALEXANDER HENRY (1739-1824)
Travels and Adventures in Canada and the Indian Territories, between the Years 1760 and 1776 (New York, Riley, 1809) 330p.

JOSEPH HOWE (1804-1873)
Confederation Considered in Relation to the Interests of the Empire (London, Stanford, 1866) 37p.

Poems and Essays (Montreal, Lovell, 1874) 341p.

The Speeches and Public Letters of the Hon. Joseph Howe. Edited by William Annand; Revised and Augmented by J.A. Chisholm (Halifax, Chronicle Pub. Co., 1909) 2 vols.

The Heart of Howe: Selections from the Letters and Speeches. Edited by D.C. Harvey (Toronto, Oxford, 1939) 197p.

Western and Eastern Rambles. Travel Sketches of Nova Scotia. Edited by M.G. Parks (Toronto, University of Toronto Press, 1973) 220p.

JOHN HUNTER-DUVAR (1830-1899)
John A'Var: His Lays (East Boston, H.F. Hodges & Company, 1874)

The Enamorado. A Drama (Summerside, Graves, 1879) 120p.

De Roberval (St. John, New Brunswick, McMillan, 1888) 192p. [Also includes "The Emigration of the Fairies" and "The Triumph of Constancy: A Romaunt."]

The Stone, Bronze and Iron Ages. A Popular Treatise on early Archaeology (London, Swan Sonnenschein, 1892) 285p.

Annals of the Court of Oberon. Extracted from the Records (London, Digby Long, 1895) 246p.

ANNA JAMESON (1794-1860)
A First or Mother's Dictionary for Children (London, Adlard, 1825)

The Diary of an Ennuyée (London, Colburn, 1826) 354p. [First published anonymously as *A Lady's Diary.*]

Loves of the Poets (London, Colburn, 1829) 2 vols. [Also published as *Memoirs of the Loves of the Poets* (London, Colburn, 1831) and as *The Romance of Biography* (London, Saunders and Otley, 1837) 2 vols.]

Memoirs of Celebrated Female Sovereigns (London, Colburn, 1831) 2 vols.

Memoirs of the Beauties of the Court of Charles II (London, 1831)

Characteristics of Women (London, 1832) 2 vols.

Visits and Sketches at Home and Abroad (London, 1834) 2 vols.

Winter Studies and Summer Rambles in Canada (London, Saunders & Otley, 1838) 3 vols. [Also a selection from this work published as *Sketches in Canada, and Rambles Among the Red Men* (London, Longmans, 1852) 314p. Another selection, *Winter Studies and Summer Rambles in Canada.* Edited with an Introduction by Clara Thomas (Toronto, McClelland and Stewart, 1965) 172p.]

Memoirs of the Early Italian Painters (London, 1845) 2 vols.

Memoirs and Essays on Art, Literature and Social Morals (London, Bentley, 1846) 298p.

The Relative Position of Mothers and Governesses (London, 1846)

Sacred and Legendary Art (London, Longman, 1848) 2 vols.

Legends of the Monastic Orders (London, Longman, 1850) 481p.

Legends of the Madonna (London, 1852)

A Commonplace Book of Thoughts, Memories and Fancies, Original and Selected (London, Longman, 1854) xiv + 371p.

Sisters of Charity, Catholic and Protestant, At Home and Abroad (London, 1855)

The Communion of Labour (London, Longman, 1856) 156p.

Mrs. Jameson's Works (Boston, Ticknor and Fields, 1866) 10 vols.

*Anna Jameson, Letters and Friendships
1812-1860*. Edited by Mrs. Stewart Erskine
(London, Unwin [1915]) 350p.
Letters of Anna Jameson to Ottilie von Goethe.
Edited by G. H. Needler (London,
Oxford University Press, 1939) xxv +
247p.
Early Canadian Sketches. With an Introduc-
tion by G. H. Needler (Toronto, Burns
and MacEachern, 1958)

PAULINE JOHNSON (1861-1913)
The White Wampum (London, Lane, 1895)
88p.
Canadian Born (Toronto, Morang, 1903)
67p.
Legends of Vancouver (Vancouver, Thomp-
son Stationery Company, 1911) 89p.
The Shagganappi. With an Introduction by
Ernest Thompson Seton (Toronto,
Briggs, 1912) 257p.
Flint and Feather (Toronto, Musson [1912])
156p. Revised and enlarged with an
Introduction by Theodore Watts-
Dunton (Toronto, Musson, 1913)
The Moccasin Maker. With an Introduction
by Sir Gilbert Parker, and an Apprecia-
tion by Charles Mair (Toronto, Briggs,
1913) 248p.

WILLIAM KIRBY (1817-1906)
*Counter Manifesto to the Annexationists of
Montreal*. By Britannicus [pseud] (Niag-
ara, Davidson, 1849) 16p.
*The U.E.: A Tale of Upper Canada in XII
Cantos* [Anon] (Niagara, "Mail", 1859)
178p.
The Golden Dog (Le Chien D'Or). A Legend
of Quebec (Montreal, Lovell, 1877)
678p.
The Hungry Year (Toronto, Methodist
Book, 1878) 15p.
Canadian Idylls (Welland, 1884) [Also
enlarged edition (Welland, 1894) 175p.]
The United Empire Loyalists of Canada.
Illustrated by Memorials of the Servos
Family (Toronto, Briggs, 1884) 20p.
Annals of Niagara (Welland, Tribune,
1896) 269p.
Alfred, Lord Tennyson and William Kirby.
Unpublished Correspondence, to which
are added some Letters from Hallam,
Lord Tennyson. Edited by Lorne Pierce
(Toronto, Macmillan, 1929) 71p.

ARCHIBALD LAMPMAN (1861-1899)
Among the Millet and Other Poems (Ottawa,
Durie, 1888) 151p.
Lyrics of Earth (Boston, Copeland & Day,
1895) 56p.

Alcyone (Ottawa, Ogilvy, 1899) 110p.
The Poems of Archibald Lampman. Edited
with a Memoir by Duncan Campbell
Scott (Toronto, Morang, 1900) 473p.
Lyrics of Earth: Sonnets and Ballads. With an
Introduction by Duncan Campbell Scott
(Toronto, Musson, 1925) 276p.
At the Long Sault and Other New Poems. With
a Foreword by Duncan Campbell Scott
and an Introduction by E. K. Brown
(Toronto, Ryerson, 1943) 45p.
Selected Poems of Archibald Lampman.
Chosen and with a Memoir by Duncan
Campbell Scott (Toronto, Ryerson,
1947) 176p.
*Archibald Lampman's Letters to Edward
William Thomson (1890-1898)*. Edited with
an Introduction, Annotations, a Bibliog-
raphy with Notes, and [Lampman's]
"Essay on Happiness" by Arthur S.
Bourinot (Ottawa, Bourinot, 1956) 75p.
*At the Mermaid Inn, Conducted by A.
Lampman, W. W. Campbell, Duncan C. Scott.*
Being selections from Essays...which
Appeared in the Toronto *Globe,* 1892-
1893. Edited by Arthur S. Bourinot
(Ottawa, Bourinot, 1958) 96p.
*Some Letters of Duncan Campbell Scott,
Archibald Lampman, and Others*. Edited by
Arthur S. Bourinot (Ottawa, Bourinot,
1959) 63p.
*Lampman's Kate, Late Love Poems of
Archibald Lampman 1887-1897*. Edited with
an Introduction by Margaret Coulby
Whitridge (Ottawa, Borealis Press,
1975) 52p.
Selected Prose of Archibald Lampman. Edited
with an Introduction by Barrie Davies
(Ottawa, The Tecumseh Press, 1975)
127p.
Lampman's Sonnets 1884-1899. Edited with
an Introduction by Margaret Coulby
Whitridge (Ottawa, Borealis Press,
1976) xxvi + 194p.

STEPHEN LEACOCK(1869-1944)
Elements of Political Science (London,
Constable, 1906) 417p.
*Baldwin, Lafontaine, Hincks; Responsible
Government* (Toronto, Morang, 1907)
371p. [Enlarged and revised edition,
MacKenzie, Baldwin, Lafontaine, Hincks
(Toronto, Oxford, 1926) 395p.]
Literary Lapses. A Book of Sketches
(Montreal, Gazette Printing Co., 1910)
125p.
Nonsense Novels (London, Lane, 1911)
230p.

Sunshine Sketches of a Little Town (London, Lane, 1912) 264p.

Behind the Beyond, and Other Contributions to Human Knowledge (London, Lane, 1913) 195p.

Adventures of the Far North. A Chronicle of the Frozen Seas (Toronto, Glasgow Brook, 1914) 152p.

Arcadian Adventures With the Idle Rich (London, Lane, 1914) 310p.

The Dawn of Canadian History. A Chronicle of Aboriginal Canada and the Coming of the White Man (Toronto, Glasgow Brook, 1914) 112p.

The Mariner of St. Malo. A Chronicle of the Voyages of Jacques Cartier (Toronto, Glasgow Brook, 1914) 125p.

Moonbeams from the Larger Lunacy (New York, Lane, 1915) 282p.

Essays and Literary Studies (New York, Lane, 1916) 310p.

Further Foolishness. Sketches and Satires on the Follies of the Day. (New York, Lane, 1916) 312p.

Frenzied Fiction (New York, Lane, 1918) 240p.

The Hohenzollerns in America. With the Bolsheviks in Berlin and Other Impossibilities (New York, Lane, 1919) 269p.

The Unsolved Riddle of Social Justice (New York, Lane, 1920) 152p.

Winsome Winnie, and Other New Nonsense Novels (Toronto, Gundy, 1920) 243p.

My Discovery of England (London, Lane, 1922) 219p.

College Days (New York, Dodd Mead, 1923) 169p.

Over the Footlights, and Other Fancies (London, Lane, 1923) 278p.

The Garden of Folly (Toronto, Gundy, 1924) 282p.

Winnowed Wisdom. A New Book of Humour (New York, Dodd Mead, 1926) 288p.

Short Circuits (Toronto, Macmillan, 1928) 336p.

The Iron Man and the Tin Woman, With Other Such Futurities (New York, Dodd Mead, 1929) 309p.

Economic Prosperity in the British Empire (Toronto, Macmillan, 1930) 246p.

Laugh With Leacock (New York, Dodd Mead, 1930) 330p.

The Leacock Book. Selections...Arranged with an Introduction by Ben Travers (London, Lane, 1930) 248p.

Wet Wit and Dry Humour, Distilled from the Pages of Stephen Leacock (New York, Dodd Mead, 1931) 260p.

Afternoons in Utopia. Tales of the New Time (Toronto, Macmillan, 1932) 240p.

Back to Prosperity: The Great Opportunity of the British Conference (Toronto, Macmillan, 1932) 103p.

The Dry Pickwick and Other Incongruities (London, Lane, 1932) 271p.

Mark Twain (London, Davies, 1932) 167p.

Charles Dickens, His Life and Work (London, Davies, 1933) 275p.

Lincoln Frees the Slaves (New York, Putnam, 1934) 178p.

Humor, Its Theory and Technique, with Examples and Samples (New York, Dodd Mead, 1935) 268p.

Funny Pieces. A Book of Random Sketches (New York, Dodd Mead, 1936) 292p.

Hellements of Hickonomics, In Hiccoughs of Verse Done in Our Social Planning Mill (New York, Dodd Mead, 1936) 84p.

Here are My Lectures and Stories (New York, Dodd Mead, 1937) 251p.

Humour and Humanity. An Introduction to the Study of Humour (London, Butterworth, 1937) 254p.

My Discovery of the West. A Discussion of East and West in Canada (Toronto, Allen, 1937) 272p.

Model Memoirs and Other Sketches from Simple to Serious (New York, Dodd Mead, 1938) 316p.

Too Much College; or, Education Eating Up Life, with Kindred Essays in Education and Humour (New York, Dodd Mead, 1939) 255p.

Laugh Parade. A New Collection of the Wit and Humor of Stephen Leacock (New York, Dodd Mead, 1940) 326p.

Canada: the Foundations of Its Future (Montreal: Distillers Corp. Ltd., 1941) 257p.

Montreal: Seaport and City (New York, Doubleday, 1942) 340p.

My Remarkable Uncle, and Other Sketches (New York, Dodd Mead, 1942) 313p.

Our Heritage of Liberty, Its Origin, Its Achievement, Its Crises. A Book for War Time (New York, Dodd Mead, 1942) 86p.

Happy Stories, Just to Laugh At (New York, Dodd Mead, 1943) 240p.

How to Write (New York, Dodd Mead, 1943) 261p.

Canada and the Sea (Montreal, A. M. Beatty, 1944) 63p.

Last Leaves (Toronto, McClelland and
   Stewart, 1945) 213p.
*While There is Time: the Case Against Social
   Catastrophe* (Toronto, McClelland and
   Stewart, 1945) 136p.
The Boy I Left Behind Me (New York,
   Doubleday, 1946) 184p.
*The Leacock Roundabout. A Treasury of the
   Best Works of Stephen Leacock* (New
   York, Dodd Mead, 1946) 422p.
The Bodley Head Leacock. Edited with an
   Introduction by J. B. Priestley (London,
   Bodley Head, 1957) 464p. [Also pub-
   lished as *The Best of Leacock* (Toronto,
   McClelland and Stewart, 1957) 464p.]
The Unicorn Leacock. Edited by James
   Reeves (London, Hutchinson, 1960)
   191p.
A Feast of Stephen. A Leacock Anthology.
   Edited by Robertson Davies (Toronto,
   McClelland and Stewart, 1970) 160p.

PAUL LE JEUNE (1591-1664)
*Brieve Relation Du Voyage De La Nouvelle
France* (Paris, Sebastien Cramoisy,
1632) 68p.
*Relation De Ce Qui S'Est Passé En La Nouvelle
France En L'Année 1633* (Paris, Sebastien
Cramoisy, 1634) 216p. Le Jeune also
   edited the *Relations* for the years
   1634-40 and 1658-61. [Translations
   appear in *The Jesuit Relations and Allied
   Documents.* Edited by Reuben Gold
   Thwaites (Cleveland, The Burrows
   Brothers Company, 1896-1901) 72
   vols.]

ROSANNA LEPROHON (1829-1879)
*Antoinette de Mirecourt; or, Secret Marrying
and Secret Sorrowing.* A Canadian Tale
(Montreal, Lovell, 1864) 369p. [Also
   French translation by J. A. Genand
   (Montreal, Beauchemin, 1865) 342p.
Armand Durand; or A Promise Fulfilled
   (Montreal, Lovell, 1868) 77p.
The Poetical Works of Mrs. Leprohon
   (Montreal, Lovell, 1881) 228p.
Le Manoir de Villerai. Un Roman Canadien.
   Traduit de l'Anglais. (Montreal,
   Beauchemin, 1884) 383p. [The English
   original appeared in the *Family Herald*
   (Montreal, 1859-1860). The French
   translation by E. L. De Bellefeuille first
   appeared in Montreal (1861) 405p.]
*The following works were published only
in serial form:*
   Ida Beresford. 1848.
   Florence Fitz-Hardinge. 1849.
   Eva Huntingdon. A Tale. 1850.

Clarence Fitz-Clarence. 1851.
Eveleen O'Donnell. 1859.
My Visit to Fairview Villa. 1870.
Clive Weston's Wedding Anniversary.
   1872.

MARC LESCARBOT (1570-1642)
*Adieu A La France Sur L'Embarquement du
Sieur de Poutrincourt et de son equipage faisant
voile en la terre de Canadas dicte la France
Occidentalle* (Rouen, Jean Petit, 1606) 8p.
*La Defaite des Sauvages Armouchiquois Par le
Sagamos Membertou & ses alliez Sauvages en
la Nouvelle France, au mois de Juillet dernier,
1607* (Paris, Jeremie Perier, 1608) 24p.
Histoire de la Nouvelle France (Paris, Jean
   Millot, 1609) 888p. [Translated by W. L.
   Grant with an Introduction by H. P.
   Biggar as *The History of New France by
   Marc Lescarbot* (Toronto, The Champ-
   lain Society, 1907-14) 3 vols.]
Les Muses de la Nouvelle France (Paris, Jean
   Millot, 1609) 66p. Includes "Le Théâtre
   de Neptune" which was translated by
   Harriet Taber Richardson as *The Theatre
   of Neptune in New France* (Boston,
   Riverside Press, 1927)
*La Conversion des Sauvages qui ont eté baptizés
en la Nouvelle France, cette année 1610*
   (Paris, Jean Millot, 1610) 46p.
*Relation Dernière De ce qui s'est passé au
voyage du sieur de Poutrincourt en la Nouvelle
France* (Paris, Jean Millot, 1612) 40p.

NELLIE MCCLUNG (1873-1951)
Sowing Seeds in Danny (New York, Double-
   day, 1908) 313p.
The Second Chance. (New York, Doubleday,
   1910) 369p.
*The Black Creek Stopping House and Other
Stories* (Toronto, Briggs, 1912) 224p.
In Times Like These. Addresses (New York,
   Appleton, 1915) 217p.
The Next of Kin. Stories of Those Who Wait
   and Wonder (Boston, Houghton, 1917)
   256p.
Purple Springs (Toronto, Allen, 1921)
   335p.
The Beauty of Martha (London, Hutchin-
   son, 1923) 288p.
When Christmas Crossed "The Peace" (To-
   ronto, Allen, 1923) 149p.
Painted Fires (New York, Dodd Mead,
   1925) 316p.
All We Like Sheep and Other Stories (Toronto,
   Allen, 1926) 261p.
Be Good to Yourself. A Book of Short Stories
   (Toronto, Allen, 1930) 179p.

Flowers for the Living. A Book of Short Stories (Toronto, Allen, 1931) 212p.
Clearing in the West. My Own Story (Toronto, Allen, 1935) 378p.
Leaves from Lantern Lane (Toronto, Allen, 1936) 199p.
More Leaves from Lantern Lane (Toronto, Allen, 1937) 201p.
The Stream Runs Fast. My Own Story (Toronto, Allen, 1945) 316p.

THOMAS MCCULLOCH (1776-1843)
Popery Condemned by Scripture and the Fathers (Edinburgh, Pillans, 1808) 385p. [Also published as *Popery Again Condemned* (Edinburgh, Neill, 1810) 429p.]
Colonial Gleanings: William and Melville (Edinburgh, Oliphant, 1826) 144p.
Memorial from the Committee of Missions of the Presbyterian Church of Nova Scotia to the Glasgow Society for Promoting the Religious Interests of the Scottish Settlers in British North America (Edinburgh, Oliver & Boyd, 1826) 75p.
A Review of the Supplement to the First Annual Report of the Society for Promoting the Religious Interests of Scottish Settlers in British North America (Glasgow, Young, 1828) 50p.
Calvinism, the Doctrine of the Scriptures (Glasgow, Collins, [1849]) 270p.
Letters of Mephibosheth Stepsure [pseud] (Halifax, Blackader, 1860) 143p. [Also published as *The Stepsure Letters* (Toronto, McClelland and Stewart, 1960) 160p.]

J. MACKAY
Quebec Hill; or, Canadian Scenery. A Poem in Two Parts (London, Blackader, 1797) 34p.

WILLIAM LYON MACKENZIE (1795-1861)
The Legislative Black List of Upper Canada; or, Official Corruption and Hypocrisy Unmasked (York, *Colonial Advocate*, 1828) 39p.
A New Almanac for the Canadian True Blues. With which is Incorporated the Constitutional Reformer's Text Book, for the Millenial and Prophetical Year of the Grand General Election for Upper Canada and Total and Everlasting Downfall of Toryism in the British Empire. By Patrick Swift [pseud] [2nd edition (York, Baxter, [1833?]) 23p.]
Sketches of Canada and the United States (London, Effingham Wilson, 1833) 504p.
Mackenzie's Own Narrative of the Late Rebel-

lion (Toronto, Palladium Office, 1838) 23p.
The Sons of the Emerald Isle; or, Lives of One Thousand Remarkable Irishmen, including Memoirs of Noted Characters of Irish Parentage or Descent (New York, Burgess Stringer, 1845) 108p.
An Almanac of Independence & Freedom for the Year 1860. Containing a Plea for the Relief of the Inhabitants of Canada from a State of Colonial Vassalage or Irresponsible Rule (Toronto, Author, 1860) 62p.
Selected Writings, 1824-1837. Edited by Margaret Fairley (Toronto, Oxford University Press, 1960) 383p.

ALEXANDER MCLACHLAN (1818-1896)
The Spirit of Love, and Other Poems (Toronto, Cleland, 1846) 36p.
Poems (Toronto, Geikie, 1856) 192p.
Lyrics (Toronto, Armour, 1858) 151p.
The Emigrant, and Other Poems (Toronto, Rollo & Adam, 1861) 236p.
Poems and Songs (Toronto, Hunter Rose, 1874) 223p.
The Poetical Works of Alexander McLachlan (Toronto, Briggs, 1900) 424p.

CHARLES MAIR (1838-1927)
Dreamland and Other Poems (Montreal, Dawson, 1868) 151p.
Tecumseh. A Drama (Toronto, Hunter Rose, 1886) 205p.
Tecumseh, A Drama, and Canadian Poems (Toronto, Briggs, 1901) 276p.
Through the Mackenzie Basin. A Narrative of the Athabasca and Peace River Treaty Expedition of 1899 (Toronto, Briggs, 1908) 494p.
Tecumseh, A drama, and Canadian Poems: Dreamland and Other Poems; The American Bison; Through the Mackenzie Basin; Memoirs and Reminiscences. With an Introduction by Robert Norwood (Toronto, Radisson Society, 1926) 72 + 470p.

SUSANNA MOODIE (1803-1885)
Enthusiasm and Other Poems (London, Smith & Elder, 1831) 214p.
Roughing It in the Bush; or, Life in Canada (London, Bentley, 1852) 2 vols.
Life in the Clearings Versus the Bush (London, Bentley, 1853) 384p.
Mark Hurdlestone, the Gold Worshipper (London, Bentley, 1853) 2 vols.
Flora Lyndsay; or, Passages in an Eventful Life (London, Bentley, 1854) 2 vols.

Matrimonial Speculations (London, Bentley, 1854) 352p.

Geoffrey Moncton; or, The Faithless Guardian (New York, DeWitt, 1855) 362p. [Also published as *The Monctons* (London, Bentley, 1856) 2 vols.]

The World Before Them (London, Bentley, 1868) 3 vols.

The Victoria Magazine 1847-1848. Edited by Susanna and J.W.D. Moodie. Reprinted with an Introduction by W.H. New (Vancouver, University of British Columbia Library, 1968) 294p.

Works attibuted to Susanna Moodie:

Spartacus. A Roman Story [Anon] (London, Newman, 1822) 131p.

The Little Prisoner; or, Passion and Patience (London, Newman, 1829)

Ashton Warner, A Native of St. Vincents [Anon] (London, Maunder, 1831)

The History of Mary Prince, A West Indian Slave [Anon] (London, Maunder, 1831)

Negro Slavery Described by a Negro. Being the Narrative of Ashton Warner, a Native of St. Vincents. [Anon] (London, Maunder, 1831)

Profession and Principle. Tales (London, Dean, 1833)

Rowland Massingham, the Boy That Would be His Own Master (London, Dean, 1837)

The Little Black Pony, and Other Stories (Philadelphia, Collins, 1850)

The Soldier's Orphan; or, Hugh Latimer (London, Dean, 1853)

Something More About the Soldier's Orphan (London, Dean, 1853)

George Leatrim; or, the Mother's Test (Edinburgh, Hamilton, 1875)

EMILE NELLIGAN (1879-1941)

Emile Nelligan et son oeuvre. Préface par Louis Dantin (Montreal, [Beauchemin], 1903) 164p.

Poésies (Montreal, Fides, 1945) 232p.

Poésies complètes 1896-1899 (Texte établi et annoté par Luc Lacourcière (Montreal, Fides, 1952) 331p.

Selected Poems. Translated by P.E. Widdows (Toronto, Ryerson, 1960) xv + 39p.

Poèmes choisis. Présenté par Eloi de Grandmont et précédé d'une chronologie, d'une bibliographie et de jugements critiques (Montreal, Fides, 1967) 166p.

JONATHAN ODELL (1737-1818)

The American Times. A Satire in Three Parts... by Camillo Querno [pseud],

Poet Laureate to the Congress (London, Richardson, 1780) 40p.

The Loyalist Poetry of the Revolution. Edited by Winthrop Sargent (Philadelphia, Collins, 1857) 218p.

The Loyal Verses of Joseph Stansbury and Doctor Jonathan Odell. Edited by Winthrop Sargent (Albany, New York, Munsell, 1860) 199p.

STEPHEN PARMENIUS (1555-1583)

De Navigatione Illustris Et Magnanimi. Equitis Aurati: Humfredi Gilberto, ad deducendam in novum orbem coloniam susceptâ carmen (London, Thomam Pursutium, 1582)

Paean Stephani Parmenii Budeji. Ad psalmum Davidis CIV (London, Thomas Vautroulerius, 1582)

[A letter of the learned Hungarian Stephanus Parmenius Budeius to master Richard Hakluyt. [Newfoundland, August 6, 1583] in Richard Hakluyt's *Principall Navigations* (London, 1589)]

The New Found Land of Stephen Parmenius. Edited and translated with commentaries by David B. Quinn and Neil M. Cheshire (Toronto, University of Toronto Press, 1972) 250p.

MARJORIE PICKTHALL (1883-1922)

Dick's Desertion. A Boy's Adventure in Canadian Forests (Toronto, Musson, 1905) 128p.

The Straight Road (Toronto, Musson, [1906?]) 127p.

Billy's Hero; or, The Valley of Gold (Toronto, Musson, 1908) 128p.

The Drift of Pinions (Montreal, *University Magazine*, 1913) 94p.

Little Hearts (London, Methuen, 1915) 309p.

The Lamp of Poor Souls, and Other Poems (New York, Lane, 1916) 140p.

The Bridge. A Story of the Great Lakes (London, Hodder, 1922) 320p.

The Woodcarver's Wife, and Later Poems (Toronto, McClelland and Stewart, 1922) 105p.

Angels' Shoes, and Other Stories (London, Hodder, 1923) 320p.

The Complete Poems of Marjorie Pickthall (Toronto, McClelland and Stewart, 1925) 250p.

Little Songs (Toronto, McClelland and Stewart, 1925) 88p.

The Selected Poems of Marjorie Pickthall. Edited with an Introduction by Lorne Pierce (Toronto, McClelland and Stewart, 1957) 104p.

CHRISTOPHE REGNAUT (1613-1697)
"A Veritable Account of the Martyrdom
and Blessed Death of Father Jean de
Brébeuf and of Father Gabriel Lalement"
in *The Jesuit Relations and Allied Documents.*
Edited by Reuben Gold Thwaites (Cleveland, The Burrows Brothers Company,
1896-1901) 72 vols.

MAJOR JOHN RICHARDSON (1796-1852)
Tecumseh; or, The Warrior of The West. A
Poem in Four Cantos, with Notes. By an
English officer [pseud] (London, Glynn,
1828)
Ecarté; or, The Salons of Paris (London,
Colburn, 1829) 3 vols.
Kensington Gardens in 1830. A Satirical
Trifle [Anon] (London, Marsh & Miller,
1830) 32p.
Wacousta; or, The Prophecy. A tale of the
Canadas. By the Author of *Ecarté*
[pseud] (London, Cadell, 1832) 3 vols.
Journal of the Movements of the British Legion.
By an Officer [pseud] (London, Effing-
ham Wilson, 1836) 262p.
*Movements of the British Legion, with Stric-
tures on the Course of Conduct Pursued by
Lieut.-Gen. Evans...* Second edition, To
Which is Added... A Continuation of
the Operations from the 5th of May,
1836, to the Close of March, 1837
(London, Simpkin Marshall, 1837)
330p. [First edition London, 1836]
*The Canadian Brothers; or, the Prophecy
Fulfilled.* A Tale of the Late American War
(Montreal, Armour & Ramsay, 1840) 2
vols. [Also revised and published as
*Matilda Montgomerie; or, The Prophecy
Fulfilled* (New York, Dewitt & Daven-
port, 1851) 191p.]
The War of 1812 ([Brockville], [Author],
1842) 182p.
Eight Years in Canada (Montreal, Cunning-
ham, 1847) 232p.
The Guards in Canada; or, the Point of Honor.
Being a Sequel to Major Richardson's
"Eight Years in Canada." (Montreal,
Cunningham, 1848) 54p.
The Monk Knight of St. John. A Tale of the
Crusades (New York, Dewitt, 1850)
192p.
Hardscrabble; or The Fall of Chicago. A Tale
of Indian Warfare (New York, Dewitt &
Davenport [1851]) 99p.
Wau Nan Gee; or, The Massacre at Chicago
(New York, Long, 1852) 126p.
Tecumseh and Richardson. The Story of a
Trip to Walpole Island and Port Sarnia.

With an Introduction and Biographical
Sketch by A. H. U. Colquhoun (Toron-
to, Ontario Book Company, 1924) 124p.
[First published anonymously in 1849]
Westbrook the Outlaw; or, The Avenging Wolf.
An American Border Tale. Edited with
an Introduction by David R. Beasley
(Montreal, Grant Woolmer Books,
1973) 74p.
Wacousta Uncensored. Edited by Michael
Hurley with an Introduction by James
Reaney (London, Applegarth Follies,
1977) 150p.

CHARLES G. D. ROBERTS (1860-1943)
Orion, and Other Poems (Philadelphia,
Lippincott, 1880) 113p.
In Divers Tones (Boston, Lothrop, 1886)
134p.
Songs of the Common Day (Toronto, Briggs,
1893) 126p.
*The Raid from Beauséjour, and How the Carter
Boys Lifted the Mortgage.* Two Stories of
Acadie (New York, Hunt & Eaton,
1894) 230p. [*The Raid from Beauséjour*
was later published as *The Young Acadian*
(Boston, Page, 1907) 139p.]
*The Land of Evangeline, and the Gateways
Thither* (Kentville, Nova Scotia, Dominion
Atlantic Railway Company [1894?])
92p.
Reube Dare's Shad Boat. A Tale of the Tide
Country (New York, Hunt & Eaton,
1895) 145p. [Also published as *The
Cruise of the Yacht "Dido"* (Boston, Page,
1906) 145p.]
Around the Campfire (New York, Crowell,
1896) 349p.
The Book of the Native (Toronto, Copp
Clark, 1896) 156p.
Earth's Enigmas. A Book of Animal and
Nature Life (Boston, Lamson Wolffe,
1896) 290p.
The Forge in the Forest. Being the Narrative
of the Acadian Ranger, Jean de Mer,
Seigneur de Briart (Boston, Lamson
Wolffe, 1896) 311p.
A History of Canada (Boston, Lamson
Wolffe, 1897) 492p.
New York Nocturnes and Other Poems
(Boston, Lamson Wolffe, 1898) 84p.
A Sister to Evangeline. Being the story of
Yvonne de Lamourie (Boston, Lamson
Wolffe, 1898) 289p. [Also published as
Lovers in Acadie (London, Dent, 1924)
278p.]
The Canadian Guide-Book (New York,
Appleton, 1899) 327p.

Northland Lyrics. By William Carman
  Roberts, Theodore Roberts, and
  Elizabeth Roberts Macdonald. Selected
  and Arranged, with a Prologue (in
  verse) by Charles G.D. Roberts, and an
  Epilogue by Bliss Carman (Boston,
  Small Maynard, 1899) vii+ 12 + 86p.
By the Marshes of Minas (New York, Silver
  Burdett, 1900) 285p.
The Heart of the Ancient Wood (New York,
  Silver Burdett, 1900) 276p.
Poems (New York, Silver Burdett, 1901)
  222p.
Barbara Ladd (Boston, Page, 1902) 377p.
Discoveries and Explorations (London,
  Chambers, 1902) 529p.
The Kindred of the Wild. A Book of Animal
  Life (Boston, Page, 1902) 374p.
The Book of the Rose (Boston, Page, 1903)
  83p.
The Prisoner of Mademoiselle. A Love Story
  (Boston, Page, 1904) 265p.
The Watchers of the Trails. A Book of Animal
  Life (Boston, Page, 1904) 361p.
Red Fox. The Story of his Adventurous
  Career in the Ringwaak Wilds (Boston,
  Page, 1905) 340p.
The Heart That Knows (Boston, Page, 1906)
  378p.
In the Deep of the Snow (New York, Crowell,
  1907) 78p.
The Haunters of the Silences (Boston, Page,
  1907) 316p.
*Poems…*New Complete Edition (Boston,
  Page, 1907) 257p.
The House in the Water. A Book of Animal
  Life (Boston, Page, 1908) 301p.
The Red Oxen of Bonval (New York, Dodd
  Mead, 1908) 71p.
The Backwoodsmen (New York, Macmillan,
  1909) 269p.
Kings in Exile (London, Ward Lock, 1909)
  306p.
More Kindred of the Wild (London, Ward
  Lock, 1911) 264p.
Neighbours Unknown (New York, Mac-
  millan, 1911) 266p.
Babes of the Wild (New York, Cassell, 1912)
  243p.
The Feet of the Furtive (London, Ward Lock,
  1912) 277p.
Hoof and Claw (London, Ward Lock, 1912)
  267p.
A Balkan Prince (London, Everett, 1913)
  248p.
The Secret Trails (New York, Macmillan,
  1916) 212p.

The Ledge on Bald Face (London, Ward
  Lock, 1918) 255p.
In the Morning of Time (London, Hutchin-
  son, 1919) 319p.
New Poems (London, Constable, 1919) 44p.
Some Animal Stories (London, Dent, [1921])
  128p.
More Animal Stories (London, Dent, 1922)
  127p.
Wisdom of the Wilderness (London, Dent,
  1922) 218p.
They Who Walk in the Wild (New York,
  Macmillan, 1924) 212p.
The Vagrant of Time (Toronto, Ryerson,
  1927) 46p.
Eyes of the Wilderness (New York, Mac-
  millan, 1933) 269p.
The Iceberg and Other Poems (Toronto,
  Ryerson, 1934) 31p.
Further Animal Stories (London, Dent,
  1936) 128p.
Selected Poems of Sir Charles G. D. Roberts
  (Toronto, Ryerson, 1936) 188p.
Thirteen Bears. Edited by Ethel Hume
  Bennett (Toronto, Ryerson, 1947)
  254p.
Forest Folk. Edited by Ethel Hume Bennett
  (Toronto, Ryerson, 1949) 237p.
The Selected Poems of Charles G. D. Roberts.
  Edited with an Introduction by
  Desmond Pacey (Toronto, Ryerson,
  1956) xxv + 100p.
The Last Barrier and Other Stories. Edited
  with an Introduction by Alec Lucas
  (Toronto, McClelland and Stewart,
  1958) x + 153p.
King of Beasts and Other Stories. Edited with
  an Introduction by Joseph Gold (To-
  ronto, Ryerson, 1967) 240p.
Selected Poetry and Critical Prose. Edited
  with an Introduction by W. J. Keith
  (Toronto, University of Toronto Press,
  1974) xxxix + 326p.

THEODORE GOODRIDGE ROBERTS
(1877-1953)
Northland Lyrics. By William Carman
  Roberts, Theodore Roberts, and
  Elizabeth Roberts MacDonald. Selected
  and Arranged by Charles G. D. Roberts
  (Boston, Small Maynard, 1899) 86p.
The House of Isstens (Boston, Page, 1900)
Hemming, the Adventurer (Boston, Page,
  1904) 328p.
Brothers of Peril. A Story of old Newfound-
  land (Boston, Page, 1905) 327p.
The Red Feathers (Boston, Page, 1907)
  325p.

Captain Love (Boston, Page, 1908) 282p.
Flying Plover. His Stories. Told him by
Squat-by-the-fire (Boston, Page, 1909)
124p.
A Cavalier of Virginia (Boston, Page, 1910)
313p.
Comrades of the Trails (Boston, Page, 1910)
308p.
A Captain of Raleigh's (Boston, Page, 1911)
351p.
Rayton. A Backwoods Mystery (Boston,
Page, 1912) 314p.
The Harbor Master (Boston, Page, 1913)
300p. [Also published as *The Toll of the
Tides* (London, Laurie, 1913) 240p.]
Love on Smoky River (London, Long, 1913)
320p.
Two Shall Be Born (New York, Cassell,
1913) 319p.
Blessington's Folly (London, Long, 1914)
320p.
Jess of the River (New York, Dillingham,
1914) 329p.
The Wasp (New York, Dillingham, 1914)
352p.
In the High Woods (London, Long, 1916)
320p.
Forest Fugitives (Toronto, McClelland and
Stewart, 1917) 320p.
The Islands of Adventure (New York,
Hodder, 1918) 312p.
The Exiled Lover (London, Long, 1919)
320p.
*The Master of the Moose Horn, and Other
Backcountry Stories* (London, Hodder,
1919) 315p.
Moonshine (London, Hodder, 1920) 317p.
The Lure of Piper's Glen (New York,
Doubleday, 1921) 120p.
The Fighting Starkleys (Boston, Page, 1922)
250p.
Musket House (New York, Doubleday,
1922) 120p.
*Tom Akerley. His Adventures in the Tall
Timber and at Gaspard's Clearing*
(Boston, Page, 1923) 283p.
Green Timber Thoroughbreds (Garden City,
Garden City Publishing Company,
1924) 120p.
The Oxbow Wizard (Garden City, Garden
City Publishing Company, 1924) 121p.
*The Red Pirogue. A Tale of Adventure in
the Canadian Wilds* (Boston, Page,
1924) 272p.
The Stranger From Up-Along (Toronto,
Gundy, 1924) 188p.
Honest Fool (London, Hodder, 1925) 319p.

The Lost Shipmate (Toronto, Ryerson,
1926) 14p.
Prize Money (Boston, Page, 1926)
*The Golden Highlanders; or, The Romantic
Adventures of Alastair MacIver* (Boston,
Page, 1929) 308p.
The Leather Bottle (Toronto, Ryerson,
1934) 87p.

CHARLES SANGSTER (1822-1893)
*The St. Lawrence and the Saguenay, and Other
Poems* (Kingston, Creighton & Duff;
New York, Miller, Orton & Mulligan,
1856) 262p.
Hesperus and Other Poems and Lyrics
(Montreal, Lovell; Kingston, Creighton,
1860) 186p.
...Our Norland (Toronto, Copp Clark
[189?]) 14p.
*The St. Lawrence and the Saguenay, and Other
Poems* [and] *Hesperus and Other Poems and
Lyrics.* With an Introduction by Gordon
Johnston (Toronto, University of
Toronto Press, 1972) xxxvii + 186p.
Norland Echoes and Other Poems and Lyrics.
Edited with an Introduction by Frank
M. Tierney (Ottawa, The Tecumseh
Press, 1976) 117p.

DUNCAN CAMPBELL SCOTT (1862-1947)
The Magic House and Other Poems (Ottawa,
Durie, 1893) 95p.
In the Village of Viger (Boston, Copeland &
Day, 1896) 135p.
Labour and the Angel (Boston, Copeland &
Day, 1898) 59p.
...John Graves Simcoe [A Biography]
(Toronto, Morang, 1905) 241p.
New World Lyrics and Ballads (Toronto,
Morang, 1905) 66p.
Via Borealis (Toronto, Tyrrell, 1906) 21p.
Lines in Memory of Edmund Morris (n.p.,
Author, 1915) 14p.
Lundy's Lane and Other Poems (New York,
Doran, 1916) 194p.
Beauty and Life (Toronto, McClelland and
Stewart, 1921) 96p.
The Witching of Elspie. A Book of Stories
(New York, Doran, 1923) 248p.
"Pierre, A Play in One Act," in *Canadian
Plays from Hart House Theatre.* Edited by
Vincent Massey (Toronto, Macmillan,
1926) Vol. 1 pp. 51-76.
The Poems of Duncan Campbell Scott
(Toronto, McClelland and Stewart,
1926) 341p.

The Administration of Indian Affairs in Canada (Toronto, Canadian Institute of International Affairs, 1931) 27p.

The Green Cloister. Later Poems (Toronto, McClelland and Stewart, 1935) 96p.

The Circle of Affection and Other Pieces in Prose and Verse (Toronto, McClelland and Stewart, 1947) 237p.

Selected Poems of Duncan Campbell Scott. With a Memoir by E.K. Brown (Toronto, Ryerson, 1951) 176p.

At the Mermaid Inn, Conducted by A. Lampman, W.W. Campbell, Duncan C. Scott. Being Selections from Essays...which Appeared in the Toronto *Globe* 1892-1893. Edited by Arthur S. Bourinot (Ottawa, Bourinot, 1958) 96p.

Some Letters of Duncan Campbell Scott, Archibald Lampman and Others. Edited by A.S. Bourinot (Ottawa, Bourinot, 1959) 63p.

More Letters of Duncan Campbell Scott. Edited by A.S. Bourinot (Ottawa, Bourinot, 1960) 104p.

Presidential Address: Poetry and Progress (Toronto, Canadiana House, 1969) lxviip.

Selected Stories. Edited with an Introduction by Glenn Clever (Ottawa, University of Ottawa Press, 1972) 135p.

Selected Poetry of Duncan Campbell Scott. Edited by Glenn Clever (Ottawa, The Tecumseh Press, 1974) 121p.

ROBERT WILLIAM SERVICE (1874-1958)

Songs of a Sourdough (Toronto, Briggs, 1907) 116p. [Also published as *The Spell of the Yukon and Other Verses* (New York, Barse, 1907)]

Ballads of a Cheechako (Toronto, Briggs, 1909) 220p.

The Trail of '98. A Northland Romance (Toronto, Briggs, 1910) 514p.

Rhymes of a Rolling Stone (Toronto, Briggs, 1912) 195p.

The Pretender. A Story of the Latin Quarter (New York, Dodd Mead, 1914) 349p.

Rhymes of a Red-Cross Man (London, Unwin, 1916) 192p.

Selected Poems (London, Unwin, 1917) 28p.

The Shooting of Dan McGrew and Other Verses (New York, Barse, 1920)

Ballads of a Bohemian (New York, Barse, 1921) 220p.

Complete Poetical Works (New York, Barse, 1921) [855]p. [Also published as *Collected Verse* (Benn, 1930) and *Complete Poems* (New York, Dodd Mead, 1933)]

The Poisoned Paradise. A Romance of Monte Carlo (New York, Dodd Mead, 1922) 412p.

The Roughneck. A Tale of Tahiti (New York, Barse, 1923) 448p.

The Master of the Microbe (New York, Barse, 1926) 424p.

The House of Fear (New York, Dodd Mead, 1927) 408p.

Why Not Grow Young? or, Living for Longevity (New York, Barse, 1928) 266p.

Twenty Bath-tub Ballads (London, Francis, Day & Hunter, 1939) 48p.

Bar-Room Ballads (New York, Dodd Mead, 1940) 169p.

The Complete Poems (New York, Dodd Mead, 1940) 735p.

The Complete Poems (New York, Dodd Mead, 1942) 1032p.

The Ploughman of the Moon. An Adventure into Memory. (New York, Dodd Mead, 1945) 472p.

Harper of Heaven (New York, Dodd Mead, 1948) 452p.

Songs of a Sun-Lover (London, Benn, 1949) 191p.

Rhymes of a Roughneck (New York, Dodd Mead, 1950) 207p.

Lyrics of a Low Brow (New York, Dodd Mead, 1951) 182p.

Rhymes of a Rebel (New York, Dodd Mead, 1952) 213p.

Songs for My Supper (New York, Dodd Mead, 1953) 192p.

Carols of an Old Codger (New York, Dodd Mead, 1954) 190p.

More Collected Verse (London, Benn, 1955)

Rhymes for My Rags (London, Benn, 1956) 191p.

Rhymes and Romance. A Robert Service Anthology (London, Benn, 1958)

Songs of the High North (London, Benn, 1958) 126p.

More Selected Verse (New York, Dodd Mead, 1971) 215p.

JOSEPH STANSBURY (1740-1809)

The Loyal Verses of Joseph Stansbury and Doctor Jonathan Odell. Edited by Winthrop Sargent (Albany, New York, Munsell, 1860) 199p.

DAVID THOMPSON (1770-1857)

New Light on the Early History of the Greater Northwest. The Manuscript Journals of Alexander Henry...and of David Thompson... 1799-1814. Edited by Elliott Coues (New York, Harper, 1897) 3 vols.

David Thompson's Narrative of His Explorations in Western America 1784-1812.
Edited by J. B. Tyrrell (Toronto, Champlain Society, 1916) 582p.
Journals Relating to Montana and Adjacent Regions, 1808-1812. Edited by M. Catherine White (Missoula, Montana University Press, 1950) 345p.
Narrative, 1784-1812. Edited with an Introduction and Notes by Richard Glover (Toronto, Champlain Society, 1962) cii + 410p.
David Thompson's Journal of the International Boundary Survey, 1817-1827: Western Lake Erie, August-September, 1819. Edited by Clarke E. Leverette (London, Ontario, Killaly Press, 1974)

EDWARD WILLIAM THOMSON (1849-1924)
Old Man Savarin, and Other Stories (Toronto, Briggs, 1895) 289p.
Walter Gibbs, The Young Boss; and Other Stories. A Book for Boys (Toronto, Briggs, 1896) 361p.
Between Earth and Sky, and Other Strange Stories of Deliverance (Toronto, Briggs, 1897) 297p.
Smoky Days (New York, Crowell, 1901)
The Many-Mansioned House, and Other Poems (Toronto, Briggs, 1909) 151p.
[Also published as *When Lincoln Died, and Other Poems* (Boston, Houghton, 1909) 146p.]
Old Man Savarin Stories. Tales of Canada and Canadians (Toronto, Gundy, 1917) 344p.
Edward William Thomson (1849-1924): A Bibliography with Notes and Some Letters.
Edited and Compiled by Arthur S. Bourinot (Ottawa, Bourinot, 1955) 28p.
The Letters of Edward William Thomson to Archibald Lampman (1891-1897). With Notes, a Bibliography, and Other Material on Thomson and Lampman. Edited by Arthur S. Bourinot (Ottawa, Bourinot, 1957) 49p.

Selected Stories of E.W. Thomson. Edited with an Introduction by Lorraine McMullen (Ottawa, University of Ottawa Press, 1973) 92p.

CATHARINE PARR TRAILL (1802-1899)
Reformation; or, The Cousin (London, 1819)
The Backwoods of Canada. Being Letters from the Wife of an Emigrant Officer (London, Knight, 1836) 352p.
Adventures of Little Downy, the Field Mouse; and The Little Princess; or Passion and Patience. New Edition. (London, Dean, 1844) 78p.
The Canadian Crusoes. A Tale of the Rice Lake Plains (London, Hall, 1852) 368p. [Also published as *Lost in the Backwoods* (London, Nelson, 1882) 319p.]
The Female Emigrant's Guide (Toronto, Maclean, 1854) 218 + 40p. [Also published as *The Canadian Settler's Guide* (Toronto, Old Countryman Office, 1855) and *The Canadian Emigrant Housekeeper's Guide* (Toronto, Lovell, 1862)]
Lady Mary and Her Nurse (London, Hall, 1856) 204p. [Also published as *Little Mary and Her Nurse, Afar in the Forest*, and *In the forest.*]
Canadian Wild Flowers. Painted and Lithographed by Agnes Fitzgibbon, with Botanical Description by C.P. Traill (Montreal, Lovell, 1869) 86p.
Studies of Plant Life in Canada (Ottawa, Woodburn, 1885) 288p.
Pearls and Pebbles; or Notes of an Old Naturalist. With Biographical Sketch by Mary Agnes Fitzgibbon (Toronto, Briggs, 1894) 241p.
Cot and Cradle Stories. Edited by Mary Agnes Fitzgibbon. (Toronto, Briggs, 1895) 239p.

GEORGE VANCOUVER (1757-1798)
A Voyage of Discovery to the North Pacific Ocean, and Round the World (London, Robinson, 1798) 3 vols.

Index

Acknowledgments

PHILIPPE AUBERT DE GASPE From *The Canadians of Old,* Translated by C.G.D. Roberts reprinted by permission of The Canadian Publishers, McClelland and Stewart Limited, Toronto

BLISS CARMAN "Low Tide on Grand Pré," "A Northern Vigil," "A Windflower," "The Ships of St. John," "Overlord," "At The Yellow of the Leaf," "Lord of My Heart's Elation." "The Great Return," "Softer than the Hill-Fog to the Forest," "Easter Eve," "Morning in the Hills" reprinted by special permission of the Bliss Carman Trust, The University of New Brunswick, Canada

EMILY CARR "D'Sonoqua" from *Klee Wyck* © 1941. Used by permission of Clarke, Irwin & Company Limited

OCTAVE CREMAZIE "The Dead," © 1978. Translator Fred W. Cogswell, by permission of Fred W. Cogswell

LOUIS FRECHETTE "The Discovery of the Mississippi," "January," from *The Poetry of French Canada in Translation* (Toronto, Oxford, 1970) by permission of John Glassco. "Cap Eternité," © 1978. Translator D.G. Jones, by permission of D.G. Jones

CHARLES GORDON "Highland Religion," from *Postscript to Adventure. The Autobiography of Ralph Conner.* Reprinted by permission of J. King Gordon.

STEPHEN LEACOCK "The Marine Excursions of the Knights of Pythias," from *Sunshine Sketches of a Little Town* by Stephen Leacock reprinted by permission of The Canadian Publishers, McClelland and Stewart Limited, Toronto

MARC LESCARBOT from *The Theatre of Neptune in New France.* Translator Harriet Taber Richardson. (Boston, Houghton Mifflin, 1927) used by permission of Houghton Mifflin Company.

NELLIE MCCLUNG "A Gentleman of the Old School," from *The Stream Runs Fast.* Reprinted by permission of Thomas Allen and Son Limited

EMILE NELLIGAN "By the Fireside," "The Garden of the Past," "Christ on the Cross," "A Woman Passing By" from *Selected Poems* by Emile Nelligan. Trans. P.F. Widdows. © 1960. Reprinted by permission of McGraw-Hill Ryerson Limited. "Old Fantasist," "The Poet's Wine," Trans. George Johnston used by permission of Les Editions Fides and George Johnston. "The Ship of Gold," Trans. A.J.M. Smith used by permission of Les Editions Fides and A.J.M. Smith

C.G.D.ROBERTS "Dedication," from *The Collected Poems of Sir Charles G.D. Roberts.* Reprinted by permission of McGraw-Hill Ryerson Limited. "The Prisoners of the Pitcher Plant," from *The Haunters of the Silences* by Charles G.D. Roberts reprinted by permission of The Canadian Publishers, McClelland and Stewart Limited, Toronto. "The Tantramar Revisited," "An Ode for the Canadian Confederacy," "In the Wide Awe and Wisdom of the Night," "In September," "The Herring Weir," "The Salt Flats," "The Pea-Fields," "The Mowing," "Marsyas," "The Skater," "The Poetry of Nature" by permission of Lady Roberts

DUNCAN CAMPBELL SCOTT "Night and the Pine," "The Piper of Arll," "Watkwenies," "The Forsaken," "On the Way to the Mission," "The Sea by the Wood," "The Wood by the Sea," "The Height of Land," "At Gull Lake: August, 1810," "At Delos," reprinted by permission of John G. Aylen, Ottawa, Canada

ROBERT SERVICE "The Shooting of Dan McGrew," "The Trail of Ninety-Eight," from *The Collected Poems of Robert Service.* Reprinted by permission of McGraw-Hill Ryerson Limited. "My Cross," from *More Collected Verse* by Robert Service reprinted by permission of The Canadian Publishers, McClelland and Stewart Limited, Toronto

We wish also to acknowledge the assistance of The Canada Council for a grant in support of the translations of Octave Crémazie's "The Dead" and Louis Frechette's "Cap Eternité."